OpenSocial™ Netwo

Introduction xvii
Chapter 1: Social Network Programming 1
Chapter 2: Introduction to OpenSocial 55
Chapter 3: Gadget XML and Gadget API 87
Chapter 4: JavaScript API 111
Chapter 5: OpenSocial RESTful API 169
Chapter 6: Programming Fundamentals 221
Chapter 7: Sample Applications 235
Chapter 8: Performance, Scalability, and Monetization 277
Chapter 9: OpenSocial Templates, Markup, and Emerging Technologies 325
Index 375

OpenSocial™
Network Programming

Lynne Grewe

WILEY

Wiley Publishing, Inc.

OpenSocial™ Network Programming

Published by
Wiley Publishing, Inc.
10475 Crosspoint Boulevard
Indianapolis, IN 46256
www.wiley.com

ISBN: 978-0-470-44222-7

Manufactured in the United States of America

10 9 8 7 6 5 4 3 2 1

Library of Congress Cataloging-in-Publication Data:

Grewe, Lynne, 1965-
   OpenSocial network programming / Lynne Grewe.
     p. cm.
   Includes index.
   ISBN 978-0-470-44222-7 (paper/website)
 1.   Online social networks — Computer software. 2.   Online social networks — Design.
 3.   Application program interfaces (Computer software) I. Title.
   HM742.G74 2009
   006.7'54 — dc22
                                                              2009001915

To my family, Ben, Allen, and Jake, thank you for sharing this life and love with me.
To my best friend and mother, Joyce, thank you for all of your love and support.
To my father, Larry, and brother, Jeff, thanks for believing in me.

About the Author

Lynne Grewe, Ph.D., is founder and director of ILab at California State University East Bay, where she as a professor in Computer Science. She created the first class in a university to teach social network programming, using the platforms of OpenSocial, Facebook, and others. Previously, she worked at IBM as a media specialist. She received her Ph.D. in Electrical and Computer Engineering from Purdue. She has collaborated with numerous companies in social networking. She has published in professional journals and presented at many conferences and symposiums. Lynne has contacts in industry that are spearheading social network platforms and including Sun, Yahoo!, and Google. She is also a leader in the community developing personalization/socialization of the social network experience and is a member of the OpenSocial foundation.

Credits

Executive Editor
Carol Long

Development Editor
Kevin Shafer

Technical Editor
Ken Walton

Production Editor
Liz Britten

Copy Editor
Kim Cofer
Foxxe Editorial Services

Editorial Manager
Mary Beth Wakefield

Production Manager
Tim Tate

Vice President and Executive Group Publisher
Richard Swadley

Vice President and Executive Publisher
Barry Pruett

Associate Publisher
Jim Minatel

Project Coordinator, Cover
Lynsey Stamford

Proofreader
Josh Chase (Word One)

Indexer
J & J Indexing

Acknowledgments

I would like to thank a number of people for helping me create the best book possible. Thank you to Kevin Shafer, my development editor at Wiley, who with his considerable experience made this book shine. Thank you to Carol Long, executive acquisitions editor at Wiley, a great editor who guided me through the process. Also, thanks to the Wiley publishing team, including Sara Shlaer and Kirk Bateman.

A special thanks to Ken Walton, director of business development and chief software architect at Klick-Nation, who served as technical editor and spent many hours reviewing the book, making suggestions, and helping to ensure that there are no errors.

I also interviewed a number of people to create this book and want to thank the following for their invaluable assistance:

- ❑ Ken Walton, director of business development and chief software architect, KlickNation
- ❑ Cody Simms, Yahoo!, senior director, Yahoo! platforms
- ❑ Prakash Narayan, Zembly
- ❑ Jia Shen, CTO and founder, RockYou
- ❑ Lan LiaBraaten, Sara Jew-lim, Jan Penner, Google
- ❑ David Young, Slide
- ❑ Paul Linder, platform architect, hi5
- ❑ Rod Boothby, vice president, Joyent
- ❑ Ali Partovi, CEO, iLike
- ❑ Vikas Gupta, cofounder/CEO, Jambool
- ❑ Charlene Li, emerging technologies and coauthor of "Groundswell"
- ❑ Kevin Chou, CEO, Watercooler
- ❑ Rhett Mcnulty, COO, Shopit
- ❑ Stefano Pochet, Nealab Technologies, Freebar
- ❑ Jeff Roberto, Friendster
- ❑ Gina Olsen, imeem
- ❑ Pieter De Schepper, Netlog

Contents

Introduction   **xvii**

Chapter 1: Social Network Programming   **1**

Social Network Platforms   **2**

MySpace   2

hi5   5

orkut   7

Friendster   8

imeem   9

Freebar   9

Netlog   11

Yahoo!   12

Other Networks   14

Social Network Applications   **14**

Application Discovery   15

Application Installation   16

Application Appearance   17

Control of Applications   25

Making Applications Social and Viral   **29**

Application Goals   **29**

Growth   30

Engagement   30

Good Look and Feel   32

Dynamic Evolution   32

Self Expression   32

Social Exposure   33

Relationship Building   33

Real-World Problem Solving   33

Application Trends   **33**

Reach (General Appeal) Applications   35

Vertical (Targeted) Applications   36

Template-Based Application Development   36

Brand Applications   39

Destination Applications   39

Contents

Longer Engagement 39

Use of Media 39

Internationalization 41

Self Expression 43

Partnering 43

Virtual Currencies, Goods, and Points 43

Mobile Applications 45

Increased Use of Social Data 45

Increased Use of Application Data 46

Viral Channels and Features **46**

Social Network Identity **48**

Marketing — The Next Step **50**

Retention **53**

Tips for Good Application Development **53**

Summary **54**

Chapter 2: Introduction to OpenSocial **57**

OpenSocial History **57**

OpenSocial Architecture **59**

Client-Based API 60

Server-Based API 61

Application Architecture **65**

Sample Application **66**

OpenSocial Data Formats **67**

JSON 67

Atom 68

XML 68

Application Deployment **69**

MySpace Deployment 69

hi5 Deployment 76

orkut Deployment 77

Netlog Deployment 80

imeem Deployment 80

Friendster Deployment 82

Freebar Deployment 85

What You Need to Get Started **85**

Summary **88**

Chapter 3: Gadget XML and Gadget API **89**

Gadget XML **89**

Gadget API **97**

Core Gadget API 97
Feature-Specific Gadget API 104
Multiple Views **109**
Changing Views Dynamically 111
Lifecycle Support **111**
Summary **112**

Chapter 4: JavaScript API 113

A Simple Application in OpenSocial **113**
OpenSocial API Features **117**
People **118**
VieweData Example 119
GetFriends Example 121
Info Example 124
IdSpec 124
Activities **132**
Messages — Email and Notifications 133
Activity Posting (Updates) 136
Invitations to Install 139
Persistence **141**
Information Storage 142
Information Retrieval 142
Detail of OpenSocial JavaScript API **146**
Summary **170**

Chapter 5: OpenSocial RESTful API 169

Getting to Know REST **169**
Purely RESTful Architecture 171
RESTful-RPC Hybrid Architecture 171
Looking at an Example of REST 171
OpenSocial RESTful Server-Side Programming **173**
Completely Server-Based OpenSocial RESTful API Application 173
Hybrid OpenSocial JavaScript and RESTful API Application 175
OpenSocial RESTful Application Architecture **175**
OpenSocial REST Authorization and Authentication (OAuth) **176**
OAuth Steps 177
OAuth Parameters 179
OAuth Requests 179
OAuth Signing Requests 180
OAuth Tokens (the Response) 181
OAuth in PHP 181

Contents

HTTP Errors   195
OpenID   195
Key Cache and Token Management   195
OAuth Libraries   196
What You Need   196
hi5 Authentication Scheme   196
OpenSocial RESTful API Details   **198**
OpenSocial REST Request Construction   198
OpenSocial REST API Specification   200
Data Formatting and Atom/AtomPub   203
HTTP Method Type   210
OpenSocial REST Response   211
What You Need   212
OpenSocial REST Application Deployment   **212**
HTTP Status Codes   **213**
OpenSocial REST Support Discovery   **213**
OpenSocial Security with the REST API   **216**
OpenSocial REST API Future   **216**
OpenSocial RPC Protocol   **216**
Summary   **219**

Chapter 6: Programming Fundamentals   **223**

Application Testing   **223**
Front-End GUI Design Tips   **224**
Navigation Tabs   224
Look and Feel   226
Social Network-Specific Looks   227
External Resources   **228**
Caching Issues   230
POST Request   231
Signed Request   232
Performance Improvement Using Preload   234
Capabilities Inquiry   **234**
Action Requests and Permissions   **234**
Summary   **235**

Chapter 7: Sample Applications   **235**

Person/People Applications   **235**
Requesting a Maximum Number of Friends   236
Using Multiple Requests for Friends   236
Requesting Only Friends Who Have the Application Installed   237

Producing a Paginated Friends List   238
Using Pronouns   239
Creating a Friend Selector   241
Testing If Two Users Are Friends   243
Finding Top Friends Who Have the Application Installed   244
Friends of Friends   246

Communications Applications   **246**
Making Signed Requests   247
Creating Minimessages   249
Creating Gadget Message Bundles   250
Using Message and Activity Templates   251
Using Message Summaries   254
Using Media Items in Activities   254

Clearing AppData   **258**
Understanding Environment — Support and Domain   **259**
Handling Errors   **262**
Container Compliance and NOT_IMPLEMENTED   262

Checking and Asking for Permissions   **263**
Working with Container-Specific Extensions   **264**
hi5 Lifecycle Extension   265
DataRequest Extension   266
Fields Extension   266
hi5 Template Library   266

Using Internationalization, Localization, and Globalization   **267**
Using Flash Media   **271**
Option 1: Using the Gadget API   271
Option 2: Using the SWFObject JavaScript Library   272
More Configuration Options   273
Container Support   274

JavaScript Tools for Applications   **274**
Summary   **275**

Chapter 8: Performance, Scalability, and Monetization   **279**

Understanding Scalability and Performance   **280**
Defining Scalability   280
Using Scalability Metrics   281
Performance Problem Areas   282
Scaling Up or Out   282

Understanding Architecture   **282**
Understanding Subsystems   **284**
Web Server   285
Application Server   285

Contents

Load Balancing	286
Caching	286
Content Delivery Networks (CDNs)	292
Understanding Hosting Solutions	**292**
What They're Saying about Hosting Solutions	294
Amazon Web Services (AWS)	294
Joyent	300
Other Hosting Solutions	301
Case Studies	**301**
Understanding Database Issues	**302**
Distributed Systems (Scale Out)	303
Database Sharding	303
Understanding Redundancy	**304**
Using Monitoring	**304**
Understanding Software Design	**305**
Language Choice	307
Versioning	307
OpenSocial Performance Tuning	**308**
Minimizing the Number of HTTP Requests	308
Batching Multiple Requests	308
Using OpenSocial AppData as a Container Cache	309
Reducing the Number of DNS Lookups	309
Reducing the Number of Files	309
Turning on the Persistence Feature in a Web Server	309
Compressing Content Using GZIP	310
"Minifying" JavaScript	310
Using CSS in a Header	310
Locating JavaScript at the Bottom	311
Caching versus Requests for External Files (JavaScript, CSS)	311
Flushing a Server Response	311
Monitoring Client Code Performance	311
Preloading OpenSocial Content	313
Achieving Good Load Times	314
Using OpenSocial get from Cache	314
Using CSS Image Sprites	314
Using Analytics	**314**
Google Analytics	315
Yahoo! Web Analytics	317
Sometrics	318
Social Network-Provided	318
Using Scalable User Interface Design	**318**
Making the Most of User/System Support	**319**

Monetization   **320**
  Advertising   320
  Affiliate Programs   321
  Partnering   322
  Virtual Goods and Virtual Currency   322
  Real Goods and Micropayments/Micro-Transactions   323
  Monetization Case Studies   323
Summary   **325**

Chapter 9: OpenSocial Templates, Markup, and Emerging Technologies   **325**

OpenSocial Templates Standard   **325**
  Requiring a Feature   326
  Understanding Basic Template Construction and Use   327
  Naming Templates   328
  Using Expressions in Templates   329
  Using Variables and Passing Data to a Template   330
  Calling Templates with Parameters   331
  Using the repeat Attribute for Looping   332
  Using Conditional Tests   332
  Localization with Templates   332
  Using a Separate Definition File for Templates   333
  OpenSocial Markup Language   334
  OpenSocial Data Pipelining   345
  OpenSocial Template Examples   350
OpenSocial Proxied Content   **352**
OpenSocial Client Libraries   **353**
Yahoo! Open Strategy   **353**
  Y!OS Architecture   354
  Yahoo! User Profiles   355
  Yahoo! User Updates   355
  Yahoo! Applications (YAP)   356
  YAP Application Development Steps   360
  YAP OpenSocial Application Development   361
  Yahoo! Query Language   364
  Understanding the Yahoo! User Interface (YUI)   365
  Using Yahoo! Markup Language (YML)   365
  Y!OS Application Examples   366
iWidgets   **367**
Zembly   **368**
  Understanding the Zembly Application Structure   369
  Understanding a Zembly Service   370
  Understanding a Zembly Widget   371

Contents

Understanding a Zembly Snippet   371
Understanding a Zembly Key Chain   371
Creating an OpenSocial Application in Zembly   371
Publishing an Application   373
Creating Your Own Service   373
Summary   **374**

Index   **375**

Introduction

OpenSocial is a new and exciting platform that allows you to create and deploy social networking applications on multiple networks, including MySpace, hi5, imeem, Friendster, Netlog, orkut, and more. It is an alternative to the single-container Facebook-only API used by Facebook. This book teaches you step by step how to create viral and engaging social network applications using OpenSocial. Also discussed are front-end and back-end issues, how to make money with social network applications, and marketing strategies. This book also features new emerging technologies that let you "mash/mix" a social application.

Who This Book Is For

The primary target audience of this book is programmers interested in state-of-the-art social network programming with OpenSocial. While a brief introduction to JavaScript is provided, some familiarity with it and Web development is ideal. The parts of this book dealing with a discussion of social applications and emerging technologies are appropriate for the broader audience of tech-savvy social network users who want to easily make their own applications.

What This Book Covers

This book gives a programmer a well-rounded education in the creation of applications for the most popular social networks using OpenSocial. What sets this book apart from others in social network application development is that it shows you how to develop applications for more than one platform, featuring OpenSocial in a "write once, deploy to many social networks" fashion. In addition, the book features a discussion of how to make viral, social applications, and discusses issues surrounding both front-end and back-end needs. Finally, this book is unique in that it also includes a discussion of some emerging platforms that allow even non-programmers to create applications.

Some of the highlights of this book include the following:

- ❑   Learning the OpenSocial API
- ❑   Understanding the OpenSocial architecture, including both client (JavaScript API) and server (RESTful) APIs
- ❑   Learning how to develop OpenSocial applications (including deployment on multiple platforms)
- ❑   Learning about front-end and back-end solutions
- ❑   Discovering marketing and monetization ideas
- ❑   Learning about emerging technologies

How This Book Is Structured

Following is a breakdown of the contents of this book:

❏ *Chapter 1: Social Network Programming* — This chapter provides an overview of some of the most popular social network platforms from a user's perspective. Next, the chapter discusses what a social network application is, and how applications can be found in different platforms and controlled. This chapter also provides an overview of some of the most popular techniques used in creating both "social" and "viral" applications. Tips and tricks from industry experts are provided.

❏ *Chapter 2: Introduction to OpenSocial* — This chapter discusses OpenSocial as an open API for social network development that is meant for use in multiple social network platforms. This chapter also discusses the basic anatomy (architecture) of OpenSocial. Here, you will also learn about OpenSocial data formats. The chapter concludes with an examination of how to deploy it on multiple containers (social networks).

❏ *Chapter 3: Gadget XML and Gadget API* — This chapter provides an examination of the Gadget XML and Gadget API specifications.

❏ *Chapter 4: OpenSocial API* — This chapter provides an in-depth discussion of the OpenSocial JavaScript API, with numerous code samples.

❏ *Chapter 5: OpenSocial RESTful API* — This chapter examines the new OpenSocial RESTful API, which allows server-side programs to access OpenSocial data directly.

❏ *Chapter 6: Programming Fundamentals* — This chapter examines some of the fundamental concepts you should know when working with an OpenSocial application.

❏ *Chapter 7: Sample Applications* — This chapter shows how to create applications that feature different social hooks.

❏ *Chapter 8: Performance, Scalability, and Monetization* — This chapter discusses scalability, and provides tips on maximizing this important characteristic of OpenSocial applications. The discussion examines the inner components making up an application, as well as a variety of available hosting solutions. The chapter examines how to fine-tune applications for better performance, as well as how to maximize the benefits of a scalable design. The chapter concludes with a look at how to use your application to make money.

❏ *Chapter 9: OpenSocial Templates, Markup, and Emerging Technologies* — This chapter examines the OpenSocial Templates standard, OpenSocial proxied content, OpenSocial client libraries, and other emerging technologies.

What You Need to Use This Book

This book assumes that you are a user of social networks and have an account on one or more networks (such as MySpace or hi5). Having an understanding of JavaScript and basic Web development technologies is ideal. Finally, as described in the book, to create and deploy your own application, you will need an account on an appropriate server.

Conventions

To help you get the most from the text and keep track of what's happening, a number of conventions are used throughout the book.

> Boxes like this one hold important, not-to-be forgotten information that is directly relevant to the surrounding text.

Tips, hints, tricks, and asides to the current discussion are offset and placed in italics like this.

As for styles in the text:

- ❏ New terms and important words are *highlighted* like this when they are introduced.
- ❏ Keyboard strokes are shown like this: Ctrl+A.
- ❏ Filenames, URLs, and code within the text are shown like this: `persistence.properties`.
- ❏ Code is shown in two different ways:

```
New and important code is highlighted in code examples with a gray background.
The gray highlighting is not used for code that's less important in the
    present context, or has been shown before.
```

Source Code

As you work through the examples in this book, you may choose either to type in all the code manually or to use the source code files that accompany the book. All of the source code used in this book is available for downloading at `http://www.wrox.com`. Once at the site, simply locate the book's title (either by using the Search box, or by using one of the title lists) and click the Download Code link on the book's detail page to obtain all the source code for the book.

Because many books have similar titles, you may find it easiest to search by ISBN; this book's ISBN is 978-0-470-44222-7.

Once you download the code, just decompress it with your favorite compression tool. Alternately, you can go to the main Wrox code download page at `http://www.wrox.com/dynamic/books/download.aspx` to see the code available for this book and all other Wrox books.

Errata

We make every effort to ensure that there are no errors in the text or in the code. However, no one is perfect, and mistakes do occur. If you find an error in one of our books (such as a spelling mistake or faulty piece of code), we would be very grateful for your feedback. By sending in errata, you may save another reader hours of frustration and, at the same time, you will be helping us provide even higher-quality information.

To find the errata page for this book, go to `http://www.wrox.com` and locate the title using the Search box or one of the title lists. Then, on the book details page, click the Book Errata link. On this page, you can view all errata that has been submitted for this book and posted by Wrox editors. A complete book list (including links to each book's errata) is also available at `www.wrox.com/misc-pages/booklist.shtml`.

If you don't spot "your" error on the Book Errata page, go to `www.wrox.com/contact/techsupport.shtml` and complete the form there to send us the error you have found. We'll check the information and, if appropriate, post a message to the book's errata page, and fix the problem in subsequent editions of the book.

p2p.wrox.com

For author and peer discussion, join the P2P forums at p2p.wrox.com. The forums are a Web-based system for you to post messages relating to Wrox books and related technologies, as well as to interact with other readers and technology users. The forums offer a subscription feature to email you topics of interest of your choosing when new posts are made to the forums. Wrox authors, editors, other industry experts, as well as your fellow readers, are present on these forums.

At http://p2p.wrox.com you will find a number of different forums that will help you not only as you read this book but also as you develop your own applications. To join the forums, just follow these steps:

1. Go to p2p.wrox.com and click the Register link.

2. Read the terms of use, and click Agree.

3. Complete the required information to join, as well as provide any optional information you wish, and click Submit.

4. You will receive an email with information describing how to verify your account and complete the joining process.

You can read messages in the forums without joining P2P, but in order to post your own messages, you must join.

Once you join, you can post new messages and respond to messages other users post. You can read messages at any time on the Web. If you would like to have new messages from a particular forum emailed to you, click the "Subscribe to this Forum" icon by the forum name in the forum listing.

For more information about how to use the Wrox P2P, be sure to read the P2P FAQs for answers to questions about how the forum software works, as well as many common questions specific to P2P and Wrox books. To read the FAQs, click the FAQ link on any P2P page.

1

Social Network Programming

The most recent explosive growth on the World Wide Web (WWW) is *social networking*. Social networking allows you to make and connect to friends in unique and fun ways, in what are known as *build communities*. Consider the explosive growth of social networks such as MySpace and Facebook in the United States. This new paradigm of Web use is taking hold not only in the U.S., but also worldwide. Social networks are considered the new interface, the new transaction process of the WWW in large part because of the concept behind the word "social," and its implementation through the development and use of *social network applications*. This book provides you with the skills necessary to create dynamic, viral, engaging applications for multiple platforms.

This book provides the programmer and (in the case of mash-up and authoring technologies) the casual or beginning tech-savvy person with the necessary knowledge to enable them to create their own social network applications.

Not all social networks allow third-party organizations or individuals to create social network applications. This capability really emerged with the Facebook API, which is why you see so many applications on Facebook.

Most recently, a new standard has emerged called OpenSocial. It was spear-headed by Google to be an Open Source multi-container (network) solution. It was explicitly created to allow developers to create applications that could be deployed on multiple social networks (containers), unlike the previous Facebook-only API. This is a powerful idea, because it provides the capability to create once and deploy to many. OpenSocial has the added advantage of being Open Source, which enables developers to take lead roles in how it will evolve. Many of the most popular social networks such as MySpace, hi5, Friendster, and others, are now supporting OpenSocial as the standard for application development. New social networks are signing on rapidly. New OpenSocial applications are being generated for these containers every day.

To create successful social networking applications, a developer must understand how each social network is run, and how users utilize these networks and their applications. This chapter reviews a number of OpenSocial container networks from a user's perspective. These interfaces can (and do) change, and what is shown in this discussion reflects the state as of this writing. However, even with changes, you will notice many of the same utilities and similar user interface (UI) features.

This chapter also examines good application goals, and shows you some application trends. You will learn about the most effective viral channels and application features. Later in this chapter, you will learn about marketing strategies and the important topic of user retention. This chapter concludes with some tips for good application development.

Social Network Platforms

Today, there are many social networks, and more are being created every day. The biggest players change frequently, depending on the country. Following are a few of the most popular social networks:

- ❏ MySpace
- ❏ hi5
- ❏ orkut
- ❏ Friendster
- ❏ imeem
- ❏ Freebar
- ❏ Netlog
- ❏ Linkedin
- ❏ Facebook

While many of these networks are general, some have targeted audiences. For example, LinkedIn is used mostly for professional networking. imeem is targeted (centered?) around music, artists, producers, and consumers.

Now, let's take a brief look at some of the most popular social networks.

MySpace

MySpace is one of the earliest and most successful social networks in existence, often billed as the most popular social network. It has been around since 2003/2004, and its user demographics include a large percentage of U.S. teenagers. Fox Interactive Media has owned MySpace since 2005.

The Internet marketing research firm, comScore, compiles and provides marketing data and services to many of the largest Internet-based companies. In the United States, Fox is ranked fifth, above Facebook's number 16 in comScore's measure of the number of unique visitors. In terms of OpenSocial, MySpace was one of the initial launch partners, and offered its MySpace Developer Platform that supported OpenSocial in 2007. For many English-based applications, you will want to deploy your OpenSocial application on MySpace because of the sheer size of the potential audience.

Figure 1-1 shows the main interface, referred to in OpenSocial as the "home" view. This is seen by a typical MySpace user and consists of an upper navigation bar, followed by three vertical sections populated with boxed areas, each containing specific utilities. The left column is dominated by an image of the user and details about the user, followed by a listing of currently installed applications. The middle column contains MySpace-controlled utilities such as "Status and Mood" (both yours and your friends'), "Friend Updates" (what your friends are doing), "Bulletin Space," and "Friend Spaces" (listing of friends). The far right column on the main interface displays installed applications running in this "home" view. You have access to some of these items through OpenSocial. For example, OpenSocial allows an application to get the current status of a person. Knowing where and how users on a network might use this feature can be important for your application. Becoming intimately familiar with a network from a user's perspective is critical.

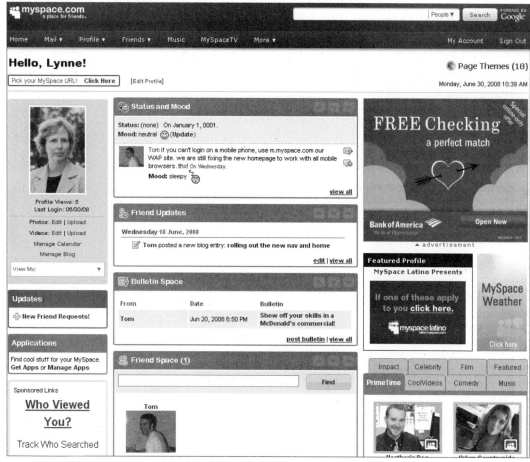

Figure 1-1: MySpace main user interface ""home" view"

The main MySpace navigation bar (which remains on most pages) contains the following links:

❑   Home takes you to the main ("home") view shown in Figure 1-1.

❑   Mail takes you to the interface that lets you send and receive messages with others on MySpace

❑   Profile contains the information the user chooses to "share" with friends and others on the network. The "Tom" user profile is provided to everyone as a friend when you join MySpace.

❑　Friends shows both current friends and ways to find new friends.

❑　Music shows media pages delivered by MySpace (much like the media you see at the Yahoo! Web site).

❑　More displays a series of MySpace-sponsored applications, as shown in Figure 1-2.

Figure 1-2: More applications sponsored by MySpace

As users add more information, applications, and friends, their profiles grow in size. But, regardless of the amount, the information is divided into categories showing information about the user on the left-hand side of the profile page (such as interests, details, schools, networking, and so on). On the right side of the profile page are categories for Blurbs, Friends' Comments, and Friend Space. Also featured on the profile are user-added applications that are deployed to run in the "profile" view. When users decide to add an application, they can determine if it appears in their profile or not.

Later in this chapter, you will learn about the size limitations of applications on different views for all of the social networks, including MySpace. It is important to keep these restrictions in mind when developing your application.

hi5

Launched in 2003, hi5 is one of the world's largest social networks, ranked as a top 20 Web site globally, and the number 1 social network in 25 countries across Latin America, Europe, Asia, and Africa. According to comScore, more than 56 million individuals every month visit hi5, which is currently available in 27 language options. Recently, hi5 experienced one of the fastest growth rates of social networks. hi5 is a privately held company, headquartered in San Francisco, California.

Figure 1-3 shows the main interface (or "home" view) seen by a typical hi5 user. Note that this interface consists of an upper navigation bar, as well as three vertical sections populated with boxed areas, each containing specific utilities.

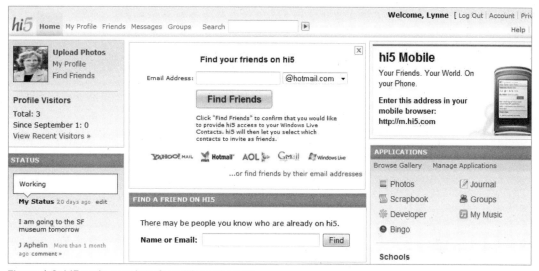

Figure 1-3: hi5 main user interface ("home" view)

The main navigation bar that appears on most pages seen by the user has links for Home (home view), Profile (profile view), Friends (listing of friends), Messages, and Groups (user and friend's groups subscribed to). The left column is dominated by an image of and details about the user. The middle column contains such hi5-controlled utilities as "Find Friends." The far-right column features a list of installed applications.

As shown in Figure 1-4, a user profile page has a secondary navigation bar that provides links to elements such as Profile (profile info), Photos (photo albums), Scrapbook (where you and your friends can make postings), Journal (where you can make journal entries and share with friends), Groups (that is, topical groups of which users can be members), Friends (that is, a list of a user's friends), Developer (this is present if the user has registered as a developer, and links to main development page), and Applications (currently installed applications, a link to a gallery, featured applications, and so on). Underneath this navigation bar is the current user profile data, with the current applications installed that run in "profile" view appearing beneath the navigation bar.

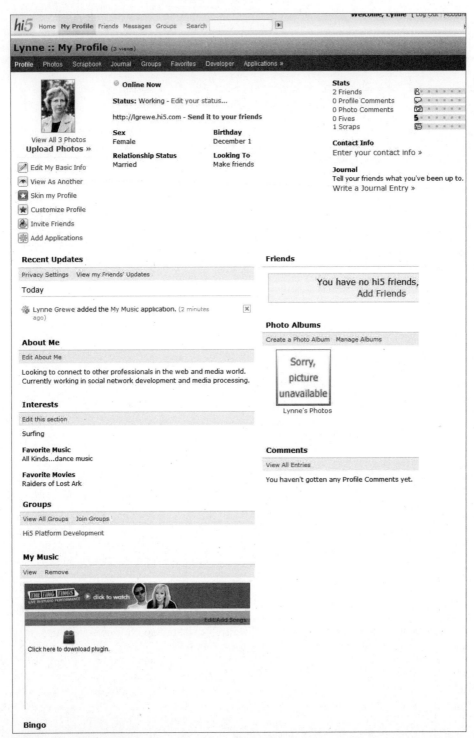

Figure 1-4: Profile in hi5

Of particular interest in a user's hi5 profile is the Applications link on the navigation bar. Clicking this link takes you to a page that first displays hi5-featured applications, followed by a list of applications currently installed. Featured applications can be determined by factors such as applications most recently installed by a user's friends.

orkut

orkut was founded in 2004 and, as of this writing, has more than 50 communities, with more than 37 million total members and nearly 1.3 million daily visitors. The majority of users are from Brazil, followed by smaller minorities in India and United States, as well as (to a much lesser degree) a handful of other countries. The large majority of users are in the age bracket of 18-30 years old.

Figure 1-5 shows the main interface ("home" view) that consists of an upper navigation bar, and, underneath the navigation bar, three vertical sections populated with boxed areas that contain links to specific utilities.

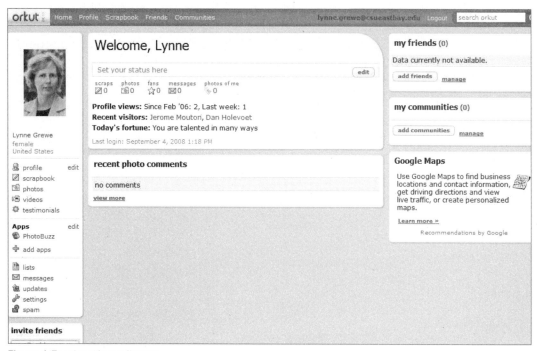

Figure 1-5: orkut "home" page

The main navigation bar provides links for Home (home view), Profile (profile view), Scrapbook (user postings such as twitters or blogs), Friends (listing of friends), and Communities (user-joined communities).

The left column on the "home" page shows an image of the user, followed by details about the user. A list of currently installed applications appears below the user profile information. The middle column provides information about the user's status, people who have visited the user's profile, and more. The right column contains a list of friends and communities a user belongs to.

Friendster

Launched in 2002, Friendster was one of the earliest social networks, appearing on the scene even before MySpace. With more than 80 million members worldwide, Friendster is a leading global online social network that is popular in Asia. Like hi5, Friendster is experiencing a good growth rate. In 2008, Friendster announced plans for users in some Asian countries to be eligible to subscribe to ''Friendster Text Alerts,'' which are Short Message Service (SMS) text messages users can receive on mobile phones to notify them of friend requests, new messages, and more. This is an intriguing possible new arena of contact for social networking applications. Friendster is headquartered in San Francisco, California.

Figure 1-6 shows the main interface (''home'' view) of Friendster that consists of an upper navigation bar, and, underneath the navigation bar, two vertical sections populated with areas that contain links to specific utilities.

Figure 1-6: Friendster's main interface, ''home'' view

The main navigation bar that appears on most pages seen by the user has links for Home (home view), My Profile (profile view), My Apps (currently installed applications), My Connections (friends, groups, and so on), Explore (people, photos, video, and so on), and Search.

The large left column below the navigation bar shows the user's image, followed by information about Friends, Groups, and so on. The smaller right column also features My Friends, Bulletins, and some advertising.

imeem

Launched in 2004, imeem is an example of a *targeted social network*, meaning that it has a specific interest or targeted audience. In this case, imeem is focused on providing users with the capability to interact by watching, posting, and sharing all kinds of digital media, particularly music. Unlike YouTube (which concentrates on the sharing of video), imeem has the look and feel of "traditional" social networks like MySpace, but is focused around music and media. Like all of the other social networks mentioned thus far, imeem generates revenue through advertising, but also generates income by providing the capability for users to subscribe to additional services. imeem has reported more than 25 million visitors per month, with more than 65,000 new users every day. imeem is a privately held company, headquartered in San Francisco, California.

As of this writing, imeem was allowing applications only to run in a *sandbox* (meaning that the applications are not available for installation and use by general users). However, because imeem is one of the larger "targeted" social networks and provides different challenges for application development, it is worth mentioning here. imeem does have plans to deploy live in the near future, and details will be posted on imeem's Web site (www.imeem.com). imeem also currently offers a REST-like Web service that developers may use to access some data. Currently, imeem supports OpenSocial 0.7, but, with the RESTful API that is part of OpenSocial 0.8, it is expected that this functionality will be subsumed by OpenSocial 0.8 when imeem supports it.

Figure 1-7 shows imeem's main interface ("home" view) that consists of an upper main navigation bar, with a second navigation bar positioned directly below. Three vertical sections underneath the navigation bars are populated with boxed areas that contain specific utilities.

The main navigation bar that appears on most pages seen by the user has links for Home (home view), Music, Video, Playlists, and Community. The second menu bar changes with the page being viewed. For example, on the Home page shown in Figure 1-7, the second menu bar deals with user-related issues such as messages and uploads of media. A user profile page, on the other hand, would have a secondary navigation bar with links for elements such as Profile (profile info), Playlists, Music, Video, Photos, Games, Blog, Friends, Groups, and, in the case of developers, Applications.

Unlike the other social networks, there is no discernible trend to the organization of the utilities in the three columns appearing below imeem's navigation bars. However, the columns feature similar kinds of utilities, such as Friend Status Updates, Friend Updates, and information about the user being featured on the page. In addition to these, there are media-related utilities such as "Media Tracker" and "Artists I am a Fan of." imeem includes a number of media-related and music-related utilities for such tasks as the creation and sharing of music playlists. Applications that use this kind of social media would be well-suited to imeem users.

Freebar

A number of predominately non-English or foreign-based social networks such as IDtail, YiQi, Hyves, Mail.ru, and Freebar are now OpenSocial containers. Freebar, a social network in Italy, is a newer player. It sprang out of a local Web community site focused regionally on Naples, Italy. Freebar now has approximately 500,000 members, predominately from Italy. Freebar is self-described as being youth-oriented, and has physical presence at youth-oriented events in Italy. As one of the first supporters of OpenSocial in Europe, Freebar is hoping to attract developers and new users alike with interesting application offers. Even though Freebar is a smaller beginning network, application developers may take advantage of Freebar's new evolution in an emerging market.

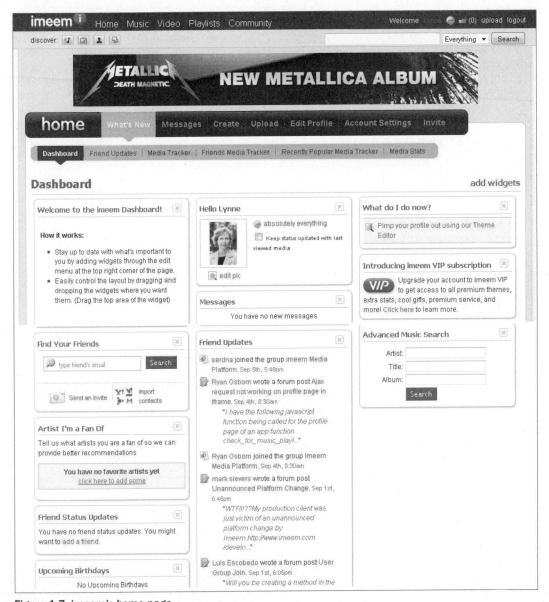

Figure 1-7: imeem's home page

Figure 1-8 shows Freebar's main interface ("home" view) that primarily consists of an upper naviga-tion bar. A unique feature of Freebar is a list of people who have visited the user profile, called the user's "space." This is similar to a feature seen on the LinkedIn professional social network. The main navigation bar takes the user to My.Space (the user profile page), Chat, Video, Forums, and Friends.

Figure 1-8: Freebar's main interface (the "home" view)

The user's profile page can be accessed by clicking on the My.Space link. The other pages are very similar in nature (like the Friends page) to what you see in other networks.

Netlog

Netlog is one of the leading European social networks. Netlog is self-described as being specifically targeted at European youth. It has been developed by Netlog NV, based in Ghent, Belgium. Netlog is currently available in 20 languages, and has more than 35 million members throughout Europe. Because of the ethnic diversity in Europe, Netlog supports many different languages, as evidenced on the opening page shown to new visitors to the site. As shown in Figure 1-9, this page queries the visitor for a preferred language. Netlog is newer to OpenSocial, and, as of this writing, has recently begun its support for applications. Because of its large user base, it will likely become a desirable container for application deployment.

Figure 1-10 shows the main interface for a user on Netlog. At the top of the page is a main navigation bar, with a secondary bar present on most main pages. The main navigation bar includes links to Explore (media, events, applications), Manage (your info, your profile, your applications, and so on), Logs (notifications and news about your friends, clans/groups, and so on), Messages (a mail Inbox), Friends (requests, add friends, and so on), and Settings (such as privacy, and so on). Netlog relies heavily on the secondary navigation bars, where the user clicks on the Application's link once at the main user's profile page in order to see applications being used.

The column layout appearing below these navigation bars includes such familiar utilities as Video, Blogs, News, New Users, and so on.

Yahoo!

As one of the largest Web companies, Yahoo! has been around since the mid-1990s. It has recently announced the creation of the Yahoo! Open strategy, called Y!OS. This opens up Yahoo!'s social infrastructure with a set of unifying APIs for social application development. Part of this is a unifying experience for the user, much like a social network. Following are some of the services that Yahoo! is integrating under Y!OS:

❑ Yahoo! Music

❑ Flickr

❑ Yahoo! Search (search monkey)

❑ del.icio.us

❑ Yahoo! Shopping

❑ YUI (Yahoo! User Interface)

❑ Yahoo! Maps

❑ Yahoo! Messenger

❑ Yahoo! Travel

❑ Yahoo! Answers

❑ Yahoo! Mail

❑ Yahoo! Blueprint Platform (Mobile applications)

❑ Yahoo! Contacts (Yahoo! Address book)

NETLOG™

Live it. Log it.

English - continue   Dansk - fortsæt

Deutsch - weiter   Svenska - fortsätt

Français - continue   Català - continua

Nederlands - ga verder   Lietuvių kalba - tarp draugų

Español - continua   Slovenščina - nadaljuj

Português - continua   Česky - pokračuj

Italiano - continua   عربي - دائم

Română - continua   中文 - 继续

Русский - продолжить   Slovenčina - pokračuj

Türkçe - devam   Magyar - tovább

Polski - kontynuuj   Afrikaans - gaan voort

Norsk (bokmål) - fortsett   Български - продължи

Figure 1-9: Netlog's entrance page for new users, querying the user for a language preference

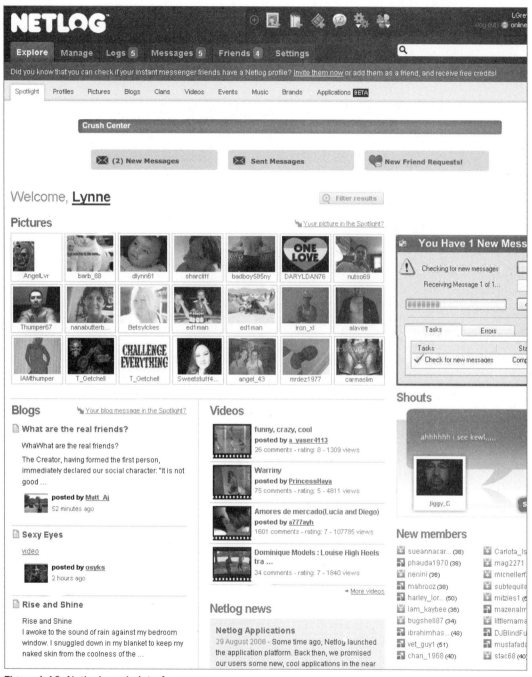

Figure 1-10: Netlog's main interface page

Extending to 233 countries, Yahoo! has more than 500 million monthly users, and 180 billion monthly page views. These are impressive numbers for an application developer to possibly leverage.

A main feature of Y!OS for the application developer is the Yahoo! Application Platform called YAP. Chapter 9 provides more details on this and other emerging technologies.

Other Networks

Other networks are involved with OpenSocial, many of which are in the beginning stages of OpenSocial support and are not yet live. The OpenSocial Web site (`http://code.google.com/apis/opensocial /gettingstarted.html`) provides a current listing of all the supporting networks. Now that you are familiar with available social networks on the Web, let's get a broad perspective of applications that can be developed for deployment on these containers.

Social Network Applications

A *social network application* is, as the name suggests, an application created and deployed on a social network, often by third-party developers. You may see this term in reference to applications that, while not on a social network, have social interactions. This book refers to these more generically as *social applications*. Some of the existing APIs used to create social interactions outside of a pure social network such as Google Friend Connect are not covered in this book. Chapter 9 discusses the Yahoo! Open Strategy (Y!OS) platform that can be used outside of a social network. In addition, OpenSocial REST (a topic examined later in the book) can be used outside of the social network application. Your imagination is the limit for what a social network application can do. Many different kinds of applications exist today. If you were to browse a list of available applications, you most likely would see categories such as Entertainment/Fun, Shopping, Sports, Financial, Travel, and more. These types of categories are not standardized between networks. There are thousands of applications available on MySpace and hi5, and, within each category, there may be many kinds of applications.

For example, consider the category of Money/Finance. In this category, you might see applications that track current stock prices, help you to maintain your personal finances, help you trade stock with others, help you create fictional portfolios, or help you loan money to friends.

In the category of Entertainment, you would most likely see many diverse applications. There are applications such as iLike that rates what music/media you like, and shares this with friends. Another example, "Kiss" by KlickNation, lets you virtually "kiss" users of the application.

The goals of an application can be varied. In the beginning stages of social network application development, many of the applications were designed for a general audience, and simple (if not often silly) in nature. Today, the trend seems to be leaning toward applications that are not meant to solely be popular (or *viral*), but also have retention and long-term use with more complex and longer interactions. Applications involving music/media, business, and education are examples of this mold. One example currently under development is an application named "USpeak," that is being created for learning "social" foreign languages.

A social application may be considered at its best when it is literally "social." This means the application has and encourages interaction between fellow friends and users of the application. It may also use social data. There are many ways that an application can achieve this, as will be discussed later in this chapter.

While it is true you could create a social network application that has no social interactions, it would not really be social. Throughout this book, you will learn how to make truly social applications for the most popular social networks.

Let's lay some groundwork, however, by examining how users find and install applications, as well as how social applications are controlled by networks.

Application Discovery

How users can find and then install your application is important. To a large extent, each network controls this. On most networks, "finding" an application can be done via the following operations:

- ❑ Browsing a subject/category index
- ❑ Searching through the use of keywords
- ❑ Being invited by a friend
- ❑ Viewing application on a user's profile
- ❑ Using a feed posting
- ❑ Using network-sponsored applications
- ❑ Using a New Application index
- ❑ Using a Most Popular Application index
- ❑ Using direct marketing (such as through email)
- ❑ Using Web site postings
- ❑ Using cross-application marketing
- ❑ Using paid advertisements
- ❑ Using purchased installments

Figure 1-11 shows a browsing index on hi5. Note that each network will have its own categorizations. Although there is no standard, networks do share many similar categories. When you create and register your application with a network, you are usually able to signify what category (or categories) your application belongs to. As you will see in Chapter 2, you are often limited to a few selections.

You may search for an application by using a simple search interface that allows you to enter a search term. Ranking of search results is done differently for each network; Figure 1-12 shows an example from hi5. The search algorithms take into account metrics such as the number of active (daily) users, the number of installs, keyword matching, recent application updates, and so on, when returning search results.

In addition to the category index, some networks offer "popular" or "new application" listings in search return lists. Popularity is often determined by the number of active users. New applications are typically listed with more recent appearing first, and, after some network-specific amount of time, being removed from the list.

Users are often introduced to a new application through an invitation by a friend. Most networks and applications allow users to create a personalized message with the invitation. Application developers should keep this personalization feature in mind. Another well-used feature of friend invitations is the creation of a graphic depicting the friend, or, better yet, something personalized to send with the invitation. Anything you can do to entice the user to install your application is a good idea.

Figure 1-11: hi5 browsing index

Notifications of what your friend is doing offer another way to spread the word about a new application. This is one of the more intriguing ways to introduce new users to your application. Think of it as using "peer pressure." What teenager doesn't want to use an application when he or she sees friends using it? Let's face it, this works even with non-teenagers. The posting of notifications about friend usage of an application is a great way to use feeds to market the application. Some networks even have built-in facilities to allow users to invite friends to use any of the applications they have installed.

A new trend is for networks to sponsor applications at the top of the search return list (as you sometimes see when using Yahoo! and Google search engines). Having your work as a developer become a network-sponsored application is another way to gain exposure for your efforts. Where and how sponsored applications appear on each network is different. They can appear in news feeds and search results. They can also appear as cross-application advertising — an arrangement under which you are not paying the network, but instead the application owner or the advertising provider the application has registered with.

Later in this chapter, you will learn about some options for this and other kinds of marketing for the discovery of applications.

Application Installation

On most networks, a user must actively choose to install an application before he or she can use it. Direct application contact by a non-user of the application is generally not allowed on social networks. There can be exceptions to this. For example, orkut currently allows users to land on a "canvas" page of a non-installed application and view it.

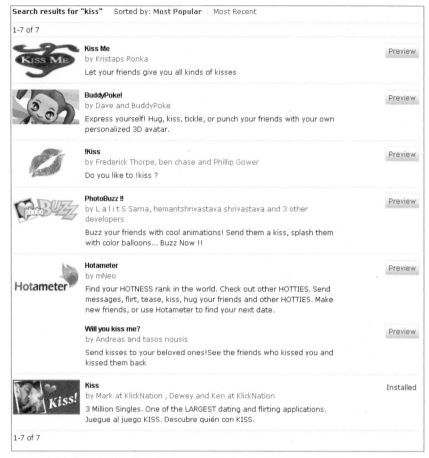

Figure 1-12: Results for searching on "kiss" for applications on hi5

Like many modern Web applications, the installation of a social network application is relatively painless. Because social networks are often very concerned about the user's level of trust, installation usually involves a stage where permissions are asked from the user to allow the application to "do" or "access" various elements related to the user's account. These typically include where the application appears on the user's pages, and how the application can contact the user. These options can be different on each social network.

After an application has been added by a user, it will appear in the user's pages. That appearance is controlled by the social network platform, as well as selected options the user made during application installation. Let's take a look at a few popular social networks, and how applications appear within them.

Application Appearance

Once an application is installed, it can appear in multiple places in a user's account.. The location of an application within the interface is different on each social network, and can possibly be influenced by user permission/account settings. As part of its "GUI design," a network will often designate an area where installed applications are listed for a user. Figure 1-13 and Figure 1-14 show how the iLike application is displayed in different views on a MySpace user's account. Typically, when creating an application, you can associate with it a logo that also appears in the user pages. Let's take a look at how a number of popular networks designate application appearance.

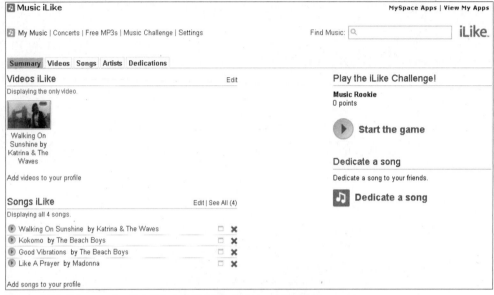

Figure 1-13: iLike application listed in "canvas" view on MySpace

Figure 1-14: iLike application
listed "profile" view on MySpace

OpenSocial applications can appear in three interfaces (called *views*) on a social network user's pages, including the following:

❑ *"Canvas" view* — This view is defined as a "full-screen" running of an application. Of course, it will be still inside of the wrapper of the social network interface, but it takes up a large percentage of the interface.

❑ *"Home" view* — This view is when the application runs on the main/home interface the user sees typically when logging into the network. Most often, this will be reduced in size compared to the "canvas" view.

❑ *"Profile" view* — This is the view when the application is running on the user's profile page. Like the "home" view, this is typically some smaller percentage of this page.

While these are the most common views, OpenSocial allows container's to create container-specific views. Table 1-1 shows the size restrictions for different views for a number of the OpenSocial social networks. Exceptions and additions to these three views are noted.

Check the container's developer documentation for possible changes in these numbers. Chapter 2 shows how to create an OpenSocial application that deploys to different views (pages).

Table 1-1: Application Size Specifications for Different Views on Different Networks

Social Network	"Home" View	"Canvas" View	"Profile" View	Other
MySpace	Width = 290 pixels	Width = 960 pixels	Left-hand column: Width = 300 pixels; Height = you set*	Preview/Profile page
	Height = you set*	Height = you set*	Right-hand column: Width = 430 pixels; Height = you set*	Directory Listing
hi5	Not supported	Width = 956 pixels	Width = 456 pixels	Preview view: Width = 620 pixels
		Height = you set	Height = you set	Height = you set
orkut	Not supported	Width = 835 pixels	Width = 543 pixels	"Preview" view: 400 pixels by 400 pixels maximum (currently uses a screen shot)
		Height = 600 pixels	Height = 280 pixels up to 500 pixels	Directory Listing

Continued

Table 1-1: Application Size Specifications for Different Views on Different Networks
(continued)

Social Network	"Home" View	"Canvas" View	"Profile" View	Other
Friendster	Not supported	Not specified; default is 500 pixels; suggested 100%	Not specified; suggested 100%	
imeem	Not supported	Width = 865 pixels	Width = 550 pixels	Preview view: Width = 635 pixels
		Height = 2000 pixels	Height = 2000 pixels	Height = 2000 pixels
Freebar	Not supported	Width = 1002 pixels	Not supported; future support.	
		Height = you set		
Netlog	Not supported	Width = 1000 pixels	Width = 490 pixels	

*Recommendations are given on the container's developer documentation.

Let's take a look at a few specific networks, and how the appearance of applications is handled in each.

MySpace Application Appearance

An application appears in the different locations in MySpace user pages. When a user first logs in to the user's home page (the "home" view), the page displays a list of all applications. For MySpace, the application can appear directly as a "box" space in the user's profile, as seen with the iLike application in the lower-left of Figure 1-15. As you can see, this can take up a lot of real estate, which means that friends and others will see the application immediately when viewing this user's profile. The user typically has the capability to simply remove the application or hide it.

A user can see a brief description of your application in the MySpace directory listing. This brief description can launch to the application's profile. When you create an application on MySpace, it has its own profile associated with it. This is sometimes called the "preview" view in other containers. This is where a user will find out information about your application. You can customize the look of your profile, but this is what the user will see before installing your application. This application profile is where you might have user forums or reviews/comments about your application. Another item on your application's profile is "friends lists." No size constraints are published on MySpace, and the profile may take up the width and remaining length of the page.

An application may run on an area of the "home" view called the User Home Page Module. It is located in a column and is limited to a smaller width (300 pixels, with height determined by developer, as reflected in Table 1-1). You can use this application to serve simply as a link to a "canvas"-sized application, or you can choose to run a version in this smaller space. This space is more "inward facing," meaning that it is seen only by the user. Hence, it would be ideal for applications that are more utilitarian or communications-oriented.

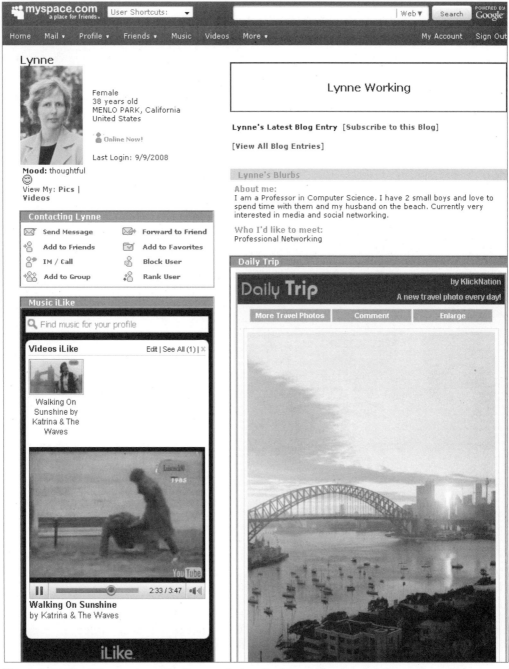

Figure 1-15: The iLike music application running on the lower-left column of the user's profile

An application launched on MySpace in "canvas" view is given a large space (960 pixels wide, as indicated in Table 1-1). The height of an application is up to you, but MySpace recommends not going beyond the page length. In practice, many applications require users to vertically scroll (sometimes because of poor design).

In "profile" view, applications can appear in either the left or right column. Applications in the left column are 300 pixels wide, and in the right column are 430 pixels wide, with the height up to the developer. MySpace's determination of which profile location (left or right) an application will appear in has changed over time.

Most applications take advantage of appearing on multiple views. This results in really long "home" and "profile" pages that can annoy users. As you add more and more applications, they may get lost in an "overlong" mess. Users have the option of removing applications from all or some of their pages to control this clutter. It seems there is no self-censoring when it comes to reducing the number of page views an application appears on. Recently, MySpace, orkut, and others have tested out limiting the number of applications that appear in "home" and "profile" views. For example, MySpace (for a brief time) tried limiting the number of applications listed on the "home" view. In some cases, these changes have been revoked, and other containers are still experimenting with this.

hi5 Application Appearance

As shown in Figure 1-16, hi5 lists currently installed applications while in "home" view, but the applications cannot be run from this view. hi5 only allows applications to run in "profile" and "canvas" views. As shown in Table 1-1, the "canvas" view is defined to be 956 pixels wide, with the height up to the discretion of the developer. The profile view has a width of 456 pixels, with the height again determined by the developer.

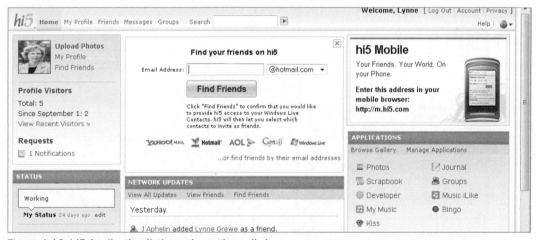

Figure 1-16: hi5 Application listing only on "home" view

hi5 has also defined a "preview" view/page. Similar to the application profile page in MySpace, this is a page that allows potential users of an application to find out more about it. Included with the listing of the application on this page is a preview link that a user may click to yield the preview view. The preview page is 620 pixels wide, with the height being determined by the developer. However, it is best to stay within page length.

orkut Application Appearance

As shown in Figure 1-17, Orkut gives a list of currently installed applications when the user is in the "home" view. However, orkut only allows applications to run in the "profile" and "canvas" views. As shown in Table 1-1, the "canvas" view on orkut is defined to be 835 pixels wide by 600 pixels high (default). The profile view on orkut is 543 pixels wide by 280 pixels high (default).

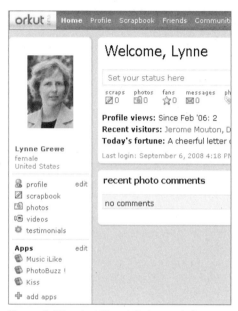

Figure 1-17: orkut "home" view only has application listings

orkut's application directory provides a concise view of an application using a title, thumbnail image (120 pixels wide, 60 pixels tall) and brief text description (maximum of 300 characters). Most containers use the 120 x 60 size for thumbnail images, but a few containers vary from this (for example,. Friendster at 75 x 75 and MySpace at 64 x 64).

Similar to hi5, orkut also uses a "preview" view/page currently defined as a screen shot. This is a page that allows potential users of an application to click a link to find out more about application.

Friendster Application Appearance

Unlike many networks, Friendster does not provide a list of user-installed applications from the "home" page. Instead, the user clicks a MyApps link from the main navigation bar to be taken to the MyApps page, where the installed applications are displayed, as shown in Figure 1-18. The user may click on the name of an application appearing in this list to run the application in "canvas" view. Also, the user may click on the Share button to invite others to share the application, or click on the Edit button to change permissions for the application (including deleting it). Also, on this page, a user can view invitations from others to use an application, as well as track invitations that have been sent.

If the application has implemented a "preview" view, a View link appears on the listing page, and when clicked, will yield a short description (and logo) of the application. Friendster also allows applications to run on a user's profile. This runs in the left-hand column of the profile page (after user details).

Figure 1-18: Friendster's MyApps page for a user

Table 1-1 provides details for size specifications in all of the various Friendster views.

imeem Application Appearance

imeem is an example of a network that has only sandbox access. This means that only developers can see and run their applications, which are not yet "live" for general users.

imeem currently has support to run in both the "canvas" and "profile" views. As shown in Table 1-1, the "canvas" view for imeem is defined to be 865 pixels wide and up to 2000 pixels high. The profile view is 550 pixels wide and up to 2000 pixels high.

imeem also supports an "about page," which is similar to MySpace's application profile page or the preview pages found in other networks. This is controlled as the "preview" view in OpenSocial. The size of this page is 635 pixels wide and up to 2000 pixels high.

Freebar Application Appearance

Currently, the only way to reach applications a user has installed on the Freebar network is through the "Applications" link under the "Extra" box located on a user's "home" page. This takes you to a page in "canvas" view, as shown in Figure 1-19. Since Freebar has just recently gone live with its OpenSocial support, the interface is rather simple. This page lists all applications — those that are installed and those that are not. The only way to distinguish whether an application has been installed is to look at the link next to the Application listing. If it says "View," the application is installed. If it says "Install," then the application obviously must be installed. Notice in Figure 1-19 that the first application, "Billardo," is not installed, but the "Ping-Pong" application is installed. Clicking on "View" launches a "canvas" view of the Application.

Netlog Application Appearance

As of the writing of this book, Netlog, is currently in a beta version for applications. Previously, Netlog only offered sandbox support.

To reach an application listing, you must first click the Explore link from the main navigation bar, which provides you with a secondary menu under the main Explore link. From this secondary menu, you click

Applications, and the resulting screen is divided into divisions for Top and New applications. From this listing, you can select an application to install.

Figure 1-19: Application listing showing both uninstalled and installed applications on Freebar

Once the application is installed, you can access it by clicking Manage from the main navigation bar, and then clicking Applications from the secondary menu. From the resulting page shown in Figure 1-20, you can elect to add the application to the user's profile.

Control of Applications

In addition to the control of an application imposed by the social network, the user and the developer also exert control on an application. Each can control different aspects of an application.

Network Control

Social networks limit applications in a number of ways, including the following:

- ❑ The capability to contact users
- ❑ The capability to contact non-users
- ❑ Where an application appears in the interface
- ❑ Through a myriad of facilities effecting communications and data access

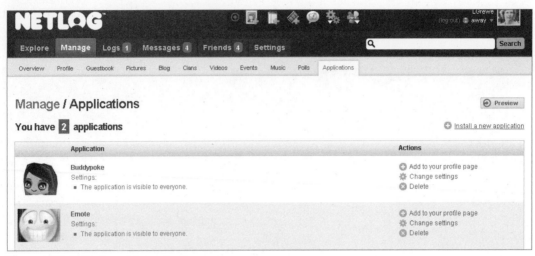

Figure 1-20: Netlog's user's application page

How this is accomplished is, unfortunately, not uniform, and is specific to the social network. Sometimes these services are even disabled. These controls are among the things that often change with social networks.

More specifically, the social network can control applications in the following ways:

- Controlling options through application setup
- Enforcing user-specified permission settings
- Using browsing indices and associated keyword searches
- Limiting "canvas" screen space
- Limiting access to user data
- Limiting (or preventing) access to non-user data
- Limiting the use of messaging, notifications, and other communication options
- Limiting the number of invitations you can send
- Enforcing the network's "Terms of Use Policy," including those pertaining to language and objectionable content
- Limiting data storage (when provided)
- Limiting media access
- Limiting client-side technologies
- Implementing an approval process for application development and application content/media

Each container is different in how it controls an application. These policies are sometimes not published, and may often change. Because of this, developers must continually educate themselves on the changes in any network's application policies. For example, orkut has a limit on activity streams of one update per day, per application, per user.

The first stage of network control comes in the registration of an application. Commonly, this will include limitations on the name of the application, logo used, terms of use, information about pages, as well as the application URL configuration. Chapter 2 provides more detail for different networks.

Placement of an application in browsing indices (as well as placement in returned search results) is determined differently for each network. Each network has different browsable categories. Among the attributes that should be considered is the information given at registration time (such as the application category).

Chapter 4 discusses how different networks support and limit access to social data through the JavaScript (OpenSocial) API. Besides differences between versions of OpenSocial, the greatest difference is in the implementation of optional OpenSocial data fields.

Terms of use policies are enforced by each network. How this is done is proprietary for each network. However, there have been cases of applications being removed because of violations of these policies. Some of the container rules are motivated by applications that seemingly "scam" users into recommendations and other operations.

Checking the terms of use for applications is critical for any developer, and the terms are unique to the network platform. For example, the MySpace Web site provides a complete list of rules for developers that include what an application must do and what it must not do. (See `http://developer.myspace.com/community/myspace/applicationguidelines.aspx` for complete information.)

In addition to Web pages documenting current social network application policies, some social networks (including MySpace) sponsor a forum on the topic. (For a MySpace example, see `http://developer.myspace.com/Community/forums/45.aspx`.) This is a good place to post questions, or even make requests.

Typically, if an application is in violation of a social network's terms of use and guidelines for stated policies, the developer will be notified and have some time to fix the problem. Rules surrounding notification are different for each network. The social network may also, under certain conditions, impose certain sanctions on the developer and the application. Again, using MySpace as an example, specific remedies are outlined for developers to correct violations (see `http://developer.myspace.com/Community/blogs/devteam/archive/2008/08/21/when-good-apps-go-bad.aspx` for complete details.)

Limitations on all forms of communications such as messages, postings to feeds, and notifications are set for applications, and are network-specific. When this limit is exceeded, further requests are refused until the limitation (typically an elapsed time period) is no longer true. Unfortunately, these rules do change, and developer's must read the network's current policies on these issues. Each network also limits the number of invitations an application can send out per user in a fixed amount of time.

Some other forms of network limitation include if and how an application can access network media, and the amount of data storage given an application (when it exists). Additionally, there can be control on the kind of output your application is allowed to give.

User Control

A user can control applications in the following ways:

❑   Installation and removal

❑   Setting permissions at installation time

❑   Changing permissions

❑   Reporting on application

Upon installation of an application, the user may set the original permissions associated with the application. The user may also have the capability to alter these permission settings after installation, as shown in Figure 1-21. Basic user actions such as installation and removal can be tracked by your application. This is done through the recently added OpenSocial lifecycle support, which is discussed in more detail in Chapter 3.

Applications You Are Using

Applications you are currently using appear in this list. You may control where application modules appear, what kinds of notes and updates you receive, and what information is shared.

🎵 Music iLike	About	Settings	Access to private photos and videos disabled.	Remove
🔭 Cities I've Visited	About	Settings	Access to private photos and videos disabled.	Remove
⚫ Photo Shout Out	About	Settings	Access to private photos and videos disabled.	Remove
🦗 SuperPoke!	About	Settings	Notifications disabled. Access to private photos and videos disabled.	Remove
🛍 Shopit Store	About	Settings	Access to private photos and videos disabled.	Remove
✈ Daily Trip	About	Settings	Access to private photos and videos disabled.	Remove
📰 News Merger	About	Settings	Access to private photos and videos disabled.	Remove
◼ Minigolf	About	Settings	Access to private photos and videos disabled.	Remove
Friend Finder Friend Finder	About	Settings		Remove
🖼 Likeness	About	Settings	Access to private photos and videos disabled.	Remove

Figure 1-21: A MySpace user's list of applications, where applications can be removed, and permissions changed

Users can also influence the success of an application via reporting and voting on it. A user can report an application to the network for things such as the application not working properly, infringements on conditions of use, or the use of objectionable material. Each network has policies to investigate these reports, and network responses can include removal of an application.

Developer Control

Developers control their applications simply by how they code and deploy them. It is interesting to note that through the simple act of deployment, the developer can determine how the application appears in a network, and how it is found.

Now that you are familiar with social networks (containers) and have a broad understanding of applications that can be deployed to these, let drill down a bit to see what distinguishes a good social network application from one that is not as successful.

Making Applications Social and Viral

Of primary interest to social network application developers is making an application viral and social. A *viral* application is one that is "wildly" popular. A distinctive feature of social network applications is that they can experience an explosive user growth rate in very short time periods. Another kind of application might take weeks and months to achieve a sizable user base, but a social application can expand its user base in a matter of days (and sometimes hours). This is exciting, but can also be challenging.

There is no uniform metric for viral growth. It is a relative concept. Regardless of the numerous formulas that "experts" apply, viral growth is related directly to the user growth rate. Following are some of the common metrics used in the calculation of viral growth:

❑   Average number of invitations a user will send out in a given time period

❑   Retention rate equals the percentage of users lost (application is uninstalled) in a time period

❑   Capacity equals the total number of potential users (with the maximum being the number of network members, or it can be less, and based on demographics)

❑   Invite conversion rate equals the percentage of invitees who accept

The reality is that each of these metrics is not constant, but instead each changes over the life of an application. Modeling the viral nature of your application involves tracking all of this information from the birth of the application.

Both new and experienced social network application developers must also answer the question of how to make their applications *social*. The goal is to create engaging interactions between users. Interactions may be between friends or other application users, possibly people outside of the application, or even the encompassing social network. Interactions can be specific to the function of the application. For example, in the iLike application, you get to share what you like with other friends and users.

Application Goals

The failure of application development often is the result of not defining and understanding an application's objectives. Following are good goals to consider when developing your application:

❑   Growth

❑   Engagement

❑ Good look and feel

❑ Dynamic evolution

❑ Self expression

❑ Social exposure

❑ Relationship building

❑ Real-world problem solving

Let's take a look at each of these application objectives.

Growth

Growth is defined as building a user base. Without this, your application is dead. Having an application go viral is often a desired goal. The definition of viral growth should vary greatly by the application purpose and intended audience. Techniques to achieve this goal are a main focus of this chapter, and discussed throughout.

Engagement

Engagement is defined as the holding of attention and the participation of an application user with the application, other users (through the application), or the "brand" of the application. What you want is early engagement with your application. Across social networks, there is a tendency for a user to try a new application, and then quickly remove it (or no longer use it). Applications such as these obviously lack early engagement.

As an application developer, what you must focus on is how you can achieve these different aspects of engagement early — say, in a 1-minute time period. To make this time period the most effective, you might consider the following:

❑ Clearly demonstrate purpose of the application

❑ Show appropriately interesting content, tying it to friends and other related groups, if possible.

❑ Make the initial interface simple

❑ On the first interface, allow some form of "ownership"/capability of a user to start to use the application, and customize it to his or her needs

❑ Highlight identity of the application through logo placement

❑ Pay attention to the responsiveness in the loading of the application, and in response to user interactions

The term "engagement" has been defined in a number of important ways, and may be achieved by the developer through many different means. Let's take a quick look the following ways to achieve engagement:

❑ Distribution

❑ Exposure

❑ Attentiveness

❑ Communication

❑ Persuasion

❑ Response

The key to engagement is all about making it relevant to the user.

Distribution

Distribution is an aspect of engagement dealing with the loyalty a user has to an application. This can be measured by the regularity a user visits. Sometimes this is called the "stickiness" of an application. Measuring this is important, and there are many tools available to accomplish this, including Google and Yahoo analytics, as well as sites such as Quantcast (www.quantcast.com). Another way to measure loyalty is through the concept of subscriptions and renewals, which can be appropriate for some kinds of applications.

Exposure

One measure of *exposure* is through "completion," meaning that a user uses an application to its "completion." For example, in a gaming application, this could mean finishing a game. Other measures of exposure include how long an application is used, and if users recommend it. You should design your application for increased exposure, which can be accomplished through direction of use, incentives, and recommendation opportunities. For example, you might offer users "virtual currency" in your application if they recommend it to their friends. In the case of direction of use, you might again offer an incentive if users reach a level of "play" or "use" in the application.

Attentiveness

Attentiveness describes the concentration a user applies with each of his or her senses when using an application. It also relates to the quality of thought used to think about the information users are processing. A direct measure of this, also related to exposure, is how long a user uses an application. For example, one way that you could increase the attentiveness of your users would be to introduce dynamic and changing content.

Communication

Communication is a type of engagement where users are actively involved in communicating "within" and "about" the application. Communications "within" the application could include the sending of media/widgets to others. Communication "about" the application might be sending messages to friends or others about the application or the use of it. Creating a comment wall or review board are some options. Other possibilities for communication include pokes, simple gestures, instant messaging, and direct email.

Persuasion

Persuasion is really an aspect of communication whereby the user of the application is endorsing the application to friends or others. This could be accomplished directly through messages, or invitations generated from the application. Indirectly, it might be through the placement of an application on a user's profile.

Response

Response in this context indicates a direct interaction with the application. This is a measure of active use (as opposed to inactive observation) of the application. Increased response means increased exposure of an application, which introduces the important possibility of interactions.

Good Look and Feel

Look and feel describes the main appearance and interactive features in an application's interface. In social network applications, you see two basic trends with regard to look and feel: those that look like the social network interface, and those that do not.

A developer may design an application to look like a social network interface (for example, MySpace or hi5) to create consistency, potential ease of use, and perhaps greater trustworthiness (because it may appear to the user as though the social network might "own" this application).

The choice to use a different look from the social network creates a stronger sense of application identity. This look can be directed toward the targeted audience, and may be more appropriate for the content of the application.

Dynamic Evolution

Dynamic evolution addresses both the concept of the application experience being interactive (dynamic), as well as changing over time (evolution). Regardless of the purpose of the application, incorporating built-in ways for the user to interact is crucial for engagement. Having interchanges that are social in nature (such as involving friends) is ideal.

A static application (one that does not evolve over time) will often quickly lose its user base. The nature of the application will sometimes determine the timetable over which changes are made, as well as what changes are made. Some applications can change weekly, and, in little ways, possibly on a daily basis. Change can be a result of the changing social graph. Change can result from friends' actions, new content, or as a result of altering application functionality. This is discussed in more detail later in this chapter in the section, "Retention."

Self Expression

Self expression can take many forms in social networks. It can also be present in different locations (page views) on a network. For example, there is the profile page that represents each user. Also there are communications postings (for example, status lines) that serve self expression. Selection of a user's friends and a user's friend's expression can be considered part of the user's own self expression. So, applications that feature these elements allow for greater self expression in a social context.

The nature of the application (such as some of the graffiti drawing applications) allow for content development as a means of self expression. Another example is gifting in applications. Direct communication of preferences through recommendations and references are another form of self expression implemented in social applications. Some may consider self expression equivalent to a user "showing off." With this definition, anything that promotes the user in a public way is desirable.

Social Exposure

A good way to make an application viral is through *social exposure*, which is the direct use of a user's personal social graph (their friends and friends' friends). For example, an application can show a user what his or her friends who are using this application have recently done, or are currently doing. This kind of social activity stream is a great driver of retention and exposure engagement within an application.

Going beyond friends and reaching further into the social graph to friends of friends can be appropriate for some applications, and can be a means of advancing both engagement and growth. Within the confines of the application, this can introduce users to new potential friends, and possibly increase interactions within the application.

Relationship Building

Besides looking at a user's own social graph, an application can try to link unrelated users by such things as common interests or usage of the application as a means to build relationships. Shared interests can come directly from user-generated data in the application, or may come from user profile data (if accessible to the application). Creating new relationships (and possibly groups and communities) will increase loyalty (that is, distribution engagement) and retention.

Real-World Problem Solving

Many of the first social network applications were fun, but were considered by many to be silly and with little purpose. One particular way of building retention in your application is to have it solve some real-world problem. There are lots of possibilities in each application domain. For example, in your application, you could include aspects of project management, event management, shopping, recommendations, education, communications, content creation and distribution, information management, and sharing.

Application Trends

The importance of current and emerging trends is that they show where current and future innovation is headed. Trends at best can reflect user desires and needs. Trends often appeal to the public. You want your application to achieve these goals. Studying trends, and picking ones that work for your application, is part of a good application-development design strategy.

This section presents some of the current and emerging social network application trends. Later in this chapter, the concept of retention is examined in more detail. While not the opposite of "trendy," retention is a good (or better) goal.

A recent report by Morgan Stanley (see http://www.socialtimes.com/2008/04/social-applications-are-the-hottest-trend for complete details) on Internet trends compared two of the top social networks, and came to the conclusion that one was achieving a greater user growth rate because of the following attributes:

❑   Ads being less intrusive

❑   Early newsfeed use and personalization

- ❏ Simple/concise user interface
- ❏ Feature friend information
- ❏ Personalized ads
- ❏ Mobile phone capabilities

These are trends you might consider for your own social application.

Figure 1-22 shows a breakdown of the most popular application categories to date on MySpace. This was compiled by adding up the total install numbers from the top 10 applications in each of the 23 application categories on MySpace. Some major applications (mostly games) are counted in multiple categories.

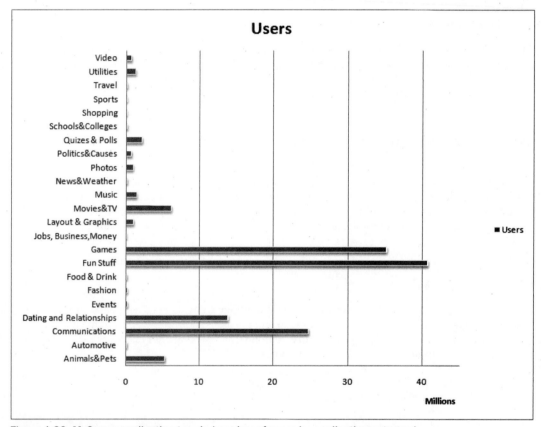

Figure 1-22: MySpace application trends (number of users by application category)

What the chart in Figure 1-22 doesn't show you is that a few applications are really dominating the numbers in the most popular categories. Figure 1-23 shows the numbers for the top 10 applications in the most popular "Fun Stuff" category.

While the focus of this book is on OpenSocial, because the Facebook application platform has been around longer, it is important to look at application trends on Facebook. A great site to check out is Adonomoics (http://adonomics.com/), which offers Facebook analytics. In particular, that site shows rankings of companies involved in application development on Facebook. Looking at the applications from some of the more successful companies can give you ideas for successful formulas.

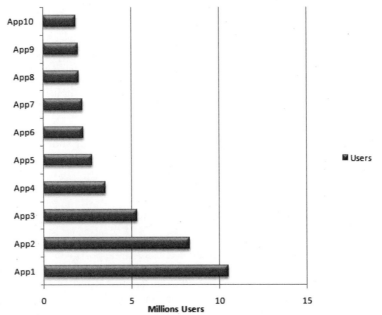

Figure 1-23: User numbers for the top 10 applications in the "Fun Stuff" MySpace category

There is an ongoing discussion in the developer community regarding *application purpose* — that is, creating applications "solely" for entertainment or creating "useful" applications. Many critics of the social network application business say that most (or all) of the applications produced are "silly" and of no purpose. It is true that there are a number of applications that can fit this mold. Also, it is true that statistics show that there is a lifetime to these (and, perhaps, all) applications. But, does this make them unviable as a business model? Some developers say "yes," and others say "no." What developers agree on is that an application must be engaging to users, and this is the one common trait that all applications must have.

Let's take a look at some different trends in terms of application development. (There is no implied importance to the order in which they are examined.)

Reach (General Appeal) Applications

Some companies (in particular many with longer histories, such as application developers RockYou and Slide) have developed a number of wide-reaching, general-appeal applications. These are applications built for *reach*, which is the concept of trying to gain the most users spread across demographics and interests. Many of these applications have simple premises, and are based on simple messaging.

The advantage of these kinds of applications is that they have the largest potential market. The disadvantage is that often, in their general appeal, these applications may have a shorter lifespan because users may quickly lose interest. One argument made by developers who prefer this kind of application is that the application can be made quickly, and can quickly become viral because of ease of use.

Some of the simpler applications of this genre are often criticized as being silly. But, as pointed out in the article, "Silly is Serious Business" by Keith Rabois, Vice President of Strategy & Business Development at Slide (see http://voices.allthingsd.com/20080513/silly-is-serious-business), statistics can support "silly" or entertaining as good business. Rabois provides a number of examples where more entertaining media is the preference for the general audience. For example, he points out that during the recent United States Presidential campaign broadcasts, shows such as *American Idol* and *Dancing with the Stars* had the greatest audience. This definitely points to the fact that "entertaining" is important, but, given a choice of different forms of entertainment, would silly always rule?

Not all applications that fall into this category are simple. A good example of this are the "profile pimping" applications that let users develop and share graphics such as slide shows.

Vertical (Targeted) Applications

A number of developers are finding users by targeting a specific category. A couple of great examples of this are iLike (which targets music) and Flixster (which targets movies).

Watercooler describes itself as the world's largest television and sports community. It is distributed across multiple social networks (for example, MySpace, Facebook, hi5, and so on). The Watercooler applications like "Pittsburgh Steeler Fans" and "Boston Red Sox Fans" (Figure 1-24) concentrate on sports. There are also the "Addicted to X" applications that focus on different television shows (Figure 1-25). Much of the content in these applications is generated by the users. The application provides effective tools for the user to report on this kind of subject.

Applications in this category focus on people who have specific likes, rather than trying to build wide-reaching applications. There is a lot of potential growth in *vertical markets*, as well as some interesting associated revenue streams.

Template-Based Application Development

This paradigm of application development surrounds the idea of creating a "template" application that can then be used to more quickly generate a series of applications. It is based on the idea that many basic applications will have many of the same features and needs, as well as similar interfaces. Some companies have used this formula to create the simple entertainment-oriented ("silly") applications previously mentioned. Others are using them to create applications that are for targeted (vertical) markets.

Slide is an example of a company that has been known to create a series of successful (viral) applications that have a template construction falling in the simpler entertainment category. These applications (denoted by developers as "throw a sheep" applications) are what the social network applications industry owes (to a great extent) its birth and boom to.

More recently, there are examples of developers creating template-based applications for vertical markets. For example, according to Adonomics.com (http://adonomics.com) Watercooler has produced more than 600 applications, and most of them are fan-oriented applications. A large number of these fan-oriented applications are focused on sports teams and television shows. Vikas Gupta, CEO of Watercooler, has described Watercooler as being the "ESPN or MTV for the social network generation."

Currently, Watercooler applications for both television shows and sporting events have set and similar formats. Translating this to the social network world can make sense for the user.

Figure 1-24: Watercooler's Boston Red Sox "fan" application

Figure 1-25: Watercooler's *Grey's Anatomy* TV Show "fan" application

Brand Applications

There are two definitions of *brand*-based applications. The first is to take an already existing brand and create an application around it. The application can be used to direct traffic to an external Web site, or used to create an awareness/advertisement vehicle. A number of applications (such as "Local Picks" by TripAdvisor) fit this description.

Developers must be careful not to abuse any of the trademark or intellectual property rules governing the use of brands. Developing a brand-based application should only be done in agreement with the company that owns the brand.

To understand the consequences of not following this tenet, you need to look no further than the famous lawsuit filed by Hasbro, Inc., over the Facebook application called "Scrabulous." This application was based on Hasbro's "Scrabble" game. As a consequence of the lawsuit, this application (much to the dismay of users) is currently no longer available, although there is an associated Web site. The final outcome of this lawsuit is still pending. This should serve as a warning regarding use of brands in an unauthorized fashion. Many believe Hasbro (which eventually developed its own application) should have purchased the "Scrabulous" application.

The second kind of "brand-based" application is discussed next as "destination" applications.

Destination Applications

Related to the concept of "branding" is what is referred to as the *destination* application. This kind of application goes beyond the simple use of a developer brand name (that is, a developer name/company such as RockYou or Slide). Instead, the application itself serves as a brand, and is a "destination," meaning that it has a higher-level of interactivity and resident features. Destination applications may have greater user response, retention, and longer life spans than the simpler "entertainment" applications. But, on the whole, whether they will be more viral remains to be seen.

iLike is an example of this kind of application. The name of the application, the company, and the supporting Web site are all called iLike. The name is self-descriptive, and has become a brand for sharing with friends and other users media that a user likes.

Longer Engagement

To achieve longer periods of user engagement, applications typically provide real services to users — they solve real-world problems. A number of emerging examples come to mind. The previously mentioned iLike is one. The "real" service provided by iLike is the discovery, sharing, and purchase of music. iLike has gone through a number of iterations (something discussed later in this chapter in the section, "Retention"). The current version of iLike is much more engaging than the initial version in terms of user attentiveness and user response. Figure 1-26 shows the 2007 version of iLike, and Figure 1-27 shows the current version of iLike.

Use of Media

The use of media can be a smart idea that can attract and keep users, or, when done poorly (such as when producing long load times), kill your application. MySpace is experiencing significant growth in its media-related utilities, and ranked with YouTube, Live.com, and Facebook as a leader in the volume of videos viewed (see http://www.socialtimes.com/2008/04/social-applications-are-the-hottest-trend). This could imply that applications featuring graphics, video, and other media will be popular (at least on MySpace).

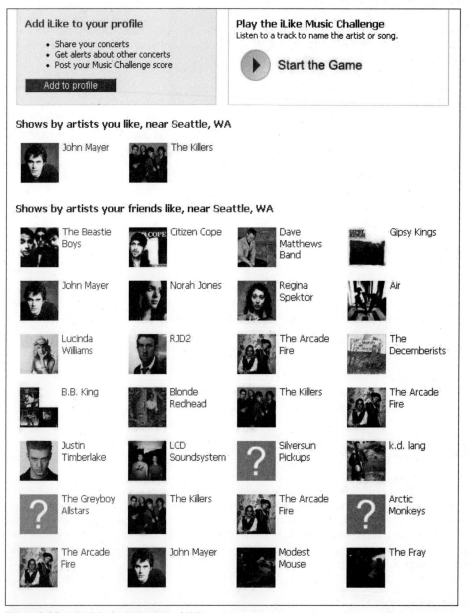

Figure 1-26: Initial/launch version of iLike

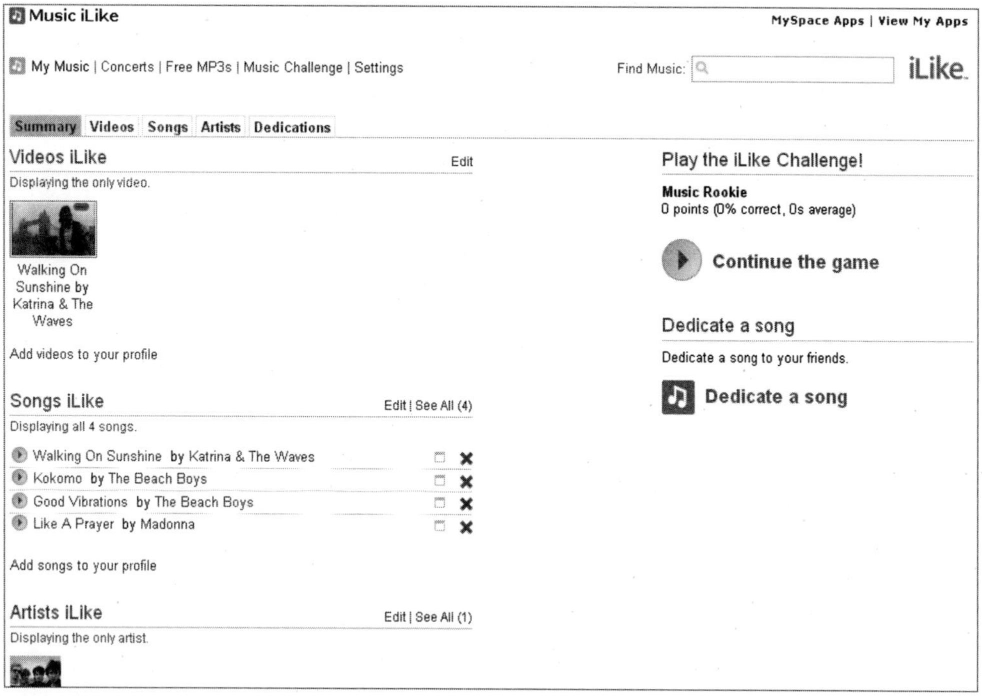

Figure 1-27: Current version of iLike with many more features, including navigation bars

A certain percentage of these types of applications are based on Flash, and many of these use ActionScript (a Flash programming language) for interactive capabilities. This is a popular way to bring higher-end game-like graphics interactions into an application. Most browsers already have installed the plug-in for Flash and, if not, it is readily available. Many of the issues with compression and faster load and run-times that you encounter with heavy graphics applications are handled well by the Flash player.

The "Maffia new" application by I-Jet is an example of combining media, storytelling, role playing, and gaming. This application is Flash-based and provides more realistic graphics, as shown in Figure 1-28. In the "Maffia new" application, the user becomes part of a clan. The role-playing in these kinds of games is addictive to users, and the applications experience a high user attentiveness and response.

Internationalization

The Morgan Stanley report mentioned previously (http://www.socialtimes.com/2008/04/social-applications-are-the-hottest-trend) discusses trends in international markets. According to this report, in the list of top ten technology, media, and telecom user countries, the United States and China are now tied for the top slot. New additions to the list include India, Brazil, and Russia. Japan, Germany, France, and Italy also are part of the top ten. This report also shows the largest growth rate for Internet use coming from China, India, Russia, Brazil, and Asian/Pacific countries, followed by other European and Latin American countries. While the U.S. still has the largest user base, it has one of the smaller growth rates. *Internationalization* is about expanding your application into these emerging (and fast-growing) markets.

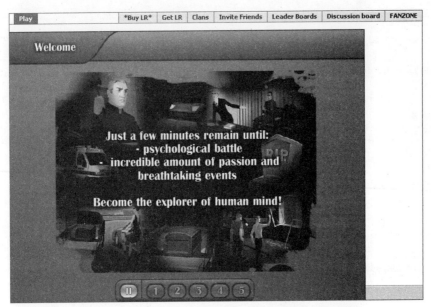

Figure 1-28: "Maffia new" application features role-playing and gaming

If you are considering mobile applications, China occupies the top slot, followed by the United States, in mobile phone subscriptions. The list of top countries also includes Russia, India, Brazil, and Japan, ahead of the top European countries of Germany, Italy, and the United Kingdom. Indonesia, Mexico, and Turkey rank ahead of France and Spain in number of mobile users.

These statistics might give you an idea why the internationalization of your applications could be a smart idea, and could make your application viral by spreading its popularity across international networks. Unlike the Facebook API, OpenSocial can provide the capability to create applications on different containers that have large audiences in (and identify with) these countries.

Following are some tips that might guide you in your application development strategy:

❑   To capture local markets, have different applications that are language-specific (and maybe functionally specific)

❑   Keep smaller markets in English

KlickNation's "Kiss" application has been developed for both the English-speaking and Spanish-speaking markets. A part of KlickNation's strategy is to reach out to networks that have strong representation in other countries. As KlickNation's first viral applications, "Kiss" experienced its initial success on the hi5 network, which has a strong presence in Spanish-speaking Latin America. According to VP of Business Development Ken Walton, KlickNation is looking to become "the developer of applications in OpenSocial like Slide/Rock You is on Facebook." KlickNation developed its Spanish version of "Kiss" using OpenSocial message bundling, its own knowledge of Spanish, and Google translation services.

Self Expression

A popular feature of many applications is the exploitation of *self expression*, which basically means that the application has a strong sense of representing the user. This can be "showing off" or "looking good" to fellow friends, or it can have a deeper meaning of "representing me."

RockYou has a number of applications that heavily feature self expression. For example, users of Rock-You's "SlideShows" application can create slideshows for friends and others to view. Initially, the application will load any pictures you have in your portfolio that you have uploaded to your social network account. This slide show will appear on your profile, "dressing up" the user's profile for others to see. RockYou's "GlitterText" application is another application that adds a "show off" element to a user's profile.

Partnering

Partnering is a primarily about business relationships and leverage. The idea here is that an application will partner with a non-social application or business to achieve more functionality or services, or provide a branding experience. A good example of this is the iLike application. iLike has partnered with both iTunes and Rhapsody. With iTunes, users are able to purchase individual songs. iLike has partnered with Rhapsody to provide iLike application users with the capability to subscribe to music. An initial number of downloads (25) will be free and, after that, the user can subscribe to the Rhapsody service. This provides a monetary stream for iLike, as well as content and more services for its users. This is a win-win situation.

Often, the partnering can be less direct, and can be for marketing rather than sales. For example, Jambool (an application development company) teamed up with Health.com and created the "Send Good Karma" application (Figure 1-29). The application allows users to send "happiness," "good health," and other "good karma" wishes. If users want to send some special "health" karma, they are directed to become a member of Health.com first.

Watercooler has partnered with some of the large television networks such as ABC, NBC, and CBS in the creation of its "Addicted to TV_X" applications. Watercooler is sometimes even able to offer its users full-length episodes of the television show. Watercooler is paid by the television networks to offer this service.

Virtual Currencies, Goods, and Points

Another trend is that of *virtual currencies, goods, and points*. This capability in applications has led to increasingly viral growth rates. More importantly, it seems there may be a trend for these applications to have higher percentages of active daily users.

Applications such as "Friends for Sale" and "Owned" feature this capability. Users have described the feature as "addictive." The drive to perform some operation to get virtual currencies, goods, or points that then enable a user do more in an application seems to be a successful pattern for extended use.

Figure 1-29: "Send Good Karma" application by Jambool partnered with Health.com

The "Send Good Karma" application described previously uses this feature in what are called "jPoints," as shown in Figure 1-30. The application developer, Jambool, also does cross-marketing with other applications it owns by advertising them as applications that use the same virtual point system.

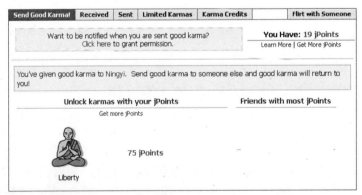

Figure 1-30: The "Send Good Karma" application uses virtual points called jPoints

Virtual goods can be important to an application in a number of ways, including revenue streams, user response, and viral growth rates. Here are some examples:

❑ Alexey Kostarev, head producer at I-Jet and producer of the "New Maffia" application, says 80 percent of his company's revenue stream comes from virtual gifting.

❑ Facebook (the longest-running container offering "virtual gifting") has been reported to generate more than $35 million annually from the gifting feature (see `http://facereviews.com/2008 /09/02/facebook-virtual-gifts-make-big-bucks`)

Virtual gifting has been a popular trend for some applications. The applications charge small amounts of money (called *micro-transactions*) for these virtual gifts that users can send friends. Why do people do this? A common response from developers has been that people don't mind spending small amounts of real money to make their friends feel good. Even though the gift is not real, the thought is, and the recipient might value it more knowing that the giver spent real money on it.

Mobile Applications

One of the biggest possible future trends will be penetration into the mobile world. Recently, MySpace announced that it was partnering with Research in Motion (RIM) to develop an integrated MySpace Mobile experience customized for RIM's BlackBerry smartphones. The new "MySpace for BlackBerry" application will be fully optimized to deliver rich content and data to users on the go. Similar agreements are being made with Apple's iPhone. This may signal a future for mobile social network applications.

Increased Use of Social Data

It is only natural that, as applications on social networks evolve, they will begin to use social data in more elaborate and unique ways. A number of developers are currently experimenting with this to evolve their applications.

Besides the traditional "see what my friend X is doing" functionality, applications could leverage profile/person data about its users. For example, you could use the data to recommend new applications that users might like, based on where they live, or on their interests.

Following are some ideas on how to use social data:

❑ Recommendation for new applications that match a user's interests or location

❑ Based on a user's demographics, suggest new friends using application

❑ Feature certain content based on user data

❑ If you serve your own advertising, do so based on user data or application use

❑ Offer features in the application based on user demographics or use

Many of these ideas are not trivial, and represent ongoing areas of research in computer science. They often involve techniques used in such areas as pattern recognition and artificial intelligence.

For example, Watercooler uses cross-application marketing by making recommendations about new applications by retrieving favorite television show information stored in a user's profile, which is a common source of user data on many social networks.

Increased Use of Application Data

In the context of this discussion, the term *application data* here is user-generated content and data inside of the application. Some applications store very little application data. However, a recent trend has been to allow users to create lots of data, and for the application to store (and then share) this data on return visits to the application. Also, applications share this information among users. Of course, the kind of data you capture will be specific to your application.

Viral Channels and Features

When developers refer to *viral channels*, they are talking about using the "social hooks" that each container offers its applications. Many of these channels are the same across social networks. However, there are some that are unique, and it is important to remember that networks regulate these channels differently.

There is the perception that, as the number of applications increases, the usefulness of these social hooks is waning. An advantage for the OpenSocial developer is that, because it is a new platform with new social networks signing on, the usefulness of social hooks is greater.

Some social hooks you may consider include the following:

- ❑ Profile View
- ❑ Feeds (news)
- ❑ Messaging
- ❑ Requests/Notifications
- ❑ Invitations (encourage more than 1 friend)
- ❑ Profile Data Access

  - ❑ Name
  - ❑ Age
  - ❑ Gender
  - ❑ Interests
  - ❑ Location
  - ❑ Work
  - ❑ Education
  - ❑ TV, Movies, Music, Books, Video, Images
  - ❑ Status
  - ❑ Languages

- ❑ Marital Status, Looking For, Sexual Orientation
- ❑ Children
- ❑ Body Type
- ❑ Smoker, Drinker
- ❑ Occupation, Income
- ❑ Religion
- ❑ Ethnicity
- ❑ Web sites
- ❑ Public/private profiles? (public link to Web site from LinkedIn)

❑ Photo Albums

❑ Music, Video

❑ Friends Access

❑ Group Access

❑ Scrapbook

❑ Journal

Interviews with a number of developers regarding how to make an application viral have revealed the following interesting tips to consider:

- ❑ Containers that allow users to send friends a lot of messages from applications tend to have more viral applications.
- ❑ Containers that allow friends to send a lot of messages from applications can lead to the perception of "spamming" and potentially be viewed as a turn-off.
- ❑ Use of social hooks is important, but the inherent application features and engagement are more important.
- ❑ Networks with tight social networks (meaning people don't have lots of remotely related friends) lead to better-quality friends and better longevity for applications.
- ❑ Networks with loose social networks can create viral applications more quickly.
- ❑ Networks with less services will allow this functionality to be represented by applications, and applications can grow more quickly.
- ❑ Networks with more services make it more difficult to create a viral application.
- ❑ Networks with many applications make it more difficult to create viral applications (or even find them).
- ❑ Require users to invite a number of people (for example, 10) before they can use or view some feature of the application.
- ❑ Give the user multiple opportunities to invite others. (You could even do this on every page view, but in different ways, with different incentives.)
- ❑ Specific invite messages and specific notifications give better results than general messages.

❑　Use address book importers to invite friends and friend selectors. Select all the friends, and make it easy (for example, have a link "invite 15 friends," so that user only must click the link).

❑　Feature user-generated content and sharing.

In addition to these viral channels, some social features can help make your application viral. Some of these will be specific to the purpose of your application. There are some that can be used in many applications, including the following:

❑　My content (user can see his or her content)

❑　Friends content

❑　Quizzes

❑　Posts/bulletin boards

❑　Voting and Most Popular (on user-developed content)

❑　Trivia games

❑　Dedicate X (dedicate something to a friend)

❑　Virtual gifting

❑　Buy virtual goods/currency

❑　Blogs

❑　Joining group of users within of application users

Social Network Identity

Understanding the identity of a social network is important. It allows you to make decisions about what applications would be popular. There are many ways to classify a network. The demographics of its audience is one. You can find some statistics offered by the social networks themselves.

There are numerous third-party organizations such as ComScore, Compete, and Alexa, that can give you network statistics. Alexa (`www.alexa.com`) recently published statistics regarding traffic on MySpace, broken down by domain as follows:

❑　`viewmorepics.myspace.com`: 28%

❑　`profile.myspace.com`: 18%

❑　`messaging.myspace.com`: 17%

❑　`home.myspace.com`: 7%

❑　`comment.myspace.com`: 5%

❑　`myspace.com`: 5%

❑　`friends.myspace.com`: 5%

❑　`bulletins.myspace.com`: 4%

❑　`collect.myspace.com`: 2%

❑　`profileedit.myspace.com`: 1%

❑ `vids.myspace.com`: 1%

❑ `blog.myspace.com`: 1%

❑ `editprofile.myspace.com`: 1%

❑ `browseusers.myspace.com`: 1%

❑ `searchservice.myspace.com`: 1%

❑ Other Web sites: 3%

(See Alexa for recent changes to these figures.)

These numbers might suggest that applications dealing with pictures, profiles, and messaging would be very successful.

There are research organizations that conduct studies to track and predict information about a social network's identity. One way to measure this identity is by its perception. These kinds of metrics should be carefully considered, since they can give you (as an application developer) some possible directions. Figure 1-31 shows a graphic produced from a study by Faber Novel (`http://fabernovel.com`) that looks at a few social Web sites (including MySpace, LinkedIn, and Facebook). As you can see, the graphic places the sites on a scale of "user identity" (from "fantasized" to "real") and on the scale of "user exposure" (from "public exposition" to "qualitative contents").

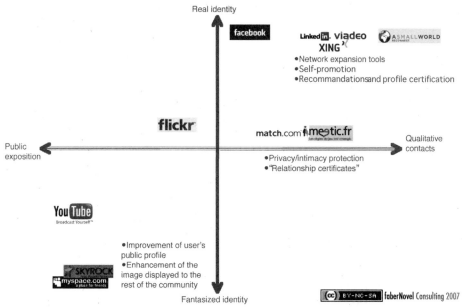

Figure 1-31: Research looks at comparing some Social Sites based on user identity and exposure

Figure 1-31 suggests that MySpace (in terms of "user-exposure") has a larger public audience, and (in terms of "user-identity") is more fantasy-oriented when compared to the the LinkedIn network. LinkedIn is placed on the opposite side of the chart, with a "user-exposure" of a smaller audience, but with a "user-identity" representing more real and qualitative contacts. Most people would probably agree with this assessment. This could mean that applications that are fantasy-based would be more successful on MySpace than on LinkedIn.

Another consideration in defining the identity of a network is the applications currently on the network themselves. Let's look at some quick statistics concerning applications and a few social networks:

❑ MySpace:

 ❑ More than 50 million application installs, with more than 20 million users

 ❑ More than 30 percent growth across all metrics (according to MySpace, without clarification of "metrics")

 ❑ More than 2,500 applications

❑ hi5:

 ❑ More than 66 million application installs

 ❑ More than 68 percent of users use applications

 ❑ More than 1,800 applications

❑ Friendster:

 ❑ More than 12 million users adding applications

 ❑ 500,000 application installs each day

 ❑ More than 500 applications certified

 ❑ More than 2,000 developers

Marketing — The Next Step

One way to feed a growing application is through effective marketing. Marketing can be used as an engagement tool with current users. Marketing can also be used at the beginning stages of application life. There are many applications on most social networks. Expecting users to find yours through simple browsing or search may not be sufficient. Marketing your application can bring new users to it. Some marketing strategies are free, and others will require a budget. Your creativity is the limit, but let's take a look at some possibilities.

First, when you design applications, treat your application's viral channels as marketing vehicles. Designing your application with this in mind can lead you toward growth.

One example of using viral channels for marketing is to offer incentives to your users to invite friends. The incentive can be in the form of virtual goods, virtual cash, or some extended application features.

The "Maffia new" application uses two kinds of incentives to get users to invite their friends. As shown in Figure 1-32, the application offers the incentive of virtual money that can be used in the game. The application also offers incentives to users to invite new friends via a direct link into the game by becoming someone important, a "Maffia Boss."

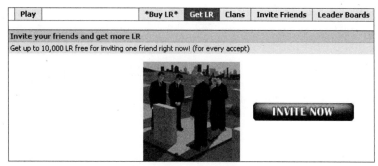

Figure 1-32: Maffia new application uses virtual currency as an incentive to invite friends

An emerging practice in applications is to direct users through a transaction that requires them to invite friends. For example, in the RockYou "Likeness" application, after taking a quiz to determine likeness when users click the Submit button, they are requested to invite friends as the next step in this transaction.

Unfortunately, many networks are limiting even more the use of these viral channels. For example, with the recent perception of application "spam" (too many messages from applications), smaller messaging limits have been set on networks. Some networks such as MySpace are currently not allowing applications to offer incentives (say, give virtual points) for users messaging others. User postings to the MySpace announcement (see http://developer.myspace.com/Community/blogs /devteam/archive/2008/05/20/new-app-guidelines-must-read.aspx) reflect a lot of negative feedback over this issue. Users like incentives. What this means for your application is that you must pay attention to the frequent changes in network policies.

A number of companies provide marketing services for applications. An example is SocialMedia, an advertising company focused on social networks and their applications. SocialMedia allows developers to set the price they want to pay for a click. This pricing is used in a real-time auction, and you can check out the live bids. SocialMedia describes this service as a way "to inject your app with thousands of core targeted users and help you transform them into a million total users."

Check out the interesting "viral calculator" they have at SocialMedia.com. For example, they calculate that, if you have a budget of $200, and each user will only refer your application to 1 other user, and this happens for 4 levels of referral, you will gain 4,000 users. With the same $200, if your referral rate is 1.25 and you have 4 levels of referral, you will gain 9,007 users. If cost is an issue, there are some newer companies that offer their marketing services in exchange for advertisement on your application.

Another model presented by OfferPal is a "new App Install program." The program comes in three available payment terms:

❑ *Cost-Per-Click* — The Cost-Per-Click program is like SocialMedia's program.

❑ *Cost-Per-Install* — In the Cost-Per-Install program, you pay only for installed users. The price is typically higher than the Cost-Per-Click rate.

❑ *Free Click Exchange* — The Free Click Exchange program guarantees a qualified click to your install page for every click you deliver to other apps within the network.

Another marketing strategy is direct cross-application advertising. You could make agreements directly with other application developers, advertising one another's applications. Once you have more than one application, you can do your own cross-application.

As an example of self cross-advertising, Jambool uses its "Reach" application called "Share Good Karma" with a large user base to create larger audiences for their new "Who's the cutest baby?" and "Ski Results" applications. Both of these new applications are intended for vertical markets. Jambool wants to build communities around these new applications, and, hence, also extend the complexity and user response and attentiveness.

Another possibility is to purchase "sponsored application" status with a network. This is similar to being a sponsored site at a search engine such as Google or Yahoo!.

If your budget allows, you can opt to pay for direct marketing. The expense of these services will usually be out of bounds for beginning applications or developers. It is best used in "branding" attempts.

Direct marketing via email is another possibility. Best results are achieved when the mailings are targeted toward your intended demographic. As with all forms of marketing, you must be careful not to annoy and lose potential users.

Another less-evasive scheme is to maintain a company/developer Web site that is advertised on all of your applications. This can be a form of self cross-application marketing.

Indirect marketing schemes such as postings and blogs can be effective. You might even create your own blog about your application. Some developers have created video and uploaded it to YouTube and other media sites. Another option is using Twitter. The genuineness of these postings can be a question, however. People like blogs and postings.

Following are a couple of services for blogs and email that you might consider:

❑   *Blogs* — Blogger (`http://www.blogger.com`), World Press (`http://www.worldpress`
`.org/blogs.htm`), Yahoo360 (`http://360.yahoo.com`), TypePad (`http://www.typepad.com`)

❑   *Email Marketing* — Constant Contact (`http://www.constantcontact.com/index.jsp`), Email
Labs (`http://www.emaillabs.com`), JangoMail (`http://www.jangomail.com`), Exact Target
(`http://email.exacttarget.com`)

Partnering is a form of co-marketing, but not necessarily with another application. For example a traditional (non-Web) company may partner with you. Recall the example of the "Share Good Karma" application and Health.com discussed previously.

Promotions you run in your application can also grow your user base. These might be in the form of a giveaway or lottery. It could be something more virtual, like being featured, in the application if you have invited many friends. You should check out a network's application guidelines before using this strategy.

A final technique to consider is sponsorship. This can go both ways. A company may decide to sponsor your application. This could include featuring you on its Web site and other forms of communications to the company's user base. Getting this kind of sponsorship requires building a relationship and sharing common business objectives. Another form of sponsorship is where your application sponsors an event, person, or product. Examples of this are common in event-oriented applications such as iLike.

A vast number of applications are not marketed beyond the use of viral channels. This includes many successful applications. A number of the larger developer companies are proud of not spending any money on marketing.

If you do choose to use some kind of marketing strategy, don't make the mistake of not tracking the results. This way you can tell into which strategy to invest more time and money.

Retention

Applications with lots of installs are great, but if you don't have good daily active use numbers, your application won't monetize and will quickly die. The best way to retain your users is through continual re-invention of your application.

Following are a few of the ways you can evolve your applications:

- ❑ New content
- ❑ Interface changes
- ❑ New functionality
- ❑ New viral channels
- ❑ Increased exposure of user and friend data
- ❑ Increased use of social data
- ❑ Increased use of user-generated content
- ❑ New marketing strategies (for example, seed to new audiences)
- ❑ Reach out to users who are fans of you application (if you have access)
- ❑ Rewards (for example, advanced features for most active users)
- ❑ Introduce (or advance) gaming elements for example, user versus user, collecting, role-playing/assignment (super user)
- ❑ Feature user-generated content
- ❑ Develop user-to-user sharing and communications
- ❑ Quickly launch on new containers
- ❑ Provide a ranking/rating mechanism

You should monitor your retention rates from the beginning — that is, upon deployment. Problems with retention, even as you are having viral growth, can be detected. Making changes to your retention strategy is important. If you are tracking retention (that is, the loss of users), then when you try a new retention idea, you can monitor if it was successful.

Tips for Good Application Development

You should put into practice a number of general application development tips that also apply to social network application development. These include making your application robust, making explicit requests, testing, and performance enhancements. Performance enhancements are tackled later in this book. For now, let's consider some forward-looking pointers on how these issues are handled in OpenSocial application development.

Robustness includes checking for errors and handling exceptions. Even when you have code that is correct, situations can happen in the containers that will return incorrect results (even temporarily). If your code does not handle these unexpected situations, it will fail. Your users will be upset. Unfortunately, container problems do arise, and you must be diligent in expecting these errors. Checking for null data (even if the container should give you back results) is an example of good exception handling.

The following OpenSocial tools will come in handy:

❑ *Built-in methods* — Built-in methods in OpenSocial classes such as `hadError()` are good to use when making data requests. A useful message for debugging possible container problems is the `getErrorMessage()` method in OpenSocial (which is discussed in more detail in Chapter 4). Another similarly useful method in OpenSocial is `getErrorCode()`.

❑ *Optional features* — OpenSocial has some optional features that will be detailed in Chapter 4. It is important when making applications in OpenSocial for multiple containers to check for support. This can be done in your program or via inquiry.

❑ *Explicit requests* — Because OpenSocial has optional features, whenever you make requests for data, you must be explicit in what you are requesting. For example, if you want to find out the name and age of a user, you must explicitly ask for this information. In OpenSocial, parameters such as `opensocial.DataRequest.PeopleRequestFields.PROFILE_DETAILS` can be used to explicitly request information. These are explored in more detail in Chapter 4.

The issues dealing with performance and hosting your applications are discussed in detail in Chapter 8. These back-end issues are critical if your application gains momentum and becomes viral. It's important even for smaller audiences when you want good user experience, and if you have a lot of media and data requests.

Another important issue to making "good" (well, in terms of money) applications is monetization. This chapter has touched upon a few trends in this area (specifically, virtual goods and partnering), but Chapter 8 looks into this area in a bit more detail.

Summary

This chapter began with a discussion of social network programming and described where OpenSocial fits in. As part of this, a number of OpenSocial containers were reviewed. Next, the topics of application discovery, installation, appearance and control were covered.

The remaining parts of this chapter focused on good application design and tips. This included the definition of application goals, viral channels and concluded with marketing and retention techniques.

Chapter 2 examines the history and architecture of OpenSocial, the architecture of an application, data formats supported by OpenSocial, and the deployment of applications.

2

Introduction to OpenSocial

OpenSocial is an exciting platform that allows you to create and deploy social networking applications on multiple networks. It is an alternative to the Facebook API that Facebook uses. This chapter begins the process of teaching you step-by-step how to create viral social network applications using OpenSocial.

OpenSocial is the newest platform for social network development. It is unique in that it was created for use with multiple social networks (called *containers*), and also has the added benefit of being an Open Source application. This is a great boon for the developer, who can write once and deploy many times. OpenSocial is, in fact, designed to ease deployment of a single application to multiple social networks.

OpenSocial is a standard that is evolving and, hence, has different versions. It is true that not all of the social networks supporting OpenSocial support the latest version, and some of these differences are explored in this chapter. You will learn how to create a simple application that uses social data, and is based on OpenSocial's JavaScript API. This application will be used in the next few chapters, so it is important to become acquainted with it here. You will learn how to deploy this application on multiple containers, including MySpace and hi5. This chapter continues the discussion of how different OpenSocial containers vary in handling applications. This chapter also includes a tour of resources available to the OpenSocial developer.

Let's begin by taking a look at the evolution of OpenSocial.

OpenSocial History

OpenSocial was initiated by Google, and has been rumored to be a response to the success of Facebook. It was launched as an Open Source project, and is hosted on Google's code repository. For the 2007 launch, a number of companies signed on, including Friendster, hi5, MySpace, imeem, Hyves, Engage.com, Orkut, Ning, Plaxo, LinkedIn, SalesForce.com, Oracle, XING, and more. Yahoo! and other companies have also signed on to support OpenSocial, and others continue to do so.

When an OpenSocial application is available to a network's users, it is said to be running as "live for all users." Not all partners have live OpenSocial containers, but many do, and others have announced upcoming support. As new versions of OpenSocial are rolled out, containers stagger in their support. Also, new containers will typically launch in what is called *open sandbox access*, which means that only developers can run the applications.

OpenSocial was launched to the public with version 0.5 in December 2007. Subsequent versions have included the following:

❑   Version 0.6, released in December 2007

❑   Version 0.7 (considered by many to be the first truly functional version) released on February 4, 2008

❑   Version 0.8, released on May 28, 2008

❑   Version 0.9, portions approved as of the writing of this book

Table 2-1 shows the list of containers and their support of OpenSocial.

Table 2-1: Social Networks OpenSocial Support*

Social Network	OpenSocial Version	Support
hi5	0.8	Live for all users
LinkedIn	0.8	Live for all users
Netlog	0.8	Live for all users
MySpace	0.8	Live for all users
Webon	0.8	Live for all users
XiaoNei	0.8	Live for all users
Yahoo!	0.8	Live for all users
51.com	0.7	Live for all users
FanBox	0.7	Live for all users
Freebar	0.7	Live for all users
Friendster	0.7	Live for all users
Hyves	0.7	Live for all Users
IDtail	0.7	Live for all users
Mail.ru	0.7	Live for all users

Continued

Table 2-1: Social Networks OpenSocial Support* *(continued)*

Social Network	OpenSocial Version	Support
Ning	0.7	Live for all isers
orkut	0.7	Live for all users
YiQi	0.7	Live for all users
lokalisten	0.8	Open sandbox access
iGoogle	0.8	Open sandbox access
imeem	0.7	Open sandbox access
Viadeo	0.7	Open sandbox access
CityIN	0.7	Application review required
Tianya	0.7	Under development
Plaxo Pulse	0.5	White-listed apps available for users

*See `http://wiki.opensocial.org/index.php?title=Main_Page#Container_Information` for any changes to this list.

An Open Source project called Shindig has been developed to enable social networks to more easily create their own containers. Shindig is an implementation of the OpenSocial specifications, and has the support of Google and other companies involved in container creation.

If a social network wants to host OpenSocial applications, it must implement the OpenSocial specification, and one way to accomplish this is by using Shindig. The social network must connect its backend to the OpenSocial Server Provider Interface (SPI) that is part of Shindig. Through the OpenSocial SPI, an OpenSocial application can access and create social data and activities, hence gaining access to the social network's back-end social data.

See `http://incubator.apache.org/shindig` *for more detailed information about Shindig.*

OpenSocial Architecture

The overall architecture of your social network application extends beyond your own code. It involves the client (Web browser), and the container (social network) itself. All social networks require that they directly serve the client, as shown in Figure 2-1. This means that when the client makes calls to your externally hosted code, the social network makes calls to your application, and those results can, in turn, be "filtered" by the social network before being delivered to the client.

Your social network application may be hosted on multiple external servers, or even hosted on the container. Depending on how you implement your application, an authentication process may be necessary.

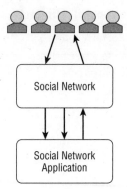

**Figure 2-1: The social
network-to-application
architecture**

With OpenSocial version 0.8, there are now two OpenSocial APIs:

❑ *Client-based API* — Relying on the client-based JavaScript technology, the OpenSocial JavaScript API (sometimes simply called the OpenSocial API) was the first API that evolved from OpenSocial's initial release. It involves making calls using an OpenSocial JavaScript API.

❑ *Server-based API* — New since the release of OpenSocial 0.8 in 2008, the server-based RESTful API first went live with the hi5 social network. This allows developers to create applications with their own server-based technology, which enables developers to write applications that are hosted on a server and make direct calls to the container. Developers can write a server-based application in any language (including PHP, Python, Java, RUBY, Perl, and many others), providing, of course, that the developer's server supports these languages.

Client-Based API

Figure 2-2 shows the transactional model of a *completely* client-based OpenSocial JavaScript API application. In this model, the entire application is developed with XML, HTML, and JavaScript. For some social networks, it is possible to host the application on the container. In other cases, the application may be preloaded/cached by the container. If the application does not need to make any further calls to the application server, the transactional model only involves the client and social network server(s).

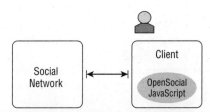

**Figure 2-2: Completely "client-based"
OpenSocial JavaScript API application**

Developers of some applications may want to store and retrieve their own application data. In these cases, developers utilize persistency as defined in the OpenSocial JavaScript API. If the developer chooses to use persistency, the transactional model still resembles Figure 2-2. The model still only involves the client and social network server(s), and, thus, is still a completely client-based OpenSocial JavaScript API application.

Developers may also want to store the data on their own database, or, perhaps, need other resources and services on their server(s). Figure 2-3 shows the transactional model for this scenario. Here, the application's server is introduced to support these external needs. In this model, resources (such as services and server-side programs) are invoked to support the application. Thus, this type of a client-based OpenSocial JavaScript application model could be described as one with server-side application support.

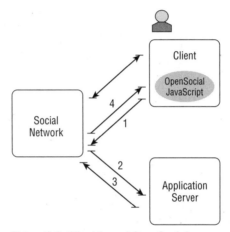

Figure 2-3: Client-based OpenSocial JavaScript application with server-side application support

Another possibility is that the application needs other external services not owned by the developer. An example of this might be an application developed for the yelp container (www.yelp.com), a site featuring user reviews and recommendations. The yelp API enables developers to include yelp data. This application would make calls to the yelp server with the third-party yelp API, as shown in Figure 2-4. This transactional model represents a variation of the client-based OpenSocial JavaScript application with server-side application support.

Server-Based API

The server-side API comes in three flavors:

- ❏ Those for a non-social network application
- ❏ Those for a social network application
- ❏ Those that are a hybrid

Some OpenSocial RESTful server-based applications are not gadgets, and are not deployed on the host container, but do use social data. (A *gadget* is a widget made by Google developers that gives users interesting and dynamic content that can be placed in any Web page.) These are often called completely server-based OpenSocial RESTful API *non-social networking applications*. Rather than using the OpenSocial JavaScript API, these applications utilize the newer OpenSocial RESTful API, which enables a server-side program to get social data directly from the social network. Such completely OpenSocial RESTful API applications are not social network applications, but could be a server program or a gadget operating within an external Web page.

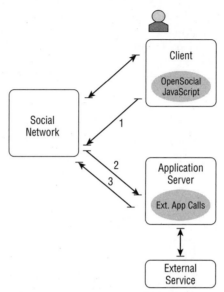

Figure 2-4: Variation in the client-based OpenSocial JavaScript application with server-side application

Let's consider a hypothetical application dealing with Flixster (www.flixter.com), a movie site. When a user views or rates a movie on the Flixter Web site, the user may want to post an activity stream to the user's MySpace account saying, for example, "Lynne rated StarWars with Flixster." Flixster would want to do this from its server, because this would be triggered by the user rating action at the Flixter site. To do this, Flixster would need access to MySpace's OpenSocial data. This is a good example where the OpenSocial RESTful API could be used.

Figure 2-5 shows the transactional model of the completely server-based OpenSocial RESTful non-social networking application. Note that this example includes a client (the user) that, when connecting to the social network (for example, MySpace) at a later time, sees the resultant activity stream. It is true that some OpenSocial RESTful API applications may not involve any client on the social network.

With OpenSocial 0.9, developers may create a completely server-based OpenSocial RESTful API social network application that is deployed on a social network. This is discussed more in Chapter 9. This is very much like the model currently employed by the Facebook API. Here, when the client requests a page where the application appears, a message sent to the social network invokes a URL of the server-based application. This application (which is hosted on the developer's server) makes calls directly to the social network using the OpenSocial RESTful API. The response is then delivered to the social network, which, in turn, integrates it and delivers it to the client.

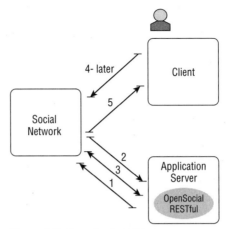

**Figure 2-5: Hypothetical Flixster
OpenSocial RESTful application**

Figure 2-6 shows the transactional model for this scenario. Currently, there is no support for this on any OpenSocial container. It will require the container to allow developers a new form of application deployment that involves the specification of this callback URL. In this case, all of the OpenSocial calls are between the application's server and the social network directly. The client is not involved in making these transactions.

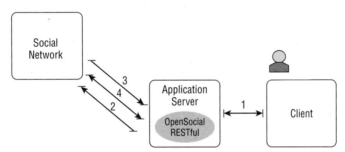

**Figure 2-6: Completely server-based OpenSocial RESTful API
social network application**

Developers may also create a *hybrid client/server* OpenSocial application. In this scenario, an OpenSocial JavaScript API social network application would make calls to a server-based OpenSocial REST API program via the OpenSocial JavaScript `makeRequest` method. This is similar to what is shown in Figure 2-3. However, as shown in Figure 2-7, the server application can make direct calls to the social network using the RESTful API. As will be explained in Chapter 6, it is possible to pass the OpenSocial data through the `makeRequest` to a server program. This can be more efficient (as will be examined in Chapter 8).

In the hybrid case, the response might include the generation of new client-side OpenSocial RESTful calls and other JavaScript code that are triggered by future user actions. It is possible in some instances where the server application may dynamically determine its social data needs and, hence, need to make OpenSocial RESTful calls. This could be a way of dynamically generating your client-side event-handling code.

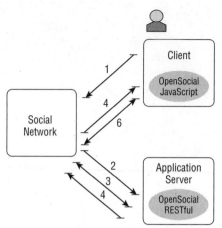

Figure 2-7: Hybrid client/server OpenSocial application, with both OpenSocial JavaScript client code and RESTful server-based code

Related to the hybrid case is the use of IFrames (from "Inline Frames"). In particular, developers separate different content into different IFrames. Sometimes these are called "widgets" or "IFrame apps". Each IFrame can be used to dynamically display part of the application and respond separately to user requests. The client code can get OpenSocial data using the JavaScript APIs, and then pass it back to the server-side program for a particular IFrame. Or, a server-side program can make OpenSocial REST calls directly.

Following is an example of an application that has an IFrame and is passed OpenSocial data. This is different in that the IFrame doesn't send back HTML to the client, but displays it and accepts user interaction. It is a way to modularize transactions and can improve performance. For example, the entire application interface is not updated; only the part that is affected. However, the developer can place the entire application interface in a single IFrame.

```
<iframe id="myframe" width="400" height="400" frameborder="0"></iframe>
<br> ...more html ...

<script type='text/javascript'>
    //call to pass viewerID (some OpenSocial data)
    document.getElementById('myframe').src = "http://U.com/u.php?id="+ viewerID;
</script>
```

In this example, some HTML is present that contains an IFrame that later (in a JavaScript block) sets the content of the IFrame associated with the output of a server-side program (u.php) that is passed some OpenSocial data.

The development of a client-based social network application using the OpenSocial JavaScript API is covered in Chapter 4. Chapter 5 discusses how to create server-based applications using the OpenSocial RESTful API.

Application Architecture

A social network application based on the OpenSocial JavaScript API can be viewed as a layered object, as shown in Figure 2-8. As you can see, an outer layer specifies the application as a Google gadget using XML. The inner content is the content of the application, and consists typically of HTML, JavaScript, CSS, and other content. This content can be in-line, or can be loaded from externally located content (for example, externally stored JavaScript code, or some kind of media such as a Flash movie).

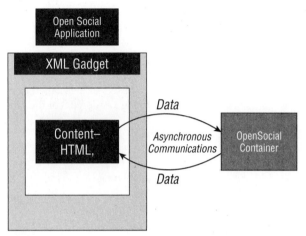

Figure 2-8: OpenSocial application layers and asynchronous communications with OpenSocial container

The JavaScript API can implement the following:

❑   *Application-specific functionality* — Supports application functions and interactions, and can make calls to other resources.

❑   *OpenSocial API calls* — Supports requests from your application to the social network to get data, store data, and do "social" operations (such as messages, invites, and so on).

❑   *Gadget API calls* — Recall that your OpenSocial application is actually a gadget. Developers may use this API to enable an application to control its presence in the social network, invoke external resources, load external media, and more.

OpenSocial client-based applications use the OpenSocial JavaScript API to make queries to the container in an asynchronous manner for most of its calls, as shown in Figure 2-8. Most of the OpenSocial methods do not directly return data. Instead, the application must request this data, and then, at some later time, the container will return the results to a callback function in the application.

The returned response object from a request is an instance of opensocial.DataResponse. A single DataRequest object can have multiple request objects added to it. An application may make several such requests during its session with a user, but can also choose to *batch* or *group* requests at one time (for improved performance). For example, a request might be to get the user's name or a user's list of friends. The class for making requests is opensocial.DataRequest. (All of the classes and methods in the OpenSocial JavaScript API begin with the namespace `opensocial`.) The application then sends this request using the `send` method of the `DataRequest` class.

Once a container receives a `DataRequest`, it goes through all of the requests associated with it, and processes each request. In the case of multiple requests, it creates a batched response. Containers should process the requests in *serial order*. For example, if you have a storage followed by a retrieval of a piece of information, the newly stored information should be returned. Similarly, if the request is first a retrieval followed by a storage operation, the old information will be returned before the new information is stored.

Sample Application

OpenSocial is built upon what Google calls *social gadgets*, which are represented by XML files. (XML, of course, is a language that is used to describe data with sets of tags called *elements*.) Listing 2-1 shows the code for a "Hello World" OpenSocial application using version 0.8 of the OpenSocial JavaScript API.

Listing 2-1: Simple OpenSocial "Hello World" Application

```
<?xml version="1.0" encoding="UTF-8"?>
<Module>
  <ModulePrefs title="Hello World!">
    <Require feature="opensocial-0.8"/>
  </ModulePrefs>
  <Content type="html">
   <![CDATA[
      Hello, world!
   ]]>
  </Content>
</Module>
```

Let's go through this code line by line:

❑   `<?xml version="1.0" encoding="UTF-8" ?>` — This indicates that you have an XML file.

❑   `<Module>` — This declares that this is a gadget.

❑   `<ModulePrefs title="Hello World!">` — This is the gadget information.

❑   `<Require feature="opensocial-0.8" />` — This indicates that you are using OpenSocial API version 0.8.

❑   `<Content type="html">` — This indicates that the gadget will be delivered as HTML. OpenSocial containers recommend this content type.

❑   `<![CDATA[` — This contains the contents of the gadget, including HTML, CSS, and JavaScript. This is similar the `body` tag of an HTML page.

Everything except the "`Hello, world!`" string is XML code that defines the application as a gadget. The structure of this XML language comes directly from Google gadgets, and is examined in detail later in this chapter.

To be able to run the OpenSocial "Hello World" application, you must place it on a server and then register the application with the desired social network(s). Figure 2-9 shows the "Hello, world" application profile running on the hi5 container.

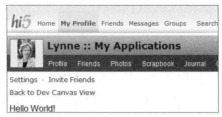

Figure 2-9: "Hello World" application
deployed in hi5

OpenSocial Data Formats

As a developer, it is important that you are aware of a number of data formats used in OpenSocial (including JSON, Atom, and XML), and it is important that you know how to use them. Let's first get acquainted with the basics surrounding these top three formats. Included in an examination of the JavaScript (OpenSocial) API in Chapter 4 is a discussion of when these formats are used.

JSON

JavaScript Object Notation (JSON) is a format that was created as a language-independent way to represent structured data. Because it is text-based, it is easy to read. JSON serializes its data using JavaScript. Because of these attributes, it has been used for Web applications, and has been adopted by OpenSocial as one of its data formats.

JSON can be used to format the following kinds of data:

- ❏ Number
- ❏ Boolean
- ❏ Null
- ❏ String
- ❏ Object
- ❏ Array

All data is given a JSON representation using either *collections* or *ordered lists*. Collections are sets of (name,value) pairs. JavaScript serializes these collections (or ordered lists) via JavaScript literals. For example, an object is represented as a collection of zero or more (name,value) pairs. An array is represented as an ordered sequence of zero or more values.

This serialization process has made the use of JSON popular in Web applications because it is able (in a serial fashion) to transmit the data over the Internet. One place JSON is used is in Ajax programming as an alternative to XML. JSON is a good fit with OpenSocial because it represents data with JavaScript literals. OpenSocial JavaScript can easily use this format, saving it to a JavaScript variable in the program. There is the added advantage that the overhead of JSON is less than XML.

JSON is used as a format for data coming from the social network to your program. This way, it is independent of the social network's underlying data representations that will change depending on the individual container (network). Similarly, you can create JSON data and send it in a request to the OpenSocial container.

To find out more about JSON go to `http:///www.json.org`.

Let's look at an example. Say that you have a `Dog` object that contains the attributes `name`, `age`, and `owner` (itself an object). Listing 2-2 shows what the JSON representation of such a `Dog` object.

Listing 2-2: JSON Representation of a Dog Object

```
{
    "name": "Butch",
    "age": 5,
     "owner": {
         "name": "Lynne",
         "city": "SF",
         "state": "CA"
     },
     "likes": "bones"
}
```

Chapter 4 discusses some of the JavaScript (OpenSocial) API calls that use JSON-formatted data. In OpenSocial, the Core Gadget API supports parsing of JSON via the `gadgets.json` object. The `gadgets.json.parse` method takes JSON and returns a JavaScript object. Another alternative is to use the JavaScript function `eval`, but for OpenSocial applications, the use of the `gadgets` method is recommended. The `gadgets.json.stringify` takes JavaScript and turns it into a JSON string.

Atom

A format used in the OpenSocial RESTful API is Atom. (Chapter 5 provides more in-depth coverage of the RESTful API.) Atom is a form of XML that describes information as feeds. The Atom format has been used on the Web to represent and deliver data such as Weblogs (blogs) and news to Web sites and clients.

The root element of an Atom-formatted data set is the `<feed>` element, which can contain a number of `<entry>` elements. Each entry is like an item in a Web feed. You will see more examples of the Atom format in Chapter 5.

XML

As you have learned, XML is a language that is used to describe data with sets of tags called *elements*. There are a number of basic rules that define XML as a standard, including stipulations such as the following:

❑   Elements are case-sensitive

❑   Elements must come in pairs (that is, have an ending tag)

The actual tags/elements are defined by the application of XML. Chapter 3 discusses XML specifications used in OpenSocial API.

See `http://xml.org` *for a complete discussion of the XML standard.*

Application Deployment

The application deployment process is unique to each container. The following discussion shows you how to deploy an OpenSocial JavaScript application on each of the more popular social networks that support OpenSocial, including MySpace, hi5, orkut, imeem, Friendster, and Netlog.

Latter in this book, the "Hello World" application is extended to get OpenSocial user and friend information, called the "Friend Finder" application. This basic application will be used in the following demonstration of application deployment.

With all of the social networks, you must have your own account. You must also go through a process of registering as a developer.

MySpace Deployment

Deployment on MySpace is a simple process. Begin by going to `developer.myspace.com` and registering as a developer. Once you have done this, you may build a new application. Click the "build" link and you will see the interface used to create a new application, as shown in Figure 2-10.

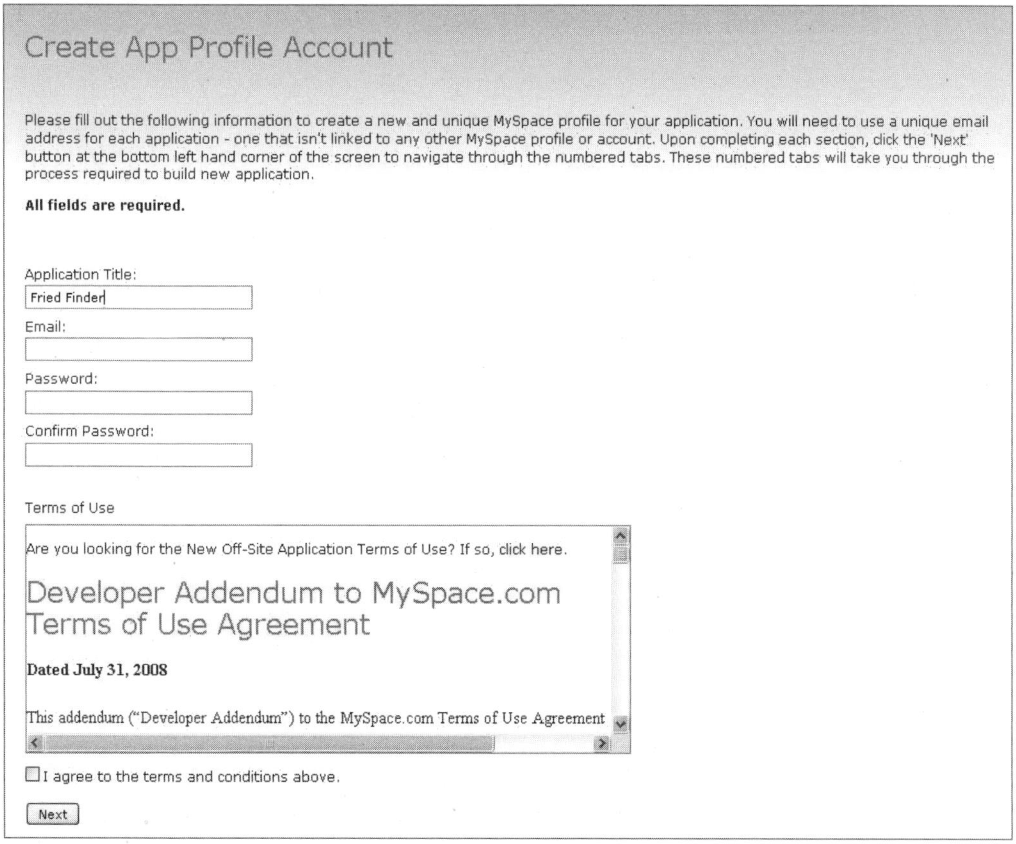

Figure 2-10: In MySpace's form for creating a new application, the information is used to create what MySpace calls an "application account"

In MySpace, an "application account" is created for each new application. You will be automatically listed as the developer, and also as a friend of this account. However, you must specify a unique email for the application. This cannot be the email you have used to create your personal developer account. Once you have set up an application account, you can go to your main developer page by directing your browser to http://developer.myspace.com. If you click on the My Apps link, you will be directed to the interface shown in Figure 2-11, which allows you to do the following:

❏ Edit applications

❏ Create new applications

❏ Delete applications

❏ Add/remove developers

❏ Publish your application

Figure 2-11: Main MySpace Developer Platform page

Click the Edit Details link appearing at the bottom of the My Applications interface shown in Figure 2-11. You will then see an interface used for entering application attributes and details, as shown in Figure 2-12. The following is the information captured:

❏ *Main App and Category/Language Settings* — This can be changed for each unique language you support.

❏ *Language* — Application language (for example, English)

❏ *Gallery Description* — A brief description of the application

❏ *Small Icon/Large Icon* — URLS to small and large application icons

❏ *Installable* — Indicates if you want your application to be able to be installed by users

❏ *Primary and Secondary Category* — Categories used to list applications in indices

❏ *Callback URLs* — These are invoked during install or uninstall:

❏ *Install* — Indicates that this is invoked when the application is installed. You can specify a program to keep track of this event, or to offer other first-time instructions to users.

❑ *Uninstall* — Indicates that this is invoked when a application is uninstalled. You might want to invoke a program that records this event, but you might also want to offer an enticement to lure the user back.

❑ *OAuth Settings* — These deal with the use of OAuth in MySpace:

  ❑ *OAuth Consumer Key* — Used for signing (authentication).

  ❑ *OAuth Consumer Secret* — Used for signing (authentication).

❑ *External Site Settings* — These are for externally hosted applications:

  ❑ *External URL* — URL of the external application.

  ❑ *External Domain* — Domain of external application.

❑ *Other* — Whatever MySpace might want (currently, age appropriateness).

You have two options with MySpace to specify the application code: hosting your code on MySpace or externally hosting it. If you host externally, much of this information will be filled in automatically, but you have the option of altering it.

Hosting on MySpace

Developers are provided an option to host their OpenSocial application code on MySpace. This may mean that you host all of your code on MySpace, or it can mean that you host the main application there, but also refer to externally located code files and other resources.

Figure 2-13 shows MySpace's Applicaton Builder interface that allows the developer to directly specify the application code for MySpace hosting. When you save the application source code, MySpace will then store and host this code. You can then return to the Application Builder to change your code.

MySpace's Application Builder lets you specify different code for each of the Canvas, Profile, and Home pages provided for MySpace applications. If you choose to only enter in the Canvas and Home page surfaces, this will mean that your application will not be displayed on the user's Profile page.

When you specify the code, you do not specify the Gadget XML, but rather only the content. Much of the Gadget XML element information (such as icons, application names, lifecycle support, and so on) is provided in the information you filled out in the MySpace application settings interface shown in Figure 2-12. Hence, for the "Friend Finder" application, only the content that was shown in Listing 2-1 should be entered. If you make the mistake of giving the complete XML application, you will get a deployment error when you try to save it.

MySpace's Application Builder requires that you specify the following application information through its Edit App Information interface:

❑ Application title

❑ Gallery description

❑ Primary category

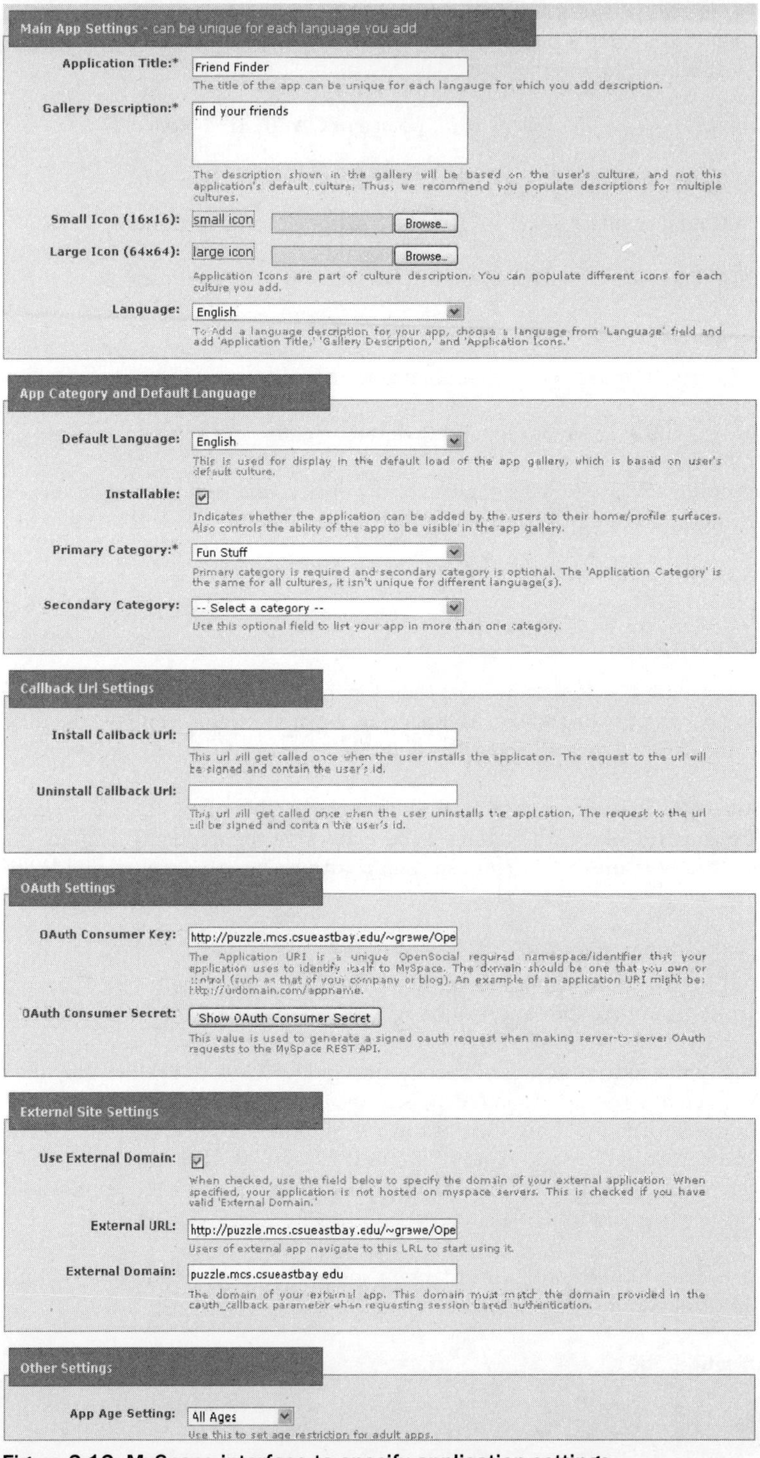

Main App Settings - can be unique for each language you add

Application Title:* `Friend Finder`
The title of the app can be unique for each language for which you add description.

Gallery Description:* `find your friends`

The description shown in the gallery will be based on the user's culture, and not this application's default culture. Thus, we recommend you populate descriptions for multiple cultures.

Small Icon (16x16): `small icon` [Browse...]

Large Icon (64x64): `large icon` [Browse...]
Application Icons are part of culture description. You can populate different icons for each culture you add.

Language: `English`
To Add a language description for your app, choose a language from 'Language' field and add 'Application Title,' 'Gallery Description,' and 'Application Icons.'

App Category and Default Language

Default Language: `English`
This is used for display in the default load of the app gallery, which is based on user's default culture.

Installable: ☑
Indicates whether the application can be added by the users to their home/profile surfaces. Also controls the ability of the app to be visible in the app gallery.

Primary Category:* `Fun Stuff`
Primary category is required and secondary category is optional. The 'Application Category' is the same for all cultures, it isn't unique for different language(s).

Secondary Category: `-- Select a category --`
Use this optional field to list your app in more than one category.

Callback Url Settings

Install Callback Url:
This url will get called once when the user installs the application. The request to the url will be signed and contain the user's id.

Uninstall Callback Url:
This url will get called once when the user uninstalls the application. The request to the url will be signed and contain the user's id.

OAuth Settings

OAuth Consumer Key: `http://puzzle.mcs.csueastbay.edu/~grswe/Ope`
The Application URI is a unique OpenSocial required namespace/identifier that your application uses to identify itself to MySpace. The domain should be one that you own or control (such as that of your company or blog). An example of an application URI might be: http://urdomain.com/appname.

OAuth Consumer Secret: [Show OAuth Consumer Secret]
This value is used to generate a signed oauth request when making server-to-server OAuth requests to the MySpace REST API.

External Site Settings

Use External Domain: ☑
When checked, use the field below to specify the domain of your external application. When specified, your application is not hosted on myspace servers. This is checked if you have valid 'External Domain.'

External URL: `http://puzzle.mcs.csueastbay.edu/~grswe/Ope`
Users of external app navigate to this URL to start using it.

External Domain: `puzzle.mcs.csueastbay.edu`
The domain of your external app. This domain must match the domain provided in the oauth_callback parameter when requesting session based authentication.

Other Settings

App Age Setting: `All Ages`
Use this to set age restriction for adult apps.

Figure 2-12: MySpace interface to specify application settings

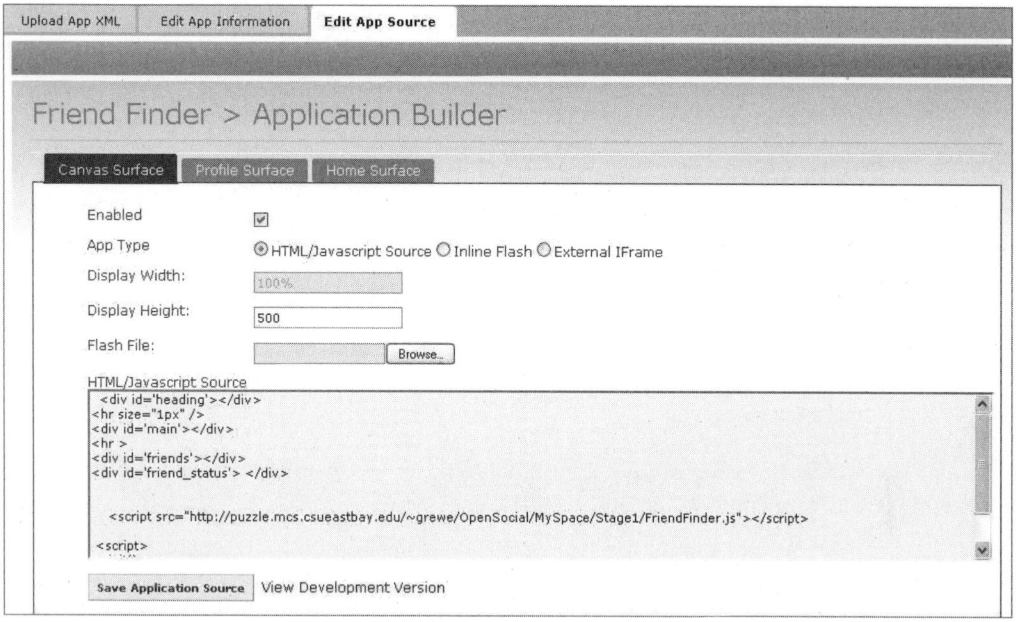

Figure 2-13: MySpace's Application Builder interface for specifying MySpace hosted code

Uploading Code from an External Server

You can choose to "host" the code yourself on some external server, and then specify its URL, simply uploading the code. Figure 2-14 shows the MySpace Upload Application XML interface where you specify the URL to your externally hosted XML code. Unlike the MySpace hosting option, developers will make changes to code on their servers and need to re-upload the code for MySpace to accept the changes.

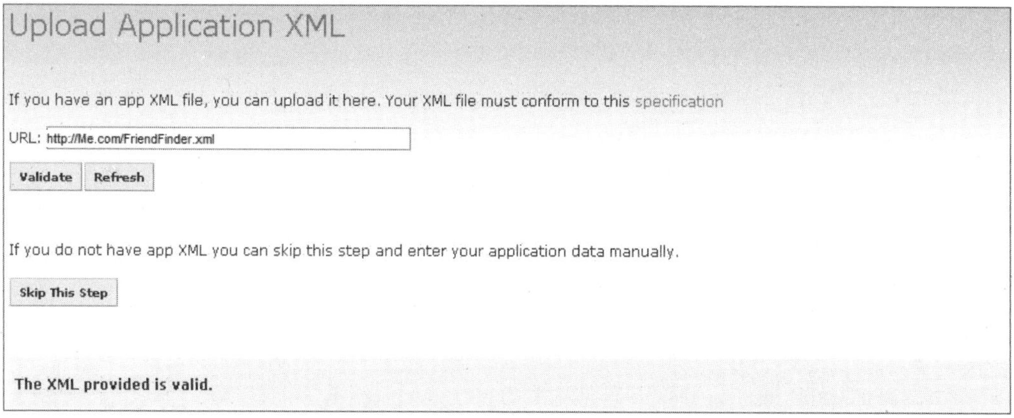

Figure 2-14: You can specify code as an externally provided XML application, but note that MySpace does not support all of the Google Gadget XML specification

MySpace requires developers to follow the Google Gadet XML specification with the following stipulations.

The following applies to <Content>:

❏ preferredHeight

  ❏ Specifies the initial height desired for the surface.

  ❏ If not provided, then the height attribute from <ModulePrefs> element is used.

  ❏ Minimum value is 20.

  ❏ Maximum value is 1000.

  ❏ If the preferredHeight is specified multiple times for the same view/surface, then the last one takes precedence.

Only one <ModulePrefs> is recognized. If multiple ModulePrefs elements are provided, the first one is used, and the rest are ignored. Following are other restrictions:

❏ title

  ❏ The short name associated with the application.

  ❏ This attribute is required to create/update an application.

  ❏ Minimum length is 1 character.

  ❏ Maximum length is 64 characters.

  ❏ Must use only the following characters: a-z, A-Z, 0-9, ', &, !, ., -, _, ?, [space].

  ❏ Must start with a letter.

❏ description

  ❏ A short description of the application, used for display in the Gallery.

  ❏ This attribute is required to create/update an application.

  ❏ Minimum length is 1 character.

  ❏ Maximum length is 256 characters.

  ❏ Must use only the following characters: a-z, A-Z, 0-9, ', &, !, ., -, _, ?, [space].

❏ thumbnail

  ❏ The URL of the thumbnail image associated with the gadget. This is displayed in the App Gallery, and the App Profile page.

  ❏ Must point to a valid .gif, .png, or .jpg file.

  ❏ Image dimensions must be 64 x 64 pixels.

  ❏ File size must be less than 300KB.

  ❏ Image will be pulled in and hosted by MySpace.

Figure 2-17: Creating a new application in hi5 by simply entering in the URL of the externally hosted OpenSocial XML file

Creating an application involves simply giving the URL to your externally hosted application. This is similar to MySpace's Upload Application XML option. The XML must contain more information than what was previously shown in Listing 2-1. For example, in Listing 2-1, you specified in the `ModulePrefs` tag the title of the application, a description of the application, and author information. The other tags define the version of OpenSocial that the application uses, as well as information about the height of the application.

hi5 requires that the `title` attribute of the `<ModulePrefs>` element must be specified. In addition, the `author_email` attribute must be equal to the developer account email address.

Figure 2-18 shows the main developer page on hi5. Figure 2-19 shows the "Friend Finder" application running in the developer sandbox in a "canvas" view. From the main developer page, and from the hi5 sandbox page, you can do the following:

- ❑ Specify the application URL
- ❑ Add more developers
- ❑ Preview or run in "canvas" mode
- ❑ View statistics
- ❑ Remove the application
- ❑ Refresh (forced when code is revised, and may not occur immediately)
- ❑ View application source
- ❑ View application in different languages
- ❑ Register to get hi5 language translations (Chapter 7 has more on internationalization)
- ❑ Submit the application for publication

Note the Reload App link near the top of Figure 2-19. The reload feature is important, and you will use it often as you are developing and changing your code. It will refresh the code, even in the sandbox, because hi5 caches it.

orkut Deployment

orkut directs you to its "Sandbox Signup" (`http://sandbox.orkut.com/SandboxSignup.aspx`) to enroll as a developer. All that is required is your name, email address (the one you used when getting your user account), and the name of your company. Once you sign up, you have the capability to deploy applications on orkut.

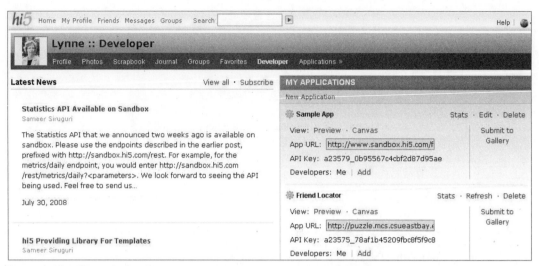

Figure 2-18: hi5's main Developer page, where you can see your applications

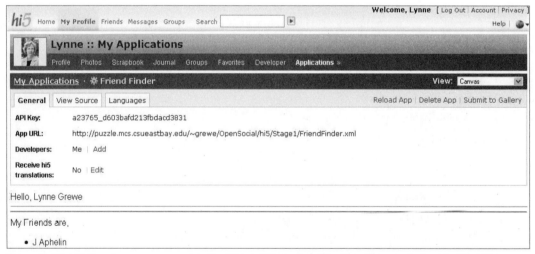

Figure 2-19: hi5 Developer page running the "Friend Finder" application ("canvas" view) in the hi5 sandbox

To reach the interface for deploying and working on your applications, you must go to the http://sandbox.orkut.com page after you log in. Note that when you log in, you will initially be in the "production" orkut machine at http://orkut.com.

Once on the "sandbox" orkut machine, you can reach the interface for deploying applications on orkut by clicking the "edit" link in the Apps area of your Home page for your orkut account. As shown in Figure 2-20, the interface is similar to hi5's, and only the application URL must be specified. From this interface, you will also find a list of applications you have deployed and installed (including installed applications not owned by you). From this interface you can do the following:

❑ Set permission for your application by clicking on the "manage" link next to it

❑ Remove your application using the "trash can" icon

❑ Run your application by clicking on its name

Figure 2-20: Deploying the "Friend Finder" application on orkut

Unlike hi5, there are no direct links in the interface to submit or reload your application. Once you are finished with the editing of your application, you can submit it to orkut by following the link from orkut's developer information page, leading to the `http://www.orkut.com/Main#AppDirectorySubmit` `.aspx` URL.

orkut caches your application even in the sandbox (before submitting it). Obviously, you will want to make changes to your XML file. To force a reload, you use "by-pass cache" (bpc) feature. You can simply add "`bpc=1`" to the URL of your running application to force a reload.

For example, let's say that you are viewing the following:

```
http://sandbox.orkut.com/Main#Application.aspx?uid=XX&appId=YY
```

You would then go to the address bar of your browser and add the "`bpc=1`" to the end of the URL, thus yielding the following:

```
http://sandbox.orkut.com/Main#Application.aspx?uid=XX&appId=YY&bpc=1
```

Other users of your application will not see the changes you have made until orkut automatically refreshes your application, which is usually done in one hour.

This bypass technique only reloads the cached XML, but not any externally referenced JavaScript or calls to external programs. You must use your browser to delete all cached files (such as JavaScript files) to see the new JavaScript. Figure 2-21 shows the dialog box for the Internet Explorer browser that enables you to delete these files. The location and look of this delete option will vary with browser and version.

Figure 2-21: Dialog box in Internet Explorer that you use to remove files so that they are refreshed with new ones

Netlog Deployment

Netlog allows developers to test their application in a sandbox, but, unlike the other containers discussed thus far (hi5, orkut, and MySpace), you do not deploy it. Instead, each time you want to test your application, you must go to the developer page (`http://en.netlog.com/go/developer/opensocial/sandbox=1`) shown in Figure 2-22. In this sense, Netlog provides more of a testing console. In this interface, you only have the option to update the code, and to change the view.

Once you have decided to go public with your application, you must fill out the developer contact form at the main developer Web site (`http://en.netlog.com/go/developer/contact`).

imeem Deployment

To deploy on imeem, go to `http://www.imeem.com/developers` and you will see the main developer control page. This is called the "developer dashboard," and is shown in Figure 2-23. From imeem's "developer dashboard," you can do the following:

❑   Manage information about an application

❑   Create new applications

❑   Check application status

❑   Delete an application

❑   Run an application in "canvas" and "profile" views

❑   See an "About" application page.

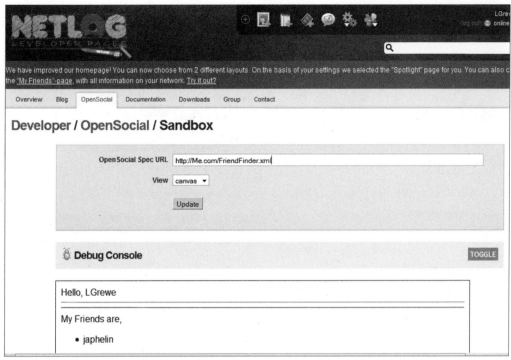

Figure 2-22: Netlog provides a simple interface for testing your Opensocial XML application

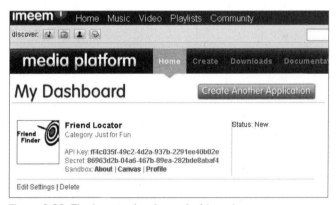

Figure 2-23: The imeem developer dashboard

Figure 2-24 shows imeem's interface to create a new application. You must enter the application name, category, email address, developers, and description. Also, you will specify if you are creating an application hosted off of or on imeem. So, like MySpace, you can host your code on imeem.

Figure 2-25 shows imeem's interface to host the application on imeem. You have the option to either enter in the code manually, or to upload an XML file to the imeem server. In the manual entry interface, you have tabs for the Canvas, Profile, and About pages. In the OpenSocial XML option (to upload an XML file), the interface only asks for the URL to your hosted XML file. Note that you only enter in the content and no Gadget XML elements in the edit space. This is similar to the MySpace-hosted code-creation process.

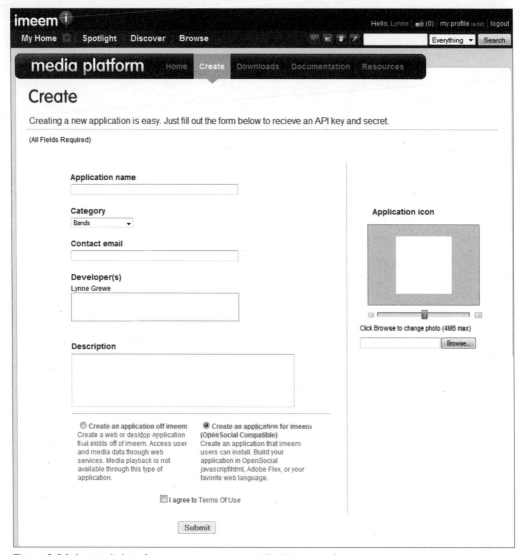

Figure 2-24: Imeem's interface to create a new application

Friendster Deployment

Friendster's developer site is located at http://www.friendster.com/developer. You reach the interface shown in Figure 2-26 by clicking on the link called "Get API key." You must enter the name of the application, platform (OpenSocial), and the URL to your XML file. Notice that this interface has a drop-down box that you use to specify the platform type. OpenSocial appears as an available option in the list, but Friendster supports other kinds of application APIs as well. Under Optional Information, the developer specifies the Category, if the application can be added to a Friendster Profile, and the URL starting with `http://widgets.friendster.com/` that the application is viewable from.

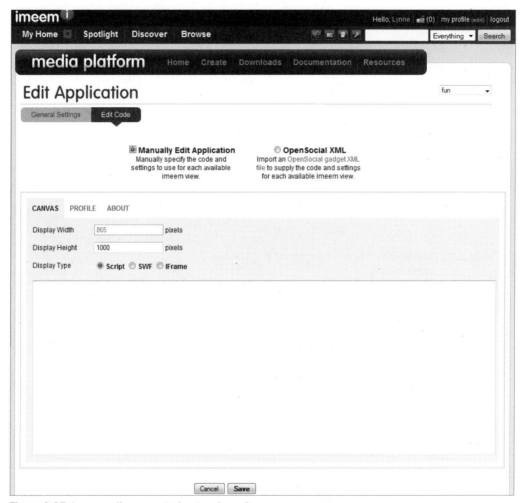

Figure 2-25: imeem allows you to host code on its server

Once you have deployed your application, you can proceed to the interface shown in Figure 2-27 by clicking the "Manage Apps" link. This interface enables you to do the following:

❑ Change the application settings

❑ Run the application

❑ Delete the application

❑ Submit the application to the gallery (publish)

Figure 2-26: Friendster's interface for creating applications

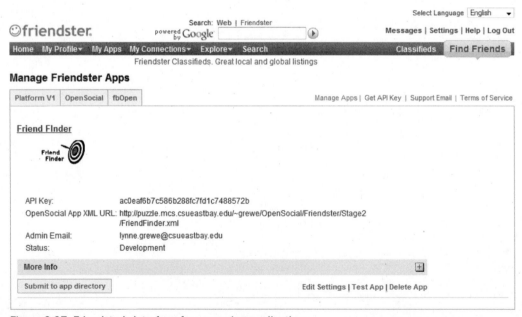

Figure 2-27: Friendster's interface for managing applications

When you click the Test App link shown at the bottom of Figure 2-27, you are taken to an interface that asks you to install the application. This is the same interface you see when installing published applications. After this, the application appears in your account pages in the same way published applications do.

Note Friendster requires that you specify the following XML elements for an application:

- ❑ `description`
- ❑ `thumbnail`
- ❑ `icon`
- ❑ `author_email`

The `thumbnail` should be 75 pixels by 75 pixels, and the `icon` should be 16 pixels by 16 pixels.

Freebar Deployment

Freebar has two options for development. One is running it in Freebar's sandbox. This is not deployment, but you must re-enter in the URL of your XML application each time you wish to test it (similar to Netlog's sandbox). Freebar's sandbox can be reached at `http://www.new.freebar.com/applications/developerzone`. This sandbox testing tool lets you alter the application view.

Another option is to upload the URL of your externally hosted XML application. You can reach this interface at `http://www.new.freebar.it/applications/developer/index`. From this interface, you can do the following:

- ❑ Publish your application
- ❑ Run your application

What You Need to Get Started

To create an OpenSocial application, you must have the following:

- ❑ Application code
- ❑ Server-to-host application (with database if necessary)
- ❑ Developer accounts on each social network/container to which you will deploy your application

Recall from the discussion earlier in this chapter that some containers offer data storage and even application hosting.

Table 2-2 provides some additional resources you might find helpful as you develop your OpenSocial applications.

Table 2-2: Additional Resources

Resource	Description	Items
OpenSocial Web site (`http://www.code.google.com/opensocial`)	This is the main resource of all things OpenSocial.	Javscript API documentation
		RESTful API documentation
		orkut (Google social network) development guide
		Google Group on OpenSocial
		OpenSocial Developer Forum to share problems/solutions (`http://groups.google.com/group/opensocial`)
		Issue Tracker to report and track bugs, make feature requests and register to receive updates about specific reports (`http://code.google.com/p/opensocial-resources/`)
		Wiki to work collaboratively on documentation (`http://code.google.com/p/opensocial-resources/`); code examples provided (`http://code.google.com/p/opensocial-resources/wiki/SampleApps`)
OpenSocial Blog (`http://www.opensocialapis.blogspot.com`)	This is the main blog for OpenSocial developers. You can see what other developers are doing, see problems and solutions, as well as events that are going on	

Continued

Table 2-2: Additional Resources *(continued)*

Resource	Description	Items
OpenSocial Foundation Web site (`http://www.opensocial.org`)	This is the home for a non-profit organization. This is another site similar to the one hosted on Google in that it contains documentation. It was jointly proposed by Yahoo!, MySpace, and Google. It is the main organization tasked to perform open development of the OpenSocial standard.	API documentation
Container Developer Forums	Forums hosted by and about individual social networks	MySpace (`http://developer.myspace.com/community/forums/`) orkut (`http://groups.google.com/group/opensocial-orkut` and `http://orkutdeveloper.blogspot.com/`) hi5 (`http://www.hi5.com/friend/group/2364084--Hi5%2BPlatform%2BDevelopment--front-html`) Friendster (`http://www.friendster.com/group/tabmain.php?gid=977483`) Ning (`http://developer.ning.com/forum/topic/listForCategory?categoryId=1185512%3ACategory%3A4646`) Plaxo (`http://groups.google.com/group/opensocial-plaxo`)

Continued

Table 2-2: Additional Resources *(continued)*

Resource	Description	Items
IRC (`http://www.irc.freenode.net/opensocial`)	Chat where you can get quick help with others online.	
OpenSocial Wiki (`http://wiki.opensocial.org`)	OpenSocial wiki	
OpenSocial Directory (`http://www.opensocialdirectory.org`)	An Open Source site that shares and rates OpenSocial applications.	

Summary

This chapter started with a brief history of OpenSocial, and then examined a number of OpenSocial architectures. You were introduced to your first OpenSocial application. You learned about OpenSocial data formats and about the deployment of OpenSocial onto a number of containers. Concluding this chapter was a breakdown of what you need to create OpenSocial applications, and a list of resources available to you.

Chapter 3 focuses on Gadget XML and API a key part of the OpenSocial standard. This includes some code examples, such as the specification of multiple views and lifecycle support.

3

Gadget XML and Gadget API

An OpenSocial application is actually a gadget that can include both Gadget XML tags and Gadget API calls. In the example shown in Chapter 2 (Listing 2-1), the content is a simple "Hello, world!" message, and the Gadget XML code makes up the rest. Gadgets are not used exclusively in OpenSocial, but they are also used to create HTML and JavaScript applications that can be embedded in Web pages and other applications supporting the Gadget standard.

This chapter examines both the Gadget XML specification and the Gadget API.

For more information about (and updates to) Google's documentation of gadgets, see http://code.google.com/apis/gadgets.

Gadget XML

An OpenSocial JavaScript application is defined by using the Google Gadget XML. In this sense, an OpenSocial application is an XML gadget. As an XML specification, it is comprised of elements and their attributes. One XML language you may be familiar with is XHTML, which is an XML specification of the HTML scripting language. Similarly, Gadget XML is an XML scripting language for the specification of gadgets.

As you saw in the "Hello World" code example in Chapter 2 (Listing 2-1), the first tag in OpenSocial gadgets is <Module>, which denotes an XML document's root element. It is similar to the <html> tag you have in an XHTML document. Inside of <Module>, you define gadgets using the following elements:

❑ ModulePrefs — Used to define a gadget and related attributes.

❑ UserPrefs — Specifies user preferences. This is optional.

❑ Content — Provides application content to the gadget.

Table 3-1 shows the attributes and sub-elements for these three main elements. Most of the attributes are optional, but this can depend on the social network to which you are deploying your application. Unfortunately, not all elements and attributes are recognized by most social networks, and some containers may place restrictions on them. (Chapter 6 dives into more detail surrounding social network restrictions.)

Table 3-1: Detail for Gadget XML

Element	Sub-element	Attribute	Description	Example
ModulePrefs		Author	Name of author.	author="L. Grewe"
		author_email	Email to contact author.	author_email= "myEmail@yahoo .com"
		author_ affiliation	Organization with which the author is affiliated. Not all social networks support this.	author_ affiliation="Your Company"
		author_location	Author's location.	author_location= "SF, CA"
		Description	A short application description.	description= "Track your Friends"
		Height	Preferred height (in pixels).	height = "200"
		Screenshot	Gadget screen shot URL, in png (preferred), jpg, or gif format. Width = 280 pixels; Height = height of gadget.	Screenshot=" http://U.com/ FindFriends.htm"
		title	Application name (short).	title ="Friend Finder"
		title_url	Title that can link to this URL. Can be used to link to an external site.	Title_url = "http:// myFriendFinder .com"

Continued

Table 3-1: Detail for Gadget XML *(continued)*

Element	Sub-element	Attribute	Description	Example
	Icon		Sub-element of the `ModulePrefs` element used to specify an application icon (an image that is 16 pixels x 16 pixels).	`<Icon>http://UServer.com/icon.gif</Icon>`
		mode	Use to specify base64-encoded image (instead of a URL).	`<Icon mode="base64" type="image/png">base64 encoded data</Icon>`
	Locale		Specifies gadget-supported locals. Optional, and you can have multiple locales.	`<Locale lang="en" country="us" />`
				`<Locale lang="ja" country="jp" />`
		lang	Specifies the language.	
		country	Specifies the country.	
		language_ direction	Specified as right-to-left (`"rtl"`) or left-to-right (`"ltr"`).	`<Locale language_direction="rtl" />`
	Link		A container-specific link. Can be used to support application lifecycle events.	Following are examples of lifecycle event notification:
				`<link rel="event"`

Continued

Table 3-1: Detail for Gadget XML *(continued)*

Element	Sub-element	Attribute	Description	Example
				`href="http://U` `.com/letmeknow"`
				`method="POST/>` `<link rel=` `"event.addapp"`
				`href="http://U` `.com/add" />`
				`<link rel="event` `.removeapp"`
				`href="http://U` `.com/remove" />`
		`rel`	Value that triggers a lifecycle event (required).	
		`href`	URL (required).	
		`method`	POST or GET. GET is default.	
	`Optional`	`feature`	Optional feature declaration. Where you specify the feature.	`<Optional` `feature="` `shareable-` `prefs"/>`
	`Preload`		Container is to get data from an external source during gadget loading. Response/data is directly placed (inline). New data will be available when the gadget is run, which improves performance.	`<Preload` `href=http://U` `.com/doit.xml />`

Continued

Table 3-1: Detail for Gadget XML *(continued)*

Element	Sub-element	Attribute	Description	Example

				You can do different preloads for different views:
				
				`<Preload`
				
				`href=http://U`
				`.com/doit.xml"`
				
				`views="profile"`
				`/>`

		href	URL of data to preload.	

	Require	feature	Required gadget feature declaration where you specify the feature.	`<Require feature=`
				`"opensocial-`
				`0.8" />`

				`<Require`
				`feature="dynamic-`
				`height" />`

UserPref			User-specific data. Can have multiple instances.	`<UserPref` `name="zipcode"`
				`display_name=` `"Zip"`
				`default_value="` `32920">`
	name		User preference name.	
	display_name		Name to display to the user.	

Continued

Table 3-1: Detail for Gadget XML (continued)

Element	Sub-element	Attribute	Description	Example
		datatype	Data type of preference, which can be the following: string (default) bool enum hidden list location	See EnumValue for examples.
		required	true or false (default is false)	required="true"
		default_value	Sets the default.	default_value="32920"
	EnumValue		Enumerates a set of possible values (Enum) for a user preference.	<UserPref name="level" display_name="Level" datatype="enum" default_value="1"> <EnumValue value="1" display_value="Beginning"/> <EnumValue value="3" display_value="Average"/>

Continued

Table 3-1: Detail for Gadget XML *(continued)*

Element	Sub-element	Attribute	Description	Example
				`<EnumValue value="3"`
				`display_value=" Advanced"/>`
				`</UserPref>`
		`value`	Value.	
		`display_value`	Defines what is displayed to user.	
Content			Contains the content of the application.	`<Content>`
				`... here it is`
				`</Content>`
		`type`	`"html"` (default) or `"url"`	`<Content type="url"`
				`href=http://U. com/doit.xml>`
				`</Content>`
		`href`	If type is `url`, this is the actual URL to the external content.	
		`view`	Specifies what view is applied to the content. Views include the following:	See the section, "Multiple Views," later in this chapter for examples and discussion.
			`profile` (user Profile page)	
			`canvas` (full view running, default view)	

Continued

93

Table 3-1: Detail for Gadget XML *(continued)*

Element	Sub-element	Attribute	Description	Example
			`profile.left` (when there is a left location on the Profile page)	
			`profile.right` (when there is a left location on the Profile page)	
			`home` (user Home page)	
			`all` (all of these)	
	`<![CDATA[ ]]>`		An escape block (allows for non-XML to be inside an XML file).	`<Content type="html">`
				`<![CDATA[`
				`YOUR HTML here...`
				`]]>`
				`</Content>`

Let's create a revised version of the OpenSocial "Hello World" application shown previously in Chapter 2, Listing 2-1. For this version, let's include more Gadget XML elements to define the application. Listing 3-1 shows the addition of a few `ModulePrefs` attributes and an `Icon` element.

Listing 3-1: Extension of the "Hello World" Application with ModulePrefs

```
<?xml version="1.0" encoding="UTF-8"?>
<Module>
  <ModulePrefs title="Hello World!" description="Hello World"
      title_url="http://www.hi5.com" author="L. Grewe"
      author_email="findme@yahoo.com" author_affiliation="iLab"
      author_location="Bay Area, CA"
      thumbnail="http://Me.com/Logo.png">

    <Icon>http://Me.com/Logo-16x16.png</Icon>
    <Require feature="opensocial-0.8"/>
```

```
    </ModulePrefs>

    <Content type="html">
      <![CDATA[
        Hello, world!
      ]]>
    </Content>
  </Module>
```

Now, let's take a look at the second half of the gadget specification, the Gadget API.

Gadget API

When a container supports OpenSocial, it also supports the corresponding version of the Google Gadget API. The Gadget API is available for use in your applications in addition to Gadget XML. This section examines a number of the Gadget API objects and methods.

> *For complete details about and updates for the Gadget API, see* `http://code.google.com/apis/gadgets/docs/reference`.

All of the objects in the Gadget API start with the `gadgets` object. Hence, when you are looking at OpenSocial code and see `gadgets.*`, you know this comes from the Google Gadget API.

The Gadget API is split up into two parts:

❑   The Core API
❑   The Feature-Specific API

Core Gadget API

For a container to be compliant with OpenSocial (and subsumed gadget) specifications, it must support and provide the Core API. This means that a developer does not need to require this API. (See the description of the `<Require>` sub-element of the `<ModulePrefs>` Gadget XML element shown in Table 3-2). Instead, the API should be automatically included when you include the following line in your gadget:

```
    <Require feature="opensocial-X.X" />
```

Table 3-2 shows most of the Core Gadget API, along with examples. These consist of the following main objects:

❑   `gadgets.io`
❑   `gadgets.json`
❑   `gadgets.util`
❑   `gadgets.Prefs`

> *Chapter 2 provides more detail about JavaScript Object Notation (JSON), which is a data format used on the Web.*

Table 3-2: Detail of Gadget Core API

Object	Method/Variable	Description	Example
gadgets.io		Allows for remote/external resource access.	
	makeRequest	static makeRequest(url, callback, opt_params) gets content from a URL and passes it to the callback function.	var params = {};
		This uses an asynchronous scheme to request and it automatically passes the response (at a later time) to the callback function.	params[gadgets.io .RequestParameters .CONTENT_TYPE] = gadgets.io .ContentType.JSON;
			gadgets.io .makeRequest ("http://U.com", response, params);
			//results passed to response function
			function response(obj) {
			//obj.txt has the returned response data
			}
	ContentType.*	Static objects that represent the following different kinds of data:	params[gadgets.io .RequestParameters .CONTENT_TYPE] = gadgets.io .ContentType.JSON;

Continued

Table 3-2: Detail of Gadget Core API (continued)

Object	Method/Variable	Description	Example
		`gadgets.io` `.ContentType.JSON` returns JSON.	`//using to set` content of type of parameters will latter use to make a data request.
		`gadgets.io` `.ContentType.DOM` returns DOM for fetching XML.	
		`gadgets.io` `.ContentType.FEED` returns JSON for RSS feed.	
		`gadgets.io` `.ContentType.TEXT` used for HTML.	
`gadgets.json`		Translations to and from JSON objects.	
	Parse	static `Object` `parse(text)` takes a JSON string and returns a JavaScript object.	`greetings = gadgets` `.json.parse(gadgets` `.util.unescapeString` `(json));`
	Stringify	static `String` `stringify(o)` takes JavaScript object o and turns it into a JSON String.	`myGiftString =` `gadgets.json` `.stringify(Gift[2]);`
			`//the JavaScript` object that is stored in `Gift[2]` is converted to a `String` `myGiftString`
`gadgets.util`		Nice utility functions.	

Continued

Table 3-2: Detail of Gadget Core API *(continued)*

Object	Method/Variable	Description	Example
	escapeString	static String escapeString(str) escapes the input as follows: newline (\n, Unicode code point 10) carriage return (\r, Unicode 13) double quote (", Unicode 34) ampersand (&, Unicode 38) single quote (', Unicode 39) left angle bracket (<, Unicode 60) right angle bracket (>, Unicode 62) backslash (\, Unicode 92) line separator (Unicode 8232) paragraph separator (Unicode 8233)	gadgets.util .escapeString(the_ string);

	unescapeString	String unescapeString(str) "unescapes" what escapeString did.	greetings = gadgets .json.parse(gadgets .util.unescapeString (json));
			
			//json is a JSON string we got back from a data request.

Continued

Table 3-2: Detail of Gadget Core API *(continued)*

Object	Method/Variable	Description	Example

	registerOnLoad Handler	static registerOnLoad Handler(callback) is used to register a callback function that is invoked when the gadget application is loaded.	gadgets.util .registerOnLoad Handler(cf);
			
			//function called at load time
			
			function cf() {
			
			... ... .your code
			
			}

	hasFeature	static Boolean hasFeature(feature) tells if a container supports a feature.	// Add a media item link if supported for hi5
			
			if(gadgets.util .hasFeature('hi5') && opensocial .getEnvironment() .supportsField (opensocial .Environment.
			
			ObjectType.ACTIVITY_ MEDIA_ITEM, hi5.ActivityMedia ItemField.LINK)) {
			
			mediaItem.setField (hi5.ActivityMedia ItemField.LINK, viewer.getField (opensocial.Person .Field.
			
			PROFILE_URL));
			
			}

Continued

Table 3-2: Detail of Gadget Core API *(continued)*

Object	Method/Variable	Description	Example
			`// code from hi5 sample code see //http://www .hi5networks.com/ platform/wiki/ SampleCode`
`gadgets.Prefs`		Class used to get information about user, such as internationalization (the country and language of user).	
	`getLang` or `getCountry`	`String getCountry()` or `String getLang()` gets Country and Language of the user.	`var prefs = new gadgets.Prefs();`
			`var name = prefs .getString("name");`
			`var lang = prefs .getLang();`
			`//later in code`
			`createMyAppActivity (viewer, lang);`

Particularly worth noting in Table 3-2 is the `gadgets.io.makeRequest` method. It is used to invoke remote applications and resources on remote servers. It returns results to the container, which, in turn, delivers them to the client. In OpenSocial JavaScript applications, you should use the `makeRequest` method to do the following:

❑   Generate HTTP requests (both GET and POST methods)

❑   Return the server response in a variety of formats

❑   Send OpenSocial data to the remote server application

❑   Support a form of signed requests

Chapter 6 discusses `makeRequest` *in more detail, including code examples.*

Let's modify the "Hello world" example using the `gadgets.io.registerOnLoadHandler` method to call a function that learns about the user's language via `gadgets.Prefs.getLang`. Listing 3-2 shows this code. The function `init()` is registered to run when the application is loaded. The `init()` function is the one that uses the Gadget API to learn the user's language, and simply displays this information back to the user.

Listing 3-2: Extension of the "Hello World" with Core Gadget API to Learn User's Language

```
<?xml version="1.0" encoding="UTF-8"?>
<Module>
  <ModulePrefs title="Hello World!" description="Hello World"
       title_url="http://www.hi5.com" author="L. Grewe"
       author_email="findme@yahoo.com" author_affiliation="iLab"
       author_location="Bay Area, CA"
       thumbnail="http://Me.com/Logo.png">

    <Icon>http://Me.com/Logo-16x16.png</Icon>
    <Require feature="opensocial-0.8"/>
  </ModulePrefs>
  <Content type="html">
    <![CDATA[
Hello World!

<div id="greeting" style="background: red;">

</div>

<script>
    // Call the init function onLoad
    gadgets.util.registerOnLoadHandler(init);

    // function to learn user's language and display it.
    function init() {

      var lang = "Not Known ";
      try{
          var prefs = new gadgets.Prefs();
          lang = prefs.getLang();
        if (lang == null)
          document.getElementById('greeting').innerHTML = "lang is
null"
          else
          document.getElementById('greeting').innerHTML = "lang is " + lang;
      }catch (e) {
          document.getElementById('greeting').innerHTML =
"exception";}
    }
</script>

]]>

</Content>
</Module>
```

In addition to the Gadget API calls, you should note the exception handling introduced in Listing 3-2. Because containers can experience problems, and (as you will later learn) may handle optional features differently, you should get in the practice of performing exception handling and error checking within your code. Some developers choose to try to re-execute (multiple times) a failed code block before responding differently in case the container is having a (very) temporary problem.

Feature-Specific Gadget API

The other part of the Gadget API is the Feature-Specific Gadget API. Unlike the Core Gadget API, to use the Feature-Specific API, you must require the desired features in your Gadget XML by using the `<Require>` element. When doing this, parts of the Feature-Specific API are grouped into different "features." Following are the Feature-Specific API objects that are currently part of the OpenSocial specification, as well as their corresponding "features":

- ❑   `gadgets.views` — Views
- ❑   `gadgets.window` — Window
- ❑   `gadgets.skins` — Skins
- ❑   `gadgets.flash` — Flash
- ❑   `gadgets.MiniMessage` — Minimessage
- ❑   `gadgets.Tab` — Tabs
- ❑   `gadgets.TabSet` — Tabs
- ❑   `gadgets.pubsub` — Publishing (Subscribing)
- ❑   `gadgets.rpc` — RPC

While most of these "features" have a one-to-one correspondence with the `gadgets.*` objects listed before, in the case of `gadgets.windows`, the functionality is split between the "dynamic-height" feature and the "settitle" feature. So, to use the methods of the `gadgets.windows` object dealing with height of your application, your XML file must require it as follows:

```
<Require feature="dynamic-height"/>.
```

Table 3-3 details some of the commonly used objects that are part of the Feature-Specific Gadget API used in OpenSocial.

Table 3-3: Detail of Feature-Specific Gadget API

Objects	Method/Variable	Description	Example
`gadgets.views`		View operations. See the section, "Multiple Views," later in this chapter for details on views, and how to set via Gadget XML.	
	ViewType	static object CANVAS results in full "screen" mode.	if (type == gadgets .views.ViewType .CANVAS)
		static object HOME results in a smaller view, run on home page.	

Continued

Table 3-3: Detail of Feature-Specific Gadget API *(continued)*

Objects	Method/Variable	Description	Example
		static object PREVIEW results in a preview view of the application.	
		static object PROFILE results in a smaller view, run on profile page.	
		Containers can also define additional views.	
	getSupportedViews	static Map <gadgets.views .ViewType, String, gadgets.views.View>	var params = {};
		getSupportedViews() gets container-supported views.	params[gadgets.io .RequestParameters .CONTENT_TYPE] = gadgets.io .ContentType.JSON;
		Note that each gadgets.view.View is keyed by its name.	gadgets.io .makeRequest("http: //U.com", response, params);
	getCurrentView	static gadgets.views.View	
		getCurrentView() gets current application view.	if(gadgets.views .getCurrentView() .getName() == "canvas")
			{ //do canvas view stuff }

Continued

Table 3-3: Detail of Feature-Specific Gadget API *(continued)*

Objects	Method/Variable	Description	Example
	requestNavigateTo	static requestNavigateTo (view, opt_params, opt_ownerId) tries to navigate and bring up the indicated application view. You can pass parameters (opt_params) for optional container support. opt_owerid gives the owner of the page navigating to, with optional container support. The default is the current owner.	gadgets.views .requestNavigateTo(new gadgets.views.View('canvas'));
			//created a canvas view with no //parameters to pass and owner of page //is current owner.
gadgets.window		Window-related issues.	
	adjustHeight	static adjustHeight() or static adjustHeight(height) adjusts the height of window the gadget is inside of to the height specified in pixels. If no height is specified, it adjusts to the gadget content.	// Call this method to adjust the app's IFrame height if necessary
			gadgets.window .adjustHeight();
			See the getViewport Dimensions method for another example.

Continued

Table 3-3: Detail of Feature-Specific Gadget API *(continued)*

Objects	Method/Variable	Description	Example
	getViewport Dimensions	static Object getViewport Dimensions() gets information about the dimensions available for your gadget.	var height = gadgets .window .getViewport Dimensions() .height;
			gadgets.window .adjustHeight (height);
gadgets.skins		Establishes the look and feel of a container (for example, font color and background).	
	getProperty	static String getProperty (propertyKey) retrieves the value of the Property. See gadgets.skins .Property.	var bgcolor = gadgets .skins.getProperty (gadgets.skins .Property.BG_COLOR);
			//use bgcolor to set the background of some document element to this color
	Property	Specifies possible skin properties, including the following: static object ANCHOR_COLOR — link color used static object BG_COLOR — gadget background color static object BG_IMAGE — gadget background image	See the previous example.

Continued

Table 3-3: Detail of Feature-Specific Gadget API *(continued)*

Objects	Method/Variable	Description	Example
		static object FONT_COLOR — gadget font color	
gadgets.flash		Deals with Flash files. See discussion in Chapter 7 on issues with this.	
	embedFlash	static Boolean embedFlash(swfUrl, swfContainer, swfVersion, opt_params) lets you embed Flash files.	See discussion in Chapter 7 for details.

Listing 3-3 shows how the "Hello World" application can be modified to add the feature of dynamically adjusting the height of the application using the gadgets.window.adjustHeight method.

Listing 3-3: Extension of the "Hello World" Application to Adjust the Height of the Application

```
<?xml version="1.0" encoding="UTF-8"?>
<Module>
  <ModulePrefs title="Hello World!" description="Hello World"
      title_url="http://www.hi5.com" author="L. Grewe"
      author_email="findme@yahoo.com" author_affiliation="iLab"
      author_location="Bay Area, CA"
      thumbnail="http://Me.com/Logo.png">

    <Icon>http://Me.com/Logo-16x16.png</Icon>

    <Require feature="dynamic-height"/>
    <Require feature="opensocial-0.8" />
  </ModulePrefs>
  <Content type="html">
    <![CDATA[

      Hello World!

      <script>
        // Call the init function onLoad
        gadgets.util.registerOnLoadHandler(init);

        function init() {
          gadgets.window.adjustHeight(50);
        }
```

```
      </script>
    ]]>
  </Content>
</Module>
```

Multiple Views

In Chapter 1, you learned about how different networks allow applications to appear. OpenSocial refers to this as the *view of an application*. A *view* is the page (or area of a page) on a social network where your application can appear. For example, in MySpace, an application can be viewed on the user's Home page, Profile page, and in a Canvas page. Let's take a look at how you specify the view in your application.

You may want your application to appear on all of the possible views, or only some. You may want your content to vary depending on the view. OpenSocial allows all of these possibilities through the <Content> tag that is part of the Google Gadget XML specification.

You can have more than one <Content> element in your OpenSocial XML application. The view attribute of the <Content> tag allows you to specify what views the contained content will apply to. All <Content> sections should be at the same level in the document tree. For example, to create different content for the "profile" and "canvas" views, you would use something similar to the XML code shown in Listing 3-4.

Listing 3-4: Application with Contents for "Profile" View and for the "Canvas" View

```
<?xml version="1.0" encoding="UTF-8" ?>
<Module>
  <ModulePrefs title="View Silly Example">
    <Require feature="opensocial-0.8" />
  </ModulePrefs>
  <Content type="html" view="profile">
  <![CDATA[
    <h1>Profile Content</h1>
  ]]>
  </Content>
  <Content type="html" view="canvas">
  <![CDATA[
    <h1>Canvas Content</h1>
  ]]>
  </Content>
</Module>
```

Consider some other possibilities and their associated meanings:

❑   <Content views="canvas, home"> — This means the contained content will be displayed for both "canvas" and "home" views.

❑   <Content> — This will be the default content displayed for all views not specified with a <Content views="XX"> tag.

❑   Only <Content views="profile"> — If this is the only content tag in your XML application, it means that the application will only be shown in the user's profile and not other possible views.

Listing 3-5 shows an example that uses multiple content tags.

Listing 3-5: Application Directing the Content to Different Views

```xml
<?xml version="1.0" encoding="UTF-8" ?>
<Module>
  <ModulePrefs title="Another Simple Views Example">
    <Require feature="opensocial-0.8" />
  </ModulePrefs>

  <Content type="html" view="home">
  <![CDATA[
    <h1>Home</h1>
  ]]>
  </Content>

  <Content type="html" view="profile">
  <![CDATA[
    <h1>Profile</h1>
  ]]>
  </Content>

  <Content type="html" view="canvas">
  <![CDATA[
    <h1>Canvas</h1>
  ]]>
  </Content>

  <Content type="html" view="canvas,profile">
  <![CDATA[
    I am in both the canvas and profile view but, NOT in the home view.
  ]]>
  </Content>

  <Content type="html">
  <![CDATA[
    I am in any view that is not specified. (the preview view)
    ]]>
  </Content>

</Module>
```

The output of the code in Listing 3-5 is as follows for the different views:

❑ "Home" view:

```
<h1>Home</h1>
```

❑ "Profile" view:

```
<h1>Profile</h1>
I am in both the canvas and profile view but, NOT in the home view.
```

❏ "Canvas" view:

```
<h1>Canvas</h1>
I am in both the canvas and profile view but, NOT in the home view.
```

❏ "Preview" view:

```
I am in any view that is not specified. (the preview view)
```

Changing Views Dynamically

Sometimes you may want to redirect the user from one view to another. This can be useful when your application is transitioning from a typically smaller "profile" view to a "canvas" view. This can be done by using the `gadgets.views.navigateTo` method of the Gadget API.

Let's modify the code in Listing 3-5 to have a link in the "preview" content that will take the user to a "canvas" view.

```
<input type="button" value="Canvas"
        onclick="var views =gadgets.views.getSupportedViews();
                gadgets.views.requestNavigateTo(views["canvas"]);">
```

Lifecycle Support

The *lifecycle* for an application involves the idea of stages of existence between an application and a user. Lifecycle stages include the following:

❏ Application not yet installed
❏ Application in use
❏ Application removed
❏ Application is being recommended (invite)
❏ Application has a change in policy

It is useful for an application developer to know when an application changes stage. OpenSocial provides support for this in what is known as *lifecyle events*, which are events leading to the transition from one stage to another. The lifecycle events include the following:

❏ `addapp` — Application installation
❏ `removeapp` — Application removal
❏ `invite` — A user is being invited to add the application from another user

When the `<Link>` element is used in the Gadget XML, OpenSocial allows the developer to specify a URL for each kind of event. This URL will be invoked when the event occurs. You should have your link point to a program that records this information, but you may also choose to do further actions.

When the registered URL program is invoked by the container with a lifecycle event, it will pass appropriate data. For example, when the application is installed, it will pass an `id` attribute, which is the user ID of the installer. Optionally, there is a `from` attribute the container may support that has the values of `"invite"`, `"gallery"`, and `"external"`, letting you know where the user originated from.

Listing 3-6 shows the sample "Hello World" application that adds `<Link>` elements to track when the application is installed and removed.

Listing 3-6: Extension of the "Hello World" Application to Include Lifecycle Support

```xml
<?xml version="1.0" encoding="UTF-8"?>
<Module>
  <ModulePrefs title="Hello World!" description="Hello World"
      title_url="http://www.hi5.com" author="L. Grewe"
      author_email="findme@yahoo.com" author_affiliation="iLab"
      author_location="Bay Area, CA"
      thumbnail="http://Me.com/Logo.png">

    <Icon>http://Me.com/Logo-16x16.png</Icon>
    <Require feature="opensocial-0.8"/>
    <Link rel="event.addapp" href="http://me.com/recordAppadded">
    <Link rel="event.removeapp" href="http://me.com/AppRemoved">
  </ModulePrefs>

  <Content type="html">
    <![CDATA[
      Hello, world!
    ]]>
  </Content>
</Module>
```

Summary

This chapter started with a brief history of OpenSocial, and then examined a number of OpenSocial architectures. You were introduced to your first OpenSocial application, and, with it, you learned how to use the Gadget XML and Gadget APIs. This chapter went into greater detail on how to create multiple views for your application. You also learned about lifecycle support.

Chapter 4 takes a closer look at the OpenSocial API, including the Person, the Persistence and the Activity API components.

4

JavaScript API

The JavaScipt API provides access to user and friend data, as well as providing the capability to share this data and create activities. The OpenSocial API addresses the following three functional areas:

❑   People

❑   Activities

❑   Persistence

This chapter begins by walking you through the development of a simple application that uses social data and is based on OpenSocial's JavaScript API. After examining this sample application, the chapter takes a detailed look at the structure of the OpenSocial JavaScript API and its communications procedures.

A Simple Application in OpenSocial

In Chapter 2, you learned how OpenSocial applications (at their most basic level) are based on the OpenSocial JavaScript API, and how they are XML files (gadgets) containing content encoded with HTML and CSS. This section goes through the development of a simple application that uses the OpenSocial Javascript API to access some social data. Chapter 2 introduced simple application called "Hello, world," which didn't make any calls while loading the JavaScript (OpenSocial) API. Let's now create a simple application that makes use of social data. This application, called "Friend Finder," presents a user with a list of friends after giving a personalized greeting to the user.

As you learned in Chapter 2, when deploying an application, one of the differences between containers (social networks) is whether or not the application is hosted by the container. Often times, when this is the case, you will not need to explicitly load the JavaScript (OpenSocial) API, as was done in the previous "Hello, world" application.

To facilitate ease in deployment, let's separate the new "Friend Finder" application into two files: an XML gadget file and a separate JavaScript file. While it is possible to have inline JavaScript inside the XML file, let's separate it for clarity. This will make the most sense as your code grows beyond the trivial stage.

Listing 4-1 shows the XML gadget file and Listing 4-2 shows the JavaScript file for the new "Friend Finder" application.

Listing 4-1: XML (Gadget) File for the "Friend Finder" Application

```
FriendFinder.xml

<?xml version="1.0" encoding="UTF-8"?>
<Module>
  <ModulePrefs title="Friend Finder" description="Friend tracker"
               title_url="http://FriendFinder.com" author="L. Grewe"
               author_email="ff@yahoo.com"
               author_affiliation="iLab" author_location="Bay Area, CA"
               thumbnail="http://UServer/Logo.PNG">
    <Icon>http://UServer/Logo_16_16.PNG</Icon>
    <Require feature="dynamic-height"/>
    <Require feature="opensocial-0.8"/>
  </ModulePrefs>
  <Content type="html">
    <![CDATA[


        <div id='heading'></div>
        <hr size="1px" />
        <div id='main'></div>
        <hr>
        <div id='friends'></div>


        <script src="http://UServer/FriendFinder.js"></script>

        <script>
            init();
        </script>
]]>


  </Content>
</Module>
```

Listing 4-2: JavaScript Code for the "Friend Finder" Application

```
FriendFinder.js
var os;
var dataReqObj;
var html = '';
var heading = '';
var friends_html = '';

function init() {

    dataReqObj = opensocial.newDataRequest();
```

```
        var viewerReq = dataReqObj.newFetchPersonRequest(opensocial.IdSpec.
            PersonId.VIEWER);

        dataReqObj.add(viewerReq, 'viewer');
        var idspec = opensocial.newIdSpec({"userId": "VIEWER",
            "groupID" : "FRIENDS"});
        viewerReq = dataReqObj.newFetchPeopleRequest(idspec);
        dataReqObj.add(viewerReq, 'viewerFriends');

        dataReqObj.send(onLoadViewerResponse);

    }


    function onLoadViewerResponse(data) {

        var viewer = data.get('viewer').getData();
        heading = 'Hello, ' + viewer.getDisplayName();
        var thumb = viewer.getField(opensocial.Person.Field.THUMBNAIL_URL);
        var profile = viewer.getField(opensocial.Person.Field.PROFILE_URL);

        document.getElementById('heading').innerHTML = heading;
        document.getElementById('main').innerHTML = html;

        var viewer_friends = data.get('viewerFriends').getData();

        friends_html  = 'My Friends are, ' ;
        friends_html = friends_html + '<ul>';

        viewer_friends.each(function(person) {
          friends_html = friends_html+ '<li>' + person.getDisplayName() +
                '</li>';
        });


        friends_html = friends_html + '</ul>';


        document.getElementById('friends').innerHTML = friends_html;

    }
```

FriendFinder.xml contains some simple HTML that invokes the init() method in the JavaScript file. Let's look at the details of the init() method:

- ❑ dataReqObj = opensocial.newDataRequest(); — This creates a new DataRequest. object, which is the object in OpenSocial that is used to request social data.

- ❑ viewerReq = dataReqObj.newFetchPersonRequest(opensocial.IdSpec.PersonId.VIEWER);) ; — This creates a request to fetch the current viewer's information.

- ❑ dataReqObj.add(viewerReq,'viewer'); — This adds the request just created.

- ❑ var idspec = opensocial.newIdSpec({"userId": "VIEWER", "groupID" : "FRIENDS"}); viewerReq = dataReqObj.newFetchPeopleRequest(idspec); — This creates a request to fetch the current viewer's friends.

- ❏ `dataReqObj.add(viewerReq, 'viewerFriends');` — This adds the friends request and associates it with the string key `'viewerFriends'`.

- ❏ `dataReqObj.send(onLoadViewerResponse);` — This sends the current request object and registers the method `onLoadViewerResponse` as the callback function. (This is invoked when the container has finished processing the request.)

The `datReqObj` object in the `init` method is an instance of the `DataRequest` object in the OpenSocial API. It is important to understand that invoking the `send` method on this object turns into a call to the container (social network), which returns the results in JavaScript Object Notation (JSON) format. The JSON format is converted via OpenSocial to a JavaScript object called `DataResponse` that is received by the `onLoadViewerResponse` method. These kinds of asynchronous calls are at the heart of many OpenSocial interactions. As you will see shortly, one of the characteristics of the JavaScript (OpenSocial) API is that it is asynchronous.

> **You should batch the data you want into a single `DataRequest`. The results are returned via a single `DataResponse`. Batching as much as you can into a single call will make your application perform better, resulting in a better user experience.**

The `onLoadViewerResponse` method does the bulk of the work in this sample application. Let's look at it in detail. The object data it receives is an instance of the OpenSocial `DataResponse` object.

The following lines of code get the viewer data and store it in the `viewer` variable. The name of the viewer (`viewer`), the thumbail URL (`thumb`), and profile URL (`profile`) are stored in the respective variables.

```
viewer = data.get('viewer').getData();
heading = 'Hello, ' + viewer.getDisplayName();
thumb = viewer.getField(opensocial.Person.Field.THUMBNAIL_URL);
profile = viewer.getField(opensocial.Person.Field.PROFILE_URL);
```

The following line sets the HTML (associated with the HTML `div`) with an ID `heading` to a personalized greeting using the name of the viewer.

```
document.getElementById('heading').innerHTML = heading;
```

From the `DataResponse` object, the following code gets the viewer's friends. The `get` method returns an OpenSocial `ResponseItem` object. Recall that in the request made, the data is associated with the string key `'viewerFriends'`, and this key is used to retrieve the response information. The `getData` method of the `ResponseItem` object retrieves the data associated with this response. What is returned is the generic JavaScript object.

```
viewer_friends = data.get('viewerFriends').getData();
```

The following code constructs a list of the viewer's friends by cycling through them using the `each` statement in JavaScript, meaning that, for each person found in the friend's response, the code grabs the name and makes it an element in a list.

```
friends_tml  = 'My Friends are, ' ;
friends_html = friends_html + '<ul>';
viewer_friends.each(function(person) {
friends_html = friends_html +  '<li>' + person.getDisplayName() + '</li>';
});
friends_html = friends_html + '</ul>'
```

The following line sets the HTML (associated with the div) with an ID 'heading' to the friends list.

```
document.getElementById('friends').innerHTML = friends_html;
```

Figure 4-1 shows this simple "Friend Finder" application running in MySpace. You will learn how to retrieve and create many other kinds of social data later in this chapter.

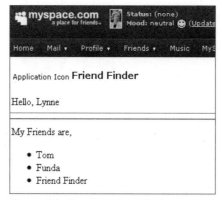

**Figure 4-1: Simple "Friend Finder"
application deployed on MySpace**

Now that you have seen the JavaScript API in action, let's take a deeper look at what this important collection of tools actual entails.

OpenSocial API Features

To understand the OpenSocial JavaScript API, you should first become familiar with some common features seen throughout. This section discusses a few, including the following:

❑   Data type creation

❑   Asynchronous communications

❑   Naming conventions

A common criticism about JavaScript is the fact that it lacks a strong sense of data type. While it could be argued that this allows for greater freedom in programming, it also creates greater difficulties when handling data exchanges such as those needed by OpenSocial (between the container and the application). In an attempt to avoid problems, OpenSocial is written as if JavaScript were strongly typed. To assist with this, a number of static data fields are defined. A couple of examples are `opensocial.Activity.Field` and `opensocial.Message.Field`. Other examples are the `opensocial.BodyType.*` fields used to represent the string data returned when requesting the user's body type.

Another OpenSocial API characteristic is that many of the API calls use asynchronous communications in the form of a full asynchronous callback methodology. For example, this is seen when requesting user data.

All of the OpenSocial methods and classes are under the `opensocial.*` namespace. When containers create their own OpenSocial extensions, they are required to follow a specific naming structure that mimics the `opensocial.*` naming convention. For example, if the hi5 container is to be compliant when creating extensions to the `opensocial.Person.Field.*` values, hi5 must name them as `hi5.Person.Field.new_FieldName`.

A number of methods in OpenSocial take sets of optional parameters. They are indicated with the prefix `opt_` in their names. For example, `opt_params` appears as the third argument of the `newMediaItem(mimeType, url, opt_params)` method. The `opt_params` seen in such OpenSocial methods is a kind of map/hash that associates parameter names (keys) with values. For example, the `opt_params` in the `newMediaItem` method is a map keyed with `opensocial.MediaItem.Field.*` keys.

People

Users and friends are represented as a `Person` object in OpenSocial. There are three kinds of people in OpenSocial:

❑ *Owner* — This is the person who owns the account and has installed your application. Depending on container support, this can be specified with the string `'OWNER'`, `opensocial.DataRequest.PersonId.OWNER`, or `opensocial.IdSpec.PersonId.OWNER`. The latter is the accepted standard for the latest version of OpenSocial. (Check the version you are programming to.)

❑ *Viewer* — A viewer is a person logged in to the social network who can be viewing either that person's own page that has your application on it, or another user's page that has your application on it. Depending on container support, this can be specified with the string `'VIEWER'`, `opensocial.DataRequst.PersonId.VIEWER`, or `opensocial.IdSpec.PersonId.VIEWER`. (The latter is the latest version of OpenSocial.)

❑ *Friends* — Friends appear in the social network as either the owner or viewer.

Depending on the container's support of OpenSocial (and version), these people can be signified as follows for the latest OpenSocial version:

❑ Via an `opensocial.IdSpec` object

For earlier versions of OpenSocial, you would use the following:

❑ Predefined strings (`'OWNER'`, `'VIEWER'`, `'OWNER_FRIENDS'`, `'VIEWER_FRIENDS'`)

❑ The `opensocial.DataRequest.PersonId.*` field

❑ The `opensocial.IdSpec.PersonId.*` fields

> In some examples in this book, a simple string representation will be used. Keep in mind that you will need to make substitutions as appropriate. See the section, "IdSpec," later in this chapter for details on use.

An application can get information about any of these persons through the following two-step process:

1. Request data:

    a. Create `DataRequest` object by calling `opensocial.newDataRequest`.

    b. For each request you wish to make, create it using one of the `opensocial.new*` methods.

    c. For each piece of data you want to request, add a request via `DataRequest` `.add(request)`.

    d. Make a request by registering the callback function, `DataRequest.send(callback)`.

2. Create a callback function to receive data:

    a. Once a container gets the request and it is processed, the callback function will be executed. It will be passed the `opensocial.DataResponse` object that contains the response data of the processed request. In the following code example, the `DataResponse` object is received as a parameter to the callback function, and is called dataResponse:

    ```
    function callback(dataResponse) {

        //process the response data
    }
    ```

ViewerData Example

Let's create an example that first gets the viewer's ID, display name, profile link, and thumbnail image. Then let's display this information. Listing 4-3 shows the JavaScript to achieve this.

Listing 4-3: ViewerData.Js Code to Request and Display Basic Viewer Data

```
var dataReqObj;
var heading = '';

//function called initially in XML file, this makes data request
//for viewer
function init() {
    //Create Data Request
    dataReqObj = opensocial.newDataRequest();

    //depending of version of OpenSocial, viewer reference changes
    var viewerReq = dataReqObj.newFetchPersonRequest
        ( opensocial.IdSpec.PersonId.VIEWER);
```

Continued

Listing 4-3: ViewerData.Js Code to Request and Display Basic Viewer Data *(continued)*

```
        dataReqObj.add(viewerReq, 'viewer');

        //Send Data Request
        dataReqObj.send(onLoadViewerResponse);

}

//Callback function to process Viewer data requested.
function onLoadViewerResponse(data) {
    var viewer;

    //retrieve data associated with viewer request.
    try{
        viewer = data.get('viewer').getData();
    }catch(err){
        heading = 'Error ' + err.description;
        alert (heading);}


    //Setup html to return to display viewer basic info
    try{
        heading = 'Hello, ' + viewer.getDisplayName();
        var thumb =
viewer.getField(opensocial.Person.Field.THUMBNAIL_URL);
        var profile =
viewer.getField(opensocial.Person.Field.PROFILE_URL);

        heading = heading + '<a href="' + profile +'"><img src="'
            + thumb
                        + '"></a>';
    } catch(err){
    heading = 'Error ' + err.description;
        alert(heading);}


    //Display results inside XML document at the div
    //element with id heading
    document.getElementById('heading').innerHTML = heading;

}
```

Figure 4-2 shows the result of running the application in Listing 4-3. The user's name, along with a thumbnail image (linked to the user's profile URL), is shown.

Figure 4-2: ViewerData application gets basic viewer information

Unfortunately, the newness of social network programming and OpenSocial means that all of the containers do not support the OpenSocial standard with complete compliance. This simple coding example can illustrate how this can take place. Listing 4-3 will work on the majority of social networks, including hi5, Friendster, imeem, and so on. However, as of this writing, it does not function on MySpace.

Listing 4-4 shows the necessary code substitutions for the `dataReqObj.add` and the related `data.get('viewer').getData()` calls in Listing 4-3 to work on Myspace. While both code samples should work for the currently supported version of OpenSocial in MySpace, hi5, and so on, they do not. This is one of the challenges in coding with new technologies like OpenSocial.

Listing 4-4: Code Changes from Listing 4-3 to Work in Current MySpace Container

```
//replace dataReqObj.add(viewerReq, 'viewer');

dataReqObj.add(viewerReq);  //WORKS ONLY FOR MYSPACE



//replace viewer = data.get('viewer').getData();

viewer = data.get(opensocial.DataRequest.PersonId.VIEWER)
    .getData();
```

> If you code something and it is not working, there are some things you can try. Deploy and run it on other OpenSocial containers. Look in the social network's online documentation to see if your code is supported. And, finally, post to the social network's developer forum a description of the problem (it may be a container problem).

The viewer data for some networks will only be returned if the viewer is an installed user of the application. Unfortunately, the newness of social network programming and OpenSocial means that all of the containers do not offer the same support. In orkut, for example, the viewer returned will be `null`. Your program should anticipate this case.

One possible alternative is to direct the viewer to a page to install the application. Most containers will allow you to direct the viewer to an install page if users try to take some action in your application. Another solution may be to present some alternative content that will be necessarily less personal to the viewer.

In any case, you should provide some content and functionality to non-installed viewers to entice them to install your application.

GetFriends Example

Another class of `Person` in OpenSocial is the *friend*. A common need of many applications is getting a user's friend list. This may be an integral part of the application (such as in a gaming tool or communications tool), but it is also used for the prolific "invite your friend" option to use the application.

Listing 4-5 expands on the previous `ViewerData` example to display a drop-down box containing the list of the viewer's friends. As before, this request is made through an `opensocial.DataRequest` object and the `'VIEWER_FRIENDS'` data will also be requested.

Listing 4-5: GetFriends.Js Code to Request and Display a Drop-down List of Viewer's Friends

```javascript
var dataReqObj; var heading = '';
var friends_html;
var TheFriends=new Array();

//function called initially in XML file, this makes data request
//for friend.
function init() {


    //Create Data Request
    dataReqObj = opensocial.newDataRequest();

    //create viewer request
    var viewerReq = dataReqObj.newFetchPersonRequest(opensocial.IdSpec.
        PersonId.VIEWER);
    dataReqObj.add(viewerReq, 'viewer');

    // create friends of viewer request
    var idspec = opensocial.newIdSpec({"userId": "VIEWER",
        "groupID" : "FRIENDS"});
    viewerReq = dataReqObj.newFetchPeopleRequest(idspec);
    dataReqObj.add(viewerReq, 'viewerFriends');

    //Send Data Request
    dataReqObj.send(onLoadViewerResponse);

}

//Callback function to process Viewer data requested.
function onLoadViewerResponse(data) {

    var viewer;

    //retrieve data associated with viewer request.
    try{
        viewer = data.get('viewer').getData();
    }catch(err){
        heading = 'Error ' + err.description;
        alert (heading);}

    //Set up html to return to display viewer basic info
    try{
    var thumb = viewer.getField(opensocial.Person.Field.THUMBNAIL_URL);
    var profile = viewer.getField(opensocial.Person.Field.PROFILE_URL);

    heading = heading + '<a href="' + profile +'"><img src="' + thumb +
        '"></a>';
```

```
    } catch(err){
        heading = 'Error ' + err.description;
        alert(heading);}
    document.getElementById('heading').innerHTML = heading;




    //Get Friends Information
    var viewer_friends = data.get('viewerFriends').getData();

    friends_html  = 'Your Friend , ' ;
friends_html = friends_html + '<select id=select_friend
                    onchange="getFriendStatus();">';


    viewer_friends.each(function(person) {
        friends_html = friends_html +  '<option value=' +
            person.getId() + '>'
                        + person.getDisplayName() + '</option>';
        TheFriends[person.getId()] = person;
    });
    friends_html = friends_html + '</select>';

    document.getElementById('friends').innerHTML = friends_html;
}
```

The bold text in Listing 4-5 is what is needed to request and display the friend information. The first line to note is dataReqObj.newFetchPeopleRequest('VIEWER_FRIENDS'), which sets up the request for the viewer's friends. Later, in the callback function, the data.get('viewerFriends').getData() call retrieves the related list of friends. The remainder of the highlighted code cycles through this list and generates a drop-down HTML list, and then associates it with a <div> element with ID 'friends' in the OpenSocial XML. Figure 4-3 shows the results of running this application.

Figure 4-3: GetFriends application

Listing 4-5 contains has some exception handling, but you can do more testing than this. As shown in the following code snippet, testing is done to confirm not only that the friends data was received, but also that there is at least one friend. If this is not the case, the code returns false. Note that the code uses the size() method of the OpenSocial Collections instance stored in viewer_friends.

```
if (!data || data.hadError() || data.get('viewer_friends').hadError())
    { return false; } // Error retrieving data
```

```
//Later in code...................... .
var viewer_friends = data.get('viewer_friends').getData();
if (viewer_friends.size() < 1) {
    {  return false;  } // No friends with the app
```

If a user has a lot of friends, you may want to limit the number of friends you request at one time. You can create a paginated list, if needed. The following code snippet shows how to ask for 10 of the owner's friends, starting at the 30th friend:

```
var params = {};
params[opensocial.DataRequest.PeopleRequestFields.MAX] = 10;
params[opensocial.DataRequest.PeopleRequestFields.FIRST] = 30;

var req = opensocial.newDataRequest();
req.add(req.newFetchPeopleRequest(opensocial.DataRequest.Group.OWNER_FRIENDS,
                                  params), "friends");

req.send(callBackFunction);
```

Info Example

It may seem somewhat counter-intuitive for the Object-Oriented Programming (OOP) coder, but when making a request for a person, you are only given very basic information about the person (such as the person's name and a profile URL). To get extended information about a person, you must specifically create a set of additional parameters specifying the additional information you want. You do this at request time. Only the information you requested will be sent to you.

When you consider that these transactions are going back and forth across the Internet from the program to the social network, this can be a performance hit, and you want to be able to only get the information you need. An application may only want to know the name and status of a person. To force a retrieval of the entire set of information about that person would take up unnecessary time.

Table 5-1 shows the list of fields you can request about a person in OpenSocial. These have changed over the different versions of OpenSocial, but are enumerated here as static objects of the opensocial.Person.Field class. Many of these social data fields are optional for support in OpenSocial. Each social network has chosen to support different fields. Table 4-1 shows support for these fields for a few networks. The support for these fields can change frequently for a container; refer to the container's developer documentation for current support.

> If you really need a person's data and it is currently not supported by a container, don't hesitate to contact the container and request this support. Many containers are supportive of developers needs, and have responded by adding desired functionality.

IdSpec

Some OpenSocial API calls require an instance of the opensocial.IdSpec object. An IdSpec represents a specification of IDs. An example of this is ''VIEWER' and 'VIEWER FRIENDS'. Another example could be 'OWNER'.

Table 4-1: opensocial.Person.Field.* Fields Used to Request Social Data

Field	Type/Meaning	Freebar Support	imeem Support	orkut Support	Netlog Support
ABOUT_ME	String	Yes		Yes	
ACTIVITIES	Array of strings			Yes	
ADDRESSES	Array of opensocial.Address			Yes	Yes
AGE	Number	Yes	Yes		Yes
BODY_TYPE	Specified as opensocial.BodyType				
BOOKS	Array of strings			Yes	
CARS	Array of strings				
CHILDREN	String				
CURRENT_LOCATION	opensocial.Address				
DATE_OF_BIRTH	DATE object	Yes			
DRINKER	opensocial.Enum object with keys from opensocial.Enum.Drinker				
EMAILS	Array of opensocial.Email				
ETHNICITY	String				
FASHION	String			Yes	
FOOD	Array of strings			Yes	
GENDER	opensocial.Enum object with keys from opensocial.Enum.Gender	Yes	Yes	Yes	Yes
HAPPIEST_WHEN	String				
HAS_APP	Boolean				
HEROES	Array of strings				
HUMOR	String			Yes	
ID	String	Yes	Yes	Yes	Yes

Continued

123

Table 4-1: opensocial.Person.Field.* Fields Used to Request Social Data *(continued)*

Field	Type/Meaning	Freebar Support	imeem Support	orkut Support	Netlog Support
INTERESTS	Array of strings			Yes	Yes
JOB_INTERESTS	String				
JOBS	Array of opensocial.Organization				
LANGUAGES_SPOKEN	Array of strings (format ISO 639-1 codes)			Yes	Yes
LIVING_ARRANGEMENT	String			Yes	
LOOKING_FOR	String			Yes	
MOVIES	Array of strings			Yes	
MUSIC	Array of strings		Yes	Yes	
NAME	opensocial.Name	Yes		Yes	
NETWORK_PRESENCE	String				
NICKNAME	String	Yes			Yes
PETS	String				
PHONE_NUMBERS	Array of opensocial.Phone				
POLITICAL_VIEWS	String			Yes	
PROFILE_SONG	opensocial.Url	Yes			Yes
PROFILE_URL	String	Yes	Yes	Yes	Yes
PROFILE_VIDEO	opensocial.Url				
QUOTES	Array of strings				
RELATIONSHIP_STATUS	String	Yes		Yes	
RELIGION	String				
ROMANCE	String			Yes	
SCARED_OF	String				

Continued

Table 4-1: opensocial.Person.Field.* Fields Used to Request Social Data (continued)

Field	Type/Meaning	Freebar Support	imeem Support	orkut Support	Netlog Support
SCHOOLS	Array of opensocial.Organization				
SEXUAL_ORIENTATION	String	Yes			
SMOKER	opensocial.Enum object with keys from opensocial.Enum.Smoker				
SPORTS	Array of strings			Yes	
STATUS	String	Yes			
TAGS	Array of strings				
THUMBNAIL_URL	String	Yes	Yes	Yes	Yes
TIME_ZONE	String				
TURN_OFFS	Array of strings			Yes	
TURN_ONS	Array of strings			Yes	
TV_SHOWS	Array of strings			Yes	
URLS	Array of opensocial.Url			Yes	

An instance of this object is created by passing to the constructor a parameter map using the fields in opensocial.IdSpec.Field.* as keys to set up the IdSpec object. These fields include the following:

- ❑ GROUP_ID — This represents the group of people represented by the IdSpec. This can either be 'FRIENDS' or 'SELF'.

- ❑ NETWORK_DISTANCE — This parameter is an integer and represents the number of jumps in a social graph that two people can be apart and still be in the same group. Note a number here of 1 would indicate direct friendship.

- ❑ USER_ID — This can be a singular or an array of strings representing a user's unique ID. For the singular case, 'OWNER', 'VIEWER', or an OpenSocial ID string are acceptable.

You could use the following code snippet to create an IdSpec that represents an owner and friends:

```
params[opensocial.IdSpec.Field.USER_ID] = opensocial.IdSpec.PersonId.OWNER;
params[opensocial.IdSpec.Field.GROUP_ID] = 'FRIENDS';

var myIdSpec = opensocial.newIdSpec(params);
```

Another option is to run the application shown in Listing 4-6, which requests all of the social data for the viewer and prints it out in a table.

Listing 4-6: PersonData.Js to Request a Suite of User Data and Display as a Table

```
var os;
var dataReqObj;
var html = '';
var heading = '';
var friends_html = '';
var TheFriends = new Array();
var viewer = '';

function init() {

    dataReqObj = opensocial.newDataRequest();

    //construct list of profile data you want about the user
    var param = {};


    param[opensocial.DataRequest.PeopleRequestFields.PROFILE_DETAILS] =
            [opensocial.Person.Field.MOOD,
             opensocial.Person.Field.ABOUT_ME,
             opensocial.Person.Field.AGE,
             opensocial.Person.Field.ACTIVITIES,
             opensocial.Person.Field.ADDRESSES,
             opensocial.Person.Field.BODY_TYPE,
             opensocial.Person.Field.BOOKS,
             opensocial.Person.Field.CARS,
             opensocial.Person.Field.CHILDREN,
             opensocial.Person.Field.CURRENT_LOCATION,
             opensocial.Person.Field.DATE_OF_BIRTH,
             opensocial.Person.Field.DRINKER,
             opensocial.Person.Field.EMAILS,
             opensocial.Person.Field.ETHNICITY,
             opensocial.Person.Field.FASHION,
             opensocial.Person.Field.FOOD,
             opensocial.Person.Field.GENDER,
             opensocial.Person.Field.HAPPIEST_WHEN,
             opensocial.Person.Field.HAS_APP,
             opensocial.Person.Field.HEROES,
             opensocial.Person.Field.HUMOR, opensocial.Person.Field.ID,
             opensocial.Person.Field.INTERESTS,
             opensocial.Person.Field.JOB_INTERESTS,
             opensocial.Person.Field.JOBS,
             opensocial.Person.Field.LANGUAGES_SPOKEN,
             opensocial.Person.Field.LIVING_ARRANGEMENT,
             opensocial.Person.Field.LOOKING_FOR,
             opensocial.Person.Field.MOVIES,
             opensocial.Person.Field.MUSIC,
             opensocial.Person.Field.NAME,
             opensocial.Person.Field.NETWORK_PRESENCE,
```

```
                 opensocial.Person.Field.NICKNAME,
                 opensocial.Person.Field.PETS,
                 opensocial.Person.Field.PHONE_NUMBERS,
                 opensocial.Person.Field.POLITICAL_VIEWS,
                 opensocial.Person.Field.PROFILE_SONG,
                 opensocial.Person.Field.PROFILE_VIDEO,
                 opensocial.Person.Field.PROFILE_URL,
                 opensocial.Person.Field.QUOTES,
                 opensocial.Person.Field.RELATIONSHIP_STATUS,
                 opensocial.Person.Field.RELIGION,
                 opensocial.Person.Field.ROMANCE,
                 opensocial.Person.Field.SCARED_OF,
                 opensocial.Person.Field.SCHOOLS,
                 opensocial.Person.Field.SEXUAL_ORIENTATION,
                 opensocial.Person.Field.SMOKER,
                 opensocial.Person.Field.SPORTS,
                 opensocial.Person.Field.STATUS,
                 opensocial.Person.Field.TAGS,
                 opensocial.Person.Field.THUMBNAIL_URL,
                 opensocial.Person.Field.TIME_ZONE,
                 opensocial.Person.Field.TURN_OFFS,
                 opensocial.Person.Field.TURN_ONS,
                 opensocial.Person.Field.TV_SHOWS,
                 opensocial.Person.Field.URLS];


      var viewerReq =
                 dataReqObj.newFetchPersonRequest(opensocial.IdSpec.
                 PersonId.VIEWER , param);

      dataReqObj.add(viewerReq, 'viewer');
      dataReqObj.send(onLoadViewerResponse);
}

function onLoadViewerResponse(data) {
      try{
          viewer = data.get('viewer').getData();
          heading = 'Hello, ' + viewer.getDisplayName();
          var thumb = viewer.getField(opensocial.Person.Field.THUMBNAIL_URL);
          var profile = viewer.getField(opensocial.Person.Field.PROFILE_URL);
          heading = 'Hello, ' + viewer.getDisplayName();
          heading = heading + '  <a href="' + profile + '" >
                <img src="' + thumb +
                    '"></a>';


      }catch(err){alert(err);}

      //setup table for User info
      heading = heading + '<table border=2 width="800">
                <tr valign="top">';

      //get user ABOUT me
      heading = heading + '<td>';
```

Continued

Listing 4-6: PersonData.Js to Request a Suite of User Data and Display as a Table *(continued)*

```
heading = heading + '<br> About= ';
try{
    var About = viewer.getField(opensocial.
        Person.Field.ABOUT_ME);
    if(About == null)
        heading = heading + ' None available';
    else
        heading = heading + '<br>' +  About;
} catch(err){alert(err); heading = heading + 'NOT SUPPORTED'; }
heading = heading + '</td> ';

//get user  AGE
heading = heading + '<td>';
heading = heading + '<br> Age= ';
try{
    var Age = viewer.getField(opensocial.Person.Field.AGE);
    if (Age == null)
        heading = heading + ' None available';
    else
        heading = heading + '<br>' + 'Age= ' + Age;
} catch(err){alert(err); heading = heading + 'NOT SUPPORTED'; }
heading = heading + '</td> ';

//get user ACTIVITIES
heading = heading + '<td>';
heading = heading + '<br>' + 'Activities: ' ;
try{
    var Activities = viewer.getField(opensocial.Person.Field.ACTIVITIES);
    if (Activities == null)
        heading = heading + ' None available';
    for(x in Activities){
        heading = heading + '<br> Activity' + x +
            ' = ' +Activities[x];}

}catch(e2) {alert(e2); heading = heading + 'NOT SUPPORTED';}
heading = heading + '</td>';


//get user Address
heading = heading + '<td>';
heading = heading +  '<br> Addresses= ';

try{
    var Addresses = viewer.getField(opensocial.Person.Field.ADDRESSES);
    if (Addresses == null)
        heading = heading + ' None available';
```

```
                for(x in Addresses){
                    heading = heading + '<br> Address ' + x + '<br>';
                    heading = heading +
                            Addresses[x].getField(opensocial.Address.Field.REGION);
                    heading = heading +
                            Addresses[x].getField(opensocial.Address.Field.COUNTRY);
                }
        }catch(e2) {alert(e2); heading = heading + ' NOT SUPPORTED';}
        heading = heading + '</td>';


        //get user BODY Type
        heading = heading + '<td>';
        heading = heading +  '<br> Body Type= ';
        try{
            var Body_TYPE = viewer.getField(opensocial.Person.Field.BODY_TYPE);
            if(Body_TYPE == null)
                heading = heading + ' None available';
            else {
                heading = heading + '<br>' + 'Body Type: ';
                heading = heading + '<br>' + 'Build= ' +
                    Body_TYPE.getField(opensocial.BodyType.Field.BUILD);
                heading = heading + '<br>' + 'Eye color= ' +
                    Body_TYPE.getField(opensocial.BodyType.Field.EYE_COLOR);
                heading = heading + '<br>' + 'Hair color= ' +
                    Body_TYPE.getField(opensocial.BodyType.Field.HAIR_COLOR);
                heading = heading + '<br>' + 'Height= ' +
                    Body_TYPE.getField(opensocial.BodyType.Field.Height);
                heading = heading + '<br>' + 'Weight= ' +
                    Body_TYPE.getField(opensocial.BodyType.Field.WEIGHT);
            }
        }catch(e){alert(e); heading = heading + ' NOT SUPPORTED';}
        heading = heading + '</td>';

        //get MORE data for ROW 1

        //end of row
        heading = heading + '</tr>';


        //end of Table
        heading = heading + '</table>';
        document.getElementById('heading').innerHTML = heading;
        document.getElementById('main').innerHTML = html;
    }
```

Figure 4-4 shows the results of running the code in Listing 4-6.

Person data

Hello, Lynne Grewe

About= Professional in Web Systems, Professor, Social Network and Web/Media Programming.	Age= Age= 12	Activities: None available	Addresses= Address 0 CaliforniaUnited States	Body Type= None available	Books: None available	Cars: None available	Children= None available
Current Location= country: United States	Date of Birth= Fri Dec 12 1969 00:00:00 GMT-0800 (Pacific Standard Time)	Drinker= None available	Emails: None available	Ethnicity= None available	Fashion= undefined	Food: None available	Gender= [object Object] Gender= Female
Happiest When= None available	Has App= None available	Heroes= None available	Humor= None available	ID= 79110539	Interests: Interests= Surfing	JOB Interests:	JOBs: Nor available
Languages: None available	Living Arrangements= None available	Looking For= Friends	Movies: None available	Music: music0 =All Kinds music1 = dance music	Name: family name=undefined	Net Presence:	Nickname: Lynne
Pets= None available	Phone #s: None available	Political Views= None available	Profile Song= None available	Profile URL= profile url	Profile Video= None available	Quotes: None available	Relationship status= Married
Religion= None available	Romance= None available	Scared= None available	Schools: None available	Sexual Orientation= None available	Smoker= None available	Sports: None available	Status= Working hard on writing.
Tags: None available	Thumbnail URL=	Time Zone= None available	Turn Offs: None available	Turn Ons: None available	TV: None available	URLs: None available	Mood= None available

Figure 4-4: PersonData example running on Friendster

Activities

Broadly defined, *activities* in a social network are any form of communication or information-sharing. In OpenSocial, activities can include the following:

- Direct emails to users
- Notifications
- User updates (and hence friends updates)
- Requests to install an application (invitations)

Creating activities is a great way in OpenSocial to advertise your application. OpenSocial provides the developer with the capability to request the creation of these items through its API. Let's take a look at how to do a number of these activities. Note that the containers do control how many of these activities you can create, per user of your application, per day. These restrictions change frequently, and the social network's developer documentation should provide details.

Messages — Email and Notifications

A useful feature of OpenSocial is the capability to send messages to your users. OpenSocial does this through the `opensocial.requestSendMessage` method. You must first create an instance of a message object using the `opensocial.newMessage` method. There are different kinds of messages that can be created as specified by the `opensocial.Message.Field.TYPE`. These are enumerated in `opensocial.Message.Type`, and include the following:

❑ `EMAIL` — This is a direct email to the user.

❑ `NOTIFICATION` — This is a notification that can appear in different locations on different social networks. Notifications are like short "message/requests" or "status" lines related to the application and user. Notifications can appear under the heading "Requests" in the user's home page.

❑ `PRIVATE_MESSSAGE` — This is a private message, only seen by the user.

❑ `PUBLIC_MESSAGE` — This is a public message seen by the users and possibly others.

The message itself is specified by the setting a number of parameters associated with the fields in `opensocial.Message.Field.*`, including the following:

❑ `BODY` — This contains the body of the message.

❑ `BODY_ID` — This uses gadget message templates, and specifies the ID of the template to apply.

❑ `TITLE` — This is the title of the message

❑ `TITLE_ID` — This uses gadget message templates, and specifies the ID of the template to apply.

❑ `TYPE` — This indicates the kind of message to create.

Email Message Example

Listing 4-7 (XML) and Listing 4-8 (JavaScript) show the code used to create a simple application that, when a button is clicked, will generate a new email message.

Listing 4-7: EmailMessage.xml Application with Button to Trigger Email Creation

```xml
<?xml version="1.0" encoding="UTF-8"?>
<Module>
    <ModulePrefs title="Email Message" description="Email
            Message Test" >
        <Require feature="opensocial-0.8"/>
    </ModulePrefs>
    <Content type="html">
      <![CDATA[

        <div id='heading'></div>
        <hr size="1px"/>
```

Continued

131

Listing 4-7: EmailMessage.xml Application with Button to Trigger Email Creation
(continued)

```
            <div id='main'></div>
            <hr/>
            <div id='message'> </div>

            <input type="button" value="create message" onclick="createMessage();">

            <script src="http://U.com/EmailMessage.js"></script>

            <script>    init();  </script>
        ]]>

    </Content>
</Module>
```

Listing 4-8: EmailMessage.js Application to Create Email Message from "Viewer" to "Owner"

```
var os;
var dataReqObj;
var html = '';
var heading = '';
var viewer;
var owner;

function init() {

    dataReqObj = opensocial.newDataRequest();

    var viewerReq = dataReqObj.newFetchPersonRequest(opensocial.IdSpec.
        PersonId.VIEWER);
    dataReqObj.add(viewerReq, 'viewer');

    var viewerReq = dataReqObj.newFetchPersonRequest
        (opensocial.IdSpec.PersonId.OWNER);
    dataReqObj.add(viewerReq, 'owner');

    dataReqObj.send(onLoadViewerResponse);
}

function onLoadViewerResponse(data) {
    try{
        viewer = data.get('viewer').getData();
    }catch(err)
     { alert (err); }

    try{
        owner = data.get('owner').getData();
    }catch(err)
     { alert (err); }
```

```
        heading = 'Hello, ' + viewer.getDisplayName();
        document.getElementById('heading').innerHTML = heading;
}

//create an message grabbing viewer and owner first
function createMessage(){
    if(viewer == null)
        { document.getElementById('message').innerHTML =
            "viewer is null";
        return;}

    makeMessage(viewer, owner);
}

//create an message from v to o
function makeMessage(v, o){
try{

    var opts = {};

    opts[opensocial.Message.Field.TITLE] =
                v.getDisplayName() + "'s message to "
                + o.getDisplayName() + "!!!!";

    //setup type of message EMAIL
    opts[opensocial.Message.Field.TYPE] = opensocial.Message.Type.EMAIL;

    var body = v.getDisplayName() + " says hello to "
        + o.getDisplayName() +
        " using the Message application";

    var message = opensocial.newMessage(body, opts);

    opensocial.requestSendMessage(o.getId(), message, messageMade);

}catch(e) { alert(e); }
}

function messageMade(){
    document.getElementById('message').innerHTML = "message was made";
}
```

Figure 4-5 shows the results of running the applications in Listing 4-7 and Listing 4-8.

Notification Example

Notifications are another type of message you can create. Not all social networks support notifications. The only change to the code shown in Listing 4-7 and Listing 4-8 (the EmailMessage example) is the specification of the type when creating a message, as shown here:

```
//setup type of message Notification
opts[opensocial.Message.Field.TYPE] = opensocial.Message.Type.NOTIFICATION;
```

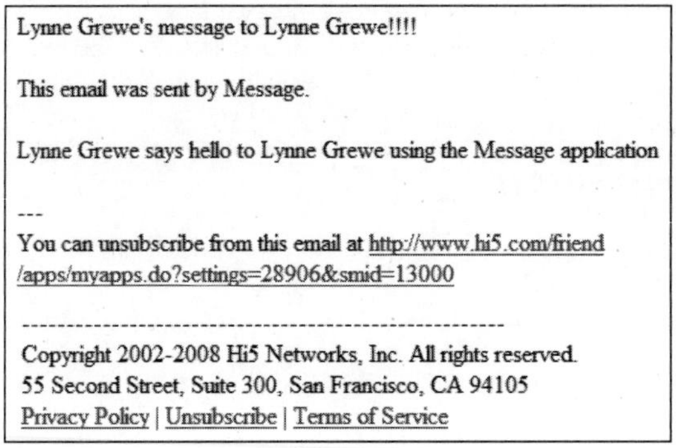

> Lynne Grewe's message to Lynne Grewe!!!!
>
> This email was sent by Message.
>
> Lynne Grewe says hello to Lynne Grewe using the Message application
>
> ---
> You can unsubscribe from this email at http://www.hi5.com/friend /apps/myapps.do?settings=28906&smid=13000
>
> --
> Copyright 2002-2008 Hi5 Networks, Inc. All rights reserved.
> 55 Second Street, Suite 300, San Francisco, CA 94105
> Privacy Policy | Unsubscribe | Terms of Service

Figure 4-5: Email created from EmailMessage application

Activity Posting (Updates)

OpenSocial has a class called `opensocial.Activity` that is a posting to an activity stream on the social network. A common appearance of these streams is under the title of "updates." In hi5, this appears in a user's profile.

An activity is represented in OpenSocial with the `opensocial.Activity` class. It can be created using `opensocial.newActivity` and takes a set of parameters keyed off of the `opensocial.Activity.Field.*` values. These include the following:

- ❏ `APP_ID` — Application ID of the application creating the activity.
- ❏ `BODY` — (Optional) This is a longer version of the activity information.
- ❏ `BODY_ID` — This uses gadget message templates, and specifies the ID of the template to apply.
- ❏ `EXTERNAL_ID` — (Optional) Additional string/ID that application can generate.
- ❏ `ID` — This is the identifier used to represent this activity.
- ❏ `MEDIA_ITEMS` — Indicates if media items are created and associated with an activity.
- ❏ `POSTED_TIME` — Gives the time (in milliseconds) when activity created.
- ❏ `PRIORITY` — This is the priority (scale 0 to 1), compared to other activities from this application.
- ❏ `STREAM_FAVICON_URL` — This is the URL for the icon representing all application activities.
- ❏ `STREAM_SOURCE_URL` — This is the URL for the source of the activity.
- ❏ `STREAM_TITLE` — This is the title of the source of the activity.
- ❏ `STREAM_URL` — This is the stream's URL.
- ❏ `TEMPLATE_PARAMS` — This is a set of (`key-value`) pairs relating to the activity.
- ❏ `TITLE` — This is the activity's title.
- ❏ `TITLE_ID` — This uses gadget message templates, and specifies the ID of the template to apply.
- ❏ `URL` — This gives the URL related to an activity.
- ❏ `USER_ID` — This is the ID of the user who "owns" this activity.

Listing 4-9 shows the JavaScript necessary to create an activity using an XML file similar to the one shown in Listing 4-7. As with the email example shown earlier in this chapter, this application has a simple interface with a button the user clicks to trigger the creation of an activity.

Listing 4-9: ActivityCreate.js Code Creating an Activity

```
var os;
var dataReqObj;
var html = '';
var heading = '';
var viewer;
var owner;

function init() {
    dataReqObj = opensocial.newDataRequest();

    var viewerReq =
        dataReqObj.newFetchPersonRequest(opensocial.
        IdSpec.PersonId.VIEWER);
    dataReqObj.add(viewerReq, 'viewer');
    var viewerReq =
        dataReqObj.newFetchPersonRequest(opensocial.
        IdSpec.PersonId.OWNER);
    dataReqObj.add(viewerReq, 'owner');

    dataReqObj.send(onLoadViewerResponse);
}

function onLoadViewerResponse(data) {
    try{
        viewer = data.get('viewer').getData();
    }catch(err)
      { alert(err); }


    try{
        owner = data.get('owner').getData();
    }catch(err)
      { alert(err); }
}

//create an activity grabbing viewer and owner first
function createActivity(){
    makeActivity(viewer, owner);
}

//create an activity to viewer from owner
function makeActivity(v, o){
 try{
    var opts = {};

    opts[opensocial.Activity.Field.TITLE] =
```

Continued

Listing 4-9: ActivityCreate.js Code Creating an Activity *(continued)*

```
                      v.getDisplayName() + " viewed " +
                      o.getDisplayName() + "'s profile with
                         the Activity application";

      opts[opensocial.Activity.Field.STREAM_FAVICON_URL] =
                      "http://U.com /Logo_16_16.PNG";


      var activity = opensocial.newActivity(opts);

      opensocial.requestCreateActivity(activity,
                  opensocial.CreateActivityPriority.HIGH,
                      activityMade);
  }catch(e) { alert(e); }
 }

 function activityMade(){
     document.getElementById('activity').innerHTML =
         "activity was made";
 }
```

Figure 4-6 shows the results in hi5 and the corresponding activity. The activity stream here is located in the user's profile.

Figure 4-6: Activity created using application code in Listing 4-9

Activities are limited by containers. For example, orkut allows one activity per user of an application per day. hi5 limits it to two activities per user per application per day.

orkut also precludes overlapping text being included in the title and body. A good tip when creating information for the body or title is to not overuse the user's name. Instead, look up `opensocial.Person.Field.GENDER` to help you with customizing a message. Here is an example of an awkward message:

```
"Lynne Grewe used Friend Finder to track Lynne Grewe's Friends"
```

Here is a better message using the gender information:

```
"Lynne Grewe used Friend Finder to track her Friends"
```

136

An even better message would be one that is more specific such as:

```
"Lynne Grewe tracked J. Aphelin on Friend Finder"
```

Invitations to Install

Providing users with the capability to invite their friends to use your application is an essential (important) function. OpenSocial creates invitations to one or more users by using the `opensocial.requestShareApp` method that takes the following parameters:

❑ `recipients` — This is an individual's ID or an array of IDs. These are the users to whom the invitation will be sent.

❑ `reason` — This is an instance of the `opensocial.Message` class. It represents the reason for the invitation. The container may govern this in the creation of the invitation message.

❑ `callback` — (Optional) This is called when the invitation has been sent by the container.

❑ `params` — (Optional) This is a set of `(key,value)` pairs (a map) that contains requests about redirection for users when they make or receive invitations.

The last optional parameter can be used to direct the user when either the invitation is sent, or an invitation is accepted. The options are keyed using the value in `opensocial.NavigationParamters` `.DesitinationType` as follows:

❑ `RECIPIENT_DESTINATION` — This is the location to redirect a user to when the user gets an invitation.

❑ `VIEWER_DESTINATION` — This is the location to redirect a user after the user sends an invitation.

Listing 4-10 shows the JavaScript code to create a user invitation. The `init()` method of this code is run at load time, making necessary person data requests that are used to set up an interface to allow the user to select a friend to invite.

Listing 4-10: Invite.js Application to Allow Users to Select a Friend and Send an Invitation

```
var os;
var dataReqObj;
var html = '';
var heading = '';
var friends_html = '';
var friend;
var viewer;
var owner;

function init() {

    dataReqObj = opensocial.newDataRequest();
```

Continued

Listing 4-10: Invite.js Application to Allow Users to Select a Friend and Send an Invitation *(continued)*

```
    var viewerReq = dataReqObj.newFetchPersonRequest('VIEWER');
    dataReqObj.add(viewerReq, 'viewer');
    var viewerReq = dataReqObj.newFetchPersonRequest('OWNER');
    dataReqObj.add(viewerReq, 'owner');
    viewerReq = dataReqObj.newFetchPeopleRequest('VIEWER_FRIENDS');
    dataReqObj.add(viewerReq, 'viewerFriends');
    dataReqObj.send(onLoadViewerResponse);

}

function onLoadViewerResponse(data) {
try{
    viewer = data.get('viewer').getData();
}catch(err)
{
  heading = 'Error2 ' + err.description;
  alert (heading);
}

try{
    owner = data.get('owner').getData();
}catch(err)
{
  heading = 'Error2 ' + err.description;
  alert (heading);
}

    heading = 'Hello, ' + viewer.getDisplayName();
    var thumb = viewer.getField(opensocial.
        Person.Field.THUMBNAIL_URL);
    var profile = viewer.getField(opensocial.
        Person.Field.PROFILE_URL);


    document.getElementById('heading').innerHTML = heading;
    var viewer_friends = data.get('viewerFriends').getData();

try{
    friends_html  = 'Invite a friend <br>';
    friends_html = friends_html + '<select id=friend>';

    viewer_friends.each(function(person) {
            friends_html = friends_html +
                '<option value=' + person.getId() +
                '>' + person.getDisplayName() + '</option>';
        });
    friends_html = friends_html + '</select>';
} catch(err)
{ friends_html ='Problem finding friends';
  alert(friends_html);
```

```
        }


        document.getElementById('friends').innerHTML = friends_html;

    }

    //create an message grabbing viewer and owner first
    function invite(){

    //get the friend that you want to invite
    var i = document.getElementById("friend");
    var id_selected = i.selectedIndex;
    friend = document.getElementById('friend').options[id_selected].value;

    try{
        var reason_body = viewer.getDisplayName() + " is inviting
               you to use the
               \"Invite\" Applciation!";
        document.getElementById('message').innerHTML = reason_body;

        var reason_message = opensocial.newMessage(reason_body);

        //create invitation
        opensocial.requestShareApp(friend,reason_message, inviteDone);

    }catch(e) {alert(e);}
    }

    function inviteDone(){
        document.getElementById('message').innerHTML =
            "Invite has been sent to " + friend;
    }
```

Persistence

Persistence is the reading and writing of application data stored on the container. Collectively, OpenSocial functions used to read and write this data are referred to as the Persistence API. Social networks place limits on their support of the OpenSocial Persistence API. For example, some networks limit the amount of storage per user per application. Only text information can be stored.

This can mean that the Persistence API will not solve all of your data needs. Even though some of the containers suggest that using the Persistence API will reduce latency, this may not always be true, and is a function of many issues (including the amount of data, kind of data, and what operations you need to perform on the data). Using the Persistence API for some or all of your application's data storage and retrieval needs can be a good decision.

OpenSocial models the storage and retrieval of data using a (key-value) association. It is a simpler model than that used by traditional relational databases. Only strings can be used for both the keys and values, but recall that the Gadgets API lets you convert JavaScript objects to strings, and vice versa.

However, storage of media items is not feasible with this service as it would take too much time to translate media objects to strings and the reverse for use.

Information Storage

You can utilize the Persistence API to store data by using the `newUpdatePersonAppDataRequest` method of the `DataRequest` class. This method takes the following parameters:

❑ `id` — This is the ID of the person you have associated the data with. Currently, only the `VIEWER`'s ID is allowed.

❑ `key` — This is a made-up key you want to associate with this data for storage and future retrieval. Only alphanumeric characters (A-Z, a-z, 0-9), _ (underscore), - (dash), and . (period) are allowed in the key.

❑ `value` — This is the data to be stored. Only text is allowed.

This method is used to store new items, as well as to update values.

Information Retrieval

You can utilize the Persistence API to retrieve data by using the `newFetchPersonAppDataRequest` method of the `DataRequest` class. This method takes the following parameters:

❑ `idSpec` — This is an instance of `OpenSocial.IdSpec` or predefined user fields.

❑ `keys` — This is either an array of keys, or an individual key, of the data to be retrieved. A key is represented by a string, and should have been used previously in a storage request.

This method maps each user in the `idSpec` given to the data retrieved. In other words, the data retrieved for each user specified in `idSpec` is itself a "map" that maps the keys to the individual data elements retrieved.

Listing 4-11 shows the JavaScript for the "Friend Blurb" application. This application allows a user to create a blurb dedicated to a friend. The blurb is a short line of text.

Listing 4-11: Persistence.js Program Using OpenSocial Persistence to Store Data

```
var os;
var dataReqObj;
var html = '';
var heading = '';
var friends_html = '';
var friend;
var viewer;
var viewer_friends;

//request viewer and friends
function init() {

    //request viewer and friends
```

```
        dataReqObj = opensocial.newDataRequest();
        var viewerReq = dataReqObj.newFetchPersonRequest('VIEWER');
        dataReqObj.add(viewerReq, 'viewer'
        viewerReq = dataReqObj.newFetchPeopleRequest('VIEWER_FRIENDS');
        dataReqObj.add(viewerReq, 'viewerFriends');
        dataReqObj.send(onLoadViewerResponse);
}

//callback function the gets viewer and friends data
//creates interface and calls function to get persistent data
function onLoadViewerResponse(data) {
    try{
     viewer = data.get('viewer').getData();
    }catch(err)
      {   alert (err);}

    heading = 'Hello, ' + viewer.getDisplayName();
    var thumb = viewer.getField(opensocial.
         Person.Field.THUMBNAIL_URL);
    var profile = viewer.getField(opensocial.
         Person.Field.PROFILE_URL);


    document.getElementById('heading').innerHTML = heading;
    document.getElementById('main').innerHTML = html;

    viewer_friends = data.get('viewerFriends').getData();

    try{
        friends_html  = '<b>Blurb a friend</b><br> To: ';
        friends_html = friends_html + '<select id=friend>';

        viewer_friends.each(function(person) {
          friends_html = friends_html +  '<option value=' +
                        person.getId() + '>' +
                        person.getDisplayName() + '</option>';
         });
         friends_html = friends_html + '</select>';
    } catch(err)
      {   alert (err);}

    document.getElementById('friends').innerHTML = friends_html;
    getAllAppData();

}

//Create the blurb and Store it using OpenSocial Persistence
function doit(){

    //get the friend that you want to invite
    var i = document.getElementById("friend");
    var id_selected = i.selectedIndex;
    friend = document.getElementById('friend').options[id_selected].value;
```

Continued

Listing 4-11: Persistence.js Program Using OpenSocial Persistence to Store Data
(continued)

```
      //get the blurb to send to the friend
      var blurb = document.getElementById('blurb').value;

      try{
       if(viewer == null)
         { document.getElementById('message').innerHTML =
             "viewer is null";
          return;}

       //create data app storage
       dataReqObj = opensocial.newDataRequest();
       //use the friend id as the key for new app data
       //associated with viewer
       dataReqObj.add(dataReqObj.newUpdatePersonAppDataRequest("VIEWER", friend,
                     blurb), 'set_data');
       dataReqObj.send(appDataDone);


      }catch(e) {alert(e);}
}


//callback when app data is set
function appDataDone(data){


    if(data.get('set_data').hadError())
       { document.getElementById('message_sent').innerHTML =
             "Data was NOT stored";
         return; }

    getAllAppData(); //refresh current apps
    return;

}


//Request all App data for the Viewer, all keys(friend ids,
//indicates blurbs
//to friends)  uses OpenSocial Persistence support
function getAllAppData(){
    //setup idSpec parameter
    var idSpec = opensocial.newIdSpec({"userId" : "VIEWER",
        "groupId" : "SELF"});

    dataReqObj = opensocial.newDataRequest();

    //Fetch ALL the keys-data
    dataReqObj.add( dataReqObj.newFetchPersonAppDataRequest
        ("VIEWER", "*"),
```

```
                        'get_data');
    dataReqObj.send(getAllAppDataDone);
}



//populate the interface when first loading the app with all
//app data stored for this user.
function getAllAppDataDone(data){

    if(data.get('get_data').hadError())
      { document.getElementById('message_recieved').innerHTML =
                    "Data was NOT retrieved for initial population";
          return; }

    var got_data = data.get('get_data').getData();
    var get_blurbs = "";
    var the_blurb;

    //retrieve data stored for each friend
    try{
      viewer_friends.each(function(person) {
          the_blurb = got_data[viewer.getId()][person.getId()];
          if(the_blurb != null)
            get_blurbs = get_blurbs + "To: " + person.
                        getDisplayName() + " (" +
                        person.getId() +")  -- " + the_blurb + "<br>";
      });
    } catch(err)
        { alert(err); }

    document.getElementById('message_recieved').innerHTML =
                    "<b>Current Blurbs:</b> <br>" +
                    get_blurbs + "<hr><br>";
}
```

Figure 4-7 shows the result of running the application in Listing 4-11.

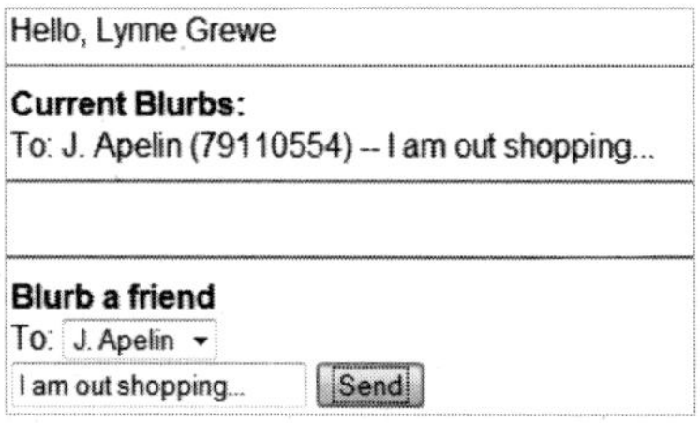

Hello, Lynne Grewe

Current Blurbs:
To: J. Apelin (79110554) -- I am out shopping...

Blurb a friend
To: J. Apelin ▾
I am out shopping...   Send

Figure 4-7: The "Friend Blurb" application

When the user submits a new blurb, the application executes the `doit` function, which uses OpenSocial's `newUpdatePersonAppDataRequest` method to store the blurb. The choice of the key in this case is the friend's ID. The application lets the user store only one unique blurb for each friend. When the application

143

loads, it calls the `getAllAppData` function, which retrieves any blurbs previously created and displays them to the user using the `newFetchPersonAppDataRequest` method. In addition to being stored, new blurbs also cause the interface to update.

Detail of OpenSocial JavaScript API

Table 4-2 details the OpenSocial API. For ease of use, it is presented in tabular format with descriptions. Examples are sprinkled throughout, but a few coding examples here augment examples presented in this and subsequent chapters.

Table 4-2: OpenSocial API Detail

Objects	Method/Variable	Description
Opensocial		This is the main object, namespace, for all of the OpenSocial API.
	getEnvironment()	Obtains the `Environment` associated with your application. Returns `opensocial.Environment`.
	hasPermission(p)	Tells if application has permission. Returns a Boolean. Parameters include `p` (an instance of `opensocial.Permission`).
	newActivity()	Creates a new instance of `opensocial.Activity`. Returns `opensocial.Activity`. Parameters specifying the activity include items such as title, body, and more. See the section, "Activities," earlier in this chapter.
	newDataRequest()	Creates a new instance of the `DataRequest` class with which to make data requests. Returns `opensocial.DataRequest`. For example, `dataReqObj = opensocial.newDataRequest();`.
	newIdSpec()	Creates a new instance of the `DataRequest` class with which to make data requests. Returns `opensocial.IdSpec`.

Continued

Table 4-2: OpenSocial API Detail *(continued)*

Objects	Method/Variable	Description
	`newMediaItem()`	Creates a media item. Returns `opensocial.MediaItem`. Parameters include `mt` (type of media, specified by `opensocial.MediaItem.Field.*`), `url` (location of media, a string), and `opt_params` (optional parameters specifying additional fields). For example, `var myVideo = opensocial.newMediaItem (opensocial.MediaItem.Field.VIDEO, "http://U.com/Video.mpg")`.
	`newMessage()`	Creates a new message. Returns `opensocial.Message`. Parameters include `body` (string, message) and `opt_params` (optional parameters, keyed with `opensocial.Message.Field.*`).
	`newNavigational Parameters()`	Redirects the user. See the `requestShareApp()` method. Returns `opensocial.NavagationalParameters`. Parameters include `p` (parameter map keyed with `opensocial .NavagationalParameters.Field.*` values that specify where to navigate to and when).
	`requestCreateActivity()`	Makes a request to the container to create the activity. Parameters include `activity` (instance of `opensocial.Activity`), `p` (priority, specified by `opensocial .CreateActivityPriority.HIGH` or `LOW`), and `opt_callback` (optional callback function to be called when activity is created).
	`requestPermission()`	Requests permission from user. Parameters include `permissions` (instance of `opensocial.Permission`), `reason` (string displayed to user when asking for this permission), and `opt_callback` (optional callback function to be called when permission request is completed; this function receives an instance of `opensocial.ResponseItem`; if there is an associated error, it means that the permission was denied).

Continued

Table 4-2: OpenSocial API Detail *(continued)*

Objects	Method/Variable	Description
	requestSendMessage()	Requests a message be sent to user(s). Parameters include users (a user ID or array of IDs [strings] or a group reference; also supports 'VIEWER', 'OWNER', 'VIEWER_FRIENDS', 'OWNER_FRIENDS'), message (instance of opensocial.Message), opt_callback (optional callback function to be called when request is completed), and opt_params (instance of opensocial.NavigationParameters that tells where to redirect user when request has been made/accepted).
	requestShareApp()	Invites user(s) to install the application. Parameters include users (a user ID or array of IDs [strings] or a group reference; also supports 'VIEWER', 'OWNER', 'VIEWER_FRIENDS', 'OWNER_FRIENDS'), reason (string displayed to user in invite), opt_callback (optional callback function to be called when request is completed), and opt_params (instance of opensocial.NavigationParameters that tells where to redirect user when request made/accepted).
opensocial.Activity		Class used to represent an activity. See the section, "Activities", earlier in this chapter.
	getField()	Gets the field information for the activity. Returns a string, the value associated with the key for this activity. Parameters include key (specifies what information to get about an activity; will be one of the fields from opensocial.Activity.Field.*, such as BODY) and opt_params (map of optional parameters; currently only key is dealing with escape type; keys of map are specified by opensocial.DataRequest.DataRequestFields.*; ESCAPE_TYPE is currently the only field).

Continued

Table 4-2: OpenSocial API Detail *(continued)*

Objects	Method/Variable	Description
	`getId()`	Gets the ID of the activity. Returns a string.
	`setField()`	Sets the `Field` associated with the key to the value. Parameters include `key` (key specified by the `opensocial.Activity.Field.*`, such as `BODY`) and `value` (a string, the value to associate with the key).
`opensocial .Activity.Field`		Class that lists the possible fields associated with an activity.
	`APP_ID`	A string, this is the ID of the application associated with the activity.
	`BODY`	A string, this is the body of the activity. Allowed HTML tags include `<a>`, `<b>`, `<i>`, `<span>`.
	`BODY_ID`	A string, this is the ID of a template message specified in Gadget XML.
	`EXTERNAL_ID`	A string, this is the optional additional ID.
	`ID`	A string, this is the ID of the activity.
	`MEDIA_ITEMS`	This is an array of `opensocial.MediaItem` objects. Each represents a different media item associated with the activity.
	`POSTED_TIME`	A string, this is the time when the activity was posted.
	`PRIORITY`	A number between 0 and 1, this is the relative priority when compared to other activities.
	`STREAM_FAVICON_URL`	A string, this is the URL to the stream's icon.
	`STREAM_SOURCE_URL`	A string, this is the URL to the stream's source.
	`STREAM_TITLE`	A string, this is the stream title.
	`STREAM_URL`	A string, this is the URL of the stream.

Continued

Table 4-2: OpenSocial API Detail *(continued)*

Objects	Method/Variable	Description
	TEMPLATE_PARAMS	Mapping of (key, value) pairs associated with the activity. Examples include the display name for the person, the ID, and so on.
	TITLE	A string, this is the title of the activity. Allowed HTML tags include <a>, <b>, <i>, <span>.
	TITLE_ID	A string, this is the ID of the template message specified in Gadget XML.
	URL	A string, this is the URL used for activity representation.
	USER_ID	A string, this is the ID of a user associated with the activity.
opensocail.Address		Class that represents all addresses.
	getField()	Gets the value associated with the Address key. Parameters include key (specified as one of the opensocial.Address.Field.* values) and opt_params (optional parameterss represented as a map <opensocail.DataRequestFields.*, object>; ESCAPE_TYPE is currently the only field).
opensocial.Address .Field		Gives the possible fields associated with an address.
	COUNTRY	A string, this is a country.
	EXTENDED_ADDRESS	A string, when an extended street address.
	LATITUDE	A number, this is a latitude.
	LOCALITY	A string, this is a locality.
	LONGITUDE	A number, this is a longitude.
	PO_BOX	A string, this is a Post Office box.
	POSTAL_CODE	A string, this is a postal (ZIP) code.

Continued

Table 4-2: OpenSocial API Detail *(continued)*

Objects	Method/Variable	Description
	`REGION`	A string, this is a region.
	`STREET_ADDRESS`	A string, this is a street address.
	`TYPE`	A string, this is a category associated with `Address` (for example, house, work).
	`UNSTRUCTURED_ADDRESS`	A string, this is a complete address in unstructured format.
`opensocial.BodyType`		Class that deals with a user's body information.
	`getField()`	Gets the value associated with the `BodyType` key. Parameters include `key` (specified as one of the `opensocial.BodyType.Field.*` values) and `opt_params` (optional parameterss represented as a map `<opensocail.DataRequestFields.*, object>`; `ESCAPE_TYPE` is currently the only field).
`opensocial.BodyType .Field`		Class that gives the possible fields associated with a `BodyType`. Container support is optional.
	`BUILD`	A string, this is build information.
	`EYE_COLOR`	A string, this is eye color.
	`HAIR_COLOR`	A string, this is hair color.
	`HEIGHT`	A number, this is height (in meters).
	`WEIGHT`	A number, this is weight (in kilograms).
`opensocial.Collection`		Common collection data structure used in OpenSocial to represent multiple items.
	`as Array()`	Gets the collection as an array. Returns an array of objects.
	`each()`	Cycles through collection items and performs function `f` on each one. Parameters include `f` (function to execute on each collection item).

Continued

Table 4-2: OpenSocial API Detail *(continued)*

Objects	Method/Variable	Description
	getById()	Retrieves the item associated with the ID in the collection. Returns the item associated with id or null if none found. Parameters include id (ID to find).
	getOffset()	If this collection is inside a larger set, it will return the offset of its occurrence. Returns the number of offset.
	getTotalSize()	Determines the size of the larger set this collection belongs to. Returns a number.
	size()	Determines the size of the collection. Returns a number, size.
opensocial .CreateActivityPriority		Class that deals with the priority of an activity.
	HIGH	This indicates "high priority." Container should create the activity even when container must seek user permission.
	LOW	This indicates "low priority." Container will not create the activity if the user has not granted permission to create activities.
opensocial.DataRequest		Class that is used to represent all data requests in OpenSocial (such as, opensocial.newDataRequest();).

	add()	Used to add requests to an opensocial.DataRequest object. You can add more than one request. Parameters include req (a request item object) and opt_key (a key with which to associate the request; used in retrieval; optional).
		
		Following is an example:
		
		`var viewerReq = dataReqObj`
		`.newFetchPersonRequest('VIEWER');`
		
		`dataReqObj.add(viewerReq, 'viewer');`

Continued

Table 4-2: OpenSocial API Detail *(continued)*

Objects	Method/Variable	Description
	`newFetchActivities Request()`	Used to create a request item to fetch activities associated with a user or users. You will add this to a `DataRequest` object. When processed, it will return a collection of `opensocial.Activity` objects. Parameters include `idSpec` (user ID or array of user IDs) and `opt_params` (mapping of `opensocial.DataRequest .ActivityRequestFields`; not currently used).
	`newFetchPeopleRequest()`	Used to create a request item to fetch `People`. You will add to a `DataRequest` object. When processed, this will return a collection of `opensocial.Person` objects. Parameters include `idSpec` (user ID or array of user IDs) and `opt_params` (mapping of `opensocial.DataRequest .PeopleRequestFields`).
	`newFetchPersonApp DataRequest()`	Used to create a request item to fetch application data stored on the container and associated with a `user.aRequest` object. When processed, this will return a collection of `opensocial.Person objects`. Parameters include `idSpec` (user ID or array of user IDs) and `opt_params` (mapping of `opensocial .DataRequest.PeopleRequestFields`). Following is an example: `viewerReq = dataReqObj .newFetchPersonRequest();` `dataReqObj.add(viewerReq, 'viewerFriends');`
	`newFetchPersonRequest()`	Used to create a request item to fetch a `Person`. When processed, this will return `opensocial.Person` objects. Parameters include `id` (user ID; can also use `opensocial.DataRequest.PersonId.*` fields or `opensocial.IdSpec.PersonId.*` fields to indicate `'VIEWER'` or `'OWNER'`) and `opt_params` (mapping of `opensocial .DataRequest.PeopleRequestFields`).

Continued

Table 4-2: OpenSocial API Detail *(continued)*

Objects	Method/Variable	Description

		Following is an example:
		
		`viewerReq = dataReqObj`
		`.newFetchPersonRequest(opensocial`
		`.IdSpec.PersonId.VIEWER);`
		
		`dataReqObj.add(viewerReq,`
		`'viewerFriends');`

	`newRemovePersonApp DataRequest()`	Removes from the container's persistence-supported storage the data associated with the keys for a user. Parameters include id (user ID that data is associated with) and key (string or array of strings; the key[s] associated with [key,value] pairs stored for the user that should be removed).
	`newUpdatePersonApp DataRequest()`	Creates or updates a new data entry in the container's persistence-supported storage. Parameters include id (user ID that data is associated with) and key (the key of the [key,value] pair that is the data to be stored; may contain alphanumeric characters, - [dash], . [dot], and _ [underscore]).
	`send()`	Sends the DataRequest to the container. Parameters include opt_callback (optional, callback function that is called when request has been processed by container).
`opensocial.DataRequest .DataRequestFields`		Class that deals with data request fields.
	`ESCAPE_TYPE`	Deals with how to escape data related to a person. The default is HTML_ESCAPE.
`opensocial.DataRequest .FilterType`		Class that deals with filters for person requests.
	`ALL`	This indicates all friends.
	`HAS_APP`	This indicates only friends that have the application installed.

Continued

Table 4-2: OpenSocial API Detail *(continued)*

Objects	Method/Variable	Description
	TOP_FRIENDS	This indicates only friends defined by user as "top" friends.
opensocial.DataRequest.PeopleRequestFields		Class that enumerates all of the fields associated with creating `People` data requests.
	FILTER	This is the filter type (default ALL). This must be one of `opensocial.DataRequest.FilterType`.
	FILTER_OPTIONS	This indicates the filter options given as a map `<string, object>`.
	FIRST	This is used in paginating. It indicates the index of the first item to fetch.
	MAX	This is the maximum number of items to fetch in a request.
	PROFILE_DETAILS	This specifies what user profile data to get. It is specified as an array of `opensocial.Person.Field.*` keys. By default, it will always include `opensocial.Person.Field.ID, NAME, THUMBNAIL_URL`.
	SORT_ORDER	This sorts the returned items. The default is `TOP_FRIENDS` sorting. Specified as an `opensocial.DataRequest.SortOrder.*` field.
opensocial.DataRequest.SortOrder		Class that specifies possible sorting techniques.
	NAME	This indicates to sort by name.
	TOP_FRIENDS	This indicates to sort by top friends.
opensocial.DataResponse		Class that represents a returned response from a data request.
	get()	Retrieves the value associated with the key. Returns `opensocial.ResponseItem`. Parameters include `key` (a specified key you want to retrieve data for).

Continued

Table 4-2: OpenSocial API Detail (continued)

Objects	Method/Variable	Description
	getErrorMessage()	Returns an error message (as a string) if it exists.
	hadError()	Indicates if an error occurred in the request. Returns a Boolean.
opensocial.Email		Class that represents an email.
	getField()	Gets the value associated with the Email key. Parameters include key (specified as one of the opensocial.Email.Field.* values) and opt_params (optional parameters represented as a map <opensocial.DataRequest .DataRequest.Fields, object>).
opensocial.Email.Field		Class that details fields associated with an email.
	ADDRESS	A string, this is the email address.
	TYPE	A string, this is the category of email (for example, work, home, and so on).
opensocial.Enum		Class that represents enum objects.
	getDisplayValue()	Returns the value (as a string) of this enum.
	getKey()	Returns the enum key, which must be an opensocial.Enum.CLASS.* field.
opensocial.Enum.Drinker		Class that gives enum keys associated with opensocial.Person.Field.Drinker.
	HEAVILY	An object, this indicates a heavy drinker.
	NO	An object, this indicates no drinking.
	OCCASIONALLY	An object, this indicates an occasional drinker.
	QUIT	An object, this indicates that the person has quit drinking.
	QUITTING	An object, this indicates the user is in the process of quitting.

Continued

Table 4-2: OpenSocial API Detail *(continued)*

Objects	Method/Variable	Description
	REGULARLY	An object, this indicates the user drinks on regular basis.
	SOCIALLY	An object, this indicates the user is a social drinker.
	YES	An object, this indicates that the user drinks.
opensocial.Enum.Gender		Class that gives enum keys associated with opensocial.Person.Field.Gender.
	FEMALE	An object, this indicates a female.
	MALE	An object, this indicates a male.
Opensocial.Enum .LookingFor		Class that gives enum keys associated with opensocial.Person.Field.LookingFor.
	ACTIVIY_PARTNERS	An object, this indicates the user is looking for people to do activities with.
	DATING	An object, this indicates the user is looking to date.
	FRIENDS	An object, this indicates the user is looking for friends.
	NETWORKING	An object, this indicates the user is looking to network.
	RANDOM	An object, this indicates the user is looking at random.
	RELATIONSHIP	An object, this indicates the user is looking for a relationship.
opensocial.Enum.Presence		Class that gives enum keys associated with opensocial.Person.Field .NetworkPresence.
	AWAY	An object, this indicates the user is currently not "in."
	CHAT	An object, this indicates the user is chatting.
	DND	An object, this indicates a "Do Not Disturb."

Continued

Table 4-2: OpenSocial API Detail (continued)

Objects	Method/Variable	Description
	OFFLINE	An object, this indicates the user is currently offline.
	ONLINE	An object, this indicates the user is currently online.
	XA	An object, this indicates an extended away.
opensocial.Enum.Smoker		Class that gives enum keys associated with opensocial.Person.Field.Smoker.
	HEAVILY	An object, this indicates that user is a heavy smoker.
	NO	An object, this indicates no smoking.
	OCCASIONALLY	An object, this indicates that user is an occasional smoker.
	QUIT	An object, this indicates that user has quit smoking.
	QUITTING	An object, this indicates that user is in the process of quitting.
	REGULARLY	An object, this indicates that user smokes on regular basis.
	SOCIALLY	An object, this indicates that user is a social smoker.
	YES	An object, this indicates that user smokes.
opensocial.Environment		Class that specifies the application environment.
	getDomain()	Gets the current domain of the container for example, hi5.com). Returns a string.
	supportsField()	Indicates if a field is supported by the container for the object. Returns a Boolean. Parameters include objectType (indicated by field in opensocial.Environment.ObjectType.*) and fieldName (field to check).

Continued

Table 4-2: OpenSocial API Detail *(continued)*

Objects	Method/Variable	Description
`opensocial.Environment` `.ObjectType`		Class that details fields related to `Environment`. Used to query if the container has support for them.
	`ACTIVITY`	Used to query Activity support
	`ADDRESS`	Used to query Address support
	`BODY_TYPE`	Used to query Body type support
	`EMAIL`	Used to query Email support
	`FILTER_TYPE`	Used to query Filter support
	`MEDIA_ITEM`	Used to query Media Item support
	`MESSAGE`	Used to query Message support
	`MESSAGE_TYPE`	Used to query Message Type support
	`NAME`	Used to query Name support
	`ORGANIZATION`	Used to query Organization support
	`PERSON`	Used to query Person support
	`PHONE`	Used to query Phone number support
	`SORT_ORDER`	Used to query Sort Order support
	`URL`	Used to query URL support
`opensocial.EscapeType`		Class that indicates how escaping can be applied to person data.
	`HTML_ESCAPE`	An object, this indicates to HTML escape data used.
	`NONE`	An object, this indicates no escaping done.
`opensocial.IdSpec`		Class that represents an ID specification.
	`getField()`	Gets the value associated with the `IdSpec` key. Parameters include `key` (specified as one of the `opensocial.IdSpec.Field.*` values) and `opt_params` (optional parameters represented as a map `<opensocial.DataRequest.DataRequest.Fields, object>`).

Continued

Table 4-2: OpenSocial API Detail *(continued)*

Objects	Method/Variable	Description
	setField()	Sets the Field associated with the key to the value. Parameters include key (key specified by the opensocial.IdSpec .Field.* such as GROUP_ID) and value (a string that is the value to associate with the key).
opensocial.IdSpec.Field		Class that gives fields associated with an IdSpec.
	GROUP_ID	A string, this represents a group of people in IdSpec. Can be either 'FRIENDS' or 'SELF'.
	NETWORK_DISTANCE	A number, this integer indicates the number of jumps in a social graph that two people can be considered to be part of this group.
	USER_ID	A string or array of strings, this indicates a user ID or array of IDs.
opensocial.IdSpec .PersonId		Class that lists predefined person IDs.
	OWNER	An object, this represents the "owner" of the application.
	VIEWER	An object, this represents the "viewer" of the application.
opensocial.MediaItem		Class that represents a media item.
	getField()	Gets the value associated with the MediaItem key. Parameters include key (specified as one of the opensocial.MediaItem.Field.* values) and opt_params (optional parameters represented as a map <opensocial .DataRequest.DataRequest.Fields, object>).
	setField()	Sets the Field associated with the key to the value. Parameters include key (key specified by the opensocial.MediaItem.Field.*, such as URL) and value (the value to associate with the key).

Continued

Table 4-2: OpenSocial API Detail *(continued)*

Objects	Method/Variable	Description
`opensocial.MediaItem` `.Field`		Class that details fields related to `opensocial.MediaItem`.
	`MIME_TYPE`	A string, this is the type of MIME media type.
	`TYPE`	`opensocial.MediaItem.Type.*` field-indicated type.
	`URL`	A string, this is the location of the media item.
`opensocial.MediaItem` `.Type`		Class that details types of media items.
	`AUDIO`	An object, this indicates an audio type of media.
	`IMAGE`	An object, this indicates an image type of media.
	`VIDEO`	An object, this indicates an video type of media.
`opensocial.Message`		Class that represents a message.
	`getField()`	Gets the value associated with the `Message` key. Parameters include `key` (specified as one of the `opensocial.Message.Field.*` values) and `opt_params` (optional params represented as a map `<opensocial .DataRequest.DataRequest.Fields, object>`).
	`setField()`	Sets the `Field` associated with the key to the value. Parameters include `key` (key specified by the `opensocial.Message.Field.*`, such as `URL`) and `value` (the value to associate with the key).
`opensocial.Message.Field`		Class that details fields associated with messages.

Continued

Table 4-2: OpenSocial API Detail *(continued)*

Objects	Method/Variable	Description
	BODY	An object, this is the body of message.
	BODY_ID	A string, this is the ID of a template message specified in Gadget XML.
	TITLE	A string, this is the title of the message.
	TITLE_ID	A string, this is the ID of a template message specified in Gadget XML.
	TYPE	A title given as a field in `opensocial.Message.Type.*`.
opensocial.Message.Type		Class that details the types of messages.
	EMAIL	An object, this indicates an email message.
	NOTIFICATION	An object, this indicates a notification.
	PRIVATE_MESSAGE	An object, this kind of message is only seen by the user.
	PUBLIC_MESSAGE	An object, this kind of message is seen by the public.
opensocial.Name.Field		Class that details information dealing with names.
	ADDITIONAL_NAME	A string representing additional name.
	FAMILY_NAME	A string representing last name.
	GIVEN_NAME	A string representing first name.
	HONORIFIC_PREFIX	A string representing prefix, i.e. Dr.
	HONORIFIC_SUFFIX	A string representing suffix, i.e. PhD.
	UNSTRUCTURED	A string representing an unstructured version of the name.
opensocial .NavigationParameters		Class that represents navigation parameters used to direct users after requests.

Continued

Table 4-2: OpenSocial API Detail *(continued)*

Objects	Method/Variable	Description
	getField()	Gets the value associated with the Navigational `Parameter` key. Parameters include `key` (specified as one of the `opensocial.NavagationParameters.Field.*` values) and `opt_params` (optional parameters represented as a map `<opensocial.DataRequest.DataRequest.Fields, object>`).
	setField()	Sets the `Field` associated with the key to the value. Parameters include `key` (key specified by the `opensocial.NavagationParameters.Field.*`, such as `URL`) and `value` (the value to associate with the key).
opensocial.NavigationParameters.DestinationType		Class that lists types of destinations for navigation parameters.
	RECIPIENT_DESTINATION	An object, this indicates the destination of the recipient.
	VIEWER_DESTINATION	An object, this indicates the destination of a viewer.
opensocial.NavigationParameters.Field		Class that details fields associated with navigation parameters.
	OWNER	A string, this is the owner ID.
	PARAMETERS	This is optional, and is a list of parameters passed with navigation to a new view.
	VIEW	This specifies the view to which to navigate.
opensocial.Organization		Class that represents an organization.
	getField	Gets the value associated with the `Organization` key. Parameters include `key` (specified as one of the `opensocial.Organization.Field.*` values) and `opt_params` (optional parameters represented as a map `<opensocial.DataRequest.DataRequest.Fields, object>`).

Continued

Table 4-2: OpenSocial API Detail *(continued)*

Objects	Method/Variable	Description
opensocial.Organization.Field		Class that lists fields associated with an Organization. All fields are optional.
	ADDRESS	This is an opensocial.Address instance.
	DESCRIPTION	This is a string.
	END_DATE	A date, this indicates the last date a person stopped being part of an organization. Null indicates the user is still a member.
	FIELD	A string, this indicates the "field" the organization is in.
	NAME	This is a string.
	SALARY	A string, this indicates how much money the user gets paid.
	START_DATE	A date, this indicates the user's start date.
	SUB_FIELD	A string, if it exists, the sub-field of an organization.
	TITLE	A string, this is the user's title in the organization.
	WEBPAGE	This is a string.
opensocial.Permission		Class that represents a permission.
	VIEWER	Permission to get viewer access.
opensocial.Person		Class that represents a person.
	getDisplayName()	Retrieves the person's name.
	getField	Gets the value associated with the Person key. Parameters include key (specified as one of the opensocial.Person.Field.* values) and opt_params (optional parameters represented as a map <opensocial.DataRequest.DataRequest.Fields, object>).
	getId()	Returns the Person ID. Returns a string.

Continued

Table 4-2: OpenSocial API Detail *(continued)*

Objects	Method/Variable	Description
	`isOwner()`	Tells if this person is the owner. Returns a Boolean.
	`isViewer()`	Tells if this person is the viewer. Returns a Boolean.
`opensocial.Person.Field`		Class that lists information fields for a person. These fields are optional for containers.
	`ABOUT_ME`	String representing info about user.
	`ACTIVITIES`	Array of strings, representing activities.
	`ADDRESSES`	Array of `opensocial.Address` objects, representing user's addresses.
	`AGE`	Number representing age.
	`BODY_TYPE`	`opensocial.BodyType` instance, representing user's body type.
	`BOOKS`	This is an array of strings representing books user likes/read.
	`CARS`	Array of strings, representing user's cars (or likes).
	`CURRENT_LOCATION`	`opensocial.Address` instance representing current location.
	`DATE_OF_BIRTH`	This is a `Date` object representing date of birth.
	`DRINKER`	Specified in `opensocial.Enum` using keys in `opensocial.Enum.Drinker.*`, indicates user's drinking preference.
	`EMAILS`	Array of `opensocial.Email` objects.
	`ETHNICITY`	String, user's ethnicity.
	`FASHION`	String, about user fashion preferences.
	`FOOD`	Array of strings, inidicating user's opinions/likes on food.

Continued

Table 4-2: OpenSocial API Detail (continued)

Objects	Method/Variable	Description
	GENDER	Gender specified in opensocial.Enum using keys in opensocial.Enum.GENDER.*.
	HAPPIEST_WHEN	String telling about when user is happy.
	HAS_APP	Boolean, indicates if user has application installed.
	HEROES	Array of strings indicating user's heroes.
	HUMOR	String related to humor.
	ID	String representing user's unique ID.
	INTERESTS	Array of strings, representing user's interests.
	JOB_INTERESTS	String, indicates user's job interests.
	JOBS	Array of opensocial.Organization objects, indicates places of user employment.
	LANGUAGES_SPOKEN	Array of strings (ISO 639-1 codes), indicating languages spoken.
	LIVING_ARRANGEMENT	String, indicating user's living arrangments.
	LOOKING_FOR	This is specified in opensocial.Enum using keys in opensocial.Enum.LookingFor.*., indicates thinks user is looking for (esp. in reference to meeting new people).
	MOVIES	Array of strings, representing movie interest.
	MUSIC	Array of strings, representing music interest.
	NAME	opensocial.Name instance, indicates user's name.
	NICKNAME	String, gives user's nickname.
	PETS	String, gives info on user's pets.

Continued

Table 4-2: OpenSocial API Detail *(continued)*

Objects	Method/Variable	Description
	PHONE_NUMBERS	Array of `opensocial.Phone` objects, representing user's phone numbers.
	POLITICAL_VIEWS	String, indicates user's political opinions.
	PROFILE_SONG	`opensocial.URL` instance, URL to song used on user's profile.
	PROFILE_URL	String, URL to user's profile.
	PROFILE_VIDEO	`opensocial.URL` instance, URL to user's video on profile.
	QUOTES	Array of strings, represents quotes provided by user.
	RELATIONSHIP_STATUS	String, represents user's relationship status.
	RELIGION	String, represents user's religion.
	ROMANCE	String, represents users opinions on romance.
	SCARED_OF	String, what user is scared of.
	SCHOOLS	Array of `opensocial.Organization` objects, schools user attended.
	SEXUAL_ORIENTATION	String, user's sexual orientation.
	SMOKER	This is specified in `opensocial.Enum` using keys in `opensocial.Enum.Smoker.*`. Represents user's smoking preference.
	SPORTS	Array of strings, user's sports information.
	STATUS	String, user's status line.
	TAGS	Array of strings, tags representing interests or tags related to user.
	THUMBNAIL_URL	String, URL to thumbnail image of user.
	TIME_ZONE	This is expressed in minutes, the difference between Greenwich Mean Time (GMT) and user's time.

Continued

Table 4-2: OpenSocial API Detail *(continued)*

Objects	Method/Variable	Description
	TURN_OFFS	Array of strings, user's list of turn offs.
	TURN_ONS	Array of strings, user's list of turn ons.
	TV_SHOWS	Array of strings, user's list of shows they watch or comments on shows.
	URLS	Array of opensocial.Url objects, represents user's URLs.
opensocial.Phone		Class that deals with a phone.
	getField()	Gets the value associated with the Phone key. Parameters include key (specified as one of the opensocial.Phone.Field.* values) and opt_params (optional parameters represented as a map <opensocial.DataRequest .DataRequest.Fields, object>).
opensocial.Phone.Field		Class that provides information about a phone.
	NUMBER	A string, this indicates the phone number.
	TYPE	A string, a label, this indicates a category for the phone.
opensocial.ResponseItem		Class that represents a response item from a DataResponse.
	getData()	Retrieves the response data.
	getErrorCode()	Retrieves any Error code if an error occurred. Defined in opensocial.ResponseItem.Error. Returns an opensocial.ResponseItem.Error.* code.
	getErrorMessage()	Retrieves an error message, if an error occurred. Returns a string.
	getOriginalDataRequest()	Gets the data request that generated this response. Returns an opensocial.DataRequest object.

Continued

Table 4-2: OpenSocial API Detail *(continued)*

Objects	Method/Variable	Description
	hadError()	Tells if an error occurred. Returns a Boolean.
opensocial.ResponseItem.Error		Class that lists possible errors in creating a response (servicing a request).
	BAD_REQUEST	An object, this indicates an invalid request.
	FORBIDDEN	An object, this indicates that an application is not allowed to make this request.
	INTERNAL_ERROR	An object, this indicates an internal container error.
	LIMIT_EXCEEDED	An object, this indicates an application has exceeded the limit on the number of these kinds of requests.
	NOT_IMPLEMENTED	An object, this indicates a container does not support this request.
	UNAUTHORIZED	An object, this indicates an application is not authorized for this request.
opensocial.Url		Class representing a URL.
	getField()	Gets the value associated with the Url key. Parameters include key (specified as one of the opensocial.Url.Field.* values) and opt_params (optional parameters represented as a map <opensocial.DataRequest.DataRequest.Fields, object>).
opensocial.Url.Field		Class detailing fields in an opensocial.Url.
	ADDRESS	A string, this indicates a URL address.
	LINK_TEXT	A string, this indicates link text.
	TYPE	A string, this indicates a type or label.

Summary

This chapter began with the creation of the "Friend Finder" application, which uses OpenSocial API calls to get the viewer's name and friend list. You then learned about the common features in the OpenSocial JavaScript API. This was followed by a fairly detailed discussion of the main components involving People, Activities, and Persistence. A number of simple applications were discussed. This chapter concluded with a detailed listing of the OpenSocial JavaScript API.

Chapter 5 delves into an examination of the newer RESTful API.

5

OpenSocial RESTful API

The OpenSocial RESTful API is a server-based API alternative to the previously discussed client-based OpenSocial JavaScript API. This chapter begins with an introduction to Representational State Transfer (REST), and this is followed by a discussion of the OpenSocial RESTful application architecture. Next, the chapter examines the OAuth authentication scheme. Finally, details of the OpenSocial RESTful API are provided, along with detailed examples.

Getting to Know REST

REST originated from Roy Fielding's 2000 doctoral dissertation at the University of California, Irvine (*Architectural Styles and the Design of Network-Based Software Architectures*). REST describes a software model that follows a set of ''REST'' principles that you'll learn about shortly. REST is designed for effective interactions and data delivery in a distributed hypermedia system.

An interpretation of REST is that of a Web-centric software system that transmits data over HTTP using HTTP methods to represent application-specific requests. In reality, the definition of REST is not specific to the Internet, nor does it require the use of HTTP. But it is based on Internet architectural concepts. The use of REST in Internet systems is its most commonly seen interpretation, and the one the discussions in this chapter focus on.

It is possible to create a system using HTTP for data requests that are non-RESTful, meaning they do not adhere to REST principles. An example of this is a number of self-declared REST Web services that are not very RESTful.

REST is based on the concept of making software that interfaces to other systems much in the way humans use the Internet. This is accomplished through the use of a browser, but under this, exchanges take place using HTTP.

REST architecture has the following properties:

❑ *Client-server — based* — This allows for system needs to be demarcated across client and server subsystems. This can separate the user interface from data-storage issues, yielding greater interface portability. Another benefit is that the resulting server needs are not complicated by user interfaces, and this greater simplicity can lead to easier scalability and performance enhancement.

❑ *Stateless* — This simplifies storage needs as compared to stateful architectures. It means that each request must possess all of the necessary information. Clients must keep track of any state information. This again simplifies the server needs, which can result in easier scalability and performance enhancements. One disadvantage of stateless architectures is that there can be an increase in the information that is repeatedly sent in requests.

❑ *Cache-enabled* — The concept of a *cache* is the use of large banks of memory to store data. Compared to database retrievals, cache retrievals are significantly faster. The REST architecture calls for the inclusion of cache response constraints, which means that the response data must be labeled as either cacheable or *non-cacheable*. When the response data is labeled *cacheable*, the client may cache this and use it as a response for future requests. Advantages here are that future requests can be served directly from the client cache. The potential problem is that the cache data may be outdated.

❑ *Uniform interface* — This constrains all interfaces to be uniform between system components. This improves understandability and separates implementations from interfaces. To achieve uniform interfaces, REST uses constraints on resource identification, resource manipulation through representations, self-descriptive messages, and hypermedia (as the engine of application state).

A main concept within REST is a *resource*, which is defined by the following properties:

❑ A resource can represent application data, application state, or application function.

❑ A resource is addressed with a unique, universal syntax.

❑ A resource can be "transferred" using a uniform interface that includes a set of well-defined operations and a set of content types.

REST is a resource-oriented architecture. As you have just learned, a resource can represent not only a function but also a state and data. A request for a resource can be segmented into two parts:

❑ *Resource method request* — This represents the operation that is being requested on the remote server.

❑ *Resource scoping information* — This can include the data to operate on and/or directions about the part of the data to operate on.

Consider searching at Google (`http://google.com`) using a Web browser. When you type in a search for the term "RESTful," the browser is directed to the following URL request:

```
http://www.google.com/search?source=ig&hl=en&rlz=1G1GGLQ_ENUS279&=&q=
    RESTful&btnG=Google+Search.
```

In this case, the method information is requested by the HTTP GET method. The scoping information is search?source=ig&hl=en&rlz=1G1GGLQ_ENUS279&=&q=RESTful&btnG=Google+Search.

Let's look at using the Yahoo! (http://yahoo.com) search engine and search for "RESTful". The following URL request is created:

http://search.yahoo.com/search?p=RESTful&fr=yfp-t-501&toggle=1&cop=mss&ei=UTF-8

In this case, the method information is represented in the URL as http://search.yahoo.com/search and the scoping information is p=RESTful&fr=yfp-t-501&toggle=1&cop=mss&ei=UTF-8. This request also is using the HTTP GET method type.

There are some differences in the Google and Yahoo! approaches to a RESTful resource request in the placement of the method request and scoping information. Using a description of RESTful architectures by Leonard Richardson, Sam Ruby, and David Heinemeier Hansson in their book, *RESTful Web Services* (Sebastopol, California: O'Reilly Media, 2007), these differences are reflected in what they call a "RESTful architecture" or a "REST-RPC Hybrid architecture." For better understanding, both types of REST resource calls are detailed next. However, many people in industry consider both implementations simply RESTful.

Purely RESTful Architecture

In a "purely" RESTful architecture the resource method information is always specified by an HTTP method, including GET, PUT, POST, DELETE, and so on. At first, this may seem very limiting. However, consider the previous Google example where GET represents well the concept of search (or "give me").

The scoping information must be part of the URL and cannot be embedded in the body of the HTTP request (as is the case in SOAP and other RPC-based architectures).

RESTful-RPC Hybrid Architecture

In this case, the resource method is not represented by the HTTP method type. Rather, it is part of the scoping information and inserted in the URL.

Like the purely RESTful architecture, the scoping information is part of the URL, and cannot be embedded in the HTTP request.

Looking at an Example of REST

By definition, your REST program will be running on your own server. There are many programming languages that could be used to create a REST program. Typically, a Web-oriented language should be chosen. But there are many possibilities, including PHP, Python, Java, ASP, and more.

Listing 5-1 shows some simple PHP code that is a generic REST program. It uses the Client URL library (curl), an optional package in PHP. The curl library allows PHP programs to connect and communicate to servers via a number of protocols, including HTTP. It supports different HTTP method types, including GET, POST, and PUT.

Listing 5-1: Simple PHP REST Program Making a Request for an HTML Resource

```php
<?php
//REST resource requests via GET , resource is a static html
$ch = curl_init("http:UServer.com /test.html");

//leave options to have response go to standard output
curl_setopt($ch, CURLOPT_HEADER, 0);

//execute the REST request
curl_exec($ch);

//close the cURL session
curl_close($ch);
?>
```

For more information about the curl *library, see* http://us2.php.net/manual/en/book.curl.php.

Using curl, a simple unauthenticated REST request takes the following steps:

1. Build a REST request by initializing a curl session with a designated request URL.

2. Set up any options associated with the session (zero or more).

3. Execute the REST request.

4. Close the curl session.

In Listing 5-1, the first line of code, $ch = curl_init("URL"), initializes a curl session with the designated URL. This points to a static HTML page. The next thing needed is to set up the session with options. This can include setting the method type, which, by default, is GET. This is done in the second line of code with the curl_setopt function. Specifically, this line of code says to not include header information in the output. Finally, the REST request is executed through a curl_exec function call. Finally, the program ends the curl session through the curl_close function.

REST Resources

The following are good resources to expand your knowledge of REST:

❑ Roy Fielding, *Architectural Styles and the Design of Network-based Software Architectures*, University of California, Irvine, 2000. (http://www.ics.uci.edu/~fielding/pubs/dissertation/top.htm).

❑ Roy Fielding and Richard Taylor, "Principled Design of the Modern Web Architecture" (PDF), *ACM Transactions on Internet Technology* (TOIT) (New York: Association for Computing Machinery) 2(2): 115–150, 2002.

❑ C. Pautasso, O. Zimmermann, and F. Leymann, "RESTful Web Services vs. Big Web Services: Making the Right Architectural Decision." International World Wide Web Conference 2008 (Beijing, China).

OpenSocial RESTful Server-Side Programming

A server-side API like the OpenSocial REST API is important to have as a programming alternative to the client-side OpenSocial JavaScript API. As discussed in Chapter 2, these options can lead to different transactional models. During a discussion with Kevin Chou, CEO at Watercooler, a social network application development company, he stressed that Watercooler develops server-based applications because their applications are media-intensive. Using the OpenSocial REST API can make it easier to build such media-based applications.

Up to now, this book has concentrated on developing client-side applications using the OpenSocial JavaScript API. As you have learned, it is possible through the Gadget API (`makeRequest`) or through Ajax to invoke server-side programs and resources. Social network applications using server-side programs facilitate the following:

❑ *Access* — This means the capability for the program to execute on a developer's server, allowing access to other functionality and data (databases) on this server.

❑ *Performance* — This is improved performance, especially when dynamic content is developed.

❑ *Work in language of choice* — This means the capability to implement possibly more complex code bases in languages other than JavaScript that offer richer OOP and other functionalities.

Let's consider an example of a social network application that manages events and projects. Let's say that the application has a rich and large database in which to store information that each user creates and shares with fellow "friends/colleagues" through the application. Because of the type or amount of data (or simply for ownership), the developer will want to store this data in the developer's own database, rather than using the persistence feature of the OpenSocial JavaScript API.

However, this means that every time the application needs to get or alter data, the application must make requests to the external database. Database access is often a performance bottleneck for many Web systems. This is aggravated even more by the fact that the application must make these requests through the Web each time. If, instead, the application were server-based and resident on the same network as the database, these calls would be much less expensive. To further improve performance, the developer could employ caching schemes (such as `memcache`) that typically require programming languages beyond JavaScript. This is just one of the many scenarios that require server-based application programming.

In Chapter 2, you learned about different OpenSocial architectures, including two transactional models using the OpenSocial RESTful API: a "completely 'server-based' OpenSocial RESTful API application," and a "hybrid client/server OpenSocial social network application" (using both OpenSocial JavaScript and RESTful APIs).

Completely Server-Based OpenSocial RESTful API Application

There are two possible interpretations of what constitutes a "completely OpenSocial RESTful API application." One is where the client works with the application, and the interface is completely on an external Web site. This means that the social network is only used to get (or set) social data about the user. The user-application experience takes place (for the most part) outside of the social network, on the external Web site.

An example of this could be a "social data aggregator" application. This application takes social data from more than one social network and aggregates it for the user and application purpose. RockYou has created an external Web site that lets users experience this for a "slideshow" application. Figure 5-1 shows the RockYou slideshow application hosted on its Web site (`http://rockyou.com`). This application lets users access their photos stored on a number of social networks they may belong to.

Figure 5-1: RockYou slideshow application

Another possibility is where the "completely OpenSocial RESTful API application" has created new user social data updates, activities, or messages that appear inside the social network, in addition to possibly inside the external Web site. User social data, activities, and messages are visible in a social network outside of an application, through the main social network's user interface. The hypothetical Flixter example discussed in Chapter 2 is an example of this. Here, the server-side OpenSocial RESTful application posts to the user's social network activity stream information about a new movie rating the user did on the Flixster Web site.

The last kind of "completely OpenSocial RESTful API application" entails the serving of a social network application completely from the server side without any OpenSocial JavaScript. This transactional model is shown in Figure 5-2. This is currently not supported by social networks, but there is ongoing discussion in the OpenSocial community aimed at providing support for it. This model most reflects how application programming for Facebook is done.

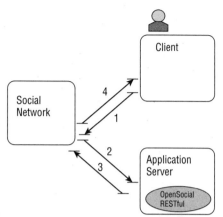

Figure 5-2: A "completely OpenSocial RESTful" social network application from the server

Hybrid OpenSocial JavaScript and RESTful API Application

Currently, to create a social network application that uses the RESTful API, it must be a "hybrid" OpenSocial application. This means that the OpenSocial JavaScript API must also be used to minimally create an XML gadget application that calls the external OpenSocial RESTful API application through a `gadgets.io.makeRequest` call. Currently, this is the only way the OpenSocial RESTful API can be used in an application deployed on a social network.

OpenSocial RESTful Application Architecture

Server-based applications can communicate directly with a social network (container) in a language-independent way using the OpenSocial RESTful API. It is not based on being a gadget but rather on how Web systems most often interact — through resource access and operations on them. More specifically, as a RESTful API, the OpenSocial REST API is defined on top of the HTTP protocol, and uses the standard HTTP methods (GET, POST, PUT, DELETE, and so on).

As shown in Figure 5-3, the architecture of an OpenSocial REST application can be broken into the following three main subcomponents:

❑ Authorization (or authentication, as shown in Figure 5-3)

❑ Discovery

❑ RESTful resource request and processing

Keep in mind that requests are coming from a server program not owned by the social network, and also (unlike the OpenSocial JavaScript application) are not invoked by the user directly. OpenSocial requires that the program go through a process of *authorization* (or *authentication*). Once completed, this allows the program to make secure OpenSocial REST requests directly to the social network container. Every request will have the appropriate authentication information associated with it. You will learn more about authorization and authentication shortly.

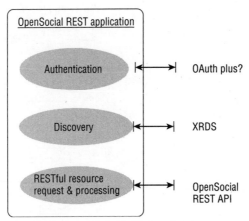

Figure 5-3: OpenSocial REST application components

Discovery is the process of the OpenSocial RESTful program detecting what services are offered by the social network. The OpenSocial REST API uses the Extensible Resource Descriptor Sequence (XRDS) protocol to convey this information. Generally speaking, XRDS is a form of XML used to discover resource information and metadata. A social network is required to declare which OpenSocial REST API features it supports via a discovery document formatted in XRDS-Simple, a constrained version of XRDS. The social network must provide developers with a URL to this document. Later, this chapter explains in detail the discovery process and provides an example.

The final component of an OpenSocial REST application is the use of the OpenSocial REST API to make REST resource calls. You have access to many of the same types of data seen in the OpenSocial JavaScript API. Later in this chapter, you will learn more about the API in detail and see some coding examples.

OpenSocial REST Authorization and Authentication (OAuth)

Authorization is the process of granting access to a resource — for example, the social network granting access to social data to an application. *Authentication* is the process of confirming the identity of an application, the container, or the user (or some combination thereof). When your OpenSocial REST application makes a request to the social network, application authorization is required, which involves a stage of application authentication. When these requests involve a user, user authentication is also required.

Most commonly, this involves the user first logging in to the social network and then providing a login and password. The application can then request an "authentication token" for this user. This can take place when the user launches the application. The application then will use this token when making requests.

Let's consider an example scenario where a Web site called "Print a Photo Album" allows a user to set up a photo album for printing. As part of this, the "Print a Photo Album" site provides the user with the capability to get photos from an album located on the MySpace container. To do this, the "Print a Photo Album" program uses an authorization and authentication protocol known as OAuth to request access from MySpace. The "Print a Photo Album" site redirects the user to the MySpace Web site, where the user logs in and confirms that the requested access is acceptable. MySpace then passes an OAuth token to the "Print a Photo Album" site, which can use this OAuth token for each request to MySpace.

OAuth was created for service providers that have Web APIs requiring authorization for some or all of its functions. For this example application, the social network is the *service provider*. In OAuth terminology, the application is called a *consumer*. For OAuth to be compliant with OAuth documentation, these OAuth terms will be used throughout the ensuing discussions.

OAuth has the following properties:

❑   It is secure for users.

❑   It is easy to implement.

❑   A consumer (application) does not have access to user passwords.

❑   It is Open Source.

❑   It provides optional OpenID support.

❑   A service provider (social network) can choose the type of authentication (that is, the encryption standard).

❑   It tests that the consumer (application) is in possession of a consumer secret and key, as well as a token and token secret.

> **OAuth does not offer the protection against eavesdropping that SSL does.**

OAuth Steps

Following are the steps followed by OAuth:

1.   The consumer asks the service provider for an "OAuth request token."

2.   The service provider returns an "OAuth request token."

3.   The consumer redirects the user to the service provider site with the "OAuth (unauthorized) request token." The user is now sent to the server provider "login" page, where the user logs in and grants access.

4.   The service provider redirects the user back to the consumer page with an "OAuth (authorized) request token."

5.   The consumer asks the service provider for "OAuth access token," giving the "OAuth (authorized) request token."

6.   The service provider takes the "OAuth (authorized) request token" and exchanges it for an "OAuth access token."

7.   The consumer stores the "OAuth access token" and uses it to make a request to the service provider for user-related resources. The service provider gets a request for user-related resources, validates the "OAuth Access Token," gets the user-related resources, and returns them. The consumer gets the user-related resources, stores them, and displays them for the user to use.

Figure 5-4 illustrates these steps.

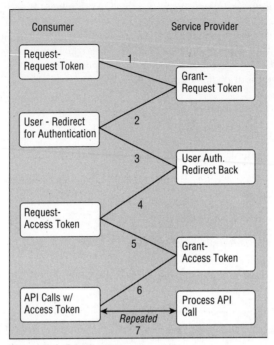

Figure 5-4: OAuth steps

As an example, let's specify the OAuth steps for the "Print a Photo Album" scenario:

1. "Print a Photo Album" (the consumer) sends a POST request to the MySpace (the service provider) URL for an "OAuth request token." As part of this request, "Print a Photo Album" sends its shared secret key.

2. MySpace returns an "OAuth (unauthorized) request token."

3. "Print a Photo Album" redirects the user to the MySpace authorization interface. The user logs in to MySpace and grants "Print a Photo Album" access to use its photos.

4. MySpace redirects the user back to "Print a Photo Album" with an "OAuth (authorized) request token."

5. "Print a Photo Album" receives the "OAuth (authorized) request token" and asks Myspace for an "OAuth access token," passing the "OAuth (authorized) request token."

6. MySpace takes the "OAuth (authorized) request token," creates an "OAuth access token," and returns it.

7. "Print a Photo Album" gets and stores the "OAuth access token." Then it requests access to the user's photos on MySpace, sending the "OAuth Access Token" with the request. MySpace gets the request for user's photos, validates the "OAuth access token," gets the user's photos, and returns them. "Print a Photo Album" gets the user's photos, stores them, and displays them for user selection in the photo-album-building process.

OAuth Parameters

Following are the parameters in OAuth, along with their meanings:

❑ oauth_consumer_key — This is assigned during consumer (application) registration by the service provider (social network) and is used to identify a consumer.

❑ oauth_token — This is given by the service provider, and represents both request and access type tokens.

❑ oauth_token_secret — This is given by the service provider, and is used for both request and access tokens.

❑ oauth_signature — All requests from the consumer to the service provider must be signed using the oauth_signature_method. This is the actual resulting signature. The signature will be verified by the service provider.

❑ oauth_signature_method — This specifies the signature protocol the consumer selected from the set the service provider stipulated.

❑ oauth_timestamp — This gives the time, typically specified as the number of seconds since January 1, 1970, 00:00:00 GMT.

❑ oauth_nonce — This is a random string used to uniquely identify a request with a given timestamp.

❑ oauth_version — This is the version of OAuth.

The following parameter is optional (but typical):

❑ oauth_consumer_secret — This is assigned during consumer registration by the service provider, and is used to identify a consumer.

All parameters are encoded via URL encoding (also called *percent encoding*).

OAuth Requests

Following are the four basic requests in OAuth that a consumer (application) makes to a service provider (social network). When making a request, the consumer must create a signature to be stored in oauth_signature that is sent with the other request information. (The signing process is discussed in the next section.)

1. Initial (unauthorized) request token request

   ❑ The request contains the parameters oauth_consumer_key, oauth_signature_method, oauth_signature, oauth_timestamp, oauth_nonce, and oauth_version (optional).

   ❑ The signature uses the parameters oauth_consumer_key and oauth_consumer_secret.

2. Authorized request token request via user authorization

   ❑ This is the HTTP GET request to the service provider's user authorization URL.

   ❑ The request contains the parameters oauth_token and oauth_callback.

179

3. Access token request giving the authorized request token

- ❑ The request contains the parameters `oauth_consumer_key`, `oauth_token`, `oauth_signature_method`, `oauth_signature`, `oauth_timestamp`, `oauth_nonce`, and `oauth_version` (optional).

- ❑ The signature uses the parameters `oauth_token_secret` (from authorized request token), `auth_consumer_key`, and `oauth_consumer_secret`.

4. API (REST) request using access token

- ❑ The request contains the parameters `oauth_consumer_key`, `oauth_token`, `oauth_signature_method`, `oauth_signature`, `oauth_timestamp`, `oauth_nonce`, and `oauth_version` (optional).

- ❑ The signature uses `oauth_token_secret` (from the access token), `auth_consumer_key`, and `oauth_consumer_secret`.

All of the OAuth request parameters can be sent in one of the following ways:

- ❑ *Via an HTTP authorization header* — Use URL encoding for names and values, separated by = with each name/value pair separated by a comma. Following is an example:

```
Authorization: OAuth realm="http://sp.example.com/",
        oauth_consumer_key="0685bd9184jfhq22",
        oauth_token="ad180jjd733klru7",
        oauth_signature_method="HMAC-SHA1",
        oauth_signature="wOJIO9A2W5mFwDgiDvZbTSMK%2FPY%3D",
        oauth_timestamp="137131200",
        oauth_nonce="4572616e48616d6d65724c61686176",
        oauth_version="1.0"
```

- ❑ *Via an HTTP* POST *request body parameters* — This is done with `content-type=application/x-www-form-urlencoded`.

- ❑ *Via a parameters added to URL query* — Append to the URL query the name/value pairs separated by `&`.

OAuth Signing Requests

Every request from the consumer to the service provider must be signed. This involves the encoding of the `oauth_consumer_secret` and `oauth_token_secret` (when it exists) parameters together. The service provider stipulates the signature method(s) that it supports, and the consumer must use one from this set.

OAuth defines the support of HMAC-SHA1, RSA-SHA1, and plain text as signature methods that can be used. The service provider typically chooses to support one or all of these methods. However, the OAuth protocol does allow service providers to implement their own methods.

The signature method that is being used is represented in the `oauth_signature_method` parameter. The many OAuth libraries provide support for creating signatures using all three of the OAuth-supported signature methods (HMAC-SHA1, RSA-SHA1, and plain text). Once the consumer has produced a signature, it will be stored in the `oauth_signature` parameter.

OAuth Tokens (the Response)

The service provider will return an HTTP response when the consumer requests a token. The token information is sent in the HTTP response body. The parameters are `oauth_token` and `oauth_token_secret`. Here is an example:

```
oauth_token=ab3cd9j4ks73hf7g&oauth_token_secret=xyz4992k83j47x0b
```

OAuth in PHP

This section covers OAuth in PHP. This library is provided free for use from Andy Smith, and can be found at `http://oauth.googlecode.com/svn/code/php`. This section details the classes in this library, and their uses.

OAuthConsumer

This class is used to create a representation of the consumer. Listing 5-2 shows how its constructor takes as its first two parameters `oauth_consumer_key` and `consumer_secret`, which were assigned when the application was registered with the service provider. The third parameter of the constructor is the callback URL of the application, given during registration.

Listing 5-2: OAuthConsumer Class

```
class OAuthConsumer {/*{{{*/
  public $key;
  public $secret;

  function __construct($key, $secret, $callback_url=NULL) {/*{{{*/
    $this->key = $key;
    $this->secret = $secret;
    $this->callback_url = $callback_url;
  }/*}}}*/
}/*}}}*/
```

OAuthToken

This class is used to represent both request and access tokens. The actual token is represented by the key variable and its secret (the `oauth_token_secret`) by the secret variable. The constructor takes the key and secret as parameter values. The only methods for this class involve getting a string containing the token value and its secret. Listing 5-3 shows the code for the `OAuthToken` class.

Listing 5-3: OAuthToken Class

```
class OAuthToken {/*{{{*/
  // access tokens and request tokens
  public $key;
  public $secret;
```

Continued

181

Listing 5-3: OAuthToken Class *(continued)*

```
/**
 * key = the token
 * secret = the token secret
 */
function __construct($key, $secret) {/*{{{*/
  $this->key = $key;
  $this->secret = $secret;
}/*}}}*/

/**
 * generates the basic string serialization of a token that a server
 * would respond to request_token and access_token calls with
 */
function to_string() {/*{{{*/
  return "oauth_token=" . OAuthUtil::urlencodeRFC3986($this->key) .
      "&oauth_token_secret=" . OAuthUtil::urlencodeRFC3986($this->secret);
}/*}}}*/

function __toString() {/*{{{*/
  return $this->to_string();
}/*}}}*/
}/*}}}*/
```

OAuthRequest

This class represents an OAuth request. This class contains the private data elements of an HTTP URL, method type (GET, PUT, POST), and request parameters. This class has a number of methods, including the following:

- ❏ _construct — This is the constructor method and takes the request method type, URL, and parameters.

- ❏ from_request — This method creates a new request based on your server configurations (for example, whether you are using HTTP or HTTPS protocols). The newly created request (an instance of the OAuthRequest) is returned from this function.

- ❏ set_parameter — This sets a parameter in the request.

- ❏ get_parameter — This retrieves a parameter in the request.

- ❏ get_signature_base_string — This returns the request as a string comprising the URL and parameters with request method type. Each parameter is URL-encoded and chained together with &.

- ❏ to_postdata — This constructs the parameters as POST data.

- ❏ sign_request — This creates the oauth_signature_method and oauth_signature parameter values.

- ❏ generate_nonce — Creates and returns a nonce value. (*Nonce* is a random string, unique for a timestamp.)

Listing 5-4 shows the code for the OAuthRequest class.

Listing 5-4: OAuthRequest Class

```php
class OAuthRequest {/*{{{*/
  private $parameters;
  private $http_method;
  private $http_url;
  // for debug purposes
  public $base_string;
  public static $version = '1.0';

  function __construct($http_method, $http_url, $parameters=NULL) {/*{{{*/
    @$parameters or $parameters = array();
    $this->parameters = $parameters;
    $this->http_method = $http_method;
    $this->http_url = $http_url;
  }/*}}}*/


  /**
   * attempt to build up a request from what was passed to the server
   */
  public static function from_request($http_method=NULL, $http_url=NULL,
                                      $parameters=NULL) {/*{{{*/
    $scheme = (!isset($_SERVER['HTTPS']) || $_SERVER['HTTPS'] != "on") ?
              'http' : 'https';
    @$http_url or $http_url = $scheme . '://' . $_SERVER['HTTP_HOST'] .
                             $_SERVER['REQUEST_URI'];
    @$http_method or $http_method = $_SERVER['REQUEST_METHOD'];

    $request_headers = OAuthRequest::get_headers();

    // let the library user override things however they'd like, if they
    // know which parameters to use then go for it, for example
    // XMLRPC might want to do this
    if ($parameters) {
      $req = new OAuthRequest($http_method, $http_url, $parameters);
    }
    // next check for the auth header, we need to do some extra stuff
    // if that is the case, namely suck in the parameters from GET or POST
    // so that we can include them in the signature
    else if (@substr($request_headers['Authorization'], 0, 5) == "OAuth") {
      $header_parameters =
                OAuthRequest::split_header($request_headers['Authorization']);
      if ($http_method == "GET") {
        $req_parameters = $_GET;
      }
      else if ($http_method = "POST") {
        $req_parameters = $_POST;
      }
      $parameters = array_merge($header_parameters, $req_parameters);
      $req = new OAuthRequest($http_method, $http_url, $parameters);
    }
    else if ($http_method == "GET") {
```

Continued

Listing 5-4: OAuthRequest Class *(continued)*

```
      $req = new OAuthRequest($http_method, $http_url, $_GET);
    }
    else if ($http_method == "POST") {
      $req = new OAuthRequest($http_method, $http_url, $_POST);
    }
    return $req;
}/*}}}*/

/**
 * pretty much a helper function to set up the request
 */
public static function from_consumer_and_token($consumer, $token,
         $http_method, $http_url, $parameters=NULL) {/*{{{*/
  @$parameters or $parameters = array();
  $defaults = array("oauth_version" => OAuthRequest::$version,
                    "oauth_nonce" => OAuthRequest::generate_nonce(),
                    "oauth_timestamp" => OAuthRequest::generate_timestamp(),
                    "oauth_consumer_key" => $consumer->key);
  $parameters = array_merge($defaults, $parameters);

  if ($token) {
    $parameters['oauth_token'] = $token->key;
  }
  return new OAuthRequest($http_method, $http_url, $parameters);
}/*}}}*/

public function set_parameter($name, $value) {/*{{{*/
  $this->parameters[$name] = $value;
}/*}}}*/

public function get_parameter($name) {/*{{{*/
  return $this->parameters[$name];
}/*}}}*/

public function get_parameters() {/*{{{*/
  return $this->parameters;
}/*}}}*/

/**
 * Returns the normalized parameters of the request
 *
 * This will be all (except oauth_signature) parameters,
 * sorted first by key, and if duplicate keys, then by
 * value.
 *
 * The returned string will be all the key=value pairs
 * concated by &.
 *
 * @return string
 */
public function get_signable_parameters() {/*{{{*/
  // Grab all parameters
  $params = $this->parameters;
```

```php
  // Remove oauth_signature if present
  if (isset($params['oauth_signature'])) {
    unset($params['oauth_signature']);
  }

  // Urlencode both keys and values
  $keys = array_map(array('OAuthUtil', 'urlencodeRFC3986'),
                    array_keys($params));
  $values = array_map(array('OAuthUtil', 'urlencodeRFC3986'),
                    array_values($params));
  $params = array_combine($keys, $values);

  // Sort by keys (natsort)
  uksort($params, 'strnatcmp');

  // Generate key=value pairs
  $pairs = array();
  foreach ($params as $key=>$value ) {
    if (is_array($value)) {
      // If the value is an array, it's because there are multiple
      // with the same key, sort them, then add all the pairs
      natsort($value);
      foreach ($value as $v2) {
        $pairs[] = $key . '=' . $v2;
      }
    } else {
      $pairs[] = $key . '=' . $value;
    }
  }

  // Return the pairs, concated with &
  return implode('&', $pairs);
}/*}}}*/

/**
 * Returns the base string of this request
 *
 * The base string defined as the method, the URL
 * and the parameters (normalized), each url-encoded
 * and the concated with &.
 */
public function get_signature_base_string() {/*{{{*/
  $parts = array(
    $this->get_normalized_http_method(),
    $this->get_normalized_http_url(),
    $this->get_signable_parameters()
  );

  $parts = array_map(array('OAuthUtil', 'urlencodeRFC3986'), $parts);

  return implode('&', $parts);
}/*}}}*/

/**
```

Continued

Listing 5-4: OAuthRequest Class *(continued)*

```
     * just uppercases the http method
     */
    public function get_normalized_http_method() {/*{{{*/
      return strtoupper($this->http_method);
    }/*}}}*/

    /**
     * parses the url and rebuilds it to be
     * scheme://host/path
     */
    public function get_normalized_http_url() {/*{{{*/
      $parts = parse_url($this->http_url);

      // FIXME: port should handle according to
      // http://groups.google.com/group/
      // oauth/browse_thread/thread/1b203a51d9590226
      $port = (isset($parts['port']) && $parts['port'] != '80') ? ':' .
               $parts['port'] : '';
      $path = (isset($parts['path'])) ? $parts['path'] : '';

      return $parts['scheme'] . '://' . $parts['host'] . $port . $path;
    }/*}}}*/

    /**
     * builds a url usable for a GET request
     */
    public function to_url() {/*{{{*/
      $out = $this->get_normalized_http_url() . "?";
      $out .= $this->to_postdata();
      return $out;
    }/*}}}*/

    /**
     * builds the data one would send in a POST request
     */
    public function to_postdata() {/*{{{*/
      $total = array();
      foreach ($this->parameters as $k => $v) {
        $total[] = OAuthUtil::urlencodeRFC3986($k) . "=" .
                   OAuthUtil::urlencodeRFC3986($v);
      }
      $out = implode("&", $total);
      return $out;
    }/*}}}*/

    /**
     * builds the Authorization: header
     */
    public function to_header() {/*{{{*/
      $out ='"Authorization: OAuth realm="",';
      $total = array();
      foreach ($this->parameters as $k => $v) {
        if (substr($k, 0, 5) != "oauth") continue;
```

```
      $out .= ',' . OAuthUtil::urlencodeRFC3986($k) . '="' .
             OAuthUtil::urlencodeRFC3986($v) . '"';
  }
  return $out;
}/*}}}*/


public function __toString() {/*{{{*/
  return $this->to_url();
}/*}}}*/


public function sign_request($signature_method, $consumer,
       $token) {/*{{{*/
  $this->set_parameter("oauth_signature_method",
       $signature_method->get_name());
  $signature = $this->build_signature($signature_method,
       $consumer, $token);
  $this->set_parameter("oauth_signature", $signature);
}/*}}}*/


public function build_signature($signature_method,
     $consumer, $token) {/*{{{*/
  $signature = $signature_method->build_signature($this,
     $consumer, $token);
  return $signature;
}/*}}}*/


/**
 * util function: current timestamp
 */
private static function generate_timestamp() {/*{{{*/
  return time();
}/*}}}*/


/**
 * util function: current nonce
 */
private static function generate_nonce() {/*{{{*/
  $mt = microtime();
  $rand = mt_rand();

  return md5($mt . $rand); // md5s look nicer than numbers
}/*}}}*/


/**
 * util function for turning the Authorization: header into
 * parameters, has to do some unescaping
 */
private static function split_header($header) {/*{{{*/
  // this should be a regex
  // error cases: commas in parameter values
  $parts = explode(",", $header);
  $out = array();
  foreach ($parts as $param) {
```

Continued

Listing 5-4: OAuthRequest Class *(continued)*

```
            $param = ltrim($param);
            // skip the "realm" param, nobody ever uses it anyway
            if (substr($param, 0, 5) != "oauth") continue;

            $param_parts = explode("=", $param);

            // rawurldecode() used because urldecode() will turn a "+" in the
            // value into a space
            $out[$param_parts[0]] = rawurldecode(substr($param_parts[1], 1, -1));
        }
        return $out;
    }/*}}}*/

    /**
     * helper to try to sort out headers for people
     * who aren't running apache
     */
    private static function get_headers() {/*{{{*/
        if (function_exists('apache_request_headers')) {
            // we need this to get the actual Authorization: header
            // because Apache tends to tell us it doesn't exist
            return apache_request_headers();
        }
        // otherwise we don't have apache and are just going to have to hope
        // that $_SERVER actually contains what we need
        $out = array();
        foreach ($_SERVER as $key => $value) {
            if (substr($key, 0, 5) == "HTTP_") {
                // this is chaos, basically it is just there to capitalize the first
                // letter of every word that is not an initial HTTP and strip HTTP
                // code from przemek
                $key = str_replace(" ", "-", ucwords(strtolower(str_replace("_", " ",
                        substr($key, 5)))));
                $out[$key] = $value;
            }
        }
        return $out;
    }/*}}}*/
}/*}}}*/
```

OAuthSignatureMethod

This is the base class used to check a signature. The single method of this class is `check_signature`, which takes the following parameters:

- ❑ `$request` — This is an instance of the `OAuthRequest` class.

- ❑ `$consumer` — This is an instance of the `OAuthConsumer` class.

- ❑ `$token` — This is an instance of the `OAuthToken` class.

- ❑ `$signature` — This a string representing a signature.

Listing 5-5 shows this class.

Listing 5-5: OAuthSignatureMethod Class

```
class OAuthSignatureMethod {/*{{{*/
  public function check_signature(&$request, $consumer, $token, $signature) {
    $built = $this->build_signature($request, $consumer, $token);
    return $built == $signature;
  }
}/*}}}*/
```

From this class, subclasses are generated that implement specific signature methods such as HMAC-SHA1 or RSA-SHA1. The RSA-SHA1 subclass is shown in Listing 5-6.

Listing 5-6: OAuthSignatureMethod_RSA_SHA1

```
class OAuthSignatureMethod_RSA_SHA1 extends OAuthSignatureMethod {/*{{{*/
  public function get_name() {/*{{{*/
    return "RSA-SHA1";
  }/*}}}*/

  protected function fetch_public_cert(&$request) {/*{{{*/
    // not implemented yet, ideas are:
    // (1) do a lookup in a table of trusted certs keyed off of consumer
    // (2) fetch via http using a url provided by the requester
    // (3) some sort of specific discovery code based on request
    //
    // either way should return a string representation of the certificate
    throw Exception("fetch_public_cert not implemented");
  }/*}}}*/

  protected function fetch_private_cert(&$request) {/*{{{*/
    // not implemented yet, ideas are:
    // (1) do a lookup in a table of trusted certs keyed off of consumer
    //
    // either way should return a string representation of the certificate
    throw Exception("fetch_private_cert not implemented");
  }/*}}}*/

  public function build_signature(&$request, $consumer, $token) {/*{{{*/
    $base_string = $request->get_signature_base_string();

    // Fetch the private key cert based on the request
    $cert = $this->fetch_private_cert($request);

    //Pull the private key ID from the certificate
    $privatekeyid = openssl_get_privatekey($cert);

    //Check the computer signature against the one passed in the query
    $ok = openssl_sign($base_string, $signature, $privatekeyid);

    //Release the key resource
```

Continued

Listing 5-6: OAuthSignatureMethod_RSA_SHA1 *(continued)*

```
        openssl_free_key($privatekeyid);

        return base64_encode($signature);
    } /*}}}*/

    public function check_signature(&$request, $consumer, $token,
            $signature) {/*{{{*/
        $decoded_sig = base64_decode($signature);

        $base_string = $request->get_signature_base_string();

        // Fetch the public key cert based on the request
        $cert = $this->fetch_public_cert($request);

        //Pull the public key ID from the certificate
        $publickeyid = openssl_get_publickey($cert);

        //Check the computer signature against the one passed in the query
        $ok = openssl_verify($base_string, $decoded_sig, $publickeyid);

        //Release the key resource
        openssl_free_key($publickeyid);

        return $ok == 1;
    } /*}}}*/
}/*}}}*/
```

This class signs requests with the application's RSA private key and the signature base string. Verification of a signature is done with the application's RSA public key. The signature base string is constructed by joining (with an &) the HTTP request method type with the URL, the normalized request parameters shortened by name.

The class in this listing is an "interface" class that is meant to be extended. Methods that currently throw exceptions should be overridden. This class has the following methods defined:

❑   `fetch_public_cert` — This method should be overridden, and should retrieve the service provider's public certificate. Note that these certificates can change, and the developer must appropriately update this information.

❑   `fetch_public_cert` — This method should be overridden, and should retrieve the service provider's private certificate.

❑   `build_signature` — This method creates a signature using the RSA methodology.

❑   `check_signature` — This method checks the validity of the signature passed in the request.

OAuth PHP Example

To better understand the process involved in OAuth, let's look at an example application using OAuth. The following test code gets a request token. With this token, it then requests and gets an access token. It then finally makes an API request using this access token. The steps in this program are as follows:

1. Create instances of OAuthConsumer.

2. Set up signature method type.

3. Create instance of OAuthRequest to serve as a request from this consumer to the service provider to ask for a request token.

4. From OAuthRequest, generate a URL and use it to make an HTTP request; using HTTPRequest, make the request.

5. Get the response from the service provider and parse it to get the oauth_token and oauth_token_secret data representing the request token. Create an instance of the OAuthToken class using this data.

6. Redirect the user to the service provider "user authorization endpoint" URL, passing the parameters of oauth_token and oauth_callback.

7. Get back from server the authorized oauth_token.

8. Request an access token.

9. Use the access token to make API calls.

Note that an "endpoint URL" represents the URL address of a resource.

Listing 5-7 shows this example code, which is a modification of the code found at http://oauth .googlecode.com/svn/code/php/example/, and is free for use.

Listing 5-7: Simple PHP Test Program That Exercises OAuth

```php
<?php
  require_once("common.inc.php");
  $access_token, $request_token;
  $sig_methods = array();

  //URL endpoints
  $base_url = "http://api.msyspace.com";
  $request_token_url="http://api.myspace.com/request_token";
  $access_token_url="http://api.myspace.com/access_token";
  $user_authorize_url ="http://api.myspace.com/authorize";

  //consumer key and secret
  $key = "http://www.myspace.com/426949207";  //myspace assigned
                                              //when registered
  $secret = "1eb60898a9fa435683f34413ebe079e6";

  //if request has token info grab it.
  $token = @$_GET['oauth_token'];
  $token_secret = @$_GET['oauth_token_secret'];


  //Step 1 - create consumer
  $test_consumer = new OAuthConsumer($key, $secret, NULL);

  //Step 2 - initialize signature method
```

Continued

Listing 5-7: Simple PHP Test Program That Exercises OAuth *(continued)*

```php
$sig_method = new OAuthSignatureMethod_HMAC_SHA1();

//program called with different options
$option = @$_GET['select'];

//Option can be to request a request_token or  access_token or
//  access_token with option specifying the token_secret
if($option == "request_token")
 { //Step 3&4
    $url = generate_token('http://api.myspace.com/request_token', $token,
                          $token_secret);
    $response = make_request($url);
    //Step 5 - get token
    get_token_from_response($response);
    //Step 6 - redirect user to get authorized token
    //should return to this program with the option of "access_token"
    redirect_user($token, $token_secret, $user_authorize_url);
 }
else
 {  //Step 7 - this is where the callback from
    //User Authorization will come
    $token_secret = urldecode($option);
    //Step 8 - request access token
    $url = generate_token('http://api.myspace.com/access_token', $token,
          $token_secret);
    $response = make_request($url);

    get_token_from_response($response);

    //generate access token object
    $acc_token = new OAuthToken($token, $token_secret);

    //Step 9 - create YOUR REST API calls, URL and Method ($url, $meth)
    makeAPI_calls($acc_token, $url, $meth);
 }



//general function that request a token at the url $req_url, passing
// for the request of an authorized token the already existing
// unauthorized token of $token and $token_secret
function generate_token($req_url, $token, $token_secret) {

    global $key,$secret;
    $consumer = new OAuthConsumer($key, $secret, NULL);
    $oAuthtoken = new OAuthToken($token, $token_secret);

    $request = new OAuthRequest('GET',$req_url, NULL);
    $request = $request->from_consumer_and_token($consumer,$oAuthtoken,
                                        'GET',$req_url,NULL);

    $signature = new OAuthSignatureMethod_HMAC_SHA1($request,
                                        $consumer, $oAuthtoken);
```

```php
    $request->sign_request($signature, $consumer, $oAuthtoken);
    $url_for_token = $request->to_url(); /* The actual URL
                                            to get a token */
    return $url_for_token;
}


//Utility function to make a request to $url and return response
function make_request($url)
{
    $request =& new HTTP_Request($url);
    if(!PEAR::isError($request->sendRequest())) {
        $response = $request->getResponseBody();
    }
    else { $response="error: ".$request->getResponseCode(); }

    return $response;
}


//function to parse $response to get token and its secret
// store them in the global variables of $token and $token_secret
function get_token_from_response($response)
{
    //response in url-encoded format oauth_token=
    // XXX&oauth_token_secret=YYYY get the token from response
    $arr = split("&", urldecode($response));
    $a = split("=", $arr[0],2);
    $token = $a[1];
    //get the token secret from response
    $a = split("=", $arr[1],2);
    $token_secret = $a[1];
}


//function to redirect to user authenticaton endpoing $url
// passing in the unauthorized token and callbackURL (with token_secret as
//option).
function redirect_user($token, $token_secret, $url) {
    //STEP 6 - redirect user to server provider's
    //user authentication endpoint
    $url = $url."?oauth_token=".urlencode($token);
    $url = $url.
            "&oauth_callback=http://U.com/
            thisprogram.php?select=".urlencode($token_secret);

    $delay = "0"; // 0 second delay

    echo '<meta http-equiv="refresh" content="'.$delay.';url='.$url.'">';
}

//function to make API calls using access token $acc_token to REST URL $url,
//method i type is $meth
function makeAPI_calls($acc_token, $url, $meth)
```

Continued

Listing 5-7: Simple PHP Test Program That Exercises OAuth (continued)

```php
{
    //MYSPACE ReST call for user
    $consumer = new OAuthConsumer($key, $secret, NULL);

    //Configure restdd

    $api_call = OAuthRequest::from_consumer_and_token($consumer,
                                    $acc_token, $meth, $url);

    $signature = new OAuthSignatureMethod_HMAC_SHA1($api_call,
                                    $consumer, $acc_token);

    $api_call->sign_request($signature, $consumer, $acc_token);

    //Step 10 - make API call request using access token,
    //uses PHP cURL library
    $url = $api_call->to_url();
    $response = make_request($url);

    //process the result as you wish
    print($response);
}
?>
```

Following are the URLs constructed for the main OAuth requests that result from running the code in Listing 5-7 on MySpace, which supports the use of OAuth for its proprietary REST API.

Note that the following URLs should appear all on one line.

1. *Request token request (initial):*

```
http://api.msyspace.com/
    request_token?oauth_version=
    1.0&oauth_nonce=27a0b5b24ecadf1546155fec809d1ad1&oauth_timestamp=
    1225775995&oauth_consumer_key=http%3A%2F%2Fwww.myspace.com%2F426949207
    &oauth_signature_method=HMAC-SHA1&oauth_signature=
    awDDBhRIwy22fJ73PmaW%2BhpKvL8%3D
```

2. *Response (raw) from Step 1:*

```
oauth_token=0WNpJ2xudna2Wut8jXSj2ZJPunaA0aZUg4v%2Frviy
    CGipJiDyHZCN3FXMhy59fTWNb3x5KfyPhF0GW8rC0zzqvg%3D%3D
    &oauth_token_secret=
    0f77234a29c5473fb00d07aa5cff59f6
```

3. *Authorized request token request via redirection to user authorization URL:*

```
http://api.myspace.com/request_token?oauth_version=1.0&oauth_nonce=
    d41d3ae96f7101133c8d4e75245591e4&oauth_timestamp=
    1226193187&oauth_consumer_key=
    http%3A%2F%2Fwww.myspace.com%2F426949207&oauth_token=
    lOOJsEcD9IWxzFb5%2Fw52v0J606CLICLjIsNrtv15x7gN%2FOuyqSLtv5Wi5
```

```
AuOvA871wzPl4dikMn7Mv6nixU24A%3D%3D&oauth_signature_method=
HMAC-SHA1&oauth_signature=8p%2Bc6fW4tQs7nLbRD0RVpEBQqu0%3D
```

4. *Access token request*:

```
http://api.myspace.com/access_token?oauth_version=1.0&oauth_nonce=
    cf5e944f330c16dd5af230720924efd4&oauth_timestamp=
    1226218131&oauth_consumer_key=
    http%3A%2F%2Fwww.myspace.com%2F426949207&oauth_token=
    EZSx7EdynZlxK5kwQgb9kLxyYobqz70Vok2aGScLEHqlTcQBWIfi
    TzTpRnLKNm%2B919RqP9DAFe593zPG4MT9mw%3D%3D&oauth_signature_method=
    HMAC-SHA1&oauth_signature=MrGBV9nfTa2bZJbXG0TYlWkyK6I%3D
```

5. *Response (raw) from Step 4*:

```
oauth_token=hW0aVH6hVNbz8AQqq0C3vSAj8KiD8dQAemMh%2Fse
    Kuxk6gShqeQSneerEwSzpZSjPyTnm23gFgEmjmUus5k2YMsGiydh
    EY0pz4Ku00RfEVZ8%3D&oauth_token_secret=
    bb485134af3e4507be9f3e37c3ed6600
```

HTTP Errors

When a service provider responds to OAuth requests, a number of HTTP errors are possible. Understanding them and having the application respond appropriately is important. Here are few of the possible HTTP errors and their meanings:

❑ *400: Bad Request* — Causes for this error include unsupported parameter(s), missing required parameters, an unsupported signature method, or a duplicate OAuth parameter.

❑ *401: Unauthorized* — Causes for this error include an invalid token, an expired token, an unauthorized request token, an invalid consumer key, a signature that doesn't match, an invalid nonce, or a used nonce.

❑ *404: Not Found* — Causes for this error include an invalid URL used for making the request.

❑ *405: Method Not Allowed* — This means this method is not allowed.

OpenID

OpenID is a protocol developed for the creation of a single ID for a user that can be used on multiple Web sites. The use of OpenID is supported in OAuth as an optional feature.

See `http://openid.net` *for further details.*

Key Cache and Token Management

Managing tokens is also important. Both request and access tokens granted to an application will have an expiration time. A typical lifetime is 24 hours. This means that you can cache and use this token for up to 24 hours. Rewriting your code to first look in the cache for a token associated with a user, and only going through the OAuth process when the token is expired, can be more efficient. You can store in the cache the expiration information for each token. However, when using cached tokens, the application should always handle exceptions of the token being expired, and consequently request a new token.

See `http://blog.springenwerk.com/2008/04/poor-man-php-key-cache-for-orkut-oauth`
`.html` *for sample code that implements a simple key cache.*

OAuth Libraries

To use OAuth, you must get the library for the programming language you are using. The first site to check out is `http://oauth.net/code`. Current language support can be found at the following:

- ❏ *C#* — `http://oauth.googlecode.com/svn/code/csharp`
- ❏ *ColdFusion* — `http://oauth.googlecode.com/svn/code/coldfusion`
- ❏ *Java* — `http://oauth.googlecode.com/svn/code/java/core`
- ❏ *JavaScript* — `http://oauth.googlecode.com/svn/code/javascript`
- ❏ *.NET* — `http://code.google.com/p/oauth-dot-net`
- ❏ *Perl* — `http://oauth.googlecode.com/svn/code/php`
- ❏ *PHP* — `http://oauth.googlecode.com/svn/code/php`
- ❏ *Python* — `http://oauth.googlecode.com/svn/code/python/oauth`
- ❏ *Ruby* — `http://oauth.rubyforge.org`

What You Need

To incorporate OAuth into your OpenSocial REST API, you need the following:

- ❏ The OAuth library for your programming language
- ❏ The authorization URLs provided by the service provider, and information on authorization options that includes the following:

    - ❏ The user authorization endpoint
    - ❏ The request token endpoint
    - ❏ The access token endpoint
    - ❏ The accepted request methods (GET, POST, PUT)
    - ❏ The signature method(s)
    - ❏ The specification of any OAuth-extended parameters (not part of OAuth, but required or optional parameters specified by the service provider)
    - ❏ The specification of request and access token expirations

You must register your application with the service provider. This typically involves minimally specifying a callback URL for the application, a description, and a developer email address. In return, you should get the `oauth_consumer_key` and `oauth_consumer_secret`.

hi5 Authentication Scheme

Currently, the only social network that supports OpenSocial REST is hi5, although orkut is about to release its support. Unfortunately, hi5 is not completely compliant in that it does not use OAuth as its

API and user authorization/authentication protocol. Instead, it uses its own proprietary scheme. This section discusses how to use this scheme. hi5 developer contacts have indicated that they have plans to support OAuth in the near future.

> **Check hi5's developer forum to see what authentication protocol it is currently supporting before using the code in this section.**

hi5 has a simpler scheme than the OAuth protocol. There is no signing of requests. Simply, an application must request a token for use. This token should be passed as the `Hi5AuthToken` parameter value in all subsequent OpenSocial REST calls. The token expires in one day, except for notifications, where it is good for four hours of use.

Following are the steps for the hi5 scheme:

1. For the `Hi5AuthToken` request, you must provide API key (assigned by hi5 when the application is registered), a username (the login of the user), and a password (the password of the user). This will typically involve a user login process. The endpoint is `http://api.hi5.com/auth/plain`. You must also make a `POST` request.

2. For the OpenSocial REST request, you must pass the `Hi5AuthTokenRequest` parameter.

Following is some example code in PHP:

```php
<?php
//requests via GET the user data
$ch = curl_init("http://api.hi5.com/social/rest/people/
    291445554/@self?format=xm
l&Hi5AuthToken=od3sA9cGSsXsPDYPx9_mlw..
    :PCb4L2uyjnWKDSzOGQ3-pCjycmaZ_OShH__SayUP
IDaMOFtxkstdnKxL0FrZ3hdeqgdwUGBDRS1a-2CCLnRuj-UG3qplZgNgQE4LU6JB8ak.");
$fp = fopen("hi5.txt", "w");

curl_setopt($ch, CURLOPT_FILE, $fp);
curl_setopt($ch, CURLOPT_HEADER, 0);

curl_exec($ch);
curl_close($ch);
fclose($fp);
?>
```

Execution of this code will yield the resulting response (when I am the user and it is formatted for readability):

```
<response>
<empty>false</empty>
<entry>
  <key>entry</key>
  <value>
    <accounts/><activities/><addresses/><books/><cars/>
```

```
                <displayName>Lynne Grewe</displayName>
                <emails/><food/><heroes/>
                <id>291445554</id>
                <ims/><interests/>
                <isOwner>false</isOwner>
                <isViewer>false</isViewer>
                <languagesSpoken/><lookingFor/>
                <movies/><music/>
                <name>
                   <familyName>Grewe</familyName>
                   <formatted>Lynne Grewe</formatted>
                   <givenName>Lynne</givenName>
                </name>
                <organizations/><phoneNumbers/>
                <photos>
                   <ListFieldImpl>
                     <type>thumbnail</type>
                     <value>http://photos1.hi5.com/0044/8335/920/
                         jm323sua825920-01.jpg</value>
                   </ListFieldImpl>
                </photos>
                <quotes/><sports/><tags/>
                <thumbnailUrl>http://photos1.hi5.com/0034/825/920/jm3sua82592021.jpg
                </thumbnailUrl>
                <turnOffs/><turnOns/><tvShows/>
                <updated>Mon Nov 03 21:55:12 PST 2008</updated>
                <urls/>
             </value>
          </entry>
          </response>
```

OpenSocial RESTful API Details

Following are the steps your application takes to use the OpenSocial REST API:

1. Get API authorization from the service provider using OAuth. This yields an oauth_token and oauth_token_secret.

2. Make an OpenSocial REST API request using OAuth token information.

3. Process the OpenSocial REST response.

OAuth authorization was discussed earlier in this chapter. Let's now examine the details of how to set up an OpenSocial REST API request, and what an OpenSocial REST API response looks like.

OpenSocial REST Request Construction

Creating an OpenSocial REST call involves the construction of a URL (referred to here as the OpenSocial REST URL), the specification of the HTTP method type, and setting up any required data and parameters. The construction of the OpenSocial REST URL, as well as the specification of the HTTP method type for the different API "requests," will be discussed shortly. Let's first take a look at the setup of required data and parameters.

As part of your creating an OpenSocial REST request, the OAuth standards (or whatever authentication protocol the social network is using) should be followed to create a signature that is sent as a request parameter. Hence, the data parameters to be sent as part of the OpenSocial REST request include not only OAuth parameters but also query parameters and REST method-specific parameters.

OAuth Parameters

When working with OAuth parameters, keep in mind the following:

- ❑ A *request* contains the parameters oauth_consumer_key, oauth_token, oauth_signature_method, oauth_signature, oauth_timestamp, oauth_nonce, and oauth_version (optional)

- ❑ A *signature* uses oauth_token_secret (from the access token), auth_consumer_key, and oauth_consumer_secret

Table 5-1 shows the query parameters.

Table 5-1: Query Parameters

Query Parameter	Meaning
count={count}	Requests the size for a paged collection (that is, a collection the user may "page" through). If not specified, the service provider chooses this.
filterBy={field}	Returns entries in a collection filtered by the field.
filterOp={op}	Specifies the operation (op) to use in filtering a collection. The default is contains. Other possibilities include equals, startsWith, and present.
filterValue={v}	The value to use in filtering. For example, you could use filterBy=name&filterOp=startsWith&filterValue=Lynne.
format={format}	This represents the format. Possibilities include atom, json, and xml. The default is xml. For example, you could use format=xml.
fields={-join|,|field}	This lists the fields to be included in members of a collection. If none is specified, the service provider determines what fields to return. For example, this may be used when asked for a "nickname" to be given for each person in a collection of people.
networkDistance={d}	(Optional) Distance refers to how many "hops" away a person is from another to be part of the "group." For example, you could ask for friends of friends.
sortBy={field}	This sorts returned items by the field.
sortOrder={o}	This specifies how to sort. Possibilities include ascending or descending.
startIndex={s}	This starts an index into a paged collection.
updatedSince={d}	This tells the service provider to only return items whose date is equal or more recent than d.

OpenSocial REST API Specification

The OpenSocial REST API, for the most part, mirrors the OpenSocial JavaScript API in capability. Specifically, an application can make requests related to the following:

❑ People

❑ Groups

❑ Activities

❑ AppData

❑ Messaging (optional)

For each category of API request listed here, there is a series of requests your application can construct. For example, with regard to People, the application can retrieve not only user data but also data about friends. Each specific API request is created by building the OpenSocial REST URL, as follows:

```
OpenSocial REST URL = "Base URL" + "REST API Specific URL Pattern"
```

The `"Base URL"` is the base URL the service provider provides for all OpenSocial REST calls. It is possible that this base URL is not the same for all OpenSocial REST calls, but, typically, it will be a constant. For example, on hi5, the `"Base URL"` is `http://api.hi5.com/social/rest` for all OpenSocial REST requests.

The `"REST API Specific URL Pattern"` will be the "extension" of the URL to specify the specific REST API call the application is making. For example, to get the user's Person data, the `"REST API Specific URL Pattern"` will be `/people/@me/@self`. Thus, for hi5, the complete URL will be `http://api.hi5.com/social/rest/people/@me/@self`.

Each of the five main types of requests is detailed in the following sections. In addition to the `"REST API Specific URL Pattern"` specification, the HTTP method types supported will be described, along with any API-specific data that is sent.

Before looking at each category, it is important to note some common constructs used in specifying the `"REST API Specific URL Pattern"`. A commonly used construct is the `{guid}`, which stands for the container-specific global user identifier (GUID). This is the user's ID. The predefined symbol `@me` indicates the user of the application (the OAuth authenticated user). The next constructor is referred to as the *selector* and specifies the person or group of people related to the user. When used, the selector is typically set to one of the following:

❑ `@self` — This indicates the user.

❑ `@all` — This indicates to select all of the related contacts.

❑ `@friends` — This indicates to select from the set of all related contacts only the ones that are the user.

❑ *User-defined local group name* — This is used to specify a group of contacts.

People

A main category of social data deals with people. Just as in the JavaScript API, the OpenSocial REST API gives a program access to this information. Table 5-2 shows examples of URL patterns for People data that an application can construct.

Table 5-2: URL Patterns for People

URL_Pattern Samples	Meaning
/people/{guid}/@all	All people connected to the user specified by guid. An example is http://api.hi5.com/social/rest/people/123456/@all.
/people/{guid}/@friends	All the friends of the user specified by guid.
/people/{guid}/{groupid}	All the people connected to user (guid) in the group specified by ID groupid.
/people/{guid}/@all/{pid}	Information about person with ID pid as "seen" by the user (guid).
/people/{guid}/@self	Information about the user with ID guid.
/people/@me/@self	Information about the user represented in Authentication (OAuth) credentials — the "requestor."
/people/@supportedFields	A list of people fields supported by the service provider.
/people/{guid}/@deleted	(Optional) A list of people connected with the user (guid) who have been deleted.

Note that the standard data that should be returned for a person from a container includes id, name, and thumbnailURL. The OpenSocial REST API allows containers to specify through its XRDS-Simple discovery document the exact form of the URL patterns that can differ from the ones given here. The ones shown in Table 5-2 are suggested URL patterns. Look at the container's developer forum and its XRDS document for variations from these and the supported list.

The standard method type indicated by the patterns shown in Table 5-2 is GET. However, there is support for the creation of a new friend by using the method type of POST for the URL pattern /people/{guid}/@friends. Note that the implementation of this and any of the REST calls is optional, as long as the service provider responds that it is not supported. It is still considered OpenSocial REST compliant. See the documentation for each container for the current list of supported calls. For example, as of this writing, hi5 supports GET operations, but not PUT or POST for people REST API calls.

Groups

"Groups" is another category of REST API calls and involves group-related requests. Table 5-3 shows the URL pattern for groups.

Table 5-3: URL Patterns for Groups

URL_Pattern Samples	Meaning
/groups/{guid}	All of the groups of which the user (guid) is a member

For hi5, a group request would look like http://api.hi5.com/social/rest/groups/12345.

Activities

"Activities" are defined as postings to activity streams on the social network. You may choose to have your program get activity information, or create a new activity. In the case of getting the activity information, the method type will be GET. In the case of creating a new activity, the method type will be POST. Table 5-4 shows the URL patterns for activities.

Table 5-4: URL Patterns for Activities

URL_Pattern Samples	Meaning
/activities/{guid}/@self	Activities associated with user (guid)
/activities/{guid}/@self/{appid}	Activities generated by the application (with ID appid) for the user (guid)
/activities/{guid}/@friends	Friends' activities (friends of user guid)
/activities/{guid}/@friends	Friends' activities generated by the application (friends of user guid)
/activities/{guid}/{groupid}	Activities for people in a group with ID groupid, that belongs to user (guid)
/activities/{guid}/{groupid}/{appid}	Activities generated by the application (with ID appid) for people in a group with ID groupid, that belongs to user (guid)
/activities/{guid}/@self/{appid}/{activityid}	A specific activity object identified by activityid that is generated by the application (appid) and belongs to user (guid)
/activities/@supportedFields	List of activity fields supported by the service provider

Note that the @app token can be used for an appid to indicate the currently requesting application. Again, the @me token can be used to indicate the user for the guid.

AppData

The final kind of OpenSocial REST request involves the retrieval or storage of application data. Recall that OpenSocial supports persistence through the storage of what is called "AppData," which are name/value pairs. Table 5-5 shows example URL patterns for this category.

Note that the predefined element of @app can be used to indicate the application making the REST request.

Messaging

This is an optional resource that OpenSocial containers can choose to support. It allows messages to be sent to a user from another user. The method type supported here is PUT, to create a message. Table 5-6 shows the URL pattern for messaging.

Table 5-5: URL Patterns for AppData

URL_Pattern Samples	Meaning
/appdata/{guid}/@self/{appid}	All application data associated with the user (guid) for the application with ID appid
/appdata/{guid}/@self/@app	All application data associated with the user (guid) for the application making this request
/appdata/{guid}/@friends/{appid}	All application data associated with the user's friends for the application with ID appid, where the user's ID is guid
/appdata/{guid}/@self/{appid}? fields=status	Only the application data named status that is associated with the user (guid) and application (appid)

Table 5-6: URL Pattern for Groups

URL_Pattern Sample, for Messaging	Meaning
/messages/{guid}/outbox/{msgid}	Message with ID msgid owned by the current user (guid)

In this case, the message data itself must contain a list of recipients. This API request will place the message in the Outbox of the user (guid). The service provider can choose to apply filters and enforcement of its mail policies in sending the mail from the user's Outbox.

Data Formatting and Atom/AtomPub

Data will be sent either in the response or the request. When making a POST or PUT request, resource-specific data will be sent. For example, when the program asks to create an activity, the program must send the activity data with the request. In the case of a response, most of the REST API requests will yield data (for example, when asking for user or friend data). This section describes how data is formatted in the OpenSocial REST API.

OpenSocial REST data can be represented in JSON, XML, or Atom formats. OpenSocial service providers must support all of these options, but can also provide their own additional data representations.

Following are the kinds of data the OpenSocial REST API supports:

- ❑ Person
- ❑ Group
- ❑ Activity
- ❑ AppData
- ❑ Message (Optional)

Let's take a look at some JSON, XML, and Atom examples for each data type.

Person Data

Person data is used to represent any person, including the user. First, let's look at a JSON representation:

```
{
  "id" : "container.com:12345",
  "displayName" : "Lynne",
  "name" : {"unstructured" : "Lynne Grewe"},
  "gender" : "female"
}
```

The sample Person data in XML format would be as follows:

```
<person xmlns="http://ns.opensocial.org/2008/opensocial">
  <id>container.com:12345</id>
  <displayName>Lynne</displayName>
  <name>
    <unstructured>Lynne Grewe</unstructured>
  </name>
  <gender>female</gender>
</person>
```

Finally, a sample Atom representation would be as follows:

```
<entry xmlns="http://www.w3.org/2005/Atom">
  <content type="application/xml">
    <person xmlns="http://ns.opensocial.org/2008/opensocial">
      <name>
        <unstructured>Lynne Grewe</unstructured>
      </name>
      <gender>female</gender>
    </person>
  </content>
  <title/>
  <updated>2009-02-03T13:30:02Z</updated>
  <author/>
  <id>urn:guid:container.com:12345</id>
</entry>
```

A number of fields can be specified about a person. The service provider must always return the `person id` and `displayName` fields. Other fields are optional, and it is up to the service provider to choose what it will support. All of the fields listed for the OpenSocial JavaScript Person object are supported for fields, including `aboutMe`, `activities`, `bodyType`, `books`, `cars`, `children`, `currentLocation`, `drinker`, `ethnicity`, `fashion`, `food`, `happiestWhen`, `heroes`, `humor`, `interests`, `jobInterests`, `languages`, `languagesSpoken`, `livingArrangement`, `lookingFor`, `movies`, `music`, `pets`, `politicalviews`, `profileSong`, `profileVideo`, `quotes`, `relationshipStatus`, `religion`, `romance`, `scaredOf`, `sexualOrientation`, `smoker`, `sports`, `status`, `turnOffs`, `turnOns`, and `tvShows`.

Table 5-7 shows the new fields for the OpenSocial REST API (in addition to those supplied by the OpenSocial JavaScript API).

Table 5-7: Individual Person Fields

Person Field	Meaning
accounts*	A list of user accounts
Addresses	A list of user addresses
Anniversary	A wedding anniversary date
Birthday	Date of birth
Connected	Boolean value indicating if user and this person have an established bidirectionally asserted connection on the container's service. The meaning of this connection can be container-specific but can include direct friends.
displayName	Person's name that is used for display
emails*	Email addresses
Gender	Gender. Possible values might be male, female, or undisclosed
Id	Unique person ID on this social network
ims*	Instant message addresses
Name	Name, separated into components (such as given name, first name)
Nickname	Casual name
Note	Notes about the person
organizations*	Current and/or past organizations to which the user belongs
phoneNumbers*	A list of user phone numbers
photos*	URL of user's photos
Published	Date person was added (for example, to the user's friend list)
preferredUsename	Preferred username.
relationships*	Bidirectionally asserted relationships, established between user and this person (for example, friends, contact, and so on)
tags*	User-defined category label
updated	Latest date person information was updated
urls*	Person-specified URLs
utcOffset	Person's time zone specified as offset from UTC

*These fields can contain multiple instances. In these cases, the following subfields are possible:
value — The actual value of the field
type — Takes values work, home, or other
primary — This takes the value true if this is the primary instance; otherwise, it is false.

The account data that can be returned for a person gives account details. An account is described with the subfields specified in Table 5-8.

Table 5-8: Subfields for Person accounts field

Account Field	Meaning
Domain	Domain for this account
username	User's username
Userid	User's ID

The Addresses field has the subfields specified in Table 5-9.

Table 5-9: Subfields for Person Addresses Field

Address Field	Meaning
formatted	The full address
streetAddress	The street address
Locality	The name of the city (or similar)
Region	The name of the state (or similar)
postalCode	The ZIP code (or similar)
country	The name of the country

The Name field has the subfields specified in Table 5-10.

Table 5-10: Subfields for Person Name field

Name Field	Meaning
Formatted	Full name with middle initial, titles, and so on.
familyName	Last name
givenName	First name
middleName	Middle name
honorificPrefix	Title (for example, "Mr.", "Dr.", and so on)
honorificSuffix	Honorable title (for example, "PhD" in "John Doe, PhD")

The organization data that can be returned for a person describes either current or past organizations the person is associated with. An organization is described with the subfields specified in Table 5-11.

Table 5-11: Subfields for organizations

Organization Field	Meaning
Name	Name of organization
department	Department in the organization
Title	Person's title within the organization
Type	Relates the organization to the person (for example, "job", "school")
startDate	Date when the person joined the organization
endDate	Date when the person left the organization
Location	Location of the organization
description	Description of what the person does (or did) in the organization

Group Data

Group data is used to represent a group. First, let's look at a JSON representation:

```
{
   "id" : "container.com: 8389/friends",
   "title" : "The Group",
}
```

The sample Group data in XML format would be as follows:

```
<group xmlns="http://ns.opensocial.org/2008/opensocial">
   <id>container.com:8389/friends</id>
   <title>The Group</title>
</group>
```

Finally, the Atom representation would be as follows:

```
<entry xmlns="http://www.w3.org/2005/Atom">
   <link rel="alternate" href="http://container.com/
       people/container.com:8389/@friends" />
   <title>The Group</title>
   <updated>2009-02-03T13:30:02Z</updated>
   <id>urn:guid:container.com: 8389/friends</id>
</entry>
```

Activity Data

Activity data is used to represent an activity in an activity stream. First, let's look at a JSON representation:

```
{
  "id" : "http://contianer.com/activities/container.com:/self/af1234",
  "title" : "<a href=\"you\">Title of Activity</a>",
  "updated" : "2009-12-12T21:35:07.266Z",
  "body" : "info about your activity",
  "bodyId" : "3333",
  "url" : "http://container.com/activity/feeds/.../af1234",
  "userId" : "example.org:34KJDCSKJN2HHF0DW20394"
}
```

The sample Activity data in XML format would be as follows:

```
<activity xmlns="http://ns.opensocial.org/2008/opensocial">
  <id>http://container.com/activities/container.com:1234/self/af1234</id>
  <title>&lt;a href=\"you\"&gt; Title of Activity &lt;/a&gt;</title>
  <updated>2009-12-12T21:35:07.266Z</updated>
  <body> info about your activity </body>
  <bodyId>3333</bodyId>
  <url>http://container.com/activity/feeds/.../af1234</url>
  <userId>container.com:1234</userId>
</activity>
```

Finally, the Atom representation would be as follows:

```
<entry xmlns="http://www.w3.org/2005/Atom">
  <category term="status"/>
  <id>http://container.com/activities/container.com:1234/self/af1234</id>
  <title><a href="you"> Title of Activity </a></title>
  <summary> info about your activity </summary>
  <updated>2009-12-12T21:35:07.266Z</updated>
  <link rel="self" type="application/atom+xml"
      href="http://container.com/activity/feeds/.../af1234"/>
  <author><uri>urn:guid:container.com:1234</uri></author>
  <content>
    <activity xmlns="http://ns.opensocial.org/2008/opensocial">
      <bodyId>1234</bodyId>
    </activity>
  </content>
</entry>
```

All of the fields listed for the OpenSocial JavaScript activity object are supported for activity fields in the OpenSocial REST API. These include: appId, body, bodyId, externalId, id, mediaItems, postedTime, priority, streamFaviconUrl, streamSourceUrl, streamTitle, streamUrl, templateParams, title, url, and userId.

AppData Data

Application data (AppData) is used in OpenSocial's service provider-sponsored persistence support. Application data is defined as sets of name/value pairs. First, let's look at a sample JSON representation:

```
{
  "status" : "good",
  "last_status" : "2009-02-03T10:30:02Z"
}
```

The sample AppData in XML format would be as follows:

```xml
<appdata xmlns="http://ns.opensocial.org/2008/opensocial">
  <entry>
    <key>status</key>
    <value>good</value>
  </entry>
  <entry>
    <key>last_status</key>
    <value>2009-02-03T10:30:02Z</value>
  </entry>
</appdata>
```

Finally, the Atom representation would be as follows:

```xml
<entry xmlns="http://www.w3.org/2005/Atom">
  <content type="text/xml">
    <appdata xmlns="http://opensocial.org/2008/opensocial">
        <status>good</status>
        <last_status>2009-02-03T10:30:02Z</last_status>
      </appdata>
  </content>
  <title/>
  <updated>2009-02-03T10:30:02Z</updated>
  <author><url>urn:guid:container.com:1234</url></author>
  <id>urn:guid:container.com:1234</id>
</entry>
```

It is also possible to have a collection of application data elements. In this case, the following will be the XML format:

```
{
  "entry" : {
    "container.com:1234" : {"status" : "good",
                            "last_status" : "2009-02-03T10:30:02Z " },
    "container.com:6789" : {"status" : "ok",
                            "last_status" : "2008-11-17T08:30:03Z" }
  }
}
```

The Atom format for a collection of application data elements looks like this:

```xml
<feed xmlns="http://www.w3.org/2005/Atom>
  <id>...</id>
  <title>...</title>
  <entry>
    <content type="text/xml">
      <appdata>
        <status>good</status>
        <last_status>"2009-02-03T10:30:02Z"</last_status>
      </appdata>
    </content>
    <title/>
```

```
        <updated>2008-11-17T08:30:03Z</updated>
        <author><url>urn:guid:container.com:1234 /url></author>
        <id>urn:guid:container.com:1234</id>
    </entry>
    <entry>
      <content type="text/xml">
        <appdata>
          <status>ok</status>
          <last_status>"2008-11-17T08:30:03Z"</last_status>
        </appdata>
      </content>
      <title/>
      <updated>2008-11-17T08:30:03Z </updated>
      <author><url>uurn:guid:container.com:6789</url></author>
      <id>urn:guid:container.com:6789</id>
    </entry>
  </entry>
```

Messaging Data

Messaging data is used to represent a message from one user to another (or others). Currently, the OpenSocial REST API only gives the format using ATOM. It should have a representation with XML and JSON syntax similar to the other data types presented earlier.

```
<entry xmlns="http://www.w3.org/2005/Atom"
       xmlns:osapi="http://opensocial.org/2008/opensocialapi">
  <osapi:recipient>container.com:3842</osapi:recipient>
  <osapi:recipient>container.com:5389</osapi:recipient>
  <title>You have an invitation from Lynne</title>
  <id>{msgid}</id>
  <link rel="alternate" href="http://container.com/invites/{msgid}"/>
  <content>
      Click <a href="http://container.com/invites/{msgid}">here</a>
      to review your invitation.
  </content>
</entry>
```

Note that {msgid} is a message ID. This should be generated by your application and should be globally unique. If you do not want to generate the message ID, the application can do a POST to /messages/{guid}/outbox and let the service provider generate the message ID. Remember that messaging is an optional feature of OpenSocial REST.

HTTP Method Type

In addition to the construction of the URL, the selection of the HTTP method type is a part of building the OpenSocial REST request. The following HTTP methods are supported:

- ❏ GET — This means to retrieve (for example, to get person data).
- ❏ PUT — This means to update.
- ❏ POST — This means to create.
- ❏ DELETE — This means to destroy.

If the application is restricted and cannot use PUT or DELETE, the application can represent these operations as a POST operation with an additional X-HTTP-Method_Override header parameter set to the value (PUT or DELETE). For example, to represent a PUT request using this idea, the following is the request header that would be generated:

```
POST /... HTTP/1.1
...
X-HTTP-Method-Override: PUT
```

OpenSocial REST Response

The format of the returned response to an OpenSocial REST request is, by default, JSON, unless specified differently in the OpenSocial REST request query parameter format. In the case of either JSON or XML, the root element is response, and must contain the following subelements:

❑ startIndex — This specifies the index of the first returned item. This is useful when paging results (see request query parameters shown earlier in this chapter in Table 5-1). Typically, this will have value of 0 (unless controlling through request query parameters).

❑ itemsPerPage — This is the number of items per page in the response. Typically, this will be equal to the count request query parameter detailed in Table 5-1 (unless the service provider has imposed restrictions).

❑ totalResults — This is the number of total possible items if no startIndex or count query parameters have been specified.

❑ entry — This represents the returned item(s). When multiple items are present, this entry element will contain an array of items.

Following is a generic example using the JSON format:

```
{
    "startIndex" : 1
    "itemsPerPage" : 10
    "totalResults" : 100,
    "entry" : [ {...first item...}, {...second item...} ... ] }
```

The following code shows a specific example from hi5 when the user data was requested using XML format. This request is for only the "standard" user data. No additional fields were requested. This is hi5's interpretation of what "standard" user data means.

```
<response>
<empty>false</empty>
<entry>
<key>entry</key>
<value>
        <accounts/><activities/><addresses/><books/><cars/>
        <displayName>Lynne Grewe</displayName>
        <emails/><food/><heroes/>
        <id>39244</id>
         <ims/><interests/>
         <isOwner>false</isOwner>
         <isViewer>false</isViewer>
```

```
            <languagesSpoken/><lookingFor/><movies/><music/>
            <name>
                <familyName>Grewe</familyName>
                <formatted>Lynne Grewe</formatted>
                <givenName>Lynne</givenName>
            </name><organizations/>
            <phoneNumbers/>
            <photos>
                <ListFieldImpl>
                    <type>thumbnail</type>
                    <value>http://photos1.hi5.com/0e44/82/930/
                        jm8sua82592001.jpg</value>
                </ListFieldImpl>
            </photos>
            <quotes/><sports/><tags/>
            <thumbnailUrl>http://photos1.hi5.com/0044/825/920/jm8sua8259201.jpg
                </thumbnailUrl>
            <turnOffs/><turnOns/><tvShows/>
            <updated>Tue Nov 04 16:03:56 PST 2009</updated>
            <urls/>
    </value>
    </entry>
    </response>
```

What You Need

You need to know the following information to be able to use the OpenSocial REST API:

❑ OAuth endpoints and specifications (see the earlier discussion in the section "OpenSocial REST Authorization and Authentication (OAuth)" for details)

❑ OAuth policies concerning token expiration

❑ OpenSocial REST API endpoint(s)

❑ Supported request methods (GET, POST, and so on).

❑ The service provider's OpenSocial discovery document, or documentation of supported OpenSocial REST calls and optional features or extensions

Most of this information should be provided by the service provider within its discovery document. The format of this document is detailed later in this chapter in the section "OpenSocial REST Support Discovery." However, social networks may choose to supply this information in other ways, including on their developer Web pages.

OpenSocial REST Application Deployment

If you recall the transactional models involving OpenSocial REST that were introduced in Chapter 2, you'll remember the hybrid case where an OpenSocial JavaScript application is deployed that communicates through makeRequest to the server-side OpenSocial REST program. In this case, the OpenSocial JavaScript application will be deployed, but not the server-based OpenSocial REST program.

In the case of the "purely REST (non-social network) application" transactional model, a server-side application has its interface on the developer's Web site. There is no social network application. However, the use of OAuth (or, in the case of hi5, the use of token technology) requires that the REST application have an API key. As of this writing, this means that a "dummy" social network application must be created on the service provider to obtain an API key for use in the OpenSocial REST program.

HTTP Status Codes

OpenSocial REST involves repeated HTTP request-and-response transactions. Your application must handle the possible HTTP response status codes appropriately. Following are some of the possible error codes and their meanings:

❑ *400: Bad Request* — This may be the result of an invalid request URL, an invalid HTTP header, an invalid HTTP body, or an unsupported parameter.

❑ *401: Unauthorized* — This may be the result of missing OAuth authorization information, or the fact that the user specified in OAuth information is not authorized for this request.

❑ *403: Forbidden* — This may be the result of the service provider refusing the request, even if the authorization information is valid.

❑ *404: Not Found* — This may be the result of the request URL not being valid.

❑ *405: Method Not Allowed* — This may be the result of this method not being not allowed.

❑ *409: Conflict* — This may be the result of some conflict with the current state of resource requested. The response body should contain information that allows the user to recognize the problem. One example might be that the application is trying to create an activity, and the maximum number per user per day has been exceeded.

❑ *500: Internal Server error* — This may be the result of a number of server-induced problems.

❑ *501: Not Implemented* — This may the result of the request not being supported by the service provider, even though the request is valid.

OpenSocial REST Support Discovery

The process of discovery involves the following steps:

1. The program (or "client") makes a request for the URL supplied by the service provider in the discovery document. The HTTP request is of method type GET, and has the Accept: application/xrds+xml header parameter value, which says that the program will accept as a response an XRDS document in XML.

2. The service provider responds with either the XRDS document in XML, or the X-XRDS-Location header parameter set to the location of the XRDS document.

3. The program (or "client") will either "read" in the document, or go to the location and read in the document. It then parses the XML to get the service information.

The actual "version" of XRDS that OpenSocial uses is XRDS-Simple, which is a simpler and more constrained XRDS version. XRDS-Simple was created out of work on the OAuth protocol used in OpenSocial.

An XRDS-Simple document defines and maps together the following elements:

❑ *Resource* — This is a service or document that is provided by the service provider.

❑ *Endpoint* — This is the URL address of a resource.

The following are the XML elements that are used in XRDS-Simple documents:

❑ `<XRDS>` — This is the root element that contains one or more `XRD` elements. The `XRDS` element must define the namespace in the form `<XRDS xmlns="xri://$xrds">`.

❑ `<XRD>` — This is used to group related `Service` elements together. It must include the `version` and `xlmns` (namespace) attributes. Other attributes can include `xlmns:simple` (which specifies the XRDS-Simple extensions) and `xlmns:os` (which is an OpenSocial extension attribute). If there is more than one XRD element in the document, each must be identified uniquely with the `xlmns:id` attribute. This must contain the child element `<Type>` in the form `<Type>xri://$xrds*simple</Type>`. This element can contain the `<Expires>` element to specify the expiration of the `XRD` element.

❑ `<Service>` — This provides a mapping between a resource description and endpoint. Keep the following in mind when using this element:

  ❑ `priority` — This is an optional attribute.

  ❑ `<Type>` — The `<Service>` element must include at least one of either `<Type>` or `<MediaType>` child elements. Zero or more `<Type>` child elements can be included. The `<Type>` child element provides an absolute URL that describes the resource and how it should be used.

  ❑ `<MediaType>` — The `<Service>` element must include at least one of either `<Type>` or `<MediaType>` child elements. Zero or more `<MediaType>` child elements can be included. The `<MediaType>` child element gives the content media type.

  ❑ `<URI>` — The `<Service>` element can have zero or more `<URI>` child elements. This is the URI (URL) of the endpoint. This is the URI you use to access the resource. Most often, you will have this element. However, if this element is missing (which is compliant), the URI is still accessible, although not in this document, but rather in some other way (for example, the service provider lists it on its Web site or in the developer forum).

  ❑ `<os:URI-Template>` — The `<Service>` element can have zero or more `<os:URI-Template>` child elements. This is an alternative to the URI. Here, the URI is given in template form. This is an OpenSocial extension tag of XRDS-Simple.

  ❑ `<LocalID>` — The `<Service>` element can have zero or more `<LocalID>` child elements. The `<LocalID>` child element gives an ID for this mapping of a resource to an endpoint. It has an optional parameter of `priority`.

Listing 5-8 provides an example XRDS-Simple discovery document that an OpenSocial container might return.

Listing 5-8: A Sample XRDS-Simple Discovery Document

```
<XRDS xmlns="xri://$xrds">
    <XRD xmlns:simple="http://xrds-simple.net/core/1.0" xmlns="xri:
```

```
       //$XRD*($v*2.0)" xmlns:os="http://ns.opensocial.org/
            2008/opensocial" version="2.0">
    <Type>xri://$xrds*simple</Type>
    <Service>
      <Type>http://ns.opensocial.org/2008/opensocial/people</Type>
      <os:URI-Template>
         http://CONTAINER.com/people/{guid}/{selector}{-prefix|/|pid}
      </os:URI-Template>
    </Service>
    <Service>
      <Type>http://ns.opensocial.org/2008/opensocial/groups</Type>
      <os:URI-Template>http://container.com/groups/
           {guid}</os:URI-Template>
    </Service>
    <Service>
      <Type>http://ns.opensocial.org/2008/opensocial/activities</Type>
      <os:URI-Template>
         http://container.com/activities/{guid}/{appid}/{selector}
      </os:URI-Template>
    </Service>
    <Service>
      <Type>http://ns.opensocial.org//2008/opensocial/appdata</Type>
      <os:URI-Template>
         http://container.com/appdata/{guid}/{appid}/{selector}
      </os:URI-Template>
    </Service>
    <Service>
      <Type>http://ns.opensocial.org//2008/opensocial/messages</Type>
      <os:URI-Template>
         http://container.com/messages/{guid}/{selector}
      </os:URI-Template>
    </Service>
  </XRD>
</XRDS>
```

As you can see, the document starts out with a single XRDS root element tag that contains a single XRD element for OpenSocial support descriptions. Following this is a series of five <Service> elements defining (in order) how the container supports the OpenSocial REST API requests:

❑   /opensocial/people — This deals with all People API requests.

❑   /opensocial/groups — This deals with all Group API requests.

❑   /opensocial/activities — This deals with all Activity API requests.

❑   /opensocial/appdata — This deals with all AppData API requests.

❑   /opensocial/messages — This deals with all Message API requests.

Note that each Service endpoint is declared with an os:URI-Template instead of simple URI. This is because each Service type is declared via its Type element as a class of OpenSocial API requests. Note that the nature of the request is such that it begins with the generic container endpoint http://CONTAINER.com (which is common) and is followed by the rest of the URI used to make up the specific endpoint. For example, http://CONTAINER.com/group/{guid} is the endpoint URI (template) used for group API requests.

Resources for XRDS Simple

The following are useful resources to learn more about XRDS-Simple:

❏   http://xrds-simple.net/core/1.0/

❏   http://www.hueniverse.com/hueniverse/2008/03/putting-xrds-si.html

❏   http://en.wikipedia.org/wiki/XRDS

OpenSocial Security with the REST API

A service provider must support OAuth to authorize an application's access to making OpenSocial REST requests. This provides one level of security. However, OAuth is not a secure communications mechanism, meaning it does not provide encryption or message body integrity checking. OpenSocial suggests that containers use SSL for this kind of security.

For security, OAuth tokens have a limited lifetime. The service provider determines its policy for this. A typical lifetime will span from hours to a day. Check the service provider's documentation to determine its token lifetime policy. For example, hi5 gives a 24-hour lifetime for its tokens.

OpenSocial REST API Future

The next version of OpenSocial will provide support for social network applications developed solely with the REST API. The specification for social network application registration with a URL (like the callback URL for Facebook applications) will be supported. Hence, the social networks will need to support a new form of deployment.

This support will be crucial for some companies that have problems with the overhead of using `makeRequst` to access server-side programs.

OpenSocial RPC Protocol

A new third OpenSocial "API" is similar to the OpenSocial REST API. The OpenSocial RPC Protocol defines an RPC-based structure to perform requests from a server-side program, rather than RESTful calls.

It is similar to the OpenSocial REST API in that it does the following:

❏   Makes calls to the service provider from a server-side program.

❏   Performs authentication through OAuth.

❏   Uses HTTP status codes.

❏   Uses JSON and XML data formats for the social data.

It differs from the OpenSocial REST API in the following ways:

❑   HTTP is not used to represent the method request but is instead inside the request data.

❑   All elements are represented with JSON and XML (not Atom).

❑   Batching is required.

❑   The discovery of service is done differently.

Let's consider the example of requesting information about a user. With the OpenSocial REST API, the request will be to the following URL using the GET HTTP request type:

```
http://container.com/people/@me/@self
```

Note that the http://container.com represents a generic endpoint, and the actual endpoint for each social network will be different. The equivalent OpenSocial RPC call would be as follows:

```
http://container.com/rpc?method=people.get&id=myself&userid=
     @me&groupid=@self
```

Again, the http://container.com represents a generic endpoint, and the actual endpoint for each social network will be different. This URL places the resource request (specified by people.get) in the request data, along with the scoping information (id=myself&userid=@me&groupid=@self).

Multiple (batched) requests are created by passing them as data in the format of a JSON array. The following listing shows the actual POST request asking for both the user and the user's friends:

```
POST /rpc HTTP/1.1
Host: Userver.com
Authorization: <1st Auth token>
Content-Type: application/json
[
  {
    "method" : "people.get",
    "id" : "me"
  },
  {
    "method" : "people.get",
    "id" : "myFriends",
    "params: {
      "groupid" : "@friends",
      "auth" : "<2nd Auth token>"
    }
  }
]
```

The following is a potential response from the service provider:

```
HTTP/1.x 207 Multi-Status
Content-Type: application/json
[
```

```
    {
      "id" : "me,
      "result" : {
        "id" : "container.com:34KJDCSKJN2HHF0DW20394",
        "name" : { "unstructured" : "Lynne Grewe"},
        "gender" : "female"
      }
    },
    {
      "id" : "myFriends"
      "error" : {
        "code" : 401
      }
    }
  ]
```

Notice how the IDs in the two JSON objects in the response correspond to those in the requests. The first request was successful, and returned the basic information about the user, Lynne Grewe. In this hypothetical example, the second request was denied by the service provider because of the user access control settings (or service provider policies).

Here are a few more OpenSocial RPC requests:

❑   Friend request (`/people/@me/@friends` REST call):

```
http://container.com/rpc?method=people.get&id=myfriends&userid=
     @me&groupid=@friends
```

❑   AppData request (PUT to /appdata/@me/@self/YourAppID REST call):

```
http://container.com/rpc?method=appdata.update&id=appdataID&appId=
        YourAppID&data.status=good&data.lastStatus=2009-12-03T19:00:00Z
```

❑   The values `data.*` are part of the data JSON object that represents the application data you are trying to store. In this case, it represents the following JSON object:

```
data : {
        status : good,
        lastStatus : "2009-12-03T19:00:00Z"
      }
```

❑   Friend (PUT) request (PUT to /people/@me/@friends REST call), creating a friend relationship between user and another user (with ID = AA332288)

```
http://container.com/rpc?method=people.create&id=createFriend&userId=@me&
        groupId=@friends&person.id=container.com:AA332288
```

Notice in these examples that the name of the resource being requested is represented by the method parameter, and has the following general form:

```
method = <service-name>.<operation>
```

The service names are identical to the names used in the REST API, and are documented in the opensocial namespace. The operation is defined as follows:

- get — Equivalent of REST GET
- create — Equivalent of REST PUT
- post — Equivalent of REST POST
- delete — Equivalent of REST DELETE

See http://www.opensocial.org/Technical-Resources/opensocial-spec-v081/ rpc-protocol *for further details on the RPC protocol.*

Summary

This chapter began with a general description of REST, including a REST example in PHP. The discussion continued with an examination of why a server-based application alternative is important. This was followed by a discussion of the OpenSocial REST transactional models.

You learned about the architecture of an OpenSocial REST application. Authorization/authentication was revealed to involve OAuth for OpenSocial-compliant REST service providers. A current modification of this for the hi5 network was presented.

You then learned about the details of the OpenSocial REST API, including a few code examples. You learned about HTTP status codes (OpenSocial REST supporting protocol), as well as OpenSocial REST support discovery.

This chapter concluded with a glimpse of the OpenSocial RPC protocol, a third "API" that offers an RPC style, server-side API with some things in common with the OpenSocial REST API.

Chapter 6 covers more advanced uses of OpenSocial and targeted application development.

6

Programming Fundamentals

This chapter examines some of the fundamental concepts you should know when working with an OpenSocial application. You will learn about testing your applications. This chapter then takes a first look at front-end and back-end issues, including a discussion of front-end GUI issues for OpenSocial applications. You will also learn how to make requests for external resources, how to inquire about a container's capabilities, and the basics of application testing.

Application Testing

Testing any Web program is not simple, and it becomes more complex for social network applications that are controlled by the container. The nature of your application and use of external resources are some of the factors that will influence how you may test your application. This section focuses on general application testing.

Unfortunately, the testing facilities that are provided don't include a set of "test" friends. So, the first recommendation is to recruit a bunch of fellow developers to act as friends. If you are a sole developer, then you can create a series of "dummy" user accounts that can be used as friends, and use these accounts to test how the application interacts within a social graph. Many times, you must make these friends developers of the application in order to install the application within the accounts. Also, you are typically limited to only being able to make a friend a developer of your application.

One of the first difficulties that new developers typically encounter is the issue of caching. Obviously, in the development and testing phases of application development, you are changing your code a lot and don't want the container to cache your application. Unfortunately, most containers do cache, even in sandbox/testing mode. So, you must be aware of this, and must know how to work around it. Earlier in this chapter, you learned a bit about how to reload your application within different containers.

Many of your errors in development will be HTML or JavaScript errors. For HTML, there are a number of good validators, including the `W3.org` validator you can find at `http://validator.w3.org`. For CSS, you can use the `W3.org` validator found at `http://jigsaw.w3.org/css-validator`.

You can find a number of JavaScript syntax checkers on the Web. The future of OpenSocial may include moving to a form of JavaScript called CAJA. CAJA is a Google-sponsored project aimed at "sanitizing" JavaScript for improved security and creating limitations (for Facebook developers, think FBJS). You can find out more about CAJA at `http://code.google.com/p/google-caja` and find a CAJA test bed where you can paste your code for validation at `http://cajadores.com/demos/testbed`.

Some containers provide development tools for testing code. For example, MySpace offers an "OpenSocial Tool/Harness" located at `http://developer.myspace.com/modules/apis/pages/opensocialtool.aspx`, which lets developers load code and run it in a self-contained environment that does not affect MySpace users.

Related to testing is the tracking of your user data. Commonly referred to as *analytics*, this can show you where you need to improve your application. Chapter 8 discusses analytic options and provides examples. Another very useful tool for debugging JavaScript is Firebug (a Firefox plug-in), which is discussed in Chapter 8 for use in performance monitoring.

Front-End GUI Design Tips

When coming up with the GUI design for your application, you should consider a number of items, including the following:

❑   *Views* — In which views will your application run?

❑   *Application (display) size* — Typically, width is controlled, while height is variable.

❑   *Title* — You must set an appropriate title.

❑   *Navigation tabs* — If you use tabs from the Gadget API, you can make a clean interface for navigation.

❑   *Look and feel* — This includes colors and backgrounds, as well as logo design.

❑   *Media* — This includes Flash and other types of media.

Earlier in this book, you learned about views and the parameters on how to set the height and title. You will learn more about the use of media in applications in Chapter 7. So, let's now take a look at the other items for consideration in the previous list, using navigation tabs and the look and feel of your application.

Navigation Tabs

Navigation tabs are a common GUI element used in applications. Navigation tabs are a useful tool for developers to use to make an application look more integrated with a social network. Navigation tabs also enable you to give your application a professional look.

Listing 6-1 shows a modification of the "Friend Finder" application that creates navigation tabs on the main interface, one called Find Friends and one called Invite (used to invite friends to install the "Friend Finder" application).

Listing 6-1: "Friend Finder" XML with New Tabs in the GUI

```
FriendFinder.xml

<?xml version="1.0" encoding="UTF-8"?>
<Module>
  <ModulePrefs title="Friend Finder" description="Friend tracker"
               title_url="http://FriendFinder.com" author="L. Grewe"
               author_email="ff@yahoo.com"
               author_affiliation="iLab" author_location="Bay Area, CA"
               thumbnail="http://UServer/Logo.PNG">
    <Icon>http://UServer/Logo_16_16.PNG</Icon>
    <Require feature="dynamic-height"/>
    <Require feature="opensocial-0.8"/>
  </ModulePrefs>
  <Content type="html">
    <![CDATA[


        <div id='heading'></div>
        <hr size="1px" />
        <div id='main'></div>
        <hr>
        <div id='friends'></div>

        <script src="http://UServer/FriendFinder.js"></script>

        <script>
         var tabs;
         var display = true;
         function guiSetup() {
           var container;
           params = {};
           params['callback'] = callback;

           tabs = new gadgets.TabSet();
           container = tabs.addTab('Find Friends', params);
           container = tabs.addTab('Invite', params);
           init();
         }

         function callback() {
          if (tabs.getSelectedTab().getName() == "Find Friends")
                 init();
          else
                 invite_friends();
         }

         function invite_friends(){
          document.getElementById('heading').innerHTML = "Invite Friends";
          document.getElementById('friends').innerHTML = "<br>coming soon...";
         }
```

Continued

Listing 6-1: "Friend Finder" XML with New Tabs in the GUI *(continued)*

```
        gadgets.util.registerOnLoadHandler(guiSetup);
    </script>
]]>

    </Content>
</Module>
```

As you can see, the XML code in Listing 6-1 still uses the `FriendFinder.js` you learned about in Chapter 4 (see Listing 4-2), and adds to it the following three inline JavaScript functions:

- ❑ `guiSetup`
- ❑ `invite_friends`
- ❑ `callback`

The following line of code in the new JavaScript registers the `guiSetup` function to execute when the application is loaded:

```
gadgets.util.registerOnLoadHandler(guiSetup)
```

The `guiSetup` function creates an instance of `gadgets.TabSet`, assigning it to the variable tabs. Two tabs are created, the Find Friends and Invite tabs, as shown in Figure 6-1. For each tab, the function `callback` is registered to handle the tab-selection event. The `callback` function tests to see which tab was selected and, based on this, changes the content the user sees.

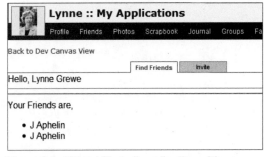

Figure 6-1: "Friend Finder" application with new tabs

Look and Feel

You should consider the following when designing the look and feel of your application:

- ❑ Background color
- ❑ Font type and color

- ❑ Icon design
- ❑ Layout
- ❑ Media and ad placement
- ❑ Navigation design

Following are some of the many factors that can influence your decisions about the look and feel of your application:

- ❑ User base demographics
- ❑ Ease of use
- ❑ Application genre
- ❑ Application purpose and function

When creating a design, try to adhere to these design tenants:

- ❑ *Repetition* — Repeat visual elements throughout application. For example, place the logo on each "page" of the application.
- ❑ *Contrast* — Add visual excitement, and draw the user's attention to important areas.
- ❑ *Proximity* — Group related items together.
- ❑ *Alignment* — Align elements vertically or horizontally together for clarity.
- ❑ *Fast load times* — Use heavyweight media only as necessary.
- ❑ *Browser safe* — Choose browser-safe colors. Design and test your application on multiple browsers.

Social Network-Specific Looks

Some social networks provide application developers with styles and tips for GUI design. This can include CSS and JavaScript files.

hi5 offers developers a template library written in JavaScript that lets you create shortcuts to some of the social data and features with a markup-like specification. Check out `http://www.hi5networks.com/platform/wiki/hi5TemplateLibraryDocumentation` for details. Since the next version of OpenSocial is scheduled to have this feature, this will not be examined in detail here.

Friendster provides developers with a set of styles used on Friendster GUI elements such as tabs, notifications, and buttons. The styles are located at `http://images.friendster.com/css/app_styles.css`, which you can link in your XML file. The file `http://www.friendster.com/developer/styles/app_styles.html` gives examples of how to use these styles.

Listing 6-2 shows how to use Friendster tab styles in the "Friend Finder" application XML code. Figure 6-2 shows the result.

Listing 6-2: Friendster-Styled Tabs for the "Friend Finder" Application

```
<link rel="stylesheet" type="text/css" href="http://images.friendster.com/cs
s/app_styles.css"/>

 <script src="http://puzzle.mcs.csueastbay.edu/~grewe/OpenSocial/hi5/TabSet/Frie
ndFinder.js"></script>

<div class="tabModuleTabs clearfixLt">
    <div class="tab selected">
      <a href="">Find Friends</a>
      <div class="plug"></div>
    </div>

  <div class="tab">
     <a href="">Invite</a>
  </div>

  </div>
  <div class="tabModuleContent boxcontent">
<div id='heading'></div>
<hr size="1px"/>
<div id='main'></div>
<hr >

<div id='friends'></div>
<div id='friend_status'> </div>
        <br/><br/><br/>
  </div>
```

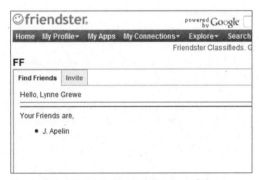

Figure 6-2: Friendster-styled version of the
tabbed "Friend Finder" application

External Resources

Chapter 2 discussed different OpenSocial architectures, including the client-based OpenSocial model. That discussion focused primarily on the application as a completely client-based OpenSocial model. Also touched upon in that discussion was an extended version of this model, referred to as the client-based OpenSocial application with server-side support. In this model, the OpenSocial JavaScript code makes a request to invoke a server-side resource. The request from the client-side OpenSocial JavaScript is handled by the social network container, which, in turn, requests the server-side resource. Results returned from the server go to the social network, which then returns it to the client.

OpenSocial facilitates calls to external resources through its `gadgets.io.makeRequest` method. This method takes two required arguments, and a third optional argument:

```
gadgets.io.makeRequest(url, callback, parameters)
```

This optional argument can be broken down as follows:

- ❑   `url` — This is the URL of the external resource.

- ❑   `callback` — This is the name of the function that serves as the asynchronous callback function.

- ❑   `parameters` — (Optional) This is a list of parameters specified in static fields of `gadgets.io.ReqeustParameters`.

Listing 6-3 shows a modification of the "Friend Finder" application that uses the simplest invocation of `makeRequest`, without any parameters.

Listing 6-3: Friend Finder Application with Call to External Resource Using makeRequest

```
FriendFinder.xml

<?xml version="1.0" encoding="UTF-8"?>
<Module>
  <ModulePrefs title="Friend Finder" description="Friend tracker"
            title_url="http://FriendFinder.com" author="L. Grewe"
            author_email="ff@yahoo.com"
            author_affiliation="iLab" author_location="Bay Area, CA"
            thumbnail="http://UServer/Logo.PNG">
    <Icon>http://UServer/Logo_16_16.PNG</Icon>
    <Require feature="dynamic-height"/>
    <Require feature="opensocial-0.8"/>
  </ModulePrefs>
  <Content type="html">
    <![CDATA[


      <div id='heading'></div>
      <hr size="1px"/>
      <div id='main'></div>
      <hr >
      <div id='friends'></div>
      <div id='friend_status'> </div>

      <script src="http://UServer/FriendFinder.js"></script>


      <script>
          var url = http://UServer/doit;
          gadget.io.makeRequest(url, callback);
```

Continued

Listing 6-3: Friend Finder Application with Call to External Resource Using makeRequest *(continued)*

```
                function callback(response) {

                document.getElementById('friend_status').innerHTML = response.text;
                }

        </script>

    ]]>

      </Content>
    </Module>
```

Listing 6-4 shows the format of the response received by the callback function, which is a JavaScript object.

Listing 6-4: Form of the JavaScript Object Received by Callback Function

```
    {
      data : the_data_parsed_when_appropriate
      errors : any_error_if_occurred
      text : raw_text_output returned
      oauthApprovalUrl :   if_OAuth_Response
      oauthError   :   if_OAuth_Response
      oauthErrorText   : if_OAuth_Error
    }
```

In Listing 6-3, the value associated with text in the response object was used. This is great for plain text or HTML content. The value associated with data is used when the response contains parsed data. For example, through the parameters attribute in makeRequest, you can request response data in JSON or DOM format. In these cases, the data value (instead of the text value) should be used. The errors value is useful in debugging request problems. The oauth* values are only used in signed requests, which are discussed in detail later in this chapter.

Caching Issues

When calling makeRequest, the container can choose to cache the results. This is done in an attempt to reduce latency, thus improving performance. Containers typically keep their cache for 1 hour. If the remote content changes, or if you are executing a dynamic program, you will not want to have the container cache the results. There are a number of possible solutions for this problem.

One option is for your server to return content with HTTP headers that have the values of Cache-Control or Expires or Last-Modified specified. The container should support these header variables appropriately.

Another solution is to use gadgets.io.RequestParameters.REFRESH_INTERVAL as a parameter to your makeRequest call. If you want no caching, you can set the interval to 0. Otherwise, it represents the number of seconds before refreshing. Listing 6-5 shows an example of this.

Listing 6-5: Setting REFRESH_INTERVAL as a Parameter to makeRequest

```
var parameters = {};
parameters[gadgets.io.RequestParameters.REFRESH_INTERVAL] = 0;
// ... ..setother parameters you want
gadgets.io.makeRequest(url, callback, paramters);
```

Another solution involves appending a new dummy parameter, cacheMe, to the URL with a unique value for each call. Because the URL is unique with each makeRequest call, the container cannot use any cached results. This is shown in Listing 6-6.

Listing 6-6: Appending a Random Number to the URL to Avoid Caching

```
var random_number = generate_random();
var newURL = url + "&cacheME=" +random_number;
gadgets.io.makeRequest(newURL, callback, parameters);
```

POST Request

The standard method type of a makeRequest request is GET. This can be set to any one of the following:

- ❑ POST
- ❑ GET
- ❑ PUT
- ❑ DELETE
- ❑ HEAD

POST is a method that encrypts the data that is sent. In this case, the parameter option will include encrypted data, as shown in Listing 6-7.

Listing 6-7: Setting POST to Include Encrypted Data

```
//create data you are going to send via POST request
//typically this would be done in a dynamic way
var  myUser = {
    name : "Lynne",
    app_userid : 7329
}

var =http://U.com/doit;

//setup POST request via parameters
var parameters = {};
parameters[gadgets.io.RequestParameters.METHOD]
    = gadgets.io.MethodType.POST; parameters
    [gadgets.io.RequestParameters.POST_DATA]
    = gadgets.io.encodeValues(myUser);

gadgets.io.makeRequest(url, callback, paramters);
```

Signed Request

If security is a concern, one solution is to sign requests to external resources. Creating a signed request makes the container verify the user's identity (the client making the request) to your external resource program. Let's first take a look at what the developer must do to create a signed request, and then discuss what the container does.

Developer Steps

To make a signed request, you need to follow these steps:

1. Get a signed key from each container to which you will deploy your application.

2. Create your makeRequest call with the authorization type set.

3. Add functionality in your server-side program to authenticate the makeRequest call. Handle errors appropriately in response construction.

The following parameter should be set for making a signed request:

```
gadgets.io.RequestParameters.AUTHORIZATION
```

This parameter can take on one of the following values:

❑ gadgets.io.AuthorizationType.NONE

❑ gadgets.io.AuthorizationType.SIGNED

❑ gadgets.io.AuthorizationType.OAUTH

Listing 6-8 shows the code necessary to create a signed request (of type SIGNED).

Listing 6-8: Signed makeRequest Call

```
var =http://U.com/doit;

//setup SIGNED request via parameters
var parameters = {};
parameters[gadgets.io.RequestParameters.AUTHORIZATION] =
    gadgets.io.AuthorizationType.SIGNED;

gadgets.io.makeRequest(url, callback, paramters);
```

Note that the response object received by the callback function (see Listing 6-4) in the case of OAuth signed requests may now have values associated with the oauth* fields with the following meanings:

❑ oauthApprovalUrl — This means that the user will need to visit this URL to give permission to the gadget for this request.

❑ oauthError — If an OAuth error occurs, this gives a status code.

❑ oauthErrorText — This is the description of a problem, if one occurred with OAuth.

What the Container Does

Before the container forwards the client's request to the external application, the container must validate the user. This information is passed on to the application via the following added request parameters:

- ❑ `opensocial_viewer_id` — This is the ID of the person making the request (client).

- ❑ `opensocial_owner_id` — This is the ID of the owner.

- ❑ `opensocial_app_url` — This is the URL of the requesting application (the container).

- ❑ `opensocial_instance_id` — (Optional) This is used when you can have multiple instances in a container. Together with `opensocial_app_url`, it makes a unique identifier for application in the container.

- ❑ `opensocial_app_id` — (Optional) This is the unique ID assigned to your application by a container.

- ❑ `xoauth_public_key` — (Optional) The container may choose to give the public key used in signing the request. The container may require developers to get this in non-programmatic ways.

Containers will take the request and these additional parameters, and then sign the request and forward it to the external resource URL provided. Notice that a few of the parameters listed here are optional. Containers can choose if and how to implement the process. For example, orkut will send a unique `opensocial_app_id`, whereas MySpace sends a unique consumer key in an `oauth_consumer-key` request parameter instead.

Containers are required to either send the public key to the developer, or to provide in its developer documentation a well-publicized site from which to get it. Following is a typical location for this on a container:

```
https://containerhost/opensocial/certificates/xoauth_public_keyvalue
```

Note that the `commonname` attribute of the certificate containing the key should be the hostname of the container, and should match the `oauth_consumer_key` request parameter.

What Your Server-Side Code Needs

The external resource program must be able to use the signature information to get the request, as well as the associated parameters to process the request. The external program must verify that the container's signature is correct. Another item to validate is the timestamp. The external application should check to ensure that the timestamp on the request is recent. OpenSocial recommends that the timestamp be within a 10-minute span (plus or minus 5 minutes) from the current time.

The optional parameters of `oauth_consumer_key` and `xoauth_public_key` can be used to determine when a container has updated its certificates. It is good practice to create a separate program to check for new certificates, download them, and set up a "certificate cache" that your external resource applications can share.

Chapter 5 provides an example of a server-side PHP program that uses OAuth for authentication.

Performance Improvement Using Preload

Because of the number of steps involved in the `makeRequest` process, as well as the possible resulting latency, making these requests should be something done in a limited, only-as-needed, fashion. Performance can be improved by preloading external resources. This is done via the `<Preload>` Gadget XML tag, as shown in Listing 6-9.

Listing 6-9: Gadget XML Preload Element Used to Load External Resource and Inline Results

```
<Preload
      href="http://U.com/doit.xml"
      views="profile" />
```

The code in Listing 6-9 will place the results in the same location as the tag in the Gadget XML, thus inlining the results. This will be performed at gadget load time, and this data will be available during gadget execution.

> Note that an optional attribute to the `<Preload>` tag is `authz`. If `authz="signed"` or `authz= "oauth"` is specified, it tells the container to prepare a signed request for processing the preload.

Capabilities Inquiry

As mentioned, OpenSocial has some optional features that containers may or may not choose to implement. In addition, some social networks may not be fully compliant. It is important to know how to dynamically inquire about the OpenSocial capabilities on the container.

You can use the `gadgets.util.hasFeature` method discussed earlier in this chapter to query the container about what features it supports. Similarly, you can use the `openSocial.Environment` `.supportsFields` method to see if an OpenSocial field is support by the container.

> One interesting fact is that, as long as a container implements all of the OpenSocial JavaScript methods, it can be technically compliant, providing that it returns an `opensocial.ResponseItem.NOT_IMPLEMENTED` for methods it has not really implemented.

Action Requests and Permissions

Action requests are requests made to users seeking their approval for some action your application tries to take. The container will automatically handle the request and process the user response for any necessary permission. These requests can be specific to the container and its application regulations.

For example, when your application wants to create an activity through `opensocial`
`.requestCreateActivity`, this can trigger the container to request permission. Other methods that might
trigger user approval include `opensocial.requestPermission`, `opensocial.requestSendMessage`,
and `opensocial.requestShareApp`.

As a developer, you must keep in mind that a user (and, consequently, the container) can deny these
requests, and your application should respond appropriately.

Summary

In this chapter, you learned about application testing and front-end issues. This included code samples
to produce gadget navigation tabs and container-specific looks.

You learned how to request external resources, as well as about the issues of caching and making signed
requests. This was followed by a quick tip on performance enhancement via preloading. (Performance
will be discussed in great detail in Chapter 8).

The chapter concluded with a discussion about capabilities inquiry, action requests, and permissions.
Chapter 7 covers more advanced examples of uses of OpenSocial and targeted application development.

7

Sample Applications

This chapter provides code for a number of sample applications that feature important elements needed by many applications. These examples include application elements related to the following:

- ❑ Person/people
- ❑ Communications
- ❑ AppData
- ❑ Environment (support and domain)
- ❑ Compliance testing
- ❑ Error handling
- ❑ Permissions
- ❑ Container-specific extensions
- ❑ Internationalization, localization, and globalization
- ❑ Flash media

Person/People Applications

This section provides a selection of code that produces useful application features dealing with a Person and/or People. This discussion includes code for the following:

- ❑ Requesting a maximum number of friends
- ❑ Using multiple requests for friends
- ❑ Requesting only friends who have the application installed
- ❑ Producing a paginated friend list
- ❑ Using pronouns
- ❑ Creating a friend selector

❏   Testing if two users are friends

❏   Finding top friends who have the application installed

❏   Friends of friends

Requesting a Maximum Number of Friends

Some OpenSocial containers (such as orkut) limit the default number of returned friends from a friend request (for example, 20). In this case, the request can be modified to ask for a maximum number of friends using the MAX parameter, as shown in Listing 7-1. The maximum can be any integer number, and in Listing 7-1, it is set to 50. The actual number of friends retrieved (a user can have less than 50 friends) is the output of this code snippet.

Listing 7-1: Requesting a Maximum Number of Friends

```
function makerequest() {
    var req = opensocial.newDataRequest();
    var param = {};
    param[opensocial.DataRequest.PeopleRequestFields.MAX] = 50;

    var idspec = opensocial.newIdSpec(
                { "userId" : "OWNER", "groupId" : "FRIENDS" });
    var Req = dataReqObj.newFetchPeopleRequest(idspec, param);
    req.add(Req, 'req');

    req.send(getresponse);
};

function getresponse(data) {
    output(data.get("req").getData().size());
};

makerequest();
```

Using Multiple Requests for Friends

Often, the you may only want the application to get a defined set of friends at a time, rather than retrieving all of them. This can be done via OpenSocial JavaScript calls using the opensocial.DataRequest .PeopleRequestFields.FIRST parameter (which represents the index of the first friend to retrieve), along with the MAX parameter. By setting these parameters and updating the FIRST parameter for each call (thus, keeping track of the friends currently retrieved), multiple calls can be performed to retrieve the friends in batches. Listing 7-2 shows code that recursively makes calls to get 10 friends at a time until all the friends are requested.

Listing 7-2: Multiple Requests for Friends

```
var flag_no_more_friends = false;
var index = 0;
var max = 10;

function makerequest(i) {
```

```
    var req = opensocial.newDataRequest();
    var param = {};
    param[opensocial.DataRequest.PeopleRequestFields.FIRST] = i;
    param[opensocial.DataRequest.PeopleRequestFields.MAX] = max;
    var idspec = opensocial.newIdSpec(
                { "userId" : "VIEWER", "groupId" : "FRIENDS" });
    var Req = dataReqObj.newFetchPeopleRequest(idspec, param);
    req.add(Req, 'req');

    req.send(getresponse);
};

function getresponse(data) {
    var num = data.get("req").getData().size();

    output(num + " more friends");
    gadgets.window.adjustHeight();
    if(num < max)
       flag_no_more_friends = true;

    index = index + num;

    if(flag_no_more_friends == false)
       paginatefriends();
};

function paginatefriends(){
    makerequest(index);
};

paginatefriends();
```

Requesting Only Friends Who Have the Application Installed

One common operation that many applications need to make is the retrieval of only friends who have currently installed the application. This can be used to populate application information such as "friend's app data." Certainly, the application can be written to retrieve the current friend list (of those with the application installed) from a database or AppData storage. However, a better way to do this is by applying a filter in the OpenSocial request for friends to limit the return to only those who have the application installed. This requires that the OpenSocial container provides support for the HAS_APP Person field.

Listing 7-3 shows code that requests only the friends who have this application installed. For testing purposes, the output is the number of friends who currently have the application.

Listing 7-3: Requesting Only Friends Who Have the Application Installed

```
function makerequest() {
  var req = opensocial.newDataRequest();
  var param = {};
  param[opensocial.DataRequest.PeopleRequestFields.MAX] = 50;
  param[opensocial.DataRequest.PeopleRequestFields.FILTER] =
```

Continued

Listing 7-3: Requesting Only Friends Who Have the Application Installed *(continued)*

```
                                    opensocial.DataRequest.FilterType.HAS_APP;

    var idspec = opensocial.newIdSpec(
                    { "userId" : "OWNER", "groupId" : "FRIENDS" });
    var Req = req.newFetchPeopleRequest(idspec, param);
    req.add(Req, 'req');
    req.send(getresponse);
};

function getresponse(data) {
    output(data.get("req").getData().size() + " friends have this app");
};


    makerequest();
```

Producing a Paginated Friends List

A common need is to page through a set of user's friends. This is important because some users can have hundreds of friends. Listing 7-4 shows code that implements the pagination of a friends list. The results are shown in Figure 7-1.

Listing 7-4: Paginating a Friends List

```
<Content type="html">
    <![CDATA[


Here it is
<div id='friends'> me the friends </div>

<script>
    var first = 1;
    var max = 2;
    var perPage;
    var friends_html;

    function init(){
        var param = {};
        param[opensocial.DataRequest.PeopleRequestFields.FIRST] = first;
        param[opensocial.DataRequest.PeopleRequestFields.MAX] = max;


        var dataReqObj = opensocial.newDataRequest();
        var viewerReq = dataReqObj.newFetchPersonRequest('VIEWER');

        dataReqObj.add(viewerReq, 'viewer');


        var idspec = opensocial.newIdSpec(
                    { "userId" : "VIEWER", "groupId" : "FRIENDS" });
```

```
          var Req = dataReqObj.newFetchPeopleRequest(idspec);
          dataReqObj.add(Req, 'friends');

          dataReqObj.send(onLoadViewerResponse);
      }

    function onLoadViewerResponse(data){
        var viewer_friends = data.get('friends').getData();

        friends_html = "Select a friend: <br> <ul>";
        perPage = 0;
        viewer_friends.each(function(person) {
            friends_html = friends_html +  '<li>' +
                  person.getDisplayName() + '</li
>';
            perPage++;
        });
        friends_html = friends_html + '</ul>';
        friends_html = friends_html + '<input type=submit onclick
                          ="movePage(-1)" value="Prev" />';
        friends_html = friends_html + '<input type=submit onclick
                          ="movePage(1)" value="Next"/>';
        document.getElementById('friends').innerHTML = friends_html;
    }

  function movePage(delta) {
      first = first + (delta * perPage);
      if(first < 0)
          first = 1;
      init();
  }

    init();
</script>

]]>
    </Content>
```

Figure 7-1:
Paginated
friends list

Using Pronouns

A common need in social applications is to refer to a user by an appropriate pronoun (for example, "he" or "she"). Always using the person's name can be awkward, such as repeatedly saying, "Lynne does X" or "Lynne is Y." For more natural-sounding language, it is sometimes better to say, "She does X" or "She is Y."

This requires the use of the gender information referenced by opensocial.Person.Field.GENDER. Listing 7-5 shows the application code necessary to query for this information to produce and use a gender-based pronoun in the creation of a message in the viewer's "ABOUT_ME" profile information.

Listing 7-5: Using Gender Information to Create a Gender-Specific Pronoun

```
<Content type="html">
    <![CDATA[

  <style>
    #content_div {height: 800px; width: 800px; overflow: scroll; }
  </style>

  <div id="content_div">

     <div id='info'> </div>
  </div>

  <script>
      var pronoun = "";

      function init(){
         var param = {};

         //set up request to contain GENDER and ABOUT_ME fields
         param[opensocial.DataRequest.PeopleRequestFields.PROFILE_DETAILS] =
              [opensocial.Person.Field.GENDER,
               opensocial.Person.Field.ABOUT_ME];

         var dataReqObj = opensocial.newDataRequest();
         var viewerReq = dataReqObj.newFetchPersonRequest('VIEWER', param);
         dataReqObj.add(viewerReq, 'viewer');

         dataReqObj.send(onLoadViewerResponse);
      }

      function onLoadViewerResponse(data){
         var viewer = data.get('viewer').getData();

         //get gender and create pronoun
         var gender = viewer.getField(opensocial.Person.Field.GENDER);
         if(gender == opensocial.Enum.Gender.MALE)
            pronoun = "He";
         else if(gender == opensocial.Enum.Gender.FEMALE)
            pronoun = "She";
         else
            pronoun = viewer.getDisplayName();
```

```
          var the_message =  viewer.getDisplayName() +
                          " is the currently viewing this app <br><br>";
          the_message = the_message + pronoun +
                          " has the following About info: <br>"+
                      viewer.getField(opensocial.Person.Field.ABOUT_ME);


          document.getElementById('info').innerHTML = the_message;
      }

      init();
    </script>

  ]]>
  </Content>
```

The following is the output of this program. Notice how the "She" pronoun is used:

```
Lynne Grewe is currently viewing this app

She has the following About info:
Looking to connect to other professionals in the Web and media world.
Currently working in social network development and media processing.
```

Creating a Friend Selector

Being able to select friends to whom you can send messages or invitations is a common element in many applications. Listing 7-6 shows code that produces a form containing a scrollable and selectable list of the viewer's friends. Both the Thumbnail_URL and the friend's name are used in the construction of the selector.

Listing 7-6: Friend Selector Application Code

```
<Content type="html">
    <![CDATA[

   <style>
     #content_div {width: 600px;   margin:10px 0pt 0pt 20px;}
   </style>

   <div id="content_div">
       <div id='friends'> </div>
   </div>

   <script>
      var outter_html = '<div style="float:left; width: 120px; height:
          140px;">';

      var support_html = "<ul>";
      var support;
```

Continued

Listing 7-6: Friend Selector Application Code *(continued)*

```
        //function to request viewer's friends
        function init(){
           var  dataReqObj = opensocial.newDataRequest();
           var idspec = opensocial.newIdSpec(
                          { "userId" : "VIEWER", "groupId" : "FRIENDS" });
           var Req = dataReqObj.newFetchPeopleRequest(idspec);
           dataReqObj.add(Req, 'viewerFriends');
           dataReqObj.send(onLoadViewerResponse);
        }


        //function that gets response of viewer's friends and constructs selector
        function onLoadViewerResponse(data) {
           var viewer_friends = data.get('viewerFriends').getData();
           var friends_html  = 'Select Friends' ;
           friends_html = friends_html + '<form onsubmit="submitFriends(this);
                                          return false;">';
           friends_html = friends_html + '<div style="margin: 20px 0pt 0pt 20px;
                     height: 275px; overflow-y: scroll; overflow-x: hidden;">'

           //populate <div> tag - 1 for each friend with
           //an label/image and checkbox
           viewer_friends.each(function(person) {
             friends_html = friends_html + outter_html;
             friends_html = friends_html +
                          '<label style="background: transparent url(';
             friends_html = friends_html +
                          person.getField(opensocial.Person.Field.THUMBNAIL_URL);
             friends_html = friends_html +
                   ') no-repeat scroll 0pt 0pt; display: block; height: 100px;
                    width: 100px; -moz-background-clip: -moz-initial;
                    -moz-background-origin: -moz-initial;
                    -moz-background-inline-policy: -moz-initial;" for="icon_61"/>';

             friends_html = friends_html + '<div style="padding-top: 5px;">';
             friends_html = friends_html + '<input id="' + person.getId() +
                   '" type="checkbox" style="margin: 0pt; padding: 0pt;" value="' +
                   person.getId() + '" name="friend_selected"/>';

             friends_html = friends_html +
                   '<label style="padding: 0pt; font-weight: normal; font-size: 9pt;
                    color: rgb(59, 89, 152); cursor: pointer;" for="icon_61">';

             friends_html = friends_html + person.getDisplayName() + '</label>';
             friends_html = friends_html + '</div></div>';

           });
         friends_html = friends_html +
          '</div><input style="background: rgb(255,100,0);" type="submit"> </form>';


         document.getElementById('friends').innerHTML = friends_html;
    }
```

```
      init();
   </script>

]]>
</Content>
```

Figure 7-2 shows the results of running the code in Listing 7-6. Note that the code for submission of the form is not shown. It is left for the developer to decide what to do with the list of selected friends.

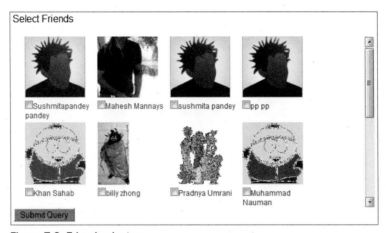

Figure 7-2: Friend selector

Testing If Two Users Are Friends

Unfortunately, there is no immediate method call you can use to determine if two users are friends. To do this, the application must retrieve one of the user's set of friends and cycle through it to see if the other user is in this list. Listing 7-7 shows code that performs this task.

Listing 7-7: Testing If Owner and Viewer Are Friends

```
<Content type="html">
    <![CDATA[

<style>
  #content_div {height: 800px; width: 800px; overflow: scroll; }
</style>

<div id="content_div">

<div id='message'> </div>
</div>


<script>
```

Continued

Listing 7-7: Testing If Owner and Viewer Are Friends (continued)

```javascript
function init(){
    var dataReqObj = opensocial.newDataRequest();
    var Req = dataReqObj.newFetchPersonRequest('VIEWER');
    dataReqObj.add(Req, 'viewer');

    Req = dataReqObj.newFetchPersonRequest('OWNER');
    dataReqObj.add(Req, 'owner');

    //get owner's friends
    var idspec = opensocial.newIdSpec(
                        { "userId" : "OWNER", "groupId" : "FRIENDS" });

    Req = dataReqObj.newFetchPeopleRequest(idspec);
    dataReqObj.add(Req, 'ownerFriends');


    dataReqObj.send(onLoadViewerResponse);
}

function onLoadViewerResponse(data){
    var owner = data.get('owner').getData();
    var friends = data.get('ownerFriends').getData();
    var viewer = data.get('viewer').getData();
    var areFriends = false;
    friends.each(function(person) {
        if(owner.getId() == person.getId())
            { areFriends = true; }
    });
    var html = owner.getDisplayName() + " and " +
                viewer.getDisplayName() + "are " ;
    if(areFriends == false)
        html = html + "not ";

    html = html + "friends.";

    document.getElementById('message').innerHTML = html;
}

    init();
</script>


]]>
</Content>
```

Finding Top Friends Who Have the Application Installed

"Top friends" is a concept in some social networks that allows users to select their "best" (or "top") friends. It may be useful for an application to exploit this feature. Listing 7-8 shows code that retrieves "top friends" who have the application installed. This is done via the parameter associated with the `opensocial.DataRequest.PeopleRequestFields.FILTER` key. As shown in Listing 7-8, this parameter is passed to the `newFetchPeopleRequest` method.

Listing 7-8: Filtering a Friends Request by Top_Friends and by HAS_APP

```
<Content type="html">
<![CDATA[

<style>
  #content_div {height: 800px; width: 800px; overflow: scroll; }
</style>

<div id="content_div">

<div id='message'> </div>
</div>


 <script>

    function init(){
        var dataReqObj = opensocial.newDataRequest();
        var Req = dataReqObj.newFetchPersonRequest('VIEWER');
        dataReqObj.add(Req, 'viewer');


        //get all friends
        var idspec = opensocial.newIdSpec({ "userId" : "VIEWER",
            "groupId" : "FRIENDS" });
        Req = dataReqObj.newFetchPeopleRequest(idspec);
        dataReqObj.add(Req, 'viewerFriends');

        //get top friends who have app installed

        var param = {};
        param[opensocial.DataRequest.PeopleRequestFields.FILTER] =
                    [opensocial.DataRequest.FilterType.TOP_FRIENDS,
                     opensocial.DataRequest.FilterType.HAS_APP];

        Req = dataReqObj.newFetchPeopleReuest(idspec, param);
        dataReqObj.add(Req, 'topViewerFriends');


        dataReqObj.send(onLoadViewerResponse);
    }
    function onLoadViewerResponse(data){

        var friends = data.get('viewerFriends').getData();
        var topFriends = data.get('topViewerFriends').getData();
        var hasAppFriends = data.get('hasAppViewerFriends').getData();
        var viewer = data.get('viewer').getData();

        var html = 'All Friends :<br><ul>';
        friends.each(function(person) {
            html += '<li>' + person.getDisplayName() + '</li>';
        });
        html += '</ul><br><hr>';
```

Continued

Listing 7-8: Filtering a Friends Request by Top_Friends and by HAS_APP *(continued)*

```
            html += 'Top Friends w/App :<br><ul>';
            topFriends.each(function(person) {
                html += '<li>' + person.getDisplayName() + '</li>';
            });
            html += '</ul><br><hr>';


            document.getElementById('message').innerHTML = html;
    }

  init();
</script>

]]>
</Content>
```

Friends of Friends

A useful feature in an application would be to find friends of friends. This is possible in OpenSocial with the `Opensocial.IdSpec.Field.NETWORK_DISTANCE` field of the `IdSpec` class. As of the writing of this book, no containers support this field. Regardless, Listing 7-9 shows a code snippet that demonstrates how to use this feature, which will hopefully be supported in the future.

Listing 7-9: How to Request an Owner's Friends of Friends

```
var idspec = opensocial.newIdSpec({ "userId" : "OWNER", "groupId" : "FRIENDS" });

//set the field for Network distance = 0 means same person, 1 means friend
// and 2 is friend of friend.
idspec.setField(opensocial.IdSpec.Field.NETWORK_DISTANCE, 2);
var req = opensocial.newDataRequest();

req.add(req.newFetchPeopleRequest(idspec), "get_friends");
req.send(response);
```

Communications Applications

This section provides a selection of code that produces useful application features dealing with communications. This discussion includes code for the following:

- ❑ Making signed requests
- ❑ Creating minimessages
- ❑ Creating gadget message bundles
- ❑ Using message and activity templates
- ❑ Using message summaries
- ❑ Using media items in activities

Making Signed Requests

Chapter 6 discussed the concept of creating a signed request from a client to the application's server-side program. Listing 7-10 shows the complete client-side OpenSocial JavaScript program necessary, and Listing 7-11 shows a PHP server-side program that accepts and validates the signed request. The OpenSocial XML application calls `makeSignedRequest()` in Listing 7-10, which constructs a signed `makeRequest` that is sent to the server code in Listing 7-11. The base of this software is given by `http://OpenSocial.org`. It is part of the OAuth software base and is freely available.

Listing 7-10: Client-Side JavaScript Code to Make a Signed Request

```
function makeSignedRequest() {


    var params = {};
    params[gadgets.io.RequestParameters.AUTHORIZATION] =
                          gadgets.io.Authorization.Type.SIGNED;
    params[gadgets.io.RequestParameters.CONTENT_TYPE] =
                          gadgets.io.ContentType.JSON;
    var url = "http://U.com/fetchme.php";
    gadgets.io.makeRequest(url, response, params);
};


function response(ret) {
    printf(ret.data);

    var html = [ ret.data.validated, "<br />",
        "oauth_consumer_key: ", ret.data.query.oauth_consumer_key, "<br />",
        "oauth_nonce: ", ret.data.query.oauth_nonce, "<br />",
        "oauth_signature: ", ret.data.query.oauth_signature, "<br />",
        "oauth_signature_method: ", "oauth_timestamp: ",
                                      ret.data.query.oauth_timestamp, "<br />",
        "oauth_token: ", ret.data.query.oauth_token, "<br />",
        "opensocial_appid: ", ret.data.query.opensocial_appid, "<br />",
        "opensocial_ownerid: ", ret.data.query.opensocial_ownerid, "<br />",
        "xoauth_signature_publickey: ", ret.data.query.xoauth_signature_publickey ]
.join("");

        printf(html);
};
```

Listing 7-11: PHP Server-Side Code to Accept and Verify a Signed Request

```
<?php
    require('OAuth.php');


    class OrkutSignatureMethod extends OAuthSignatureMethod_RSA_SHA1 {
      protected function fetch_public_cert(&$request) {
        return <<<EOD
```

Continued

Listing 7-11: PHP Server-Side Code to Accept and Verify a Signed Request *(continued)*

```
-----BEGIN CERTIFICATE-----
MIIDHzCCAoigAwIBAgIQZMuxK+KKS5wF/rjXp3z/KTANBgkqhkiG9w0BAQUFADCB
hzELMAkGA1UEBhMCWkExIjAgBgNVBAgTGUZPUiBURVNUSU5HIFBVUlBPU0VTIE9O
TFkxHTAbBgNVBAoTFFRoYXd0ZSBDZXJ0aWZpY2F0aW9uMRcwFQYDVQQLEw5URVNU
IFRFU1QgVEVTVDEcMBoGA1UEAxMTVGhhd3RlIFRlc3QgQ0EgUm9vdDAeFw0wODAz
MjYwMDEyMDdaFw0wODA0MTYwMDEyMDdaMIGuMRcwFQYDVQQKEw5oaTVtb2RibGVz
LmNvbTEZMBcGA1UECxMQRG9tYWluIFZhbGlkYXRlZDE7MDkGA1UECxMyR28gdG8g
aHR0cHM6Ly93d3cudGhhd3RlLmNvbS9yZXBvc2l0b3J5L2luZGV4Lmh0bWwxIjAg
BgNVBAsTGVRoYXd0ZSBTU0wxMjMgY2VydGlmaWNhdGUxFzAVBgNVBAMTDmhpNW1v
ZHVsZXMuY29tMIGfMA0GCSqGSIb3DQEBAQUAA4GNADCBiQKBgQCZgdrYsECeGO/Y
srDfaO/vIyMq7+DYdAmImzwg35wnti3Dr3B6kS6OeRiBAIUTvdZXX3XitJFxVlDF
H/PbRimm0d3eQvSfW3+0xIhF9C3E9QFj6LWBz6bBlh5p0pSXygAZ9AXR1OMM2lDR
R9hwQp1YVjzJk3hYW2qD591auROQvwIDAQABo2MwYTAMBgNVHRMBAf8EAjAAMB0G
A1UdJQQWMBQGCCsGAQUFBwMBBggrBgEFBQcDAjAyBggrBgEFBQcBAQQmMCQwIgYI
KwYBBQUHMAGGFmh0dHA6Ly9vY3NwLnRoYXd0ZS5jb20wDQYJKoZIhvcNAQEFBQAD
gYEABdPtdX56mPwSfPMzgSLH7RueLZi5HXqW2krojWsOv3VFnayQKuzXdy5DZrMY
/tI2AUPXicvBW3GjTfSKmUNvsOXUIC8az3K3iTs1KKekUaidLRlaRZIO0FVEJH5u
gO9HqAcXxrx99/3agvAVTKAFBFJtiWDli1LkYeqKrPQOPo8=
-----END CERTIFICATE-----
EOD;
    }
  }

    //Build a request object from the current request
    $request = OAuthRequest::from_request(null, null, array_merge($_GET, $_POST));

    //Initialize the new signature method
    $signature_method = new OrkutSignatureMethod();

    //Check the request signature
    @$signature_valid = $signature_method->check_signature($request, null, null,
                                                $_GET["oauth_signature"]);

    printf("after call");

    }catch(Exception $e){printf("exception is" + $e->getMessage());}

    //Build the output object
    $payload = array();
    if ($signature_valid == true) {
        $payload["validated"] = "Success! The data was validated";
    } else {
        $payload["validated"] = "This request was spoofed";
    }

    //Add extra parameters to help debugging
    $payload["query"] = array_merge($_GET, $_POST);
    $payload["rawpost"] = file_get_contents("php://input");

    //Return the response as JSON
     printf(json_encode($payload));

?>
```

Note that the certificate in the PHP code in Listing 7-11 is specific to the container delivering the request. This code should be expanded to test for the container being targeted, and deliver the appropriate certificate. It is further recommended that the application does not "inline" the certificate.

Creating Minimessages

The gadgets.MiniMessage Gadget API class can be used to create messages inside of the gadget. Some possible uses of this are for status messages, information/promotional messages, and possibly for handling errors.

Listing 7-12 contains the code that creates a "dismissible minimessage," which is shown in Figure 7-3. The "minimessage" Gadget API must be explicitly referenced in the <Require feature="minimessage"> line seen in the <ModulePref> tag. The creation of the minimessage is done in the makeMessage function. By default, the minimessage will appear at the top of the application, as shown in Figure 7-3. Notice the "X" in the upper-right of the message. This is to allow the user to "dismiss" the message.

Listing 7-12: A Simple Dismissible Minimessage

```xml
<?xml version="1.0" encoding="UTF-8"?>
<Module>
  <ModulePrefs title="MiniMessage" description="MiniMessage" >
    <Require feature="dynamic-height"/>
    <Require feature="opensocial-0.7"/>
    <Require feature="minimessage"/>
  </ModulePrefs>
  <Content type="html">
    <![CDATA[

<style>
  #content_div {height: 800px; width: 800px; overflow: scroll; }
</style>

<div id="content_div">
  Main Application Content

<div id='minimessage'> </div>
<div id='message'> </div>
</div>


  <script>

  function init(){
      dataReqObj = opensocial.newDataRequest();
      var Req = dataReqObj.newFetchPersonRequest('VIEWER');
      dataReqObj.add(Req, 'viewer');
      dataReqObj.send(onLoadViewerResponse);
  }
  function onLoadViewerResponse(data){

      var viewer = data.get('viewer').getData();
      var mess = viewer.getDisplayName() +
```

Continued

Listing 7-12: A Simple Dismissible Minimessage *(continued)*

```
                        " --New Video feature launching next week!--";
        makeMessage(mess);
    }
    function makeMessage(mess){

        //create minimessage
        var miniMessage = new gadgets.MiniMessage();

        //make a dismissible message
        // default location is at the top of the application
        var html = miniMessage.createDismissibleMessage(mess);
    }

    init();
    </script>
]]>
    </Content>
```

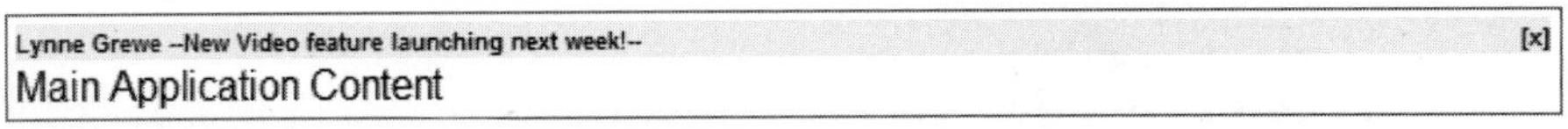

Lynne Grewe --New Video feature launching next week!--	[x]
Main Application Content	

Figure 7-3: Simple dismissible minimessage used for promotional information

Additionally, the developer can create timed messages (which disappear after so many seconds) or static messages (which cannot be dismissed by the user, but only via the `gadgets.MiniMessage` `.dismissMessage(mini_message_object)` application Gadget API call).

Creating Gadget Message Bundles

A useful concept when working with gadgets is that of *message bundles*. If you are repeatedly using a message or message format in an application, a message bundle can be created for it and called in the application wherever it is needed. This supports both reusability and GUI design consistency.

More than one message can be created for an application and bundled together into a message bundle. Specific application uses of message bundles can be found later in this chapter in the sections "Using Message and Activity Templates" and "Internationalization, Localization, and Globalization."

Message bundles and the messages they contain are defined with the gadget tags `<messagebundle>` and `<msg>`, respectively. They are typically stored in a separate XML file. The following is an example:

```
<messagebundle>
    <msg name="greeting">
        Friend Finder ... .track your friends now!
    </msg>
    <msg name="Item1">
```

```
        Track
    </msg>
    <msg name="Item2">
        Invite
    </msg>
</messagebundle>
```

The messages stored in a message bundle (that is, in an external XML file) are brought into an application via the `<Locale>` subelement of the `<ModulePref>` tag in the gadget specification, as shown in Listing 7-13. The message named `greeting` is referenced with the special `__MSG_` gadget substitution variable as `__MSG_greeting__`.

Listing 7-13: External Message Bundle and Reference to the Message Greeting

```
<?xml version="1.0" encoding="UTF-8"?>
<Module>
  <ModulePrefs title="Message Bundle" description="Message Bundle" >

    <Require feature="dynamic-height"/>
    <Require feature="opensocial-0.8"/>
    <Locale messages="http://U.com/messagebundle.xml"/>
  </ModulePrefs>
  <Content type="html">
    <![CDATA[

<style>
  #content_div {height: 800px; width: 800px; overflow: scroll; }
</style>

<div id="content_div">
    <div id='message'> </div>
    <b>__MSG_greeting__</b>.
</div>

]]>
  </Content>
</Module>
```

Alternatively, messages can be accessed via the gadget class `gadgets.Prefs` as follows:

```
var prefs = new gadgets.Prefs();
prefs.getMsg("greeting");
```

Using Message and Activity Templates

Both activities and messages can be created using message bundles. This is done via the parameter fields of `TITLE_ID` and `BODY_ID`, which are used when creating the message or activity. The code shown in Listing 7-14 demonstrates how to create an email message using a message bundle that contains a `<msg name="title">` and a `<msg name="body">`, both stored in the external message bundle XML file named `messagebundle.xml`.

Listing 7-14: Creating a Message with a Message Bundle

```
<?xml version="1.0" encoding="UTF-8"?>
<Module>
  <ModulePrefs title="Message Template" description="Message Template" >
    <Require feature="dynamic-height"/>
    <Require feature="opensocial-0.8"/>
    <Locale messages="http://U.com/messagebundle.xml"/>
  </ModulePrefs>
  <Content type="html">
    <![CDATA[

<style>
  #content_div {height: 800px; width: 800px; overflow: scroll; }
</style>

<div id="content_div">

<div id='message'> </div>
<b>__MSG_greeting__</b>.
<input type=button value="create message" onclick="makeMessage();">
</div>


  <script>
  var viewer, owner;

  function init(){
      dataReqObj = opensocial.newDataRequest();
      var Req = dataReqObj.newFetchPersonRequest('VIEWER');
      dataReqObj.add(Req, 'viewer');

      Req = dataReqObj.newFetchPersonRequest('OWNER');
      dataReqObj.add(Req, 'owner');
      dataReqObj.send(onLoadViewerResponse);
  }
  function onLoadViewerResponse(data){

      owner = data.get('owner').getData();
      viewer = data.get('viewer').getData();
  }


  function makeMessage(){
      if(viewer == null || owner == null) return;
      //setup Prefs object to grab the message bundle info
      var prefs = new gadgets.Prefs();
      var opts = {};
      opts[opensocial.Message.Field.TITLE_ID] = 'title';
      opts[opensocial.Message.Field.BODY_ID] = 'body';

      //set up type of message
      opts[opensocial.Message.Field.TYPE] = opensocial.Message.Type.EMAIL;
```

```
            var body = viewer.getDisplayName() + " says hello to " +
                            owner.getDisplayName() + " using the Message application";

            var message = opensocial.newMessage(body, opts);

            opensocial.requestSendMessage(owner.getId(), message, messageMade);
        }


        function messageMade(d){
            document.getElementById('message').innerHTML = "message done";
        }


        init();
    </script>

]]>
    </Content>
</Module>
```

It is possible to also "inline" the message bundle in the <Locale> tag. For activities, another option is to add template parameters so that variables can be used in the construction of the actual message. This is done with the TEMPLATE_PARAMS parameter. Both of these features are illustrated in the following code snippet:

```
<ModulePrefs>
<Locale>
    <messagebundle>
        <msg name="title ">
            ${Viewer} used Friend Finder
        </msg>
    </messagebundle>
</Locale>
</ModulePrefs>

<script>
    var viewer;

    var template_params = {
      'Viewer': viewer
    };

    //set up parameters to construct the Activity
    var params = {};
    params[opensocial.Activity.Field.TITLE_ID] = title;
    params[opensocial.Activity.Field.TEMPLATE_PARAMS] = template_params;
```

Unfortunately, a number of containers do not support the use of the TITLE_ID and BODY_ID fields. In this case, message bundles can still be used, but instead of associating the message's or activity's TITLE_ID and BODY_ID fields, you would associate the messages with the TITLE and BODY fields directly. This is demonstrated in the following code snippet for a message where the <msg> tags used are named `title` and `body`:

```
var prefs = new gadgets.Prefs();

var the_title = prefs.getMsg("title");
var the_body = prefs.getMsg("body");
opts[opensocial.Message.Field.TITLE_ID] = the_title;
opts[opensocial.Message.Field.BODY_ID] = the_body;
```

Using Message Summaries

Containers have limits on the number of activities per user per day that can be created from an application. Related to this is the fact that some containers summarize activities. They do this by creating "activity summaries," which involves the condensing of multiple activity postings to one activity. This reduces the number of activities displayed and can reduce visual clutter.

It is possible to use message bundles to suggest summaries to containers. Activity summaries will summarize around a key in a key/value pair. The message created for summarization should have an ID = `"messageID of main template":"key"`, as shown in the following examples:

```
<messagebundle>
  <msg name="VIDEO:Director">
    ${Subject.Count} friends have suggested listening to videos by ${Director}
  </msg>
  <msg name="VIDEO:Title">
    ${Title} has been watched by ${Subject.Count} friends</msg>
</messagebundle>
```

Using Media Items in Activities

Adding media can enrich and make activity postings more interesting. This is a good technique to use to attract new users to an application. Recall that activity streams are often seen as "updates" by friends.

OpenSocial supports the creation of audio, image, and video media items. More than one media item can be included in an activity. However, some containers restrict this, as well as the type of media items allowed in an activity. Check out the container-specific developer documentation for current rules.

OpenSocial creates new media items with the `opensocial.newMediaItem` method. The resulting media item can be placed in an array of media items that can then be passed as an optional parameter when creating the activity. Listing 7-15 shows how to accomplish this. In this code, a media item is created that is associated with an image URL.

Listing 7-15: Creating a Media Item Associated with an Activity

```
<Content type="html">
<![CDATA[

<style>
  #content_div {height: 800px; width: 800px; overflow: scroll; }
</style>
```

```
<div id="content_div">

<div id='activityGUI'>

<input type=button value="send smiley update"
      onclick="makeActivityMedia('http://puzzle.mcs.csueastbay.edu/
      ~grewe/OpenSocial/hi5/ActivityMediaItems/smiley.jpg');">
<div id='activity'></div>
</div>
</div>


  <script>

   var viewer;
   var owner;

   function makeActivityMedia(ImageURL){
       var opts = new Array();

       //make activity title using viewer and owner names
       opts[opensocial.Activity.Field.TITLE] = viewer.getDisplayName() +
                " is sending " + owner.getDisplayName + " a smile";
       var mediaItems = new Array();

       //setup media Item related to acitivy
       var media_param = {};
       media_param[opensocial.MediaItem.Field.TYPE] =
                [opensocial.MediaItem.Field.IMAGE];
       var mediaItem  = opensocial.newMediaItem("text/jpeg", ImageURL, media_param);


       // Add a media item link if supported
       if(gadgets.util.hasFeature('hi5') && opensocial.getEnvironment().
           supportsField(opensocial.Environment.ObjectType.ACTIVITY_MEDIA_ITEM,
                hi5.ActivityMediaItemField.LINK))
        {
          mediaItem.setField(hi5.ActivityMediaItemField.LINK,
                        viewer.getField(opensocial.Person.Field.PROFILE_URL));
        }

       mediaItems.push(mediaItem);
       opts[opensocial.Activity.Field.MEDIA_ITEMS] = mediaItems;


        //create activity
       var activity = opensocial.newActivity(opts);


       //activity request
       opensocial.requestCreateActivity(activity,
                        opensocial.CreateActivityPriority.HIGH, activityMade);
   }
```

Continued

Listing 7-15: Creating a Media Item Associated with an Activity *(continued)*

```
        function activityMade(){
            document.getElementById('activity').innerHTML = "activity was made";
        }


        //setup request for viewer and owner - used in activity info
        function init(){
            dataReqObj = opensocial.newDataRequest();
            var Req = dataReqObj.newFetchPersonRequest('VIEWER');
            dataReqObj.add(Req, 'viewer');

            Req = dataReqObj.newFetchPersonRequest('OWNER');
            dataReqObj.add(Req, 'owner');

            //get owner's friends
            var idspec = opensocial.newIdSpec(
                            { "userId" : "OWNER", "groupId" : "FRIENDS" });
            Req = dataReqObj.newFetchPeopleRequest(idspec);
            dataReqObj.add(Req, 'ownerFriends');


            dataReqObj.send(onLoadViewerResponse);
        }


        function onLoadViewerResponse(data){

            owner = data.get('owner').getData();
            var friends = data.get('ownerFriends').getData();
            viewer = data.get('viewer').getData();
        }




        init();
        </script>

    ]]>
        </Content>
    </Module>
```

Unfortunately, a number of containers do not support media items, and the alternative is to create HTML inside the activity title or body. Listing 7-16 shows how to create the same effect using this workaround. Figure 7-4 shows the results on orkut, a container that currently does not support media items.

Listing 7-16: Using HTML as an Alternative to a Media Item

```
<Content type="html">
    <![CDATA[

<style>
```

```
    #content_div {height: 800px; width: 800px; overflow: scroll; }
</style>

<div id="content_div">

<div id='activityGUI'>
  <input type=button value="send smiley"
        onclick="makeActivityMedia('http://U.com/smiley.jpg);">
  <div id='activity'></div>
</div>
</div>


  <script>

   var viewer;
   var owner;

   function makeActivityMedia(ImageURL){
        document.getElementById('activity').innerHTML = "hi";
        var opts = new Array();
        opts[opensocial.Activity.Field.TITLE] = viewer.getDisplayName() +
                        " it's  Smiley time :";
        opts[opensocial.Activity.Field.BODY] = viewer.getDisplayName() +
                        " is making  a smile <img src=\"
                        " + ImageURL + "\">";


        var activity = opensocial.newActivity(opts);

        opensocial.requestCreateActivity(activity,
                        opensocial.CreateActivityPriority.HIGH,
                        activityMade);

    }


   function activityMade(status){

        if (status.hadError())
         {
           alert("Error creating activity.");
         }
         else
        {
           alert("Activity successfully created.");
        }
     }



   function init(){
        dataReqObj = opensocial.newDataRequest();
        var Req = dataReqObj.newFetchPersonRequest('VIEWER');
```

Continued

257

Listing 7-16: Using HTML as an Alternative to a Media Item *(continued)*

```
        dataReqObj.add(Req, 'viewer');

        Req = dataReqObj.newFetchPersonRequest('OWNER');
        dataReqObj.add(Req, 'owner');

        //get owner's friends
        var idspec = opensocial.newIdSpec(
                            { "userId" : "OWNER", "groupId" : "FRIENDS" });
        Req = dataReqObj.newFetchPeopleRequest(idspec);
        dataReqObj.add(Req, 'ownerFriends');


        dataReqObj.send(onLoadViewerResponse);
    }
  function onLoadViewerResponse(data){

        owner = data.get('owner').getData();
        var friends = data.get('ownerFriends').getData();
        viewer = data.get('viewer').getData();
    }
  init();
  </script>

]]>
  </Content>
```

Figure 7-4: Using HTML in the body of the activity to insert an image

Clearing AppData

Recall that a feature of OpenSocial is persistence storage of AppData via the `opensocial.DataRequest`
`.newUpdatePersonAppDataRequest(id,key,value)` method. This data can also be removed using the
`opensocial.DataRequest.newRemovePersonAppDataRequest(id,keys)` method, as shown in the following code snippet that removes the data associated with the viewer and key="theKey":

```
var Req = opensocial.newDataRequest();
Req.add(
    Req.newRemovePersonAppDataRequest("VIEWER", "theKey"),
    "clear_data");
Req.send(callback_function);
```

The following code clears data associated with keys k1, k2, k3, and k4:

```
req.add(
    req.newRemovePersonAppDataRequest("VIEWER", ["k1", "k2", "k3", "k4"]),
    "clear_data");
```

To clear all data associated with the viewer, use the following code:

```
req.add(
    req.newRemovePersonAppDataRequest("VIEWER", "*"),
    "clear_data")
```

Understanding Environment — Support and Domain

OpenSocial allows an application to test for container support using the opensocial.Environment object that can be obtained through the opensocial.getEnvironment() method call. The returned container's Environment object can be queried for support through its supportsField method, which can test for support for fields related to the following:

- ❑   Activity
- ❑   Address
- ❑   BodyType
- ❑   Email
- ❑   Filter_Type
- ❑   MediaItem
- ❑   Message
- ❑   MessageType
- ❑   Name
- ❑   Organization
- ❑   Person
- ❑   Phone
- ❑   Sort_Order
- ❑   URL

The supportsField method takes two parameters: the opensocial.Environment.ObjectType.* value and the corresponding field support value. For example, if you are testing the opensocial.Environmnet.ObjectType.Person object, then opensocial.Person.Field.NAME is one of the many opensocial.Person.Field.* fields that can be checked for support.

The other method of this Environment class that is useful is the getDomain method that will return a string representing the container's domain. This can be used when requesting container-specific resources or developing a container-specific GUI.

Listing 7-17 shows sample code that tests a few environment features. In this code, the domain is retrieved, as well as testing for various Email, Address and Person fields for support. Figure 7-5 shows the results of running this code on orkut.

Listing 7-17: Environment Support and Domain Example Code

```
<Content type="html">
   <![CDATA[

<style>
  #content_div {height: 800px; width: 800px; overflow: scroll; }
</style>

<div id="content_div">

<div id='domain'> </div>
<hr>
<div id='support'> </div>
</div>


  <script>
   var support_html = "<ul>";
   var support;

   function init(){

       //get the environment
      var e =  opensocial.getEnvironment();

       //get domain like "hi5.com"
       var domain = e.getDomain();
       document.getElementById('domain').innerHTML = "Domain is " + domain;


       //test for support of different fields
       //email support for person data
       support = e.supportsField(opensocial.Environment.ObjectType.EMAIL,
                            opensocial.Email.Field.ADDRESS);
       support_html = support_html + "<li> Email-Address : " + support + "</li>";

       //longitude support for address
       support = e.supportsField(opensocial.Environment.ObjectType.ADDRESS,
                            opensocial.Address.Field.LONGITUDE);
       support_html = support_html + "<li> Address-Longitude: " + support + "</li>";
       //country support for address
       support = e.supportsField(opensocial.Environment.ObjectType.ADDRESS,
                            opensocial.Address.Field.COUNTRY);
       support_html = support_html + "<li> Address-Country: " + support + "</li>";

       //About_me support for person
       support = e.supportsField(opensocial.Environment.ObjectType.PERSON,
                            opensocial.Person.Field.ABOUT_ME);
       support_html = support_html + "<li> Person- ABOUT_ME: " + support + "</li>";

       //GENDER support for person
       var support = e.supportsField(opensocial.Environment.ObjectType.PERSON,
```

```
                                        opensocial.Person.Field.GENDER);
        support_html = support_html + "<li> Person- GENDER: " + support + "</li>";


        //person email support for person
        var support = e.supportsField(opensocial.Environment.ObjectType.PERSON,
                                      opensocial.Person.Field.EMAILS);
        support_html = support_html + "<li> Person- Emails: " + support + "</li>";


        support_html = support_html + "</ul>";
        document.getElementById('support').innerHTML = support_html;
    }


    init();
  </script>

]]>
</Content>
```

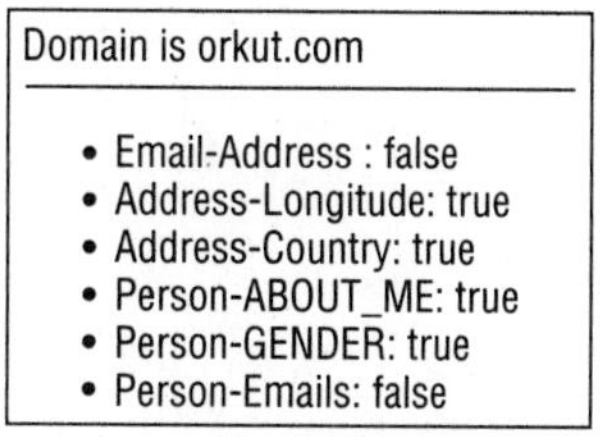

```
Domain is orkut.com

 • Email-Address : false
 • Address-Longitude: true
 • Address-Country: true
 • Person-ABOUT_ME: true
 • Person-GENDER: true
 • Person-Emails: false
```

**Figure 7-5: Application testing
for environment support**

Using the `Environment` object and its `supportsField` method to check for container support are both highly recommended options. Another possibly quicker (but more static) option is to test for the domain the application is running on and hard-code logic for each domain as necessary. This requires that the application be altered each time a container changes its support. The following code snippet shows how this is structured:

```
if (MySpace) {
  ...
} else if (hi5) {
  ...
} else if (orkut) {
  ...
} else {
...
}
```

While this may not be a great option, and doesn't respond to container changes, it is still commonly seen in application code.

Handling Errors

Expecting errors and handling them is important in creating robust code. An application can use the `hadError()` and `getErrorMessage()` methods, as shown in the following generic OpenSocial code inside a callback function. Note that `"req"` is the key associated with the request.

```
function response(data) {
    if (!data.hadError()) {
        ...
    } else if (data.get("req").hadError()) {
        alert(data.get("req").getErrorMessage());
    } else {
        alert("An unknown error occurred");
    }
};
```

In the previous code, note that the `getErrorMessage()` call returns container-specific messages. While showing these messages is useful for debugging, it is not a great interface for users when things are failing.

Alternatively, the application can test for the kind of error using the `getErrorCode()` method, as shown in the following code:

```
function response(data) {
    if (!data.hadError()) {
        ...
    } else if (data.get("req").hadError()) {
        switch (data.get("req").getErrorCode()) {
          case opensocial.ResponseItem.Error.BAD_REQUEST:
            ...
            break;
          case opensocial.ResponseItem.Error.INTERNAL_ERROR:
            ...
            break;
    }
    } else {
        ...
```

Table 7-1 shows examples of error codes in OpenSocial, their meanings, and suggestions on how to handle each.

Container Compliance and NOT_IMPLEMENTED

One interesting point regarding OpenSocial compliance is that a container may be considered compliant even if it does not implement a documented OpenSocial API method, as long as the container returns a `NOT_IMPLEMENTED` error code. This can be returned to any kind of callback function from a request.

Table 7-1: OpenSocial Error Codes

Error Code	Meaning	How to Handle
`opensocial.ResponseItem .Error.FORBIDDEN`	The application can never have access to this data.	This means the application should not request this. Need to change the code.
`opensocial.ResponseItem .Error.INTERNAL_ERROR`	Server problem (not having to do with the application).	Notify the user to make the request again, or to reload. The message to the user should indicate that there is a problem with the container (not the application).
`opensocial.ResponseItem .Error.LIMIT_EXCEEDED`	Over quota (for example, the application is trying to send too many messages or post too many times to any activity stream).	Depending on the exact regulations on the item, the application can tell the user that in X days/minutes, the user can make this request again.
`opensocial.ResponseItem .Error.NOT_IMPLEMENTED`	No container support.	The application must either present an alternative or simply skip over this element.
`opensocial.ResponseItem .Error.UNAUTHORIZED`	The gadget does not have access to this data.	The application could alternatively request authorization.

So, it becomes very important to always test for the error code NOT_IMPLEMENTED before proceeding. Some of the methods that register such callback functions include the following:

❑ requestCreateActivity

❑ requestPermission

❑ requestSendMessage

❑ requestShareApp

Checking and Asking for Permissions

Currently, there is only one permission field, opensocial.Permission.VIEWER, which is used to determine whether an application can have/get access to viewer data. Remember, a viewer may not necessarily have the application installed. The viewer may be viewing the application from someone else's profile.

An application can test to see if a viewer has this permission by using the `hasPermission` method as follows:

```
var permission = opensocial.hasPermission(opensocial.Permission.VIEWER);
```

The value of `permission` will be `true` if the application has access to the viewer data, and `false` otherwise. This application can ask for permission using the `requestPermission` method, as shown in the following code snippet. The first parameter of this method specifies the kind of permission (`opensocial.Permission.VIEWER`). The second parameter is a string used in the prompt for permission. The third is a callback function. This callback function will be called once the permission request process is finished. Rather than calling the callback function, the container can choose to reload the application from scratch.

```
function response(data) {
    if (!data.hadError()) {
        ...
    } else if (data.get("req").hadError()) {
        switch (data.get("req").getErrorCode()) {
            case opensocial.ResponseItem.Error.UNAUTHORIZED:
                opensocial.requestPermission([opensocial.Permission.VIEWER],
                    "give application access to your data", callback_function);
                break;
            case opensocial.ResponseItem.Error.INTERNAL_ERROR:
                ...
                break;
        }
    } else {
        ...
    }
}
```

If the callback function is invoked, it will be passed an `opensocial.ResponseItem` object. The error code will be set on this `Response` object if there were any problems. If there were no problems, this means that all permissions were granted. Following is a possible callback function:

```
function callback_function(data) {

    if(data.hadError() == true){
        switch(data.getErrorCode()){
            case opensocial.ResponseItem.Error.UNAUTHORIZED:
             //viewer has denied access
              //can handle as wish ... tell user can not run application
                break;
        }
    }
}
```

Working with Container-Specific Extensions

OpenSocial allows containers to provide their own container-specific extensions. But what about the "write once deploy many" idea? The answer is complex. Some social networks have very different purposes than others. Consider the imeem (which is heavily focused on media) or LinkedIn (which surrounds professional networking) containers. The needs of these social networks and applications focused on their specialties will be very different, and even the latest version of OpenSocial may not fulfill these needs. So, it is a good thing that OpenSocial allows for these extensions.

If developers are careful, they can still adhere to the "write once and deploy many" philosophy. It may mean that extended capabilities in the application only exist on the container(s) that have the supporting OpenSocial extensions. However, if the application really is specialized and uses specialized extensions extensively, then it really isn't (at least not in its fullest functionality) for every container.

hi5 Lifecycle Extension

Following is some code that creates a media item (an image) for an activity. (Listing 7-15 contains the complete code.)

```
var opts = [], items = [];
var mediaItem = opensocial.newActivityMediaItem(
    opensocial.Activity.MediaItem.Type.IMAGE, "http://imageurl");

items.push(mediaItem);
opts[opensocial.Activity.Field.MEDIA_ITEMS] = items;
var activity = opensocial.newActivity(opts);
opensocial.requestCreateActivity(activity,opensocial.CreateActivityPriority.HIGH);
```

This code will work on all compliant OpenSocial containers. However, hi5 has added the capability of associating a link with this media item. This is a hi5 extension, and it is coded as follows:

```
mediaItem.setField(
    hi5.ActivityMediaItemField.LINK, "http://linkurl");
```

This code will only work on hi5. The application can test if it is on hi5 with the following boldfaced modifications:

```
var opts = [], items = [];
var mediaItem = opensocial.newActivityMediaItem(
    opensocial.Activity.MediaItem.Type.IMAGE, "http://imageurl");
if (gadgets.util.hasFeature('hi5')) {
    mediaItem.setField( hi5.ActivityMediaItemField.LINK,"http://linkurl");
}
items.push(mediaItem);
opts[opensocial.Activity.Field.MEDIA_ITEMS] = items;
var activity = opensocial.newActivity(opts);
opensocial.requestCreateActivity(activity,opensocial.CreateActivityPriority.HIGH);
```

The application must include the hi5 extension code using the `<Optional>` subelement of the `<ModulePref>` tag. For example, to include the hi5 optional feature called the "hi5-lifecycle," the XML additions must be made. The following code shows how this is done for the "hi5-lifecycle" extension (changes appear in boldface):

```
<?xml version="1.0" encoding="UTF-8" ?>
<Module>
  <ModulePrefs title="Optional features are fun">
    <Require feature="opensocial-0.7" />
```

```
    <Optional feature="hi5-lifecycle">
      <Param name="installPingUrl"
             value="http://myserver/install"/>
      <Param name="removePingUrl"
             value="http://myserver/uninstall"/>
    </Optional>
  </ModulePrefs>
  ...
</Module>
```

DataRequest Extension

DataRequest is one of the OpenSocial classes that have been extended. As an example, MySpace allows an application to request photos associated with a viewer, as shown in the following code snippet:

```
function request() {
    var request = container.newDataRequest();
    var photoReq = MyOpenSpace.DataRequest.newFetchPhotosRequest(
                              opensocial.DataRequest.PersonId.VIEWER);
    request.add(photoReq, 'photos');
    request.send(response);
};
```

Fields Extension

The fields associated with a Person are another common container extension. MySpace has extended it to use its own specially defined fields like MOOD, HEADLINE, and DESIRE_TO_MEET as follows:

```
var opt_params = {};
opt_params[opensocial.DataRequest.PeopleRequestFields.PROFILE_DETAILS] =
    [ MyOpenSpace.Person.Field.MOOD,
      MyOpenSpace.Person.Field.HEADLINE,
      MyOpenSpace.Person.Field.DESIRE_TO_MEET];
```

hi5 Template Library

The hi5.template library is a browser-side, JavaScript library that enables the fusion of JavaScript data and logic with HTML. It simplifies writing applications by providing a message resource tag as follows:

```
<os:message key="resource" />
```

See http://www.hi5networks.com/developer/2008/07/hi5-providing-library-for-temp.html for details.

Chapter 9 discusses OpenSocial templates, which formalize this concept as an OpenSocial standard. It is recommended that the developer follow this standard over the hi5-only template library. The OpenSocial Templates standard is developed (as is all of OpenSocial) by a consortium of people and companies like hi5. In this case, hi5 led the way by providing this concept in its hi5 extension first, before OpenSocial templates even existed.

Using Internationalization, Localization, and Globalization

Internationalization and *localization* are terms that are frequently used (as synonyms) to mean that an application is set up to adapt to different regions and languages. Specifically, localization is the process of loading into the application different locale-specific text and elements. Sometimes the terms are mashed together into a numeronym called i18n and L10n. Another term used to indicate this process is *globalization*.

Localization is important because many social networks have a broad international user base. Some networks predominately have users from non-English-speaking countries. In these cases, localizing to include these languages and cultures is critical.

Developers commonly create the translated text via human experts or rely on the results of running the text through translation programs.

Developers can use a number of ways to achieve localization, including the use of message bundles (introduced earlier in this chapter). Message bundles make it easy to localize an application's text without introducing language-specific application logic. This is the case because message bundles can be associated with specific locales. An application can have as many message bundles as it wishes.

Following are the localization steps for using message bundles in an OpenSocial application:

1. Create the application.
2. For any text that should be translated in the application, represent it with a message in an English-based message bundle.
3. Translate the English-based message bundle to each language (or country) to be supported.
4. Modify the application Gadget XML to reference these new message bundles.

Message bundles can be "inlined" in the application XML, or, as discussed earlier in this chapter, it can be placed in a separate XML file. In the latter case, the naming convention suggested for the XML message bundle file is A_B.xml, where A is the language code and B is the country code. Thus, en_ALL.xml would be the name of the English-based message bundle file for all English-speaking countries, and de_ALL.xml would be the German-based message bundle file.

The following code snippet shows how to use the <Locale> tag to associate the different message bundle files with the appropriate language:

```
<ModulePrefs title="__MSG_title__" description="__MSG_desc__">
  <Require feature="opensocial-0.7"/>
  <Locale messages="http://U.com /ALL_ALL.xml"/>
  <Locale lang="en" messages="http://U.com/en_ALL.xml"/>
  <Locale lang="es" messages="http://U.com/es_ALL.xml"/>
</ModulePrefs>
```

In this example, notice that the default file used for all locales not specified is ALL_ALL.xml. If, in addition to language, the country should be specified, this can be done with the country attribute shown in the following line for U.S. (not U.K.) based English:

```
<Locale lang="en" country="US" messages="http://U.com/en_US_ALL.xml"/>
```

Following is another alternative with the same meaning:

```
<Locale lang="en-US" country="US" messages="http://U.com/en_US_ALL.xml"/>
```

It is possible to specify a default message bundle that is used when the country does not correspond to any of the country-specific message bundles of that language. The following shows how this is done for English:

```
<Locale lang=="en"  messages="http://U.com/ en_ALL.xml"/>
<Locale lang="en" country="US" messages="http://U.com/en_US_ALL.xml"/>
```

Now, it becomes a simple matter of using the messages in the message bundle for text and other content in the application. For example, suppose the following represents the en_ALL.xml file:

```
<?xml version="1.0" encoding="utf-8" ?>
<messagebundle>
   <msg name="title">Friend Finder</msg>
   <msg name="info1">Track</msg>
   <msg name="info2">Invite</msg>
</messagebundle>
```

This can be used inside of the application content as follows:

```
<div id="main_content">

   <h1>__MSG_title__</h1>
   <table><tr><td>__MSG_info1__</td><td>__MSG_info2__</td> </tr></table>
</div>
```

Figure 7-6 shows the results of running this when English is the user's language, and Figure 7-7 shows results when Spanish is the user's language.

Friend Finder

Track   Invite

Figure 7-6: Application using English message bundle

Buscador del Amigo

Siga   Invite

Figure 7-7: Application using Spanish message bundle

A useful application for translation of message bundles, i18n, can be found at `http://code.google` `.com/p/osi18ntool/download/list`. This desktop application is shown in Figure 7-8. The results of translating the previous message bundle will yield the following Spanish message bundle:

```xml
<?xml version="1.0" encoding="utf-8" ?>
<messagebundle>
    <msg name='title'><![CDATA[Buscador de amigos]]></msg>
    <msg name='info1'><![CDATA[Pista]]></msg>
    <msg name='info2'><![CDATA[Invitar]]></msg>
</messagebundle>
```

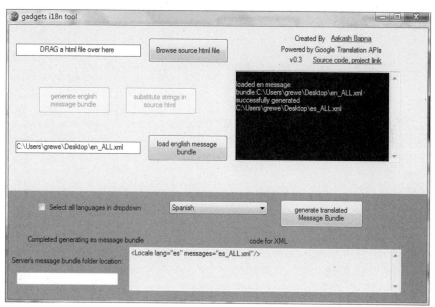

Figure 7-8: Gadgets i18n tool for translation of message bundles

Note that the translation is different from what is seen in Figure 7-7, which uses a different translation online service. The Gadgets i18n tool is easy to use because you provide a message bundle in one language, and it returns a message bundle in the specified language or can do all languages at once. Given the discrepancies between language translation services, it can make sense to have a human language expert confirm the translations. Consider the famous automobile example of the "Nova," which had to belatedly change its name for the Spanish-speaking countries where this translates to "it doesn't go."

Another useful translation service is provided by hi5 (see `http://www.hi5networks.com/developer /2008/09/translation-service-for-openso.html`). Figure 7-9 shows the hi5 developer interface and the "languages" tab that provides translation of application message bundles.

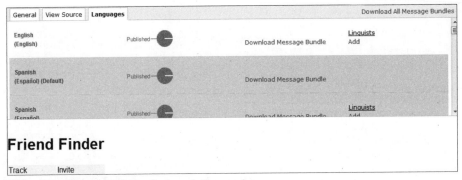

Figure 7-9: hi5 message bundle translation service

In the case of a hybrid OpenSocial application, the client application can send (via the `gadgets .io.makeRequest` call) information about the user's language and country code as parameters. Localization can be done on the server program or the response can use message bundles again. The following code shows how to build these request parameters:

```
var prefs = new gadgets.Prefs();
var country = prefs.getCountry();
var lang = prefs.getLang();


var requestUrl = 'http://example.com/hello/getGreeting.php?' + 'country=' + country
    + '&lang=' + lang;

gadgets.io.makeRequest(requestUrl, callback);
```

If the budget and schedule do not allow for localization, English is the best "universal" language for application development. However, there are cases (such as for the container `YiQi.com`) where this will most likely not be sufficient, and even developer information is not available in English.

Localization Resources

Following are some localization resources to check out:

- ❏ http://code.google.com/apis/gadgets/docs/i18n.html

- ❏ http://code.google.com/p/opensocial-resources/wiki /OrkutLocalization

- ❏ http://www.hi5networks.com/platform/wiki/Internationalization

- ❏ http://wiki.opensocial.org/index.php?title=Localizing_OpenSocial_ applications

- ❏ http://www.hi5networks.com/developer/2008/09/translation-service- for-openso.html

- ❏ http://wiki.opensocial.org/index.php?title=Gadgets_i18n_Tool

---

Using Flash Media

Using media in an application is a great way to increase an application's installed base and retention. Flash is a very popular kind of interactive media. Some developers create applications almost entirely using Flash.

A couple of possibilities to embed Flash in an application include the use of the gadget API, and the alternative use of an additional JavaScript library.

Option 1: Using the Gadget API

The Gadget API (which is part of the OpenSocial standard) includes support for embedding Flash files. Specifically, the gadgets.flash.embedFlash method can be used to embed a Flash document into the Document Object Model (DOM) tree of the XML application. Listing 7-18 shows a simple application that uses this method call.

Listing 7-18: Application with Gadget Embedded Flash

```
<div id='heading'></div>
<hr size="1px"/>
<div id='movie'> </div>


<script>
    var swfUrl = http://UServer.com/UFlash.swf;
    gadgets.flash.embedFlash(swfUrl, "movie",
              {id: flexAppId, width: 500, height: 500 });
</script>
```

The swfUrl variable is the URL to the externally hosted Flash file. The embedFlash method takes the following parameters in order: the URL to the Flash file, the ID of the DOM element into which to embed the Flash movie, and other optional parameters.

Option 2: Using the SWFObject JavaScript Library

Unfortunately, not all the OpenSocial containers support the gadgets.flash object. For example, neither MySpace nor hi5 currently support it. If this is the case, you can use the solution presented here that utilizes the SWFObject JavaScript library. This is a free-for-use library found at http://code.google.com/p/swfobject. Listing 7-19 shows an OpenSocial XML application that uses this library to embed a Flash file.

Listing 7-19: XML Application Embedding Flash with the SWFObject Library

```
<div id='heading'></div>
<hr size="1px"/>
<div id='main'></div>
<hr>
    <script src="http://UServer.com/swfobject.js"></script>
<script type="text/javascript">
    swfobject.registerObject("movie", "9.0.0", "expressInstall.swf");
</script>
<div>
    <object id='movie' classid=
          "clsid:D27CDB6E-AE6D-11cf-96B8-444553540000"
          width="780" height="420">
        <param name="movie" value="http://UServer.com/UFlash.swf" />
        <object type="application/x-shockwave-flash"
          data="http://UServer.com/UFlash.swf"
          width="780" height="420">
        </object>
    </object>
</div>
```

The code in Listing 7-19 can be broken up into the following steps:

1. Load the SWFObject JavaScript Library:

```
<script src="http://UServer.com/swfobject.js"></script>
```

This code loads the SWFObject JavaScript library, which must be uploaded to the developer's server.

2. Embed the Flash content:

```
<object id='movie' classid="clsid:D27CDB6E-AE6D-11cf-96B8-444553540000"
    width="780" height="420">
        <param name="movie" value="http://UServer.com/UFlash.swf" />
        <object type="application/x-shockwave-flash"
```

```
                              data="http://UServer.com/UFlash.swf" width="780"
                              height="420">
                  </object>
              </object>
```

The following are the required attributes of the `object` tags shown in this code:

- ❏ `classid` — The outer object element only. The value is always `clsid:D27CDB6E-AE6D-11cf-96B8-444553540000`.

- ❏ `type` — The inner object element only. The value is always `application/x-shockwave-flash`.

- ❏ `data` — The inner object element only. This defines the URL of a SWF file.

- ❏ `width` — Both object elements. This defines the width of a SWF file.

- ❏ `height` — Both object elements. This defines the height of a SWF file.

  The listed `param` element is required and specifies the following:

- ❏ `movie` — The outer object element only. This defines the URL of a SWF file.

3. Register the Flash content with the `SWFObject` library:

```
<script type="text/javascript">
    swfobject.registerObject("movie", "9.0.0", "expressInstall.swf");
</script>
```

The first parameter of the `registerObject` method is the ID in the markup of the object associated with the Flash content. The last parameter is optional and is used to activate the Adobe Express Install application (`http://www.adobe.com/cfusion/knowledgebase/index.cfm?id=6a253b75`). It specifies the URL of the express install SWF file. Express Install displays a standardized Flash plug-in download dialog instead of the application Flash content when the required plug-in version is not available. A default `expressInstall.swf` file is packaged with the library. It also contains the corresponding `expressInstall.fla` and `AS` files (in the `SRC` directory) to allow developers to create their own custom Express Install experience.

More Configuration Options

There are additional attributes and parameters that are useful in creating a custom Flash experience. For the `Object` element, these include `id`, `name`, `class`, and `align`.

In addition, the following are optional Flash-specific `param` elements (see `http://www.adobe.com` for more details on Flash): `play`, `loop`, `menu`, `quality`, `scale`, `align`, `wmode`, `bgcolor`, `base`, `swliveconnect`, `flashvars`, `devicefont`, `allowscriptaccess`, `seamlesstabbing`, `allowfullscreen`, and `allownetworking`.

You may want to consider adding alternative content inside of the `Object` element.
If the Flash plug-in is not supported, this alternative content will be displayed.
Here is an example:

```
<object classid="clsid:D27CDB6E-AE6D-11cf-96B8-444553540000"
    width="780" height="420">
        <param name="movie" value="http://UServer.com/UFlash.swf" />

        <object type="application/x-shockwave-flash"
                data="http://UServer.com/UFlash.swf" width="780"
                height="420">

                <p>Alternative content</p>
        </object>
</object>
```

Container Support

Social Networks sometimes require a review process for Flash content before allowing it to be used in an application. Sometimes this is true even during development, before submission for publication. This is the case for hi5, but not the case for MySpace. Unfortunately, this information is not documented. Should you have a problem with Flash or other media appearing, take advantage of the developer forums for the social network and inquire if there is a review process.

JavaScript Tools for Applications

Two JavaScript items, Dojo (a toolkit) and Coderunner (an OpenSocial JavaScript testing application), can be useful in creating OpenSocial JavaScript applications.

The Dojo Toolkit is an Open Source JavaScript toolkit with a set of tools for DOM manipulation, Ajax, animations, event and keyboard normalizations, Localization (i18n), and Accessibility (a11y). It is also lightweight and free for use. Check out `http://sitepen.com/labs/guides/?guide=DojoQuickStart` for details.

Coderunner is an application in orkut that you can install to test OpenSocial JavaScript calls (see `http://opensocial-resources.googlecode.com/svn/samples/coderunner/trunk/index.html`). Figure 7-10 shows Coderunner running some OpenSocial JavaScript code.

Figure 7-10: CodeRunner running live OpenSocial JavaScript code in orkut's sandbox

Summary

This chapter covered a number of application features that are important and common in many applications. The discussion examined a number of person-related functionalities (such as the friend selector), as well as communication-related functionalities (such as the creation of messages, signed requests, and media items). Other topics of discussion included testing for support, error handling, container-specific extensions, internationalization, and, finally, the inclusion of media.

Chapter 8 discusses OpenSocial Templates and Markup Language and takes a quick look at emerging OpenSocial-related platforms.

8

Performance, Scalability, and Monetization

This chapter explores performance, scalability and monetization issues. A phrase I often repeat to my student developers is "just do it." It is a mantra I believe in. However, this doesn't mean that you shouldn't plan and think about the future. It does mean that you can sometimes become overly concerned about issues such as performance and scalability, issues that remain throughout all lifecycle stages of a system.

There are a number of "funny" stories about developers who have released already successful social network applications, with hundreds of thousands of users running around to buy more hardware to meet the demands of the new social network applications. What you can learn from this is that there will always be times when you must respond quickly, and that an application will always have performance and scalability problems. Smart developers will understand this from the beginning, and, as budget and time allow, create their social network applications with performance and scalability in mind.

The discussions in this chapter delve into the following topics:

❑ *Scalability and performance* — What are they? How do you measure performance and scalability?

❑ *Architecture* — The discussions that follow explore single to "N" layers of an architecture.

❑ *Important subsystems* — These are architecture components. The discussions examine both necessary and optional components used for improving performance and scalability.

❑ *Case studies* — Throughout this chapter, you will see examples of what social network application developers are doing to make well-performing and scalable architectures.

❑ *Hosting solutions* — These include shared server, host providers, cluster computing, and private dedicated servers.

❏ *Database issues* — You will learn about general database issues, including scaling up or scaling out. You will also learn a bit about database sharding.

❏ *Monitoring* — This can help with issues of scaling. (For example, you can add more servers and other hardware upgrades, or simply focus on source code improvement.)

❏ *Redundancy* — This is used for performance, reliability, and backup.

❏ *Software design* — When examining software design, topics discussed here include design, modularity, file loading, language choice, and versioning software.

❏ *OpenSocial performance tuning* — How can you improve the performance of your OpenSocial code?

❏ *Analytics* — This discussion examines how to track your users and how they use your application.

❏ *Scalable user interface design* — You will learn how interface design can grow with the application's changing operations.

❏ *User/system support* — This discussion delves into handling user's requests, comments, and bug reports. This is a great place to get ideas for future revisions.

❏ *Monetization* — This is a discussion of how to make money, related services, and providers.

Understanding Scalability and Performance

To "scale a Web system" means to change (usually by increasing) the "size" or "capacity" of the system or its individual components. *Scalability* is a measure of how much the system can be changed (and sometimes at what cost). Typically, systems are scaled (up) to improve performance.

Performance has been defined by a number of metrics that include the following:

❏ *Throughput* — This is defined as the number of requests per second.

❏ *Efficiency* — This is the work rate of system processors.

❏ *Delay* — This represents the delay in delivering a response.

❏ *Response time* — This represents the average response time.

❏ *Quality of service and user experience/satisfaction* — This is represented by both qualitative and quantitative measures of the level of service or user satisfaction.

Some of these metrics (such as "user experience/satisfaction") can be rather esoteric. In this discussion, the throughput (number of processed requests per second) will be used as the primary measure of performance.

Defining Scalability

Many scalability metrics look at the exchange of improved performance for the entailed cost of scaling. While there is no one best metric to be used, let's look at the work published by Prasad Jogalekar and Murray Woodside on scalability (see "Evaluating the Scalability of Distributed Systems," *IEEE Transactions on Parallel and Distributed Systems*, Vol. 11, No. 6, June 2000), where they define a scalability metric that compares the "productivity" (defined as a performance-cost metric) between two differently scaled systems by calculating the ratio of their productivities. *Productivity* is defined as the "valued delivered per second" divided by "the cost per second." *Value delivered* is defined as a product of the throughput and the average "value" of each response, which is a function of the quality of service.

Using this information, the following equations can be derived:

❑ Productivity (@scale *i*) = Value / Cost;

❑ Value = Throughput * Value_Response (Quality_of_Service)

❑ Scalability (scale *i&j*) = Productivity(@scale *i*) / Productivity(@scale *j*)

While there are arguably many good metrics for measuring performance and scalability, these capture the essence of the goal — to scale for better performance, while understanding the cost. When considering cost, you should not only take into account the purchase of any hardware or software, but also factor in the configuration and maintenance cost and/or usage costs (when you are purchasing services). The Value_Response metric and Quality_of_Service metric can encompass delay measures, availability measures, probability of timeouts, data loss, and system failures. Jogalekar and Woodside use the following simple metric for Value_Response:

❑ Value_Response (@scale *i*) = 1/ (1+ T(*i*)/T)

❑ T(*i*) = Average response time at scale *i*

❑ T = Target (ideal) response time

This metric of Value_Response will approach 1 as the average response time approaches 0. It will have a smaller value approaching 0 as the average response time becomes larger (to infinity).

The goal is to have the highest value possible for a given scale. Jogalekar and Woodside suggest calculating the productivity for each scale you are considering. Using these values, you can then select where it makes the most sense to currently scale. Look at their work for an analysis where they define the level of scale *i* as representing the number of database processors and replicas.

Using Scalability Metrics

Having theoretical formulations like the ones just discussed can provide some tips on scaling. However, the reality is often different, and many times practitioners depend on their own experiences and case studies or anecdotal information to make scaling decisions. Another approach (which is more feasible when paying for use, instead of purchasing owned resources) is to do benchmarking tests, or simply "just try it out." For example, the developer examines a part of the Web system (say, database retrieval) and measures how throughput is improved when increasing the scale (such as adding more database servers). This can be expensive, so I suggest first understanding the costs involved and potential performance increase.

If cost turns out to be reasonable, a developer might decide to scale up. However, with scaling comes additional resources, added management, and unexpected failures. So, unless performance is a problem, leave it alone (a philosophy often described in the adages, "Don't fix something that isn't broken," or "Keep it simple stupid").

Performance Problem Areas

This chapter provides tips for improving performance, as well as handling a number of performance problems. Before getting into details, let's establish that many performance bottlenecks are related to one of the following issues:

❑   Application server response time

❑   Database server response time

Later discussions in this chapter focus on architectural decisions that make a big impact on performance. In addition, this chapter covers other scalability issues related to source code development and performance "tuning."

Scaling Up or Out

When considering scaling options, developers talk about the two paradigms of *scale up* (also known as *vertical scaling*) and *scale out* (also known as *horizontal scaling*). "Scaling up" is the replacement of a resource with a single, better-performing resource. An example is replacing a server with one that has additional memory, more processors, and increased processor speeds. "Scaling out" is the replacement of a set of N resources with $N + K$ resources. An example is replacing one database with four database servers.

Understanding Architecture

Web system architecture involves the conceptual design and implementation of the components in a Web system. The simplest Web system for a social network application is none. Recall that it is possible to host an OpenSocial JavaScript application on some of the social networks (or containers). If the application has no need for back-end services (such as database storage), then this is sufficient.

OpenSocial REST applications are, by definition, always server-side. Many OpenSocial JavaScript applications will have proprietary data for which the simple OpenSocial persistence service will not suffice. In this case, server-side storage and retrieval is needed. Also, many applications have business logic that the developer wants to have on the server side (rather than on the client side) for a variety of reasons, including the following:

❑   Ownership

❑   Performance

❑   Security

A good architecture is important for successfully running applications. It becomes critical when an application goes viral. Sometimes, developers start out using a shared single-server environment. In this case, the server must handle all requests and provide presentation, business logic, and data logic not only for your application(s) but also for others sharing the server. This is fine as a learning environment, but, with the growth of a user base, it can quickly become a performance problem.

Minimally, at the beginning, your architecture should consist of a Web server and a database server. However, this is usually not enough as applications go viral. Later in this chapter, you'll see case studies that show how other developers or companies have solved this problem. The main focus of the current discussion is how to architect multiple servers into well-performing and scalable systems.

When creating the architecture for a Web system that serves a social network application(s), the following should be taken into consideration:

- ❑ Number of users (requests)
- ❑ Budget and costs
- ❑ Performance
- ❑ Scalability
- ❑ Maintenance
- ❑ Reliability
- ❑ Backup

A common concept of application logic is separate presentation, business, and data services and logic. A common description for this is a *three-layer architecture* (using a model-view-controller, or MVC, framework).

The Presentation layer is the part of the application that is responsible for constructing presentation information that involves the creation of a user interface. The Business layer is the "computational" layer, where operations on data are performed to achieve application logic and are returned to the Presentation layer logic. The Data layer is responsible for all storage and retrieval data operations, and typically involves a database(s).

Another conceptual architecture separates the system into an Application/Client layer, a Middleware layer, and an Infrastructure layer. There are some similarities with the Presentation-Business-Data model. The Application/Client layer is composed of the technology and software components that directly serve the client. The Middleware layer focuses on services to the client that utilize the Infrastructure layer. Following are some examples of Middleware layer services:

- ❑ Authentication
- ❑ Authorization
- ❑ Encryption
- ❑ Communications (via sockets, and so on)
- ❑ Database pooling
- ❑ Messaging
- ❑ HTTP/Web services

The Infrastructure layer represents the physical equipment, data, and resources used in the system. Examples of Infrastructure layer components include the following:

- ❑ Database
- ❑ Proxies

- ❑ Load balancing
- ❑ Security (for example, firewalls)
- ❑ Operating system and server configuration

While these are conceptual models of architecture, they often translate into modularization of software and partitioning of hardware to handle each layer separately.

Another useful separation for improved performance is to have separate layers for static versus dynamic Web/application content. Developers may serve up Static layer content with a "lighter-weight" Web server or cache.

As for the Dynamic layer content (sometimes called the Application layer), developers also commonly separate it (the Infrastructure layer) into two separate layers: a stateless layer and a persistence (stateful) layer. If there is a separate stateless application layer, it can be infinitely scalable.

There is no single standard methodology for developing Web system architectures. This can be approached in many different ways, focusing on data-driven, user-driven, or function-driven method-ologies. Software engineering principles of requirements analysis and design can be employed. An example of a more formalized method for Web system architecture is the Open Group Architectural Framework (TOGAF) Method (see `http://www.opengroup.org/architecture/togaf8-doc/arch`).

The next few sections of this chapter delve deeper into Web system design. First, let's take a look at a treatment of the necessary (for example, Web server) and optional (for example, caching) subsystems. Issues of performance and scalability are highlighted. Later, you'll learn about the roles of current hosting solutions and databases in architecture design.

Understanding Subsystems

Figure 8-1 shows a generic Web system architecture that has a number of commonly used subsystems. The first layer's components are called Front-end Scalers. The purpose of the Front-end Scaler(s) is to distribute requests for improved performance. Requests can be sent to the Web servers, or directed to the application servers supporting the separation of dynamic and static content. The Front-end Scaler(s) can have an embedded cache for fast retrieval, and can involve the following subsystems:

- ❑ Load balancer(s)
- ❑ Proxy servers
- ❑ Caching/Squid
- ❑ Connection pooling to back-end machines

Rounding out the design in Figure 8-1 are sets of Web and application servers, a caching layer, and database layer.

The following discussions examine each of the components in Figure 8-1, and provide information about current products as appropriate. (The discussion of database issues appears later in this chapter.)

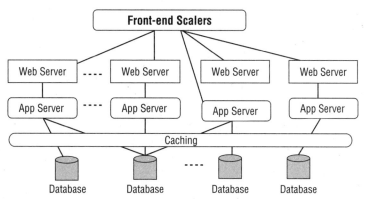

Figure 8-1: Generic Web system architecture with multiple layers and components

Web Server

Web servers are machines that run a program that accepts HTTP requests from clients and, in return, gives an HTTP response.

> *There are a number of commercial Web servers on the market. Go to* `http://en.wikipedia.org/wiki/Comparison_of_web_servers` *for a comparison of some of them.*

Many developers use Apache as their Web server for both dynamic and static content. Apache is Open Source and free. It is considered by many a good, general-purpose Web server, and many large Web sites use it. It currently is the most used Web server on the Internet. Apache can be extended in a number of ways through additional modules. For example, Apache can be extended to serve as an application server with support from modules such as `mod_perl` and `mod_python`.

Apache can serve as a reverse proxy with the `mod_proxy` module. (Proxy servers are examined in more detail later in this chapter.) In conjunction with this, the `mod_cache` module can be configured to be a caching proxy. (Caching is also discussed in more detail later in this chapter.)

Because Apache supports a number of services, it can also be more than is required and slower than desired. This is particularly true if what are requested are static documents. An alternative is a lightweight Web server such as lighttpd, which uses less memory and has a lighter CPU load. It has been often used for delivering not only static content but also media-heavy, large content. lighttpd can also be used as a load balancer and reverse proxy (both of which are discussed later in this chapter). Another server, Nginx (discussed later in this chapter), can also serve as a faster performing Web server.

Application Server

There are many dynamic application engines/environments a developer can use for serving dynamic (Web) requests. Each application server program supports a particular language, such as PHP, Python, Perl (PerCGI), Java (J2EE), and so on. Installation and configuration of the application server software is specific to the application server software chosen, and the developer should follow the corresponding documentation.

Load Balancing

As more servers are added (via replication, which is discussed later in this chapter in the section, "Distributed Systems (Scale Out)") to handle performance needs, some mechanism must be used to direct incoming traffic among the multiple (replicated) servers. This is the job of a *load balancer*, which can be a piece of software and/or hardware. For improved speed, hardware-implemented load balancers should be used, and these can involve switches for fast routing.

There are a number of products available, and each has its own algorithm for determining how to direct the incoming requests. For directing traffic among a set of Web servers, a common technique used is called *round robin rotation*. This technique directs incoming requests (in a rotational order) to the servers in its pool. For example, if there are three servers, A, B, and C, the first request goes to A, the next to B, and the third to C, with the fourth request going back to A.

Another algorithm employed is *random selection*. In this case, the traffic is directed to a "randomly" selected server.

These are simple and fast algorithms. Some load balancers consider the load and response time of each of the servers in determining where to pass the request. The load balancer must quickly make its decision about routing a request to avoid adding too much delay in its processing.

More complicated configurations with load balancers are possible. For example, the balancer can be set up in an asymmetric fashion so that some servers receive more traffic than others. Another possibility is an "on-demand" setup, where more servers are dynamically brought into the pool as the traffic increases. There are even some load balancers that let you create script programs to be used for the traffic distribution.

An intelligent load balancer attempts to determine which server is least loaded, and route the request to the server most likely to be able to handle the request quickly. Following are a few things to consider when selecting a load balancer:

❑ High-quality software load balancers are more expensive than the round-robin variety.

❑ Hardware-based load balancers are, in general, more expensive than software load balancers.

A concept related to load balancing, *partitioning*, is the splitting up of different application information and services into clusters or groups of servers and/or storage. For example, one set of servers could deal with messaging operations. Another set of servers could process application business logic. Intelligent load balancers can then direct traffic to a cluster of servers, as well as to a particular server in this cluster, based on the request information.

Caching

Caching is the process of storing requested information in special-purpose memory for fast retrieval. Retrieving information from cache is significantly faster than database retrieval or an application creating a response. Depending on the amount of data, caching can be many times faster. A caching "system" can be implemented to facilitate different architecture layers. It can be used to store static content, such as static Web pages or Web content. Caching can be used to store commonly requested database items. It can also be used to store even the results of dynamic application programs. In this case, the cache content will have a more limited lifetime, and will be refreshed more frequently.

Caching improves performance by reducing response latency. It also diminishes server loads and reduces network traffic. A Web cache stores copies of documents passing through it; subsequent requests may be satisfied from the cache if certain conditions are met.

For the social network application, caching can be done at the client, the social network container, the proxy server (front end) and at back-end servers. Social network application developers can control how (and if) caching is done on their servers. Also, developers can directly make requests regarding caching on the social network container. For OpenSocial REST applications, developers can send directives (via HTTP headers, and so on) for client caching.

In the case of the client, content will be stored in the cache of the user's machine. The client cache is often called the *user agent cache*, and is set up and managed by the user's Web browser (or *user agent*). Users have the capability through the browser's controls to clear the cache and, in some cases, to disable it.

Server caching can be implemented at different stages and in different ways, including the following:

- ❑ Proxy server (forward proxy cache or Web cache)
- ❑ Reverse proxy server
- ❑ Database cache
- ❑ Distributed cache

Performance improvements from cache are limited by the size of the cache and number of cache servers. *Pre-fetching* is the anticipation and placing into cache responses to requests that are likely to happen in the future. Pre-fetching can increase the hit rate and, hence, improve the performance of using caches. Common use patterns can predict what items will be needed and, hence, pre-fetched.

Cache and HTTP Headers

While caching on the server and client are great ways to improve performance, it must be used with care so that stale content is not retrieved. The following HTTP headers involve caching and are important to remember when making requests to systems that use cache:

- ❑ `IF-Modified-Since` — This means do not send a response if not modified since this date/time.
- ❑ `Pragma no-cache` — This means do not return a response from cache.
- ❑ `Last-Modified` — This gives a date/time when last modified.

Client caching can make a huge difference. For example, when visiting a popular site that has been cached by a browser, it can load in less than a second. By comparison, when visiting the same page after cache has been cleared, it can take more than 2 seconds to load. (The exact times will vary, of course, based on traffic conditions, the client machine, and other issues.) What is important in this anecdotal information is the number of times faster the site with caching loads compared to the same client in similar network conditions.

The use of HTTP headers can help control how caching is done on a client. The following HTTP headers pertain to caching on the client:

❑   `Expires` — This HTTP header is set to a date when content is no longer good. This tells the client cache how long the content is good for. After the time specified, the client will forward the request on to the server, instead of retrieving the item from its cache. A problem with `Expires` is that the server and client must have the same synchronized date, or problems may occur. For static content, this should be set to a far future date. For dynamic content, this can be used if you know the date the dynamic content will next change. For example, this would be the case if it is the application policy to load in new messages at the same time each day.

❑   `Cache-Control` — This HTTP header provides more options than `Expires` for setting cache-related specifications. You can use the following header values:

    ❑   `max-age=second` — Sets the maximum time content as good. This is like `Expires` header.

    ❑   `public` — Sets authenticated responses as cacheable (the default is uncacheable).

    ❑   `no-cache` — Like `Expires`, this means submit requests to the server.

    ❑   `must-revalidate` — Even in special situations (allowed in HTTP), the client must adhere to specifications of the `Cache-Control` header.

See `http://www.w3.org/Protocols/rfc2616/rfc2616-sec14.html#sec14.9` *for more details.*

The following is an example of a `Cache-Control` header:

```
Cache-Control: max-age=3600, must-revalidate
```

Check out `http://www.mnot.net/cacheability` *for a tool that can assist you in figuring out how cacheable an application's responses are.*

Other techniques can be used for avoiding the cache when desired. One not uncommon technique is creating request URLs that have appended to them random strings that do not affect the content requested but are treated as requests that are unique from what currently is cached.

Proxy Server

The general definition of a *proxy server* is a server that accepts requests, possibly filters them, and then passes them on to another server. The purpose of proxy servers typically relates to security but can also involve caching. In the latter case, they are called *caching proxy servers*. When these servers are focused only on Internet traffic, they are called *Web proxy caching servers* and are implementations of *Web cache*. Another name for this kind of Web cache is a *forward proxy cache*.

Reverse Proxy Server

A *reverse proxy server* is a server that receives all requests for a set of servers. The reverse proxy server should be physically close to its servers for fast forwarding. Other names for the reverse proxy server include the following:

❑   Gateway cache

❑   Surrogate cache

❑   Web accelerator

Reverse proxy servers are used for load balancing. A *Web accelerator* can improve performance by caching content and, thus, service incoming requests readily.

The difference between a (forward) proxy server and a reverse proxy server is that a forward proxy server is set up so that it is "closer" to a set of clients, and services these clients by caching information. In this case, the forward proxy server serves a limited number of clients. The reverse proxy takes the opposite tact and is set up close to the servers. The reverse proxy is intended to serve an unlimited number of clients for a limited number of Web servers.

A Web accelerator (reverse proxy server) designed for heavy content delivery is Varnish (`http://varnish.projects.linpro.no`), and the provider claims that it is faster than Squid (which is discussed shortly). It is Open Source, free software. Varnish is designed as a high-performance caching reverse proxy, unlike Squid, which is a forward proxy that can be configured as a reverse proxy.

While a reverse proxy server sits in front of Web servers (as represented by the Front-end Scalers shown in Figure 8-1), receives all requests, and dispatches them to one of a set of Web servers routed through the proxy server, it can also handle the request itself. The reverse proxy server can direct requests for static data to different servers than requests from the dynamic application.

Multiple Cache

Multiple cache servers can be managed using protocols such as Internet Cache Protocol (ICP) and Hyper Text Caching Protocol (HTCP). ICP is a lightweight protocol used to find the most appropriate location to get something from the cache when multiple cache servers are used. HTPC discovers, manages, and queries an HTTP cache. Covering this in detail is outside of the scope this book, but the following are some resources to check out:

- ❑ *ICP documentation* — `http://tools.ietf.org/html/rfc2186`
- ❑ *Application of ICP to Web caching* — `http://tools.ietf.org/html/rfc2187`
- ❑ *HTCP* — `http://www.htcp.org`

Following are a few of the servers that use ICP or HTPC:

- ❑ *Squid server* — Squid is an Open Source (forward) proxy server and Web cache. As an Open Source project, it is free for use. Squid supports not only HTTP but also FTP and other protocols (such as SSL and HTTPS). Although a forward proxy server, Squid can also be configured to run as a reverse proxy server. For more details on Squid, see `http://www.squid-cache.org` and `http://www.visolve.com/squid/whitepapers/reverseproxy.php`.

- ❑ *Microsoft Internet Security and Acceleration (ISA) server* — ISA server is an edge security gateway that is described as offering both security and fast access to applications (application server) and data. ISA supports both scaling out and scaling up. It is now supported on hardware virtualization.

- ❑ *Cisco Content Delivery Engine/System* — These are both hardware and software solutions provided by Cisco for content ingest, storage, caching, personalization, and streaming functionality.

Distributed Cache

Memcached is a general-purpose, distributed memory-caching system that is used by some large Web sites, including YouTube, Digg, Twitter, and Slashdot. It creates one global cache distributed across a number of servers. A common use is to improve performance of dynamic database-driven Web sites by caching data to reduce the number of the database retrievals. Memcached is free for use.

Memcached is supported in a number of languages. APIs can be found at `http://www.danga.com/memcached/apis.bml`.

Memcached works as follows:

1. Memcached creates a large hash table distributed across multiple machines.

2. When the table is full, subsequent inserts cause older data to be removed in least recently used (LRU) order.

3. Applications using Memcached put Memcached requests into application code and, if it fails to retrieve the item, the application code then makes a call to the database.

Memcached is implemented using two-layer hashing as follows:

❏ The first layer sends a request to a Memcached server it finds by hashing the key onto a list of virtual buckets, each one representing a Memcached server.

❏ The second layer (at each of the distributed Memcached servers) uses a hash table to store the data.

Listing 8-1 shows application code that services a request to retrieve data. First, Memcahced is tried, and if this fails, the request passes to the database.

Listing 8-1: Memcached Pseudo Code to Get Data

```
function retrieve_data (int userid) {
    value = memcached_fetch("userrow:" + userid);    //try to get from memcached
    if (!value) {            //if not in cache then must do database call
        value = db_select("SELECT * FROM users WHERE userid = ?", userid);
        memcached_add("userrow:" + userid,  value);   //ask to store in cache
                                                       //key is userid .
    }

    return result;
}
```

Listing 8-2 shows the application code that performs a request to store data. Here, both the database and Memcached are updated.

Listing 8-2: Memcached Pseudo Code to Store Data

```
function store_data(int userid, string dbString) {
    value = db_execute(dbString);
    if (value) {
        d = createUserDataFromDBString(dbString);
        memcached_set("userrow:" + userid, d);
    }
}
```

When using Memcached, set the expiration for every Memcached record created. This is done through the Time to Live (TTL) parameter. When this expires, Memcached will return a "404: Not Found" error code. This ensures that a cache record will not be used after its expiration.

Memcached can be used not only to cache database records but also for application requests, as shown in the next discussion regarding Nginx.

Nginx

There are a number of products that combine components previously discussed. One such system, Nginx, is rapidly gaining popularity. It combines a reverse proxy server with cache (see `http://wiki.codemongers.com/Main` and `http://nginx.net`). Nginx comes preloaded with Memcached, which means that requests can bypass the application server and be served directly from cache. KlickNation and others have successfully used Nginx to improve performance. Some companies report increases such as a 400 percent throughput increase (for example, from 400 requests per second to 1,600 requests per second).

There are caching modules available for Apache (`http://code.google.com/p/modmemcachecache`) and lighttpd (`http://trac.lighttpd.net/trac/wiki/Docs`). However, they require additional setup and configuration, whereas this feature is standard in Nginx. Like lighttpd, the memory footprint and resource usage is lower (as compared to Apache). A number of sites (see `http://wiki.codemongers.com/Main`) have reported that Nginx is now more popular than lighttpd.

Nginx works when it gets a request by first querying the cache. If it does not find the item, it will respond with a "404: Not Found" error code. This error can be caught, and then a redirect is made to the application server to process the request. Also, the application should return a response and send it to Memcached to be stored for future retrieval. Following is an example of the configuration used to do this:

```
upstream appserver {server 127.0.0.1:9010;}
server {
    location / {
        set $memcached_key $uri;
        memcached_pass  127.0.0.1:11211;
        error_page      404 = @dynamic_request;
    }
    location = @dynamic_request {
            proxy_pass appserver;
    }
```

The following points help explain this script:

❑   memcached_key is the key that Nginx will query Memcached with. Here, the Nginx variable $uri is used.

❑   If the resource is not found (404 in the code sample) in Memcached, the request (via @dynamic_request) is passed on to your application server at appserver, which, in turn, should return a response.

Some developers have also used Nginx for serving (and caching) static content, finding that using it results in such fast delivery that as users increase, the bottleneck becomes a server's I/O capacity before maxing out memory or CPU usage on a server.

Content Delivery Networks (CDNs)

For a heavy-content application, using a Content Delivery Network (CDN) can improve performance. A CDN is a set of computers networked across the Internet that work together to deliver content to end users. The improved performance from using a CDN is achieved through placement of servers closer to the clients. In this way, the clients can be more quickly served, and there is less traffic on the developer's network backbone. This design is sometime referred to as *edge server placement*.

CDNs advertise themselves as a commercially available set of grid computers purposed to serve and store heavy-demand data. Typically, this is served out of memory. Some providers include Akamai, Limelight Networks (LLNW), and CDNetworks. The number of servers (nodes) making up a CDN varies, depending on the architecture, with some reaching thousands of nodes with tens of thousands of servers. There is a trend for larger Web sites with heavy-data needs to build their own CDNs.

Some of the CDNs not only offer content storage but are also application service providers (ASPs) which means that they host applications. One such provider is Akamai. Akamai will host all kinds of content, including HTML, CSS, audio, graphics, animation, and video that mirrors the content at the customer servers. When a client accesses the customer's site, content can be delivered from a nearby Akamai server instead of from the customer's site. The Akamai server is automatically picked depending on the type of content and the client's Internet (network) location.

This frees up resources on the customer's network and produces a fast response time to the client. In addition to static content caching, Akamai provides application services that (because of being nearby to the client location) can accelerate dynamic content delivery. Akamai hosts J2EE-compliant applications and streaming media, among other applications.

> Note that S3 (an Amazon storage solution) shouldn't be confused with a CDN. It is not a distributed caching service, and it doesn't have global locations like a CDN does. S3 will be discussed later in this chapter in the section "Hosting Solutions."

Understanding Hosting Solutions

The range of possible solutions for hosting a social network application includes the following:

- ❑ Shared hosting
- ❑ Collocated hosting
- ❑ Unmanaged leased dedicated hosting
- ❑ Managed dedicated hosting
- ❑ Cloud computing hosting
- ❑ Internal/owned/proprietary hosting

Shared hosting is sharing a server with other customers. This is okay as a learning environment but not something that can be used for serious application hosting. This is a starting point for many beginning developers that they will quickly outgrow when their applications start to experience some success. If the application takes up too many resources, the shared-server administrator will often ask the developer to find a better solution. Another drawback of using shared servers is that these servers are controlled by the provider, and getting special software installed may not be possible.

Collocated hosting means the developer purchases a host, and it is placed on a network by the hosting provider. The network (and hopefully redundant power supply) is supplied by the hosting provider. Sometimes server management will be offered.

Unmanaged leased dedicated hosting is the similar to collocated hosting, but, in this case, you are leasing the machine. In addition, no management of the servers is given, and because of this lack of support, this is generally not a good solution for social network application developers.

Managed dedicated hosting means that the provider also manages the servers. Both models, where you lease, as well as where you provide, the server are available, but the former (leasing) is more typical. Support can be variable among managed hosting providers, and can include uptime monitoring, hardware warranties, security updates, and more. Of the options mentioned so far, this can be a viable solution for part of (or all) your hosting needs.

Cloud computing is a set of computers on the Internet that form a "cloud," which are used in concert to provide computing resources. *Grid computing* is often associated with cloud computing, and it is a topic of discussion later in this chapter. Cloud computing is considered by many to be a new computing paradigm that excels above other Web-hosting solutions. The provider will manage the computing cloud resources, networks, and so on, and the developer pays for use of the system. Companies such as Amazon and Joyent provide cloud computing resources, and are commonly used by social network application developers.

The last form of hosting solutions is the *owned/proprietary system* solution, where the developer owns all of the computers/servers and the network. This means a larger initial capital outlay that will not be feasible for most startup organizations. Hosting solutions that allow developers to rent the use of resources to host their applications do not require this large initial investment, nor do developers have to have staff to maintain the hardware.

For the leased hosting solutions, resource use is typically rented by the hour and/or by the amount of storage and number of transfers. Benefits of this model are the access to scalable resources a developer could not initially afford and the capability to expand resource use dynamically as demand rises. The hosting providers can have hundreds or thousands of machines, typically consisting of commodity hardware that will change frequently. As users of these systems, developers do not need to care about their changing configuration and maintenance, only that performance and scalability needs are met.

In general, renting resources (like renting a car) can be more expensive in the long run. However, when factoring in the reduced personnel, it can still be economical. For "smaller" organizations, it can be the only viable alternative. That being said, a number of large companies use managed or cloud hosting solutions.

Some developers may only use external (systems they don't own and/or manage) hosting solutions for part of their systems. An example of this is using external hosting only for large-volume content storage and delivery, but maintaining developer-owned application servers and other resources. In this hybrid solution, it may make sense to retain the most frequently requested (for example, top 10 percent of) resources on the developer's own servers (preferably with caching).

The reason is that, for these limited resources (which will have a high percentage of use), the developer will not have to pay for the transfer fees from the hosting provider. Not only can this save significant money, but also performance will be improved if the frequently used objects are stored in cache, or efficiently retrieved. This kind of cost analysis will be highly dependent on application needs. Going to the trouble of having a hybrid system will usually mean that you have a very popular application, or are in the business of creating a number of applications.

With this additional complexity, there are some benefits such as redundancy — that is, if a hosting provider is down, your application can write to your proprietary storage. But, this means writing your code with these fail-safes built in.

What They're Saying about Hosting Solutions

Developers are using all kinds of solutions. I interviewed a number of developers at an OpenSocial event, and here are some the trends and comments regarding the topic of hosting solutions:

- ❑ Popular hosting providers (in no order) are Amazon and Joyent. More recently, some developers are trying out Google App Engine.

- ❑ The free account provided by Joyent is popular, especially with new developers.

- ❑ Developers find there is a difference among the hosting providers in costs for their application architecture configuration needs.

- ❑ No consensus has evolved on what provider is the best in terms of service. However, some providers (such as Amazon, Joyent, and App Engine) provide cloud/cluster computing support that is different from other more traditional "managed server" providers.

Here are some tips to consider when looking at different hosting solutions:

- ❑ Understand what kind of hosting the provider is offering (shared server, collocated, managed, cloud computing, and so on).

- ❑ Consider the scalability limitations. What is the size of the available resources?

- ❑ What support exactly (free, fee-based) is provided? How do you reach the support staff? How qualified are the employees?

- ❑ What are the costs? Look at different scenarios so that you know what you are getting into.

- ❑ Look for data centers that have redundant power sources and redundant connectivity.

- ❑ Look at security — both physical and network.

- ❑ As for connectivity, how many lines are being offered? What is the typical utilization (meaning what bandwidth is left for you to use)?

- ❑ Know what the bandwidth limitations are and what happens if the application exceeds them.

- ❑ How do former and current customers rate them?

Amazon Web Services (AWS)

Amazon Web Services (AWS) is Amazon's Web-hosting solution, which provides access to a number of developer services using the HTTP, REST, and SOAP protocols. Let's take a look at a few services useful for hosting social network applications that AWS provides — Elastic Compute Cloud (EC2), Elastic Block Store (EBS), Simple Storage Server (S3), and CloudFront.

Elastic Compute Cloud (EC2)

EC2 allows developers to rent computer resources for hosting their applications in a cloud computing environment. EC2 provides the use of a large number of machines that a developer utilizes by creating a desired number of "virtual machines" (server instances). Each virtual machine can be configured to contain developer-specified software. A developer can create and remove server instances as performance demands. These new server instances can be brought online in seconds/minutes, and truly make the application scalable. This is where the term "elastic" comes from.

After creating an EC2 account, a developer has the capability to set up (virtual) server instances. Amazon will allocate resources (such as CPU, memory, and instance storage through the specification of "instance type," which will be discussed shortly). Other resources (such as network and disk subsystems) are shared among instances (possibly including ones owned by other customers). Shared resources are distributed equally among similar "instance types" with higher-performing "instance types" getting a higher amount of shared resources.

EC2 instance types are currently classified as standard instance types and high CPU instance types.

Standard instance types have the following specifications:

❑   *Small Instance (Default)* — 1.7GB of memory, 1 EC2 Compute Unit (1 virtual core with 1 EC2 Compute Unit), 160GB of instance storage, 32-bit platform, I/O performance is moderate

❑   *Large Instance* — 7.5GB of memory, 4 EC2 Compute Units (2 virtual cores with 2 EC2 Compute Units each), 850GB of instance storage, 64-bit platform, I/O performance is high

❑   *Extra Large Instance* — 15GB of memory, 8 EC2 Compute Units (4 virtual cores with 2 EC2 Compute Units each), 1690GB of instance storage, 64-bit platform, I/O performance is high

High CPU instance types have the following specifications:

❑   *High-CPU Medium Instance* — 1.7GB of memory, 5 EC2 Compute Units (2 virtual cores with 2.5 EC2 Compute Units each), 350GB of instance storage, 32-bit platform

❑   *High-CPU Extra Large Instance* — 7GB of memory, 20 EC2 Compute Units (8 virtual cores with 2.5 EC2 Compute Units each), 1690GB of instance storage, 64-bit platform

Developers should decide on what kind of instance(s) to use based on resource needs and budget. One idea is to try out the different instance types to see how they perform for an application — in essence, doing a benchmark test. Amazon recommends standard instances for most general-purpose applications, and high-CPU instances for compute-intensive applications.

In addition to choosing what type of instance(s) to use, developers will set up each instance with a software configuration determined in advance. A software configuration is represented by an *Amazon Machine Image (AMI)*. The desired architecture will designate the number of instances and which AMI to install on each. Recall the generic architecture used (with some variations) by many developers with high-use popular applications shown in Figure 8-1. In reference to Figure 8-1, AMIs must be generated to represent the Web servers, application servers, and database servers.

An AMI specifies the operating system, machine configuration, libraries, and service programs, in addition to developer application-specific content and programs. Amazon provides a number of pre-configured template images that can be used as a starting point. You should use one of these templates and customize it to create your own AMI.

Amazon provides the following options in terms of operating systems:

❑ Red Hat Enterprise Linux

❑ Windows Server 2003

❑ OpenSolaris

❑ Oracle Enterprise Linux

❑ openSUSE Linux

❑ Ubuntu Linux

❑ Fedora

❑ Gentoo Linux

❑ Debian

Amazon provides the following database software options:

❑ Oracle 11g

❑ Microsoft SQL Server Standard 2005

❑ MySQL Enterprise

❑ Microsoft SQL Server Express

Amazon provides the following batch-processing software options:

❑ Hadoop

❑ Condor

❑ Open MPI

Amazon provides the following Web server software options:

❑ Apache HTTP

❑ IIS/ASP.Net

Amazon provides the following application server software options:

❑ Java Application Server

❑ JBoss Enterprise Application Platform

❑ Support for a number of languages (PHP, Perl, Python, and more)

❑ Ruby on Rails

There are many other kinds of software provided for use by Amazon, as detailed on its Web site. For example, the following video-encryption and streaming software is available:

❑   Wowza Media Server Pro

❑   Windows Media Server

There are a number of good articles at the EC2 Web site that show, step by step, how to use its services. The following steps outline the basic steps to use the EC2 service:

1.   Create accounts on EC2 and S3. (S3 will be discussed shortly.)

2.   Create an AMI for each kind of server instance needed.

3.   Upload the AMI(s) into Amazon S3. S3 is Amazon's storage service, and Amazon will create new virtual machine instances from AMI(s) stored there.

4.   Set up security and network access.

5.   Select multiple locations, if desired.

6.   Choose the appropriate instance type(s) and operating systems. "Start" instances (each associated with an AMI).

7.   Monitor (as desired) instances using Web service APIs.

8.   Determine (if desired) persistent block storage.

9.   Developer will be billed for resource use.

Details for setting up your account, creating AMIs, and creating instances are covered at `http://docs.amazonwebservices.com/AWSEC2/2007-03-01/GettingStartedGuide`. Another article to look at is one dedicated to using Amazon for Facebook social network application development at `http://developer.amazonwebservices.com/connect/entry.jspa?entryID=1044`. As of this writing, there is not yet an equivalent for OpenSocial, but the tips are easily translated for OpenSocial.

Sign up for Amazon Web Services at `http://amazon.com/ec2`. In addition to a login and password, you will be given both an Access Key ID with Access Key Secret and an X.509 certificate.

When making a request to the Amazon system, the access identifiers are used as identification for the requestor. Any authenticated requests must be signed by including a "signature" calculated by using the pair of public/private access identifiers. AWS supports the use of its Access Key information and the X.509 certificate as follows:

❑   AWS Access Key Identifiers are used to calculate HMAC-SHA1 request signatures, and these are included in query, REST, and SOAP requests.

❑   X.509 certificates can be used as an alternative to the Access Key Identifiers for authentication of requests. This certificate can be generated by Amazon when you set up your account, but you may also upload a certificate of your own. You can use X.509 certificates only with SOAP requests.

Never give out this information to third parties. Keep it in a private, protected location.

Grid/Cluster Computing

An advantage of the Amazon EC2 cloud computing service (as well as some other hosting providers that offer cloud computing) is that they can be set up to do a form of "parallel" computing referred to as *grid* or *cluster computing*. This actively uses a set number of server instances in EC2 to resolve a single task in a parallel distributed fashion. One of the software packages offered by Amazon for use in the creation of AMIs is Hadoop, which can be used to implement grid computing solutions.

Hadoop is based on running a map/reduce algorithm with a distributed file system. Hadoop can be used to take care of instance failure and perform data replication.

> *See* `http://hadoop.apache.org/core` *for more details on Hadoop.*

Elastic Block Store

Elastic Block Store (EBS) gives persistence storage to Amazon EC2 instances that currently can range from 1GB to 1TB. It is designed to provide better latency and throughput than the storage in the Amazon EC2 instances, and is why a developer may want to use it over the storage on an EC2 instance.

An EBS volume can only be used by one EC2 instance, but multiple volumes can be used by one EC2 instance. This storage persists independently from the life of an instance. An EBS is used like a hard drive with its own file system.

One use of the Amazon EBS is to place data across multiple volumes to increase access throughput (like a distributed file system). If an instance fails, the EBS volume that was associated with it can be assigned to another working instance. This provides a form of fail-safe information storage.

Simple Storage Server

Amazon Simple Storage Server (S3) is a storage service that is used by EC2, but it can also be used independently. It is used by a number of Web sites to store and serve static content. It is reported by many developers to be a highly scalable, fast, and reasonably priced solution. Data objects in S3 are currently defined as ranging from 1 byte to 5GB, and S3 can (theoretically) store as many objects as desired. Both REST and SOAP are used to store, retrieve, and delete data objects.

> *Note that S3 shouldn't be confused with a CDN. It is not a distributed caching service, and it doesn't have global locations like a CDN does.*

A nice Web client for accessing S3 is the Firefox add-on called S3Firefox Organizer or S3Fox (see `https://addons.mozilla.org/en-US/firefox/addon/3247`). S3Fox Organizer helps you organize/manage/store your files on Amazon S3.

CloudFront

Amazon CloudFront is a newer Amazon service that enables developers to deliver content using a global network of edge servers. This is a type of CDN. Like CDNs, CloudFront is used to deliver content quickly to the user by locating servers near the user (called *edge servers*).

CloudFront works as follows:

1. Use Amazon S3 (bucket) to store original files.

   2. Using an Amazon CloudFront API call, register the S3 bucket to a CloudFront "distribution."

   3. Use domain name of the "distribution" (for example, `me.cloudfront.net`) to reference all of the content files.

   4. When a client makes a request to a "distribution" domain name (for example, `me.cloudfront.net`), the call will be automatically routed by Amazon to the nearest edge server.

Currently, Amazon has edge servers in the United States, Europe, Hong Kong, and Japan.

For more information about CloudFront, see `http://aws.amazon.com/cloudfront`.

Pricing Summary

Following is a breakdown of Amazon pricing information as of this writing. Payment is a function of the instance type, the hours of use (rounding up partial hours), and the bandwidth use (data transfer).

- ❏ *Amazon EC2 running Linux/UNIX*:

   - ❏ $0.10 per small instance (`m1.small`) instance-hour (or partial hour)

   - ❏ $0.40 per large instance (`m1.large`) instance-hour (or partial hour)

   - ❏ $0.80 per extra large instance (`m1.xlarge`) instance-hour (or partial hour)

   - ❏ $0.20 per high-CPU medium instance (`c1.medium`) instance-hour (or partial hour)

   - ❏ $0.80 per high-CPU extra large instance (`c1.xlarge`) instance-hour (or partial hour)

- ❏ *Elastic IP Addresses*:

   - ❏ $0.01 per non-attached Elastic IP address per complete hour

   - ❏ $0.00 per Elastic IP address remap (first 100 remaps/month)

   - ❏ $0.10 per Elastic IP address remap (additional remap/month over 100)

- ❏ *Elastic Block Store*:

   - ❏ $0.10 per GB-month of provisioned storage

   - ❏ $0.10 per 1 million I/O requests

   - ❏ $0.15 per GB-month of snapshot data stored

   - ❏ $0.01 per 1,000 PUT requests (when saving a snapshot)

   - ❏ $0.01 per 10,000 GET requests (when loading a snapshot)

- ❏ *Data Transfer*:

   - ❏ $0.10 per GB Internet data transfer (all data transfer into Amazon EC2)

   - ❏ $0.17 per GB Internet data transfer (first 10TB/month data transfer out of Amazon EC2)

   - ❏ $0.13 per GB Internet data transfer (next 40TB/month data transfer out of Amazon EC2)

❑ $0.11 per GB Internet data transfer (next 100TB/month data transfer out of Amazon EC2)

❑ $0.10 per GB Internet data transfer (data transfer out of Amazon EC2/month over 150TB)

❑ $0.01 per GB regional data transfer (in/out between Availability Zones or when using public IP or Elastic IP addresses)

Data transferred between Amazon EC2 instances in the same Availability Zone using private IP addresses is free of charge. Data transferred between Amazon EC2 and Amazon S3-Europe will be charged as Internet data transfer. Data transferred between Amazon EC2 and Amazon S3-US, Amazon SDB, and Amazon SQS is free of charge. All other charges for these services will still apply.

Usage for other Amazon Web services is billed separately from Amazon EC2.

Using Amazon's cost calculator (see `http://calculator.s3.amazonaws.com/calc5.html`), a single high-CPU medium Linux/UNIX instance with 100GB data transfer in and out can be used for a month (720 hours) for $171. Change this to a high-CPU extra large Linux/UNIX instance, and the monthly fee becomes $603.

Payment for S3 storage varies by size range and is calculated on a monthly basis. For example, as of this writing, it is currently $0.15 per GB up to the first 50TB per month. Rates for additional storage become cheaper and are tiered by storage ranges. Charges are also associated with transferring data in and out of S3. Currently, the data transfer in rate is $0.10 per GB. The rate for transferring data out is $0.17 per GB for the first 10TB per month, and becomes cheaper for additional transfers. Note that there is no charge for transfers between EC2 and S3.

When using S3 to deliver content, various HTTP requests will be used. The charge for HTTP GET requests is $0.01 per 10,000 requests. The charge for HTTP PUT, COPY, and POST requests is $0.01 per 1,000 requests. There is no charge for delete requests.

Using the Amazon calculator (see `http://calculator.s3.amazonaws.com/calc5.html`), you can see that it costs $44 a month for 100GB storage with 100GB transferred in, 100GB transferred out, 100,000 PUT/LIST requests, and 1,000,000 other requests.

Joyent

Joyent is another popular hosting solution for social network application developers. Like Amazon, Joyent provides a cloud computing environment with a similar kind of pricing model.

Joyent's cloud consists of a set of what it calls *Joyent Accelerators*, which are virtualized servers. Joyent provides hardware for load balancing, storage, and database support. Like Amazon, Joyent offers pre-configured accounts. Some of the application software supported includes PHP, Ruby on Rails, Python, and Java.

Joyent has partnered with Sun and does provide OpenSolaris systems. Unlike Amazon, Joyent provides real storage instead of remote storage (for example, S3). This can mean that, if a virtualized server goes down, a new virtualized server can be up and running within seconds.

One reason for Joyent's popularity is the offer of a free account for six months. This account includes the use of two quad-core Intel Xeon processor servers, guaranteed 64 percent of the CPU, 256MB RAM, 10GB storage, and no bandwidth metering.

Other Hosting Solutions

A new and emerging hosting provider is Google through Google App Engine, a service launched in 2008. See `http://code.google.com/appengine` for details about this service.

Case Studies

This section presents a few case studies illustrating architecture decisions made by social network application developers. (Many thanks should be offered to each of the parties interviewed who provided this information.) Learning how developers working with different-sized user bases, budgets, and resources design their systems for serving social network applications is a great way to plan for growth.

RockYou (Jia Shen, Founder)

RockYou started out on shared server, but it didn't work out. The company moved to managed hosting. Following are some key RockYou characteristics worth noting:

- ❑ *Number of servers* — As of this writing, RockYou was running on 400 boxes.

- ❑ *Layering* — Their rule to live by is, "Keep separate your Application layer and your Persistence layer." The Application layer must be state free (to keep persistence separate, not here). Thus, the Application layer is infinitely scalable. They use a federated Database layer, with the database sharded off with a user ID. (Database sharding is discussed in detail later in this chapter.)

- ❑ *Load balancing* — This is accomplished with separation of static and dynamic content requests.

- ❑ *Web server* — RockYou uses Apache, with PHP.

- ❑ *Database server* — RockYou uses MySQL.

- ❑ *Caching* — RockYou uses Memcached at the front end.

KlickNation (Ken Walton, Cofounder)

The hosting provider for KlickNation is Joyent. Following are some key characteristics:

- ❑ *Application layer* — KlickNation uses PHP.

- ❑ *Load balancing* — KlickNation uses clustered, load-balanced Apache servers for dynamic content and distributed Nginx servers for static content.

- ❑ *Web server* — KlickNation uses Apache and Nginx.

- ❑ *Database server* — KlickNation uses a dedicated MySQL server.

- ❑ *Caching* — KlickNation uses caching (for example, via Nginx).

Jambool (Vikas Guptas, Founder)

Jambool uses leased computers (Amazon S3) for static media serving. Following are some key characteristics:

- ❑ *Number of servers* — Jambool uses 16 boxes.

❑ *Layering* — Jambool uses an Application layer, Service layer, and Database layers. For the Application layer, they use four servers utilizing Ruby with a thin layer of rails, as well as lighttpd. For the Service layer, they have three servers using distributed Ruby. For the Database Layer, they use five servers with MySQL, with a few servers used as database slaves.

❑ *Load balancing* — Load balancing includes a separation of static and dynamic content requests.

❑ *Web server* — Jambool uses lightttpd, Apache, with PHP.

❑ *Caching* — Jambool uses four servers with Memcached at the front end.

Slide

Slide has servers located in Los Angeles, San Francisco, and Virginia. Following are some key characteristics:

❑ *Number of servers* — Slide uses more than 300 boxes.

❑ *Layering* — Slide uses Application and Database layers, with Akamai CDN and caching. Their 64 general-purpose, Web/application servers run Apache on Linux, and PHP. They use 42 database servers running MySQL.

❑ *Caching* — Slide uses 256 high-performance servers, with lots of memory, and Flash delivery.

Watercooler (Kevin Chou, Founder)

Following are some key characteristics pertaining to Watercooler:

❑ *Layering* — Watercooler uses Application and Data layers with caching, scaling up (but not out). The Application layer consists of seven servers. The Web server runs Apache with PHP. Watercooler uses four heavy-duty database servers running MySQL.

❑ *Streaming* — Watercooler allows partners to stream and hosts content for them.

❑ *Caching* — Caching is in front of the database and front end.

Understanding Database Issues

As an application stores more data (that is, user-generated content), having a good distributed database design can be critical for performance. Following are a few fundamental ways to improve performance:

❑ Use a caching layer before the database (for example, Memcached).

❑ Scale up by upgrading database servers. Increase CPUs' capability, increase memory, increase storage, and upgrade database software.

❑ Scale out (for example, with distributed databases).

❑ Architectural shifts (for example, database sharding).

While distributed databases and good database design are topics too extensive to cover within the scope of this book, the following discussions do highlight a few ideas to consider.

If the budget allows, a developer should minimally choose to have a separate database server (and, hence, a separate Database layer). This will make the Database layer independent, and allow for scaling (both up and out).

Distributed Systems (Scale Out)

A *distributed database* is a single, "logical" database that is spread across a set of database servers. Distributed databases are a means of scaling out a Database layer. Distributing databases is a way of improving performance. For example, having data in close proximity to its requestor will yield faster results.

Following are some different approaches to creating distributed databases:

❑ *Replication* — Copies of data are distributed to different servers (sites). The advantage of replication is that it is a straightforward and relatively simple technique. Also, replication supports reliability in that, if one server is down, the replicated data is available at another server. If the replicated nodes are placed in the network near their clients, this can also reduce network traffic. The disadvantage of this model is that updates must take place on all replicated servers, thus increasing processing time for this operation. A form of replication related to "master/slave" database replication is the use of some (one) database for writing and others for retrieval. This can be useful because writing generally takes more time than a retrieval.

❑ *Horizontal partitioning* — Different rows of a table go to different servers (sites). The main concept behind horizontal partitioning is that the rows in one server are located near the clients who will need them, thus improving performance. A problem with horizontal partitioning is that it can have poorer performance when accessing data across partitions.

❑ *Vertical partitioning* — Different columns of a table go to different servers (sites). Vertical partitioning has the same benefits and disadvantages as horizontal partitioning.

❑ *Hybrid* — These are combinations of the preceding.

❑ *Database Sharding* — Data is denormalized by grouping user-related data together.

Database Sharding

Database sharding is a different form of partitioning a "logical" database based on grouping data that is used together. Such a grouping of data "used together" is called a *shard*.

For example, consider creating an application that has an interface showing a user's profile. In this case, it would make sense to group together all of that user's profile data on one shard. This is an example of a typical sharding criterion based on grouping user data. With this criterion, the data belonging to a set of X users will be stored in "shard 1," and the next data belonging to a set of X users in "shard 2," and so on.

Partitioning into shards can be done using any criteria, even timestamps. The goal is to group data by how it is used. Unlike traditional databases, with sharding, the data is denormalized. In the example application that serves a user's profile data, for sharding, this requires only one request to one shard. By comparison, in a traditional database, a number of requests to different servers must take place. For such cases, sharding can significantly improve performance.

Data sharding is a new concept, and there are no exact guidelines for determining sharding criteria. There is no requirement that all the data that can be used together must be in the same shard (and it may not be possible). For example, with the user criterion, one shard could contain a user's messages, whereas another shard could contain the same user's entire profile data. Improved performance also comes from the fact that there is no need to perform many database joins to get a set of data (that is, all of a user's messages) because they can be stored and retrieved as one shard object.

A difficulty with database sharding takes place when the data in a shard outgrows the resources of its server. It must be split, and how to do that efficiently is problematic. This is referred to as the *problem of rebalancing.*

Another issue is that programmers may be familiar with traditional databases and SQL for making queries, but not be familiar with database sharding. Some of the largest barriers to using shards occur when forming sharding criteria, coupled with the fact that there are few people who have experience with database shards. This also translates into fewer resources and tools (almost none) available for the developer interested in implementing database shards. Even with these drawbacks, a number of companies utilize database sharding, including Flickr and RockYou.

Resources for Database Sharding

The following articles are a good place to learn more about database sharding:

❑ http://lifescaler.com/2008/04/database-sharding-unraveled-part-i, http://lifescaler.com/2008/04/database-sharding-unraveled-part-ii, and http://lifescaler.com/2008/06/database-sharding-unraveled-part-iii

❑ http://www.codefutures.com/weblog/database-sharding/labels/Database%20Sharding.html

❑ http://www.codefutures.com/database-sharding/

❑ http://www.datacenterknowledge.com/archives/2007/04/27/database-sharding-helps-high-traffic-sites

❑ http://lethargy.org/~jesus/archives/95-Partitioning-vs.-Federation-vs.-Sharding.html

---

Understanding Redundancy

Redundancy is the duplication of an important component (for example, servers or services) that is system critical. The term "critical" can relate to loss of information, but also to good performance. *Cloning* is a technique that is used to replicate services or servers.

There are two basic kinds of cloning: *shared disk* and *nothing shared*. In the shared disk cloning, the clones share storage. The shared disk cloning is more difficult but can be useful for heavy-update databases.

Using Monitoring

There are a number of free software packages that monitor a networked system. Monitoring software can create graphs and present statistics on how various subsystems/components of a system are performing. This can tell you where improvements need to be made. Check out the following:

❑ *Cacti* — http://cacti.net

❑ *Multi Router Traffic Grapher (MRTG)* — `http://oss.oetiker.ch/mrtg`

❑ *PRTG Traffic Grapher* — `http://www.paessler.com/prtg`

To test client-based software (such as OpenSocial JavaScript code), a good tool is the Firefox plug-in called Firebug. Firebug not only can be used for monitoring but also to directly edit and debug live JavaScript, HTML, and CSS.

Firebug is free for use and is popular with JavaScript programmers. Figure 8-2 shows the main interface for Firebug when viewing a hi5 crossword application. Firebug has separate tab interfaces for HTML, CSS, Script, and DOM.

For more information about Firebug, see `http://getfirebug.com`.

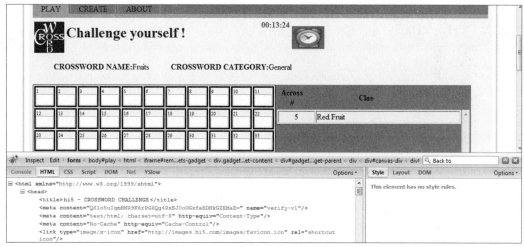

Figure 8-2: Firebug running on crossword social network application

Understanding Software Design

Good software design is necessary for achieving system performance and scalability. The following discussion provides some tips for creating a good design, selecting a language, and taking advantage of versioning support.

The process of designing software is a main topic in software engineering. The following are included in the steps and processes for creating good software:

❑ *Requirements engineering* — This includes techniques often used to understand application requirements and document them.

❑ *Design* — This includes techniques used for the design of software. This is often object oriented, and includes techniques such as waterfall, spiral, extreme programming, and many others.

❑ *Implementation* — This covers the tools used when creating software, deployment, and versioning.

❑ *Testing* — This includes techniques to test applications, including concepts such unit testing, regression testing, black-box testing, and more.

❑ *Maintenance* — This includes ideas behind maintaining software, tracking bugs, user feedback, and more.

The reality is that many developers and companies do not formalize their development process. A number of good textbooks are available if you are interested in learning more about software engineering. This discussion concentrates on more informal tips, guidelines, and suggestions.

Given the inherent social nature of a social networking application, most experienced developers of these applications stress how important it is to understand your users. Once developers determine the target audience of their applications, a software engineering technique called *role playing* can be useful in developing use cases for an application. This leads naturally to interface design and operation specifications. Some developers even go through the effort of describing different target users by creating personas (see http://en.wikipedioa.org/wiki/Personas). A tip I give to my students is to have co-developers, friends, and family try to "use" a mockup of the application and give suggestions. Refining the use case before implementation can save you from a redesign and reimplementation later.

In addition to role playing and persona building, meeting with other developers can be helpful in building an application design. There are a number of OpenSocial "meetups" and social network programming-related "meetups" that have frequent (monthly) meetings. Check out http://meetup.com for some "meetups" in your area. In addition, a number of the social networks host meetings, and some are virtual.

If your company does not have a formal documentation process, you should minimally consider using the following tools:

❑ Use versioning software, project maintenance software, and/or a wiki to document the software-creation process.

❑ There are many Unified Modeling Language (UML) tools available, and some are free for use. Create use-case diagrams with them. Some of these tools are now integrated with development tools and can be used to generate even initial code. Often, these design-to-development tools are for object-oriented languages such as Java, C# , and so on.

If you are planning to develop a number of applications, it may make sense to invest in the creation of an *application infrastructure*. This entails the development of services, libraries, and/or packages that modularize commonly needed functionality. This can be formalized with a Web service layer so that these main server-based Web services/applications can be called from any language.

With an OpenSocial hybrid client-server application, the developer must decide what application logic to implement on the client and what logic will reside on the server. The best balance is highly dependent on the application's purpose and data needs. It is possible to have the client side make many and repeated calls to the server program, which would contain the bulk of the application logic, or vice versa. Issues of performance and scalability should be of concern in making these choices. Many developers might suggest that keeping as much logic as possible on the client could improve performance and scalability. Other developers who have data-heavy applications (especially media-heavy ones) might suggest that server-side programs are superior.

Language Choice

Choosing the right language for creating an application should be a function of the application needs and how well the language can fulfill them. However, you should also use a language that the development team will be familiar with. If the development team only knows PHP, then choosing Java as the language may not be the wisest decision.

With the current container support of OpenSocial, some of the application logic must be developed in JavaScript using the OpenSocial JavaScript API. If the application has server-side programs, or is an OpenSocial REST server application, then a server-side programming language must be used. Almost any programming language that supports basic HTTP requests can be used. The most popular languages include PHP, Java, Python, ASP, Ruby, and C#. However, many other languages can be used (for example, C++, C, and Perl).

Some languages will need additional modules, interpreters, or containers in which to run. These will mean additional maintenance. Some of these language containers have additional features that can improve performance. For example, the Sun Java System Web Server not only includes support for Java but also performs load balancing, and includes a reverse proxy module.

If speed is critical, compiled software generally will be faster. The only way to know is to perform a benchmark test to compare different languages. Another resource for anecdotal feedback on language performance is fellow developers through forums or "meetups."

Following are language choices for some social network application development companies:

- *iLike* — Ruby on Rails, MySQL, with AWS for static content
- *KlickNation* — PHP, MySQL
- *I-Jet Media Inc* — Flash, Python, PHP
- *Jambool* — Ruby, MySQL
- *Watercooler* — PHP, MySQL

Versioning

Version control software enables the developer to manage multiple versions of an application. Typically, versions are indicated by a changing version number. Having access to previous versions allows for quick reversion to a previous code base, which is useful for a quick response to new software failures. It is also helpful for working with multi-developer teams, and supports collaboration through code "check-in" and "check-out" features.

Other useful features of version control software include version comparison, anonymous read access, logging, and local update operation. Following are a couple of versioning systems to consider:

- Subversion (also referred to as SVN)
- Concurrent Version System (CVS) or OpenCVS

OpenSocial Performance Tuning

This section examines some general code performance-tuning ideas, as well as some specific OpenSocial performance-tuning measures. Techniques to help improving performance include the following:

- ❏ Caching
- ❏ Minimizing the number of HTTP requests
- ❏ Batching multiple requests
- ❏ Using OpenSocial AppData as a container cache
- ❏ Reducing the number of DNS lookups
- ❏ Reducing the number of files
- ❏ Turning on the persistence feature in a Web server
- ❏ Compressing content using GZIP
- ❏ Minifying JavaScript
- ❏ Using CSS in a header
- ❏ Locating JavaScript at the bottom
- ❏ Caching versus requests for external files (JavaScript, CSS)
- ❏ Flushing a server response
- ❏ Monitoring client code performance
- ❏ Preloading OpenSocial content
- ❏ Achieving good load times
- ❏ Using OpenSocial get from cache
- ❏ Using CSS image sprites

Caching was discussed earlier in this chapter. Let's take a more detailed look at the remaining techniques in this list.

Minimizing the Number of HTTP Requests

Minimizing the number of HTTP requests can significantly improve performance. Nearly 90 percent of the end-user response time on poorly designed applications is spent waiting for a response. One way to minimize HTTP requests is through a simpler application design that has a smaller number of components to load.

Batching Multiple Requests

In OpenSocial, the program can associate multiple requests with a single DataRequest object. This batching of requests will save significant time. Batching requests and sending them as early as possible will improve performance.

Also consider not making the first request (if possible) one to create or update application data via `new updatePersonAppDataRequest`. This operation takes more time than other API calls. In a similar fashion, you should not call `requestCreateActivity` before other requests for the same reason.

Using OpenSocial AppData as a Container Cache

A common suggestion made by experienced developers is to use the OpenSocial AppData supported by containers as a cache. Retrieving this data from the container is generally faster than making a call to your server for it.

Reducing the Number of DNS Lookups

When a client receives a response with components such as images, external files, and so on referenced in it, an HTTP request for each component must take place. These components will be specified by their URLs. For each domain name in a URL not currently stored in the client's DNS cache, the client must contact a DSN to look up the associated IP address to form the HTTP request. If all of the response components have different domains, this adds up to potentially a lot of DNS lookups, each adding to the response time.

If possible, serving the response content from the same domain name will reduce the number of DNS lookups. Unfortunately, there is a downside to reducing the number of unique hostnames. This reduction will also reduce the number of parallel downloads the client will make. A client can download multiple content items at the same time but has a limited number (for example, two) it will attempt to do from the same hostname. More parallel downloads can improve performance. So, using the same hostname to reduce DNS lookups will also restrict parallel downloads. Some developers suggest a balance, using possibly two to six different hostnames for the response content.

Reducing the Number of Files

When downloading JavaScript, CSS, or other additional files, each file is a separate request. "Compressing" the JavaScript into a single file (or even integrating it directly in your OpenSocial XML file) can greatly improve performance. An article at http://yuiblog.com/blog/2007/01/04/performance-research-part-2 by Tenni Theurer states that 40 percent to 60 percent of users come to site(s) with an empty cache. For these users, it is critical that the developer design the application to load quickly by reducing the number of files. Inlining of code into a single file, while improving speed, does also result in less modularity, less reusability, and high maintenance costs.

Turning on the Persistence Feature in a Web Server

"Keep Alive On" is an HTTP feature that can be set in a Web server's configuration file. When turned on, this means that multiple HTTP requests can be sent over the same TCP connection. This can save time by avoiding repeated TCP setup and takedown operations. Apache documents turning this feature on can improve latency up to 50 percent when multiple media requests result from an HTTP response.

See http://httpd.apache.org/docs/2.2/mod/core.html#keepalive *for more details.*

Compressing Content Using GZIP

Sending compressed (textual) data rather than uncompressed data can significantly reduce the client's time to receive this content. Compression reduces the size of the data. The tradeoff is that once received, the data must be uncompressed by the client. A client can stipulate in its HTTP request `Accept-Encoding` header the kind of compression it supports. The server then can choose to compress the response using this format and must (in its header) return the type of compression used in the `Content-Encoding` header. Reports of average GZIP reductions in size are 70 percent (but, this is dependent on the content). A large percentage of Web traffic uses GZIP.

The following is the request header indicating that GZIP and deflate are supported by the client:

```
Accept-Encoding: gzip, deflate
```

The following is the response header indicating that GZIP was used to compress the response:

```
Content-Encoding: gzip
```

Currently, GZIP is one of the most commonly used compression standards, and is freely available. When using an Apache Web server, GZIP is supported using either `mod_gzip` or `mod_deflate` modules (depending on Apache version). Once the module is configured, the response will automatically be GZIPped by Apache and the `Content-Encoding` header set.

See `http://httpd.apache.org/docs/2.0/mod/mod_deflate.html` *for details on the* `mod_deflate` *module.*

Compression can be applied to HTML, XML, scripts, CSS, and other text documents. Most media content is already in a compressed format (that is, `jpeg`, `png`, `mpeg`) and should not be compressed again.

"Minifying" JavaScript

This is the idea of removing comments and all unnecessary blank spaces in a JavaScript file. The goal is to make it as small as possible, thus improving download speed and performance.

A good filtering program that does this is JSMin (see `http://www.crockford.com/javascript/jsmin.html`). Another tool can be found at `http://developer.yahoo.com/yui/compressor/`. The resulting JavaScript is called "minified JavaScript."

Another tool used not only for compacting but also for obfuscating code can be found at `http://dean.edwards.name/packer/`.

Using CSS in a Header

Placing the CSS stylesheets in the HTTP `Head` section gives the illusion of the application loading faster. This is because the application can load progressively, meaning that, as the content comes in, it is displayed. If the information (stylesheet) that styles this content is not loaded already, some browsers will wait to load any content (to prevent possibly redrawing the content with aft-loaded styles). The actual time to load the entire content is not different. It only seems faster to the user.

Locating JavaScript at the Bottom

When possible, it is best to place JavaScript code at the bottom of an application's content (response). This has to do with the fact that loading of scripts in a browser blocks parallel downloads. Recall that a *parallel download* is where downloads of separate content (for example, image 1, file 2, and so on) occur at the same time.

It is not always possible to place JavaScript at the bottom, especially if it is responsible for building the interface dynamically through operations such as `document.write`.

Caching versus Requests for External Files (JavaScript, CSS)

The benefit of putting all scripting code either in a single external file or even inline with the HTML (or XML) is the reduction in the number of requests that must be made. A corollary to this is that placing the script in a separate file can mean that it is cached by the client independently of the HTML/XML document. This can be an advantage if other HTML/XML documents use this same script. It means that they will not be loaded, and each HTML/XML document that references them externally rather than inlining the code will be smaller and, hence, load faster.

Here there is a tradeoff between number of HTTP requests (that is, two, including an HTML/XML document and a separate JavaScript file) and load size of the initial HTTP response document (that is, larger when everything is in one file). If the scripting code is used by multiple documents, it can make sense to keep them separate, hoping they will be cached by the client and, hence, not need an additional HTTP request. If the application has only one HTML/XML document, then keeping it inline makes sense. This is also the case when there are very few page views using the script.

This is the case for most OpenSocial applications, and a common tip seen on developer forums is the inlining of script. That being said, if you look at the source of many applications, you will find external JavaScript.

Flushing a Server Response

When a social network application makes a request to a server-side program, the user is waiting for the response. Rather than make the user wait until the entire response is built, with some server-side programming languages, you are able to flush the results. This will result in the client receiving the partially built response, which it can work on as the server program continues building the rest of the response.

In PHP, the function `flush()` can be invoked for this purpose. The benefit will be most evident on servers that are very busy, or when the creation of the response takes a significant amount of time. Doing a flush after the response headers are created is recommended. This will allow the client to fetch any referenced CSS or JavaScript in the header while the body of the response is being created.

Monitoring Client Code Performance

An extension called YSlow integrates into Firebug and provides performance measurement on the application. (Firebug was discussed previously in this chapter in the section "Monitoring.")

Check out `http://developer.yahoo.com/yslow` *to get YSlow, and for further details.*

Figure 8-3 shows the YSlow interface for running performance metrics on a well-known social network application. A number of the poorer performance grades are contributed by the container and are not application-specific. As a developer, you will need to go through each metric to see where you might improve performance.

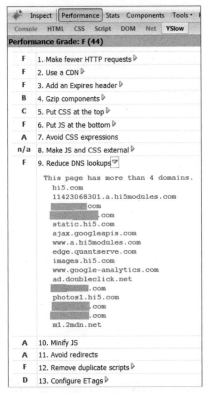

Figure 8-3: YSlow testing performance of a hi5 deployed application

Figure 8-3 shows the "Reduce DNS lookups" metric. The greyed-out areas are the servers directly owned by the application. Others are owned by the container hi5, while others are third-party services the application uses. Recall that the previous tip on reducing DNS lookups suggested a small number of unique hostnames in the two to six range. As you can see, there are more than this in this example, yielding a mediocre grade for this metric. However, most of the lookups are from the container, which is not something a developer can control.

YSlow evaluates performance on the following metrics:

❑ *Make fewer HTTP requests* — "Fewer" means that the application can run faster.

❑ *Use a CDN* — Suggests a need for a CDN. The score for this metric is computed by checking the hostname of each content object requested against the list of known CDNs. YSlow lets you register new CDN names if not in the default list.

❑ *Add an Expires header* — This suggests a need to use `Expires` or `Cache-Control` headers.

❑ *Gzip Components* — This provides a list of items not compressed using GZIP.

❑ *Put CSS at the top* — This provides a list of CSS not appearing in the header.

❑ *Put JavaScript (JS) at the bottom* — This lists JavaScript files not at the bottom of the response.

❑ *Avoid CSS expressions* — CSS expressions is a browser-specific extension of CSS and takes time to evaluate. Don't use this, or use sparingly.

❑ *Minify JavaScript (JS)* — See the previous discussion on how to "minify" the JavaScript.

❑ *Avoid redirects* — This warns the developer against using redirects. Unless entirely necessary, the use of redirects is a waste of the user's time.

❑ *Remove duplicate scripts* — This indicates multiple-loaded JavaScript files.

Some particularly useful features of YSlow's Performance utitlity and Firebug's Net utility include showing the difference with cache and without, as well as showing the load times for different response components.

Preloading OpenSocial Content

Preloading is the concept of loading content ahead of its use. Preloading can be done during client idle time. Content that is often preloaded includes images, stylesheets, and scripts.

OpenSocial supports preloading through the `Preload` element of the Gadget XML `ModulePref`. The following code preloads the XML file for the Profile view:

```
<Preload
    href=http://U.com/doit.xml"
    views="profile" />
```

Preloading can also be done for a `makeRequest` call. For example, in orkut, you can set a parameter in the `ModulePrefs` element that tells orkut to make a signed request while the application is loaded. The following is the OpenSocial JavaScript `makeRequest` call:

```
var params = {};
params[gadgets.io.RequestParameters.CONTENT_TYPE] =
                    gadgets.io.ContentType.JSON;
params[gadgets.io.RequestParameters.AUTHORIZATION] =
                    gadgets.io.AuthorizationType.SIGNED;
gadgets.io.makeRequest("http://U.com", response, params);
```

As an example, consider placing the following in the Gadget XML:

```
<ModulePrefs title="Demo Preloads" description="Demo Preloads">
  <Require feature="opensocial-0.7" />
  <Require feature="views" />
  <Preload href="http://U.com" authz="signed" />
</ModulePrefs>
```

The response from `U.com` will be inline in the application HTML. When the `makeRequest` call is made, it will use this content, rather than sending out an HTTP request.

Achieving Good Load Times

The following guidelines are given by Arne Roomann-Kurrik, Developer Programs, in the orkut Developer Forum with regard to loading times:

❑ *Good load times* — "Canvas" view should be less than 5 seconds to load. "profile" view should be less than 2 seconds to load.

❑ *Need Improvement* — "Canvas" view experiencing 5 to 10 seconds to load, and "profile" view experiencing 2 to 5 seconds to load, need improved load times.

❑ *Must Improve* — "Canvas" view with more than 10 seconds to load, and "profile" view with more than 5 seconds to load, must be improved.

Using OpenSocial get from Cache

Use the `gadgets.io.getproxyUrl` method to retrieve resources from cache before making requests to a server-side program. This method will return the URL of the cached version.

The following JavaScript code takes the URL of an image on the developer's Web site and, using the `getproxyUrl` method, retrieves the cache location if it exists. (Otherwise, the original URL will be returned.) The code uses this URL in an image tag. The cached version will be used instead, resulting in one less HTTP request.

```
function getImage() {
  Url = 'http://U.com /image.jpg';
  cached = gadgets.io.getProxyUrl(Url);
  html = ['<img src="', Url, '">'];
  document.getElementById('domId').innerHTML = html.join('');
};
```

Using CSS Image Sprites

If an application has a significant number of images, the technique of *image spriting* (which combines all of the image files into a single "sprite" file) can help with performance. Instead of performing a number of requests to retrieve all of the images, only one request is needed to retrieve the "sprite" file.

See `http://www.alistapart.com/articles/sprites` *for details on sprites.*

Using Analytics

Analytics is the tracking of application users (and application requests) as they use the application. Analytics can point to some useful information, including the following:

❑ Visit information

❑ User demographics

❑ Where users are losing interest (for example, what "application" pages they leave from)

❑ Most popular content

There is a wide variety of analytic software available. The most popular analytic software used by social network applications includes Google Analytics, Yahoo! Web Analytics, Sometrics, and container-provided analytic software. Other popular Web analytic software systems include Urchin, VisiStat, CoreMetrics, and FeedBurner. New companies are emerging, like Mixpanel.com, which is geared toward social network applications.

> Check out `http://en.wikipedia.org/wiki/List_of_web_analytics_software` *for a list and comparison of analytic software.*

Google Analytics

Google Analytics is one of the most widely used Web analytic systems for social network applications. It is free for use. After creating an account, you are given a tracking number and some JavaScript that you can include in any Web page you wish to track.

> Check out `http://www.google.com/analytics` *for details on creating an account.*

The following code is an example of the JavaScript that that Google delivers:

```
<script type="text/javascript">
    var gaJsHost = (("https:" == document.location.protocol) ?
                        "https://ssl." : "http://www.");
    document.write(unescape("%3Cscript src='" + gaJsHost +
            "google-analytics.com/ga.js' type='text/javascript'%3E%3C/script%3E"));
</script>

<script type="text/javascript">
    var pageTracker = _gat._getTracker("UA-XXXXXXX-Y");
    pageTracker._trackPageview();
</script>
```

Once you add this to your code, it will take a fixed amount of time to start tracking (for example, 24 hours). Figure 8-4 shows the main interface for a registered Google Analytics Web profile (account). The actual profile associated with the data in Figure 8-5 is a test social network application.

Information provided by Google Analytics is categorized as shown in the upper left of Figure 8-5. Information that Google Analytics provides includes the following:

❏ *Visitor Tracking*:

  ❏ *Statistics* — This includes the number of visits, unique visitors, number of page-views, average page-views, time on site, bounce rate, and new visits.

  ❏ *Visitor profile* — This includes the language and network locations.

  ❏ *Browser profile* — This includes the browser, operating system, screen colors (and resolution), Java support, and Flash version.

  ❏ Map overlay of visitors — This shows the countries colored in.

  ❏ *Connection speed* — This shows how long it took to connect.

  ❏ *Visitor loyalty* — This includes a plot of visits in a time period.

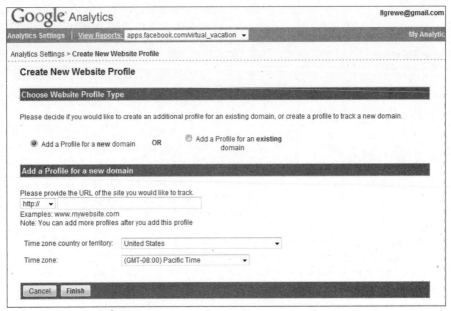

Figure 8-4: Google Analytics main page for a Web profile

- ❑ *Recency* — This includes trends in last-visit reporting.
- ❑ *Length of visit* — This includes how long a visitor is on a site.
- ❑ *Depth of visit* — This includes how many pages the visitor viewed.

❑ *Traffic Sources:*

- ❑ *Top traffic sources* — Top sources to direct traffic to your application.
- ❑ *Direct traffic info* — Information about the direction to your application.
- ❑ *Referring sites* — Sites that referred users to your application.
- ❑ *Keywords, adwords* — Keywords or adwords in search portals used to refer to your application.

❑ *Content:*

- ❑ *Navigation analysis* — Indicates navigation patterns.
- ❑ *Top content* — Content most visited.
- ❑ *Content visitation statistics* — Breakdown of different content and visitation numbers.

❑ *Goals:*

- ❑ *Setup of goal conversions* — A *goal conversion* is a Web site page that visitors reach once they complete a series of actions (such as visiting other pages first).

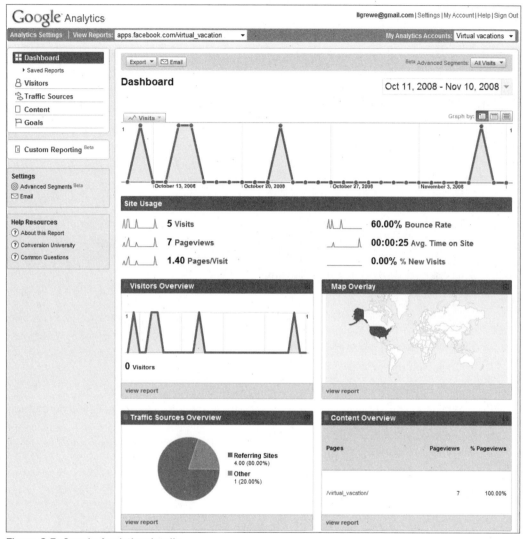

Figure 8-5: Google Analytics details

Yahoo! Web Analytics

Yahoo! Web Analytics (http://web.analytics.yahoo.com) is built out of the acquisition of IndexTools. The offering is similar to Google Analytics and is free. It also allows you to build reports and manage monetization campaigns, merchandise reporting, cost analysis of ad campaigns, and more. (Monetization is discussed in greater detail later in this chapter.)

Sometrics

Sometrics (`http://sometrics.com`) is a newly formed company that is offering analytics for social network applications. In addition, Sometrics also gathers social data beyond traditional Web analytics. Similarly to the systems previously discussed, it is free.

Social Network-Provided

It is becoming more common for social networks to provide analytic tools. An example of this is hi5 Analytics (see `http://www.hi5networks.com/developer/2008/07/historical-application-statist.html`). This is done through a REST API that has the following endpoints:

❑ `metrics/daily` — These are daily statistics (but not unique views). This API call can take a range of dates (less than 30 days).

❑ `metrics/dailyuniques` — This gives daily statistics, only allowing for unique views.

❑ `metrics/total` — These are statistics for the application since its launch.

The information provided includes the following:

❑ Number of installs

❑ Number of removes

❑ Number of Profile view calls

❑ Number of Preview view calls

❑ Number of "canvas" view calls

❑ Number of requests generated in response to application-generated emails and notifications

❑ Number of API requests made by the application

❑ Application notifications marked as spam

❑ Requests to generate a friend update

❑ Friend update requests fulfilled

❑ Invite requests fulfilled

❑ Application notification requests fulfilled

Much of this information is unique to a social network application and cannot be provided by general Web analytic systems like Google Analytics.

Using Scalable User Interface Design

A *scalable user interface* is one that can grow and be altered with new application revisions without a major redesign. This is difficult to achieve with a very long-lasting application. In some cases, making a radical change in the interface can attract new interest and improve user satisfaction. Sometimes it is necessary to include new functions. However, it can be a risky move (think "New Coke") and can end up turning away loyal users.

Making a major change in the interface of an application may be a lot of work, and quite often can lead to new bugs and application failures. A major redesign is certainly not something a developer would want to have to do earlier in an application's life.

To avoid this, you should design multiple versions of an application, scaling it back for the first. This means considering all of the possible functionalities and corresponding GUI elements that are planned for future versions before implementing the first version. Predetermine how these new functionalities can fit into version 1's interface. This may yield changes in the design of the first version's interface but will yield a more scalable interface.

When considering changes to a user interface, one technique employed by some developers is "A/B (split) testing." This is where both the current and new version of the software are offered in real time, and tested for usability and performance. This can be a good exercise to do internally before rolling out a new version, or even a small change.

Making the Most of User/System Support

A social network application's customers are paramount. The application survives only if users return (reflected in daily user numbers), and this means good user satisfaction. A great way to find out how an application is performing is to give the users a way of contacting the developer. This could include bug reporting, suggestions for future versions, and reports of inappropriate use by other users.

Using a support system is important to track these reports and resulting responses. Some different kinds of software systems you might consider for handling these tasks include the following:

- ❑ *Bug-tracking software* — For a list of some available systems, see `http://www.dmoz.org/Computers/Software/Configuration_Management/Bug_Tracking/`.
- ❑ *Issue-tracking software* — For a comparison of some systems, see `http://en.wikipedia.org/wiki/Comparison_of_issue_tracking_systems`.

Minimally, you should regularly check the email account (registered with your application at deployment) for user (or container-generated) emails. Also, you should create a "fan account" on each social network that the application is deployed on. An application "fan account" will have a profile telling users about your application, and will host a discussion board for your users to share ideas about the application with you and other users. It is also a good marketing tool to use when new versions of the application are released, or other important application news is generated.

Many applications feature user-generated content. This opens up the door for user misuse of the application through inappropriate content creation, spamming, violations of copyright, and more. With an increasing numbers of users, the amount of content can become so large that it is impossible for a sole developer to monitor.

Many Web sites (such as YouTube) and social networks (such as MySpace and Facebook) with this problem handle it by allowing their users (and others affected) to report violations. A violation will be investigated, and any proven violators will be dealt with (such as refusing services). Some social networks (like MySpace) are now requiring applications with user-generated content to have a "report abuse" functionality.

One company that has done a good job at structuring this for social network application is Watercooler, which supports the idea of volunteer moderators from its user base with whom the company works directly.

A simple way to search for potential moderators or to encourage reporting of violations is through the application "fan page" discussed previously.

Monetization

Monetization means the process of making money from a social network application. This section examines some possibilities and shows (through case studies) what other developers are doing.

All of the monetization schemes that are in use today for general Web sites can be applied for a social network application. Depending on the application and its audience, some of these techniques will be successful; others will not be.

There is a significant debate centering around the fact that social networks (such as MySpace or Facebook) monetize differently than search engines or portals (such as Google or Yahoo!). The hypothesis surrounding some of the early numbers is that there is a difference between intent and interest. *Intent* is what happens at Google or Yahoo! when a user, for example, types in "ski tickets" and the user intends to make a purchase. However, *interest* is what happens when a MySpace user brings up a ski social network application. The suggestion is that the "intent" user will click on ads and incentives more often than the "interest" user.

Despite this dour viewpoint (yet to be proven), another (yet to be seen) viewpoint is that the rich social data and the changing human interaction models on a social network will open up new avenues and richer data to exploit for mapping users to a place they will "buy."

Some of the monetization techniques that social network applications employ include the following:

- ❏ Advertising
- ❏ Affiliate programs
- ❏ Partnering
- ❏ Virtual goods and currency
- ❏ Real goods

Let's take a look at these in more detail.

Advertising

Advertising is currently a popular way that applications are earning money. There are a number of Ad Network companies in the business of trying to get developers to serve their ads, including the following (in no particular order):

- ❏ Google
- ❏ Yahoo!

- ❏ Offerpal
- ❏ Social Media
- ❏ Social Cash
- ❏ Lookery
- ❏ Zohark
- ❏ AdChap
- ❏ Cubics

Google and Yahoo! are long-time ad networks with which you may be familiar, and the others represent newer companies, many of them targeted at the social network market. Offerpal, targeted at the social Web, is a "managed offer network."

Each advertising provider has different revenue models, and some serve up different competing ads using an auction model (for example, Google and Yahoo!).

Some offer Cost per Thousand (CPM, with "M" meaning the roman numeral for "thousand") page impressions. *Impression* here means "viewing the advertising."

Another revenue model is that of Cost per Action (CPA), which can have different implementations, including the following:

- ❏ *Cost per Click (CPC)* — This is when the user actually clicks on the advertisement.
- ❏ *Cost per Lead (CPL)* — This usually involves the user doing some form of a registration through the advertisement.
- ❏ *Cost per Sale (CPS)* — This can be a fixed fee or percentage of a user sale following the advertisement on your application.

In general, CPM and many CPA revenues are fixed values. CPA ad rate is higher than the CPM rate.

Cost per Install marketing was discussed earlier in this book. The counterpart of Cost per Install marketing is Pay per Install (PPI), where you are paid if someone installs an advertised application when viewing an ad on your application. The advertised application can be another social network application, or can be a non-social application.

Affiliate Programs

Affiliate advertising is a type of advertising in which an application directs users to another Web site. There are a number of affiliate networks that connect social network application developers to affiliate programs (for example, Amazon is a large one) that matches the goals of the application. These affiliate networks also allow the developer (here called the *affiliate*) to track results and provide payments. It is free for developers to join an affiliate network.

Following are some examples of direct affiliate programs and affiliate networks:

- ❏ Amazon
- ❏ eBay

❑ Commission Junction

❑ LinkShare

❑ Millnic

Partnering

Partnerships can come in many forms but imply that the developer is working with a partnering corporation. Goals may including branding, direct sales, directing traffic (such as affiliate advertising), cross-advertising, and so on.

Some examples of previously discussed partnerships include the Send Good Karma application partnering with Health.com and Watercooler partnering with media companies such as ABC to include ABC content on applications. Both of these partnerships provide revenue streams for the social network application. KlickNation has recently begun partnerships with companies whereby they license an application on a monthly basis.

Virtual Goods and Virtual Currency

Virtual goods are "digital" goods that can be purchased, traded, and sent to other users through an application. *Virtual currency* is the offering of virtual monies that can be spent to buy services (or virtual goods) inside of an application. This is a new trend that has been used primarily in game-like social network applications.

For example, a "war-game" application could offer a more powerful gun or additional ammunition that can be purchased with a user's virtual currency. Virtual currency is gained by either completing some task or by purchasing it via a micro-transaction (a concept that is discussed in detail shortly). The task completion could be inviting friends (which has a goal of making the application viral) or could involve filling out an offer (that is, affiliate offer) that the developer is paid for completion. The micro-transaction is a direct purchase and, hence, earns real money.

Example applications discussed earlier that use virtual currency are Send Good Karma, Friends for Sale, and New Mafia. Send Good Karma uses the model of sending, a karma greeting (a virtual good). Friends for Sale allows users to purchase friends using virtual currency. The New Mafia supports virtual currency to purchase tools for its game-based application. The New Mafia site reports up to 80 percent of its revenue comes from using virtual currency.

Offerpal is one of the companies that offers virtual currency services tied to offers. There are a number of other emerging companies soon to offer services in this area. Offerpal suggests that serving advertisements (via offers) for virtual currency is a way to promote it, and is a way to engage and monetize at the same time. Offerpal suggests even advertising your virtual currency on other Web sites and other applications. Another suggestion is to send messages, activities, and emails feature virtual currency offers. At the same time, a balance is needed. If too many virtual currency offers are given, they can start to feel like spam to a user, and they can lose their value.

According CEO Anu Shukla (during a talk at Snap Summit, details of which can be found at http://www.slideshare.net/rfop/slides-706362/), Offerpal offers the following statistics regarding the use of virtual currency:

- ❑ A 10–20 percent increase in return visits is experienced when virtual currency is offered for logging in.

- ❑ A 30 percent increase in user base growth rate is experienced when virtual currency is offered for inviting friends.

- ❑ A 20 times increase in user activity is experienced when virtual currency is offered for performing an activity or task.

- ❑ $75 earned (on average) per 1,000 active daily users (compared to their figure of < $1 for "effective" CPM).

One challenge experienced by developers is how to extend the use of virtual currency outside of the game-based (or virtual goods) applications.

Real Goods and Micropayments/Micro-Transactions

One option is to sell real goods. This will make sense if the products are closely aligned with the application genre and audience. A good model of this is iLike, which sells access and downloads of music. Both iLike and Watercooler have offered ticket sales to application-related events (music and sports).

Functionally, this will minimally mean having payment support. A new form of payment is called *micropayment* (through a *micro-transaction)*, which is meant to be a small amount of money. The definition of "small" varies a lot in its implementation in social network applications. Prices can range from less than $1 to $10–$20. This new trend (used primarily to monetize virtual goods and virtual currency schemes) has created a number of new companies that offer these services, including the following:

- ❑ PayPal
- ❑ SpareChange
- ❑ Chipin

Of these, PayPal is one of the most widely used.

One form of making micropayments is with mobile devices (phones). Here are a few companies offering mobile micropayment services:

- ❑ Zong
- ❑ MobilCash
- ❑ Surfpin

Another new trend is offering "payment card" that users can purchase at retail stores.

Monetization Case Studies

Table 8-1 provides details from a few case studies to show how some developers are monetizing their applications. For each developer (company), featured techniques they are using are listed. This is not necessarily an exhaustive listing of their monetization techniques, but represents techniques discussed during interviews for this book.

Table 8-1: Monetization Case Study Details

Company	Feature Techniques
Watercooler	Advertising/partnering (traditional and targeted, sports advertising).
	Media partnership (media-streaming revenue).
	Real goods (ticket sales, merchandise sales — 10 percent of revenue).
RockYou	Advertising (both CPM and CPI — 50/50).
	Advertisement network provider. (Developed their own advertising network based on their success with their own applications. Offers advertising network services to other developers. See `https://www.rockyouads.com/ams/partner/marketing`.)
Slide	Max Levchin, Slide CEO, said, "Direct to consumer sales is what the next couple years are going to be about. I just returned from Japan and Korea, where people make billions of dollars selling virtual goods. Bringing that model from Asia worldwide is a huge component of revenues for companies like Slide." (See Keynote Speech, Web 2.0.)
I-Jet Media Inc.	Advertising (CPM — 10 percent of revenue).
	Micro-transactions/virtual currency/virtual goods (100,000 virtual currency equals $5, which, coupled with subscriptions, represents 90 percent of revenue).
	Subscription (micro-transaction, at $15/month).
	Offer-based advertising (CPM-based advertising).
Jambool	Micro-transactions/virtual currency/virtual goods.
	Partnering (drove more than 40,000 users to Health.com).
	Donations (donated more than 2,000 to kiva.org from Send Good Karma application).
KlickNation	Advertising.
	Subscription (micro-transaction at $4.99/month).
	Mobile billing.
	Licensing of applications.
ShopIt	According to Rhet McNulty, COO, this is a "cross between MySpace and eBay."
	Advertising network provider. (The purpose of the application is to provide a peer-to-peer/commerce-based advertising network.)

Summary

This chapter focused on the issues of performance and scalability. First, the definitions of performance and scalability were discussed, followed by a discussion of architectures and subsystems useful for improving performance and scalability. The topics of caching and database design were highlighted.

Next, options for hosting solutions were described. Case studies of the ways that a number of important social network application development companies are solving their hosting needs gave invaluable insight into solving this problem in different ways.

This chapter also discussed the issues of software design and OpenSocial performance tuning. Finally, scalable user interfaces, user support systems, and monetization techniques concluded the topics of this chapter.

Chapter 9 discusses the important topic of OpenSocial templates and markup language, as well as introducing a number of emerging related technologies.

OpenSocial Templates, Markup, and Emerging Technologies

This chapter focuses on new and emerging technologies related to OpenSocial and social network programming. The following technologies represent some new and exciting advances:

❑ OpenSocial Templates Standard

❑ OpenSocial Proxied Content

❑ OpenSocial client libraries

❑ Yahoo! Open Strategy (Y!OS)

❑ iWidgets

❑ Zembly

Let's take a look at these in more detail.

OpenSocial Templates Standard

The recently announced OpenSocial Templates Standard allows developers (through markup and scripting) to easily specify commonly needed application functionality and GUI elements. This supports reusability and the sharing of developer-created markup. The OpenSocial Templates Standard offers functionality similar to the Facebook Markup Language (FBML) used in Facebook applications.

Following are just a few examples of what the OpenSocial Templates Standard can do:

- ❑ Show a person
- ❑ Create a friend/friend list
- ❑ Work with tabs
- ❑ Work with vertical and horizontal layouts
- ❑ Work with lists
- ❑ Work with navigation links

Without OpenSocial templates, these functionalities are produced via JavaScript, DOM manipulation, and OpenSocial JavaScript API calls. With OpenSocial Templates, these functionalities are produced more easily and concisely with markup and template scripts. As will be discussed later in this chapter, the OpenSocial Templates Standard supports looping and conditional display, which creates unique data-driven GUI elements.

The OpenSocial Templates Standard consists of the following three components:

- ❑ *OpenSocial Templates, Part 1* — This specifies how to create templates, and how to invoke/use templates.

- ❑ *OpenSocial Markup Language, Part 2* — This markup language specification involves data requests, as well as GUI elements and layout.

- ❑ *OpenSocial Data Pipelining, Part 3* — This provides a declarative syntax for defining the data the container should provide.

In addition to these three components, the necessary extensions to an OpenSocial container (for example, ShinDig) are given at `http://wiki.opensocial-templates.org/index.php?title=OpenSocial_Template_Prototype_Implementation`.

Let's start the discussion of OpenSocial templates with a look at how a simple "HelloWorld" template can be constructed and used. Next, the discussion examines the use of expressions, variables, and control and looping statements in a template. This is followed by a discussion of the important topics of OpenSocial Markup Language (OSML) and data pipelining. This section concludes with a number of useful examples.

Requiring a Feature

To use OpenSocial templates and OSML, the developer must `Require` the corresponding feature as highlighted in the following OpenSocial XML code:

```
<ModulePrefs title="Hello World">
  <Require feature="opensocial-0.8"/>

  <Require feature="opensocial-templates"/>

  <Require feature="views"/>
</ModulePrefs>
```

Understanding Basic Template Construction and Use

OpenSocial templates are defined by a `<script>` block containing XML content that specifies the purpose and function of the template. The `<script>` element defines the name of template and declares its type as `"text/os-template"`. The XML content of the script element can include HTML, CSS, OSML, and other elements.

Listing 9-1 shows a very simple "Hello World" OpenSocial template. This is a silly template, but it is a construct that makes learning the syntax of template construction easy.

Listing 9-1: "Hello World" OpenSocial Template

```
<script type="text/os-template">
  <div style="font-size: 30px">Hello world!</div>
</script>
```

The template code in Listing 9-1 is placed inside of the OpenSocial XML application code, inlined, as shown in Listing 9-2. The os.`Container.processDocument()` function compiles all of the templates in the document and displays the results. Note that `os` is predefined as `opensocial.template`, and it is specified in the required OpenSocial Templates JavaScript library.

Listing 9-2: "Hello World" OpenSocial Template in an OpenSocial XML Application

```
<?xml version="1.0" encoding="UTF-8" ?>
<Module>
  <ModulePrefs title="Hello World">
    <Require feature="opensocial-X.X"/>
    <Require feature="opensocial-templates"/>
    <Optional feature="content-rewrite">
      <Param name="include-tags"></Param>
    </Optional>
  </ModulePrefs>
  <Content type="html">
  <![CDATA[
    <! – OpenSocial Templates library load -->
    <script type="text/javascript"
        src="http://ostemplates-demo.appspot.com/ostemplates.js">
    </script>

    <! – inlined Hello World template -->
    <script type="text/os-template">
     <div style="font-size: 30px">Hello world!</div>
    </script>

    <script type="text/javascript">
      function init() {
        <! – request container to render all inlined templates -->
        os.Container.processDocument();
      }

      gadgets.util.registerOnLoadHandler(init);
```

Continued

Listing 9-2: "Hello World" OpenSocial Template in an OpenSocial XML Application *(continued)*

```
        </script>
     ]]>
   </Content>
 </Module>
```

These inline templates must be copied in entirety at each place used in the OpenSocial application XML. This is obviously not a reusable methodology, and it does not meet the objective of OpenSocial Templates. In a moment, you will learn how to name a template and explicitly reference it (hence, making it more reusable) at any desired place in the application.

A function call seen in OpenSocial template examples is `opensocial.template.renderAll()`, which is similar to the `os.Container.processDocument` (recall `os` translates to `opensocial.template`). This function renders all of the templates in the application. The `renderAll` function can take an optional parameter that contains the data being "passed," and is accessible to all the templates in the application XML. Typically, calls to the OpenSocial JavaScript API will take place to obtain social data for use in the templates. This function is called inside of the application XML, as shown in Listing 9-3.

Listing 9-3: Using opensocial.template.renderAll to Request Rendering of All Templates

```
<script type="text/javascript">
    //socialDataFromOpenSocialApiCall =  OpenSocial API call;

    opensocial.template.renderAll(socialDataFromOpenSocialApiCall);
</script>
```

Naming Templates

OpenSocial templates (unless used only once) are typically named as shown in Listing 9-4. This is simply a matter of adding the `name` attribute to the `<script>` element. In this case, the name given to the template is `"myapp:HelloWorld"`.

Listing 9-4: Named "Hello World" OpenSocial Template

```
<script type="text/os-template" name="myapp:HelloWorld">
  <div style="font-size: 20px">Hello world!</div>
</script>
```

Any name could be given, including simply `"Hello"`. However, the structure of the name `"myapp:HelloWorld"` is representative of the formula `"namespace:template_name"`. If this formula is followed, it is possible to create a custom OSML tag to represent the template. This will be discussed later in this chapter in the section, "OpenSocial Markup Language," and is an alternative way of using named templates.

A named template can be explicitly referenced and used with the `os.getTemplate` and `template.RenderInto` functions. Listing 9-5 shows an application that does this with the `my:HelloWorld` template. Both of these functions are defined in the required OpenSocial Templates library `http://ostemplates-demo.appspot.com/ostemplates.js`.

Listing 9-5: Using the Named "HelloWorld" Template

```xml
<?xml version="1.0" encoding="UTF-8" ?>
<Module>
  <ModulePrefs title="Hello World">
    <Require feature="opensocial-X.X"/>
    <Require feature="opensocial-templates"/>
    <Optional feature="content-rewrite">
      <Param name="include-tags"></Param>
    </Optional>
  </ModulePrefs>
  <Content type="html">
    <![CDATA[
      <!- OpenSocial Templates library load -->
      <script type="text/javascript"
          src="http://ostemplates-demo.appspot.com/ostemplates.js">
      </script>

      <!- inlined Hello World template -->
      <script type="text/os-template" name="myapp:HelloWorld">
      <div style="font-size: 20px">Hello world!</div>
      </script>

      <script type="text/javascript">
        function init() {
          <!- request container to get named template -->
          var the_template = os.getTemplate('myapp:HelloWorld');
          <!- render template into div tag below -->
          template.renderInto(document.getElementById('put_it_here'));

        }

        gadgets.util.registerOnLoadHandler(init);
      </script>
      <div id='put_it_here'> </div>
    ]]>
  </Content>
</Module>
```

The `os.getTemplate('X')` call requests that the container get the template named X. The `template.RenderInto(Y)` call tells the container to associate the template output with the document element Y.

Using Expressions in Templates

You can embed an expression in the XML content of the template definition. An *expression* is a piece of "code" that is evaluated to a string and inserted in place. The general syntax of an expression is `${Exp}`. The following snippet shows the use of the expression `${Viewer}` to get the name of the viewer of the application:

```
<div>Hello ${Viewer.Name}</div>
```

Developers can create their own expressions, as long as they follow the rules for JSP expressions. These can be manipulated via comparisons and standard arithmetic functions, including the following:

- ❏ ${a + b} — This adds a to b.
- ❏ ${a - b} — This subtracts b from a.
- ❏ ${a lt b} — This tests if a is less than b.
- ❏ ${a and b} — This indicates that both a and b are true.

One exception to an expression being evaluated as a string is when it represents an object. For example, ${Viewer} will return the OpenSocial Viewer Person object.

Using Variables and Passing Data to a Template

A number of predefined variables in the OpenSocial Templates specification include the following:

- ❏ ${My} — This is used to access data passed via parameters to the template.
- ❏ ${Top} — This is used to access the data context passed into template rendering. This is the content passed in via the JavaScript call of this template.
- ❏ ${Context} — This is used when processing templates and "cycling" through a set of items. This has the following elements:

    - ❏ ${Context.UniqueId} — This is the unique ID of the template currently being rendered.
    - ❏ ${Context.Index} — This is the index of the item in set currently being rendered.
    - ❏ ${Context.Count} — This is the number of items in the set being rendered via the repeat tag.

- ❏ ${Cur} — This is the current item being rendered within a repeater.

The data coming into the template in its JavaScript invocation is accessible via the ${Top} variable. This data must be either represented as a JSON object, or another object. In this manner, ${Top.Viewer.Name} maps to data['Viewer']['Name'].

The following template code accesses the data associated with ViewerFriends via ${Top.ViewerFriends} and cycles through the list using the repeat attribute. Each time it displays the friends index in the list and the friend's name.

```
<script type="text/os-template" name="myapp:HelloWorld">

    <div repeat="${Top.ViewerFriends}">
        ${Cur.Name} is number ${Context.Index} out of ${Context.Count} Friends
    </div>
</script>
```

The code in Listing 9-6 shows an OpenSocial application that has a JavaScript block that creates a variable called data. This data variable contains a JSON object that is an array of friend's names, called ViewerFriends. Next, the application JavaScript calls the opensocial.template.processAll(data) function, which associates data with all templates in the application. This means that when the inlined template is processed, ${Top.ViewerFriends} accesses this array.

Listing 9-6: Associating the data Variable with All Templates and Accessing It in a Template

```xml
<?xml version="1.0" encoding="UTF-8"?>
<Module>
  <ModulePrefs title="Hello World" height="100">
    <Require feature="opensocial-X.X"/>
    <Require feature="opensocial-templates"/>
  </ModulePrefs>
  <Content type="html">
    <![CDATA[
      <script type="text/os-template">
        <div repeat="${Top.ViewerFriends}">
            ${Cur.Name} is number ${Context.Index}
                out of ${Context.Count} Friends
        </div>
      </script>

      <script type="text/javascript">
        var data = {
          ViewerFriends: [
              { Name : 'Lynne'},
              { Name : 'Allen'},
              { Name : 'Jake'},
              { Name : 'Butch'} ]
        };
        opensocial.template.processAll(data);
      </script>

    ]]>
  </Content>
</Module>
```

Calling Templates with Parameters

You can call a template by using parameters. Let's modify the template in Listing 9-4 so that it takes message and MessageStyle parameters, so that it no longer simply says Hello world!, but also displays the new message. Template parameters can be specified as either attributes or subelements. Listing 9-7 shows the new code.

Listing 9-7: Modified "Hello World" Template That Uses Passed Parameters

```html
<script type="text/os-template" name="myapp:HelloWorld">
  <div style="color: ${My.MessageStyle.color}">
  Your message is: ${My.message}</div>
</script>

<script type="text/os-template">
  <myapp:HelloWorld message="Hello World">
    <MessageStyle color="red"/>
  </myapp>
</script>
```

The first script in the listing is the template definition, which uses the predefined variable ${My} to gain access to the template's parameters — in this case, the parameters named message and MessageStyle.

The second script block in Listing 9-7 shows how to call the new "HelloWorld" template with the two parameters of message given as an attribute and MessageStyle as a subelement. This style of template invocation will be discussed later in this chapter in the section "OpenSocial Markup Language."

In the template definition (first script), the ${My.X} reference will first look for an attribute named X in the template call and, if it is not found, it will next look for a subelement named X. In this way, ${My.message} will get the attribute message right away. However, the reference for ${My.MessageStyle.color} will first look for an attribute called MessageStyle, which it will not find, and then next search for the MessageStyle element, which is given in the template call.

Using the repeat Attribute for Looping

A tag in a template can be executed multiple times, introducing looping that is based on the list contents of an expression. This is achieved through the repeat attribute. Any tag in the OpenSocial template XML content can have associated with it the repeat attribute that has a value equal to an expression containing a set/list to loop over. The following template code from Listing 9-6 shows a common example where the <div> tag has the repeat attribute:

```
<script type="text/os-template">
    <div repeat="${Top.ViewerFriends}">
        ${Cur.Name} is number ${Context.Index} out of ${Context.Count} Friends
    </div>
</script>
```

Using Conditional Tests

Tags in a template can be executed conditionally using the if attribute. This attribute can be associated with any tag in the OpenSocial template XML content. The value is an expression that evaluates to the Boolean values of either true or false. The tag will be executed only if the value is true. The following is an example that executes the first div tag only if ViewerFriends contains at least one item. Otherwise, the second div tag will be executed.

```
<script type="text/os-template">
    <div if="${Context.Count > 0}" repeat="${Top.ViewerFriends}">
        ${Cur.Name} is number ${Context.Index} out of ${Context.Count} Friends
    </div>
    <div if="${Context.Count == 0}">
        You have no friends
    </div>
</script>
```

Localization with Templates

Templates perform localization (the use of language-specific text) on a per-language basis using the gadget support of message bundles. Chapter 7 provides a more in-depth discussion about localization.

Using a Separate Definition File for Templates

In addition to the inlining of templates (as shown in the previous examples), it is possible to save them in a separate external file. This provides ease of use, modularity, and reusability. The tradeoff is this will be an additional file (and, hence, HTTP request) that will take additional time to load. However, because most containers will cache this on the application's behalf, this may not be an issue.

The following XML file has a generic structure:

```xml
<Templates xmlns:foo="http://foo.com/">
  <Namespace prefix="foo" url="http://foo.com/"/>

  <Style>
    <!-- Set global CSS for your library here -->
    .warning { color: red; }
  </Style>

  <JavaScript>
    <!-- Define global functions for your library here -->
    function usedByAllTemplates() { ... };
  </JavaScript>

  <!-- Template foo:bar -->
  <Template tag="foo:bar">
    <!-- Define markup for foo:bar here -->
  </Template>

  <! - "complex" Template tag foo:baz containing local CSS and JavaScript -->
  <TemplateDef tag="foo:baz">
    <Template> <!-- Define markup for foo:baz here --> </Template>
    <Style> <!-- Set CSS for foo:baz here --> </Style>
    <JavaScript>
      <!-- Define functions for the foo:baz template here -->
      function usedByFooBaz() { ... };
    </JavaScript>
  </TemplateDef>

</Templates>
```

The following XML tags are used to define the OpenSocial Templates XML file:

❑   `<Templates>` — This represents the root elements of the XML file.

❑   `<NameSpace>` — This is the tag defining the namespace to be used by all contained templates.

❑   `<Style>` — This is the set of CSS styles (globally) used by all templates defined here.

❑   `<JavaScript>` — This gets all of the JavaScript functions (globally) used by all templates defined here.

❑   `<Template>` — This contains the script block defining a (simple) template. There can be more than one defined in the file.

❑   `<TemplateDef>` — This contains a `<Template>` block defining the template, as well as additionally used `<Style>` and `<JavaScript>` code. There can be more than one defined in the file.

Following is a specific example of an external OpenSocial Templates XML file:

```xml
<?xml version="1.0" encoding="UTF-8"?>
<Templates xmlns:os="http://opensocial.org/templates">
  <Namespace prefix="os" url="http://opensocial.org/templates" />
  <Style>
    large-font: {
      font-size: 30px;
    }
  </Style>
  <Template name="os:HelloWorld">
    <div style="large-font">Hello World!</div>
  </Template>
  <TemplateDef tag="os:ViewFriends">
    <Style>
      friend-font: {
        font-size: 10px;
      }
    </Style>
    <Template>
      <div style="friend-font" repeat="${Top.ViewerFriends}">
        ${Cur.Name} is number ${Context.Index} out of
          ${Context.Count} Friends
      </div>
    </Template>
  </TemplateDef>
</Templates>
```

OpenSocial Markup Language

The OpenSocial Markup Language (OSML) is ''Part 2'' of the OpenSocial Templates Standard. OSML is a language that consists of tag elements that have predefined purposes, either related to OpenSocial data, or GUI elements that are commonly needed by developers. This will be a widely used part of the OpenSocial Templates Standard.

All OSML tag elements must appear inside of a template `<script>` block in the OpenSocial XML application `<Content>` block. In this sense, they are part of a template the developer constructs. Previous discussions explained how to create a basic template. Thus, template creation is expanded through the use of the OSML tags as part of the template content.

Let's begin by creating a simple template that contains a single OSML tag to obtain information about the owner of the application. This is done with the OSML tag `<os:OwnerRequest>`. Specifically, the ''About'' and ''Books'' information is requested.

```
<script type="text/os-data">
  <os:OwnerRequest key="Owner"  fields="about,books"/>
</script>
```

All OSML tags adhere to the following generic format:

```
<namespace:TagName attribute="value">Value</namespace:TagName>
```

The `namespace` indicates either of the following:

❑   `os` — This indicates an OSML tag.

❑   `container` — This indicates a container-specific markup tag.

The `TagName` is the name of the tag. Tables 9-1, 9-2, and 9-3 show current and proposed OSML tags. Each tag can have a number of attribute/value pairs associated with it.

Table 9-1: OSML Standard Tags

Tag	Meaning	Example
`<os:ActivitiesRequest>`	Requests activities (that is, requests are made to `opensocial.DataRequest` `.newFetchActivitiesRequest`). Returns an array of OpenSocial Activity JSON objects. Required attributes include `key` (string) and `userId` (refers to a person, group of people, comma-delimited set of IDs to use with `groupid`, each- `userid`, `@me`, `@viewer`, and `@owner`). Optional attributes include `groupId` (group of users, `@self`; with default being a list in `userId`, and `@friends`), `activityIds` (comma-separated list of activity IDs to retrieve), `appid` (application ID, with the default being the current ID), `startPage` (start, int), `count` (number to get), and `filter` (used to filter a request).	`<os:ActivitiesRequest`
		`key="ViewerActivities"`
		`.userId="@viewer" />`
		`//gets all the viewers activities`
`<os:Badge>`	Displays information about a person in the container style. Required attributes include `person` (person object).	`My friends: `

Continued

Table 9-1: OSML Standard Tags(continued)

Tag	Meaning	Example

		`<os:Badge`
		
		`repeat="${Friends}"`
		
		`person="${Cur}"/>`

`<os:DataRequest>`	Implements a `gadget.io.makeRequest` call. Returns arbitrary URL data. Required attributes include key (string) and href (valid URL to send the request to; if it is not set, it converts to an RPC call). Selected optional attributes include format (JSON or text format of returned data, with the default being JSON), method (type of request; for example, get, post, with the default being get), params (additional URL parameters like `"n1(v1&n2(v2")`), refreshInterval (time the container can cache), and authz (authentication type, such as none, signed, oauth, with the default being none). For more attributes, see the online reference. Includes a number of oauth parameters.	`<os:Request`

		`key="myData"`
		
		`authz="signed"`
		`method="get" href=`
		`http://U.com/U.php?`
		`command=`
		
		`getit&userid=`
		`${Owner.ID} />`
		
		`//in another template`
		
		`${myData.AppNickName}`
		`your score is`
		`${myData.score}`

Continued

Table 9-1: OSML Standard Tags*(continued)*

Tag	Meaning	Example
`<os:Get>`	Loads content from a URL and inserts it. Required attributes include `href` (URL of requested HTML content).	`${Viewer.Name}'s latest news`
		`<os:Get href= "http://U.com/ newsHtml?uId=$ {viewer.appData.uId}"/>`
`<os:Name>`	Gets name associated with a `person` object passed as `person` attribute. Required attributes include `person` (`person` object).	`Hello <os:Name person="${Viewer}"/>`
`<os:PeopleSelector>`	Can select (multiple) people from a provided list. Used inside of an HTML form. Required attributes include `group` (an array of `person` objects or `DataContext` key referring to array of `person` objects). Optional attributes include `inputName` (the name of form input element this creates that contains selected ID(s) to be sent as form data), `multiple` (`true` or `false`, to allow selection of multiple people), `max` (the maximum number allowed to be selected), `var` (the name of variable holding selected ID(s); supports the use of a tag outside of an HTML form), and `onselect` (JavaScript function to call when person is selected; will find selections in `contextVariable`).	`<form action= "http://U.com/u.php "`
		`method="POST">`
		`Select your best friend friend:`
		`<os:PeopleSelector`
		`group="$ {ViewerFriends}"`

Continued

337

Table 9-1: OSML Standard Tags(continued)

Tag	Meaning	Example
		`multiple="false"` `inputName="friend"/>` `</form>`
`<os:PeopleRequest>`	Used to get information about a group or list of people (can be even one person with userid specified). Returns an array of OpenSocial person JSON objects. Required attributes include key (string) and userId (refers to a person, group of people, comma-delimited set of IDs to use with groupid, each- userid, @me, @viewer, @owner). Optional attributes include groupId (group of users, @self with the default being a list in userId, @friends), startPage (start, int), startIndex (start index, int), count (number to get), and filterBy (used to filter request). See the online reference for other attributes, including sortBy, sortOrder, filterOp, and filterValue.	`<os:PeopleRequest` `key="PagedFriends"` `userId="@owner"` `groupId="@friends"` `startPage="3"` `count="20"/>`
`<os:OwnerRequest>`	Used to retrieve owner information. Returns an OpenSocial person JSON object. Required attributes include key (string). Optional attributes include fields (set of details to retrieve about the person, separated by commas; for example, name, about).	`<os:OwnerRequest` `key="owner"` `fields="name,` `birthday"/>`
`<os:ViewerRequest>`	Used to retrieve viewer information. Returns an OpenSocial person JSON object. Required attributes include key (string). Optional attributes include fields (set of details to retrieve about the person, separated by commas; for example, name, about).	`<os:ViewerRequest` `key="viewer"` `fields="name,` `birthday"/>`

Table 9-2: Possible Future OSML Tags

Tag	Meaning	Example
`<os:Layout>`	Creates a layout or partitioning.	Tag under construction.

`<os:Link><os:A>`	Links (when clicked) related HTML fetched from the server and inserted into the DOM. Offers an Ajax experience without JavaScript. Attributes include `url` (URL to retrieve), `view` (contents of a view to retrieve), `type` (either "replace" or "insert" that stipulates how retrieved content is placed), and `target` (the ID of DOM element to associate retrieved content to).	`<os:A`
		
		`url="http://U.com/info"`
		`type="replace"`
		
		`target="info_list"/>`

`<os:List>`	Creates a list in the style of the container.	Tag under construction.
`<os:PersonAppDataRequest>`	Implements same as call to `opensocial.dataReqeust.newFetchPersonAppDataRequest`. Required attributes include `key` (string) and `idSpec` (represents person to request data for). Optional attributes include `keys` (comma-separated list of data keys to retrieve — recall that AppData is stored as key/value pairs; note that * means "all data").	
`<os:Tabset>`	Creates a set of tabs.	See `<os:Tab>`.
	Creates a tab (inside a `TabSet`). Required attributes include `name` (name of tab). Optional attributes include `selected` (Boolean, `true` if tab is initially selected). Required elements include `<title>` (tab title) and `<body>` (contents of tab).	`<os:Tabset>`

Continued

Table 9-2: Possible Future OSML Tags*(continued)*

Tag	Meaning	Example
		`<os:Tab name="FF" selected="true">`
		`<title>Find Friends</title>`
		`<body>`
		`${Viewer.Name} `
		`Find your Friends`
		`</body>`
		`</os:Tab>`
		`<os:Tab name="Invite">`
		`<title>Invite Friends</title>`
		`<body>`
		`<form`
		`action="http://U.com/invite.php "`
		`method="POST"`
		`onsubmit="invite()">`
		`<os:PeopleSelector`
		`group="${ViewerFriends}"`
		`multiple="true"`
		`inputName="invite_list"/>`
		`</form>`
		`</body>`
		`</os:Tab>`
		`</os:Tabset>`
`<os:Zippy>`	Hidden text.	Tag under construction.

Table 9-3: OSML Proposed Tags (Not Yet Part of Standard OSML)

Tag	Meaning
`<os:About-view>`	Creates an "about" view
`<os:Ad>`	Creates an advertisement
`<os:Button>`	Creates a button
`<os:Collapsiblebox>`	Creates a GUI element with a collapsible area
`<os:Datetime>`	Inserts date and time
`<os:Dialog>`	Creates a dialog
`<os:Form>`	Creates a form
`<os:Friend-selector>`	Creates a selector with friends listed in it
`<os:Google-analytics>`	Inserts Google Analytics
`<os:Html>`	Outputs "unsanitized" HTML
`<os:If-is-friends-with-viewer>`	Tests to see if friends with viewer
`<os:Iframe>`	Creates an inline frame (known as an IFrame)
`<os:Image>`	Inserts an image
`<os:Locale>`	Associates language and message bundle for internationalization
`<os:Minimessage>`	Creates a message GUI element
`<os:Msgbndl>`	Represents a message bundle
`<os:Pram>`	Creates parameter value associations
`<os:PrivateData>`	Makes content visible only to specified users
`<os:Profile-pic>`	Inserts a profile picture of a person
`<os:Redirect>`	Redirects a user
`<os:Render>`	Renders specified template content
`<os:Repeat>`	Provides a loop control mechanism
`<os:Send-message>`	Executes an OpenSocial Send message

Continued

Table 9-3: OSML Proposed Tags (Not Yet Part of Standard OSML)*(continued)*

Tag	Meaning
`<os:Share-button>`	Creates an invite/share application
`<os:Showperons>`	Displays a person in the style of the container
`<os:Submit>`	Creates a Submit button
`<os:Userloggedin>`	Tests to see if the current application user is logged in
`<os:Toggle>`	Inserts a toggle

Following is another example OSML tag that will retrieve the name of the `Viewer`. In this case, the attribute name is `person` and the value is a `person` JSON object associated with the viewer of the application.

```
<os:Name person="${Viewer}"/>
```

Not all OSML tags deal with OpenSocial data. The following proposed tag creates a button GUI element:

```
<os:Button color="red">Click Me</os:Button>
```

The following is an example of a container-specific OSML tag where the `namespace` is `yahoo`:

```
<yahoo:SendMessage personId="1234">Hello there.</yahoo:SendMessage>
```

Specifying OSML as a Required Feature

To use OSML in an application, you must use `Require feature` to indicate that it is a required feature in the gadget XML, as shown here:

```
<ModulePrefs title="Hello World">
  <Require feature="opensocial-X.X"/>
  <Require feature="osml"/>
</ModulePrefs>
```

Optionally, if the OpenSocial templates feature has been required, OSML is a subset and the following will be sufficient:

```
<ModulePrefs title="Hello World">
  <Require feature="opensocial-X.X"/>
  <Require feature="opensocial-templates"/>
</ModulePrefs>
```

Accessing Social Data with Container-Specific Tags

As discussed previously, containers can create container-specific tags. Following are a few examples of this:

❑   `<yahoo:maps>`

❑   `<goog:YouTube>`

❑   `<google:analytics>`

Making Your Own OMSL Custom Tags

Developers can create a custom tag associated with a template they created and call it inside of other templates in the same way OSML tags are used. The form of the tag created is `<namespace:templateName/>`, where both the `namespace` and `templateName` are uniquely defined by the developer. The namespace must be registered by the developer using the OpenSocial templates function `os.createNamespace(namespace, URL)`. The combination of the namespace with the URL is registered with the container to make it unique. Typically, the developer's URL domain should be specified.

In addition to this, each template for which the developer wishes to create a custom tag should have the parameter `tag="namespace:templateNameX"` associated with the `<script>` element of the template definition.

For example, if you want to register the namespace of `myapp` and the URL is `http://www.U.com`, this will result in the function call shown in Listing 9-8. Notice that the first script in this listing is the template that is named with the tag attribute `myapp:HelloWorld`. The resulting tag, `<myapp:HelloWorld>`, is used in the second template of the listing.

Listing 9-8: XML Code to Have a Template Call the Named HelloWorld Template

```
<script type="text/os-template" tag="myapp:HelloWorld">
  <div style="font-size: 20px">Hello world!</div>
</script>

<!-- Call named template -->
<script type="text/os-template">
  <myapp:HelloWorld/>
</script>

<script type="text/javascript">
  function init() {
    <!-- Create a unique namespace -->
    os.createNamespace('myapp', 'http://www.U.com');
    os.Container.processDocument();
  }
  gadgets.util.registerOnLoadHandler(init);
</script>
```

OSML and Internationalization

Internationalization through the use of OSML has not been finalized, but two methods have been suggested. The first is to have the developer handle internationalization, meaning it is separate from the OpenSocial Templates Standard.

The second proposal involves the creation of an OSML tag, <os:Locale>, which borrows its syntax from the gadget message bundles. Listing 9-9 shows the use of the <os:locale> tag, which takes as parameters the lang and a reference to a <os:msgbndl> tag. This basically maps to the corresponding language message via the <msg> element that has the translated version of the message. Listing 9-9 provides translation to Spanish.

Listing 9-9: OSML Tag Used for Representation of a Spanish Message

```
<os:Locale lang="es" message="msgbundle_es"/>
  <os:msgbndl id="msgbundle_es">
    <msg name="WATCH_THIS_VIDEO">
        ${Owner}.name dijo ${Viewer}.name mirar este video
        //means owner told viewer to watch this video
    </msg>
  </os:msgbndl>
<os:Locale>
```

Rendering Partial Content

Specific partial content of a template can be rendered through the use of the <os:Render> tag. The specific content is referenced via the content parameter that has as a value of an element of this name in a template. Listing 9-10 shows the how this tag is used to render separately the "title" and "body" elements of a template.

Listing 9-10: Code Showing How to Render Content

```
<script type="text/os-template">
  <myapp:Info>
    <announce>Annoucement title</announce>
    <announce_info>
      <div>The latest announcement is XXXX</div>
      <div>from <os:ShowPerson person="${Top.Viewer}"/></div>
    </announce_info>
  </myapp:Info>
</script>
<script type="text/os-template" name=
      "myapp:Info">
  <div class="box-title"><os:Render content=
      "announce"/></div>
  <div class="box-content"><os:Render content=
      "announce_info"/></div>
</script>
```

Looping through a List of Items

The `<os:Repeat>` tag is used to loop through a set of items and, for each item, display the contents of the tag. Listing 9-11 shows how this tag is used along with the previously discussed `${Context}` and `${Cur}` template variables. The `expression` parameter contains the list of items.

Listing 9-11: Looping through a List of Friends

```
<os:Repeat expression="${ViewerFriends}">
  <div>
    Friend ${Context.Index} is ${Cur.Name}
  </div>
</os:Repeat>
```

OpenSocial Data Pipelining

Some OSML tags are designed to deal with OpenSocial data requests. This part of the OpenSocial Templates Standard (discussed in "Part 3") is called *data pipelining*. What these tags offer is the declarative (non-OpenSocial JavaScript API calls) request for OpenSocial data.

Listing 9-12 shows sample application code that uses tags to get OpenSocial data associated with the application owner. The first template in this listing involves the OSML tag `<os:OwnerRequest>`, which associates the variable `${Owner}` defined by the value in the `key` parameter with the resulting `Owner` data. The second template in this listing uses the variable `${Owner}` to display the owner's name.

Listing 9-12: Using `<os:OwnerRequest>` to Get Social Data via Markup

```
<Content type="html">
  <script type="text/os-data">
    <os:OwnerRequest key="Owner" fields="name, about, books/>
  </script>
  <script type="text/os-template">
    <div>
      Hello, ${Owner.name}. Welcome to our app.
    </div>
  </script>
</Content>
```

OpenSocial data pipelining deals with OpenSocial data access inside of templates. This section examines the details surrounding data pipelining, including the following:

❑　Data access (the `opensocial.DataContext` object)

❑　Data conditional rendering (`require` and `before` attributes of the template `<script>` tag)

❑　Listener for data changes (`listen` attribute of the template `<script>` tag)

❑　Dynamic request for data (`resendRequest`)

Data Access

As discussed previously, data can be accessed as keys that are named in template data requests. One example of this was the use of `<os:OwnerRequest key="Owner">` and the variable `${Owner}` in the code in Listing 9-12. This data is actually stored in the `opensocial.DataContext` JavaScript object, and can be equivalently accessed as `opensocial.DataContext['Owner']`.

Similarly, the developer can access properties of a data object represented by a key, or access them through the `DataContext` object as follows:

❑   `${key.property}`

❑   `opensocial.DataContext['key'].property`

❑   `os.data.DataContext['key'].property`

The scope of a `DataContext` object is related to the view name specified in the gadget `<Content>` tag containing the template. Hence, all templates in the same view share the same `DataContext` object, and templates in different views do not. This is illustrated in Listing 9-13.

Listing 9-13: OpenSocial DataContext Containing View-Specific Data

```
<Content type="html" view="home,profile">
  <script type="text/os-data">
    <os:OwnerRequest key="Owner" />
  </script>
</Content>

<Content type="html" view="home">
  <script type="text/os-template">
    <div>
       Welcome ${Owner.NAME} to the application.
    </div>
  </script>
</Content>

<Content type="html" view="profile">
  <script type="text/os-template">
    <div>
       ${Owner.NAME}'s Profile is XXX
    </div>
  </script>
</Content>
```

Data can be placed in the `DataContext` object dynamically with the `putDataSet` method, which takes an associated key and related data value. Listing 9-14 shows an example.

Listing 9-14: Dynamic Use of DataContext.putDataSet to Add Data

```
<script type="text/javascript">
  //called when user selected a GUI element ,
  //id is userid of a selected Friend
  function selectFriend(id) {
    var req = opensocial.newDataRequest();
    req.add(req.newFetchPersonRequest(id, 'Friend');
```

```
    req.send(function(data) {

      //associate the key Friend with the corresponding Person Data.
      //os.data.DataContext.putDataSet('Friend', data.get('Friend'));
    });
  }
</script>
```

Similarly, the DataContext object has a getDataSet('key') method that retrieves the data associated with the key. For example, the Friend key in Listing 9-14 can be retrieved as follows:

```
var  the_friend = os.data.DataContext.getDataSet('Friend');
```

Data Conditional Rendering

A developer can specify the conditional rendering of a template based on data availability. For example, a template that uses viewer OpenSocial data should not be rendered until this data is available. Recall that data is either accessed through its key name or via the DataContext object.

Listing 9-15 shows the modification of the <script> tag to include the attribute require. This says that the template will be rendered only if the data represented by the key ${Viewer} is available.

Listing 9-15: Template Conditionally Rendered Using the require Attribute

```
<script type="text/os-template" require="Viewer">
  Welcome ${Viewer.Name}
</script>
```

If multiple data items are needed (for example, d1, d2, d3), this can be specified by a comma-delimited list as follows:

```
<script type="text/os-template" require="d1,d2,d3" >
```

Another data conditional rendering attribute is before, which allows a template to be rendered only if the data is not yet available. This is useful when the developer wishes to show some information while waiting for data availability.

Listing 9-16 shows an example of this. When neither the application user (Viewer) nor the friends (Friends) data is loaded, the "Loading up your information ... " string is displayed. When the Viewer data is available, but not the Friends data, the "****, accessing your friends' info" string is displayed. Finally, when both Viewer and Friends data is available, it prints out "**** your friends are" followed by the names of "****'s" friends.

Listing 9-16: Template Rendered If Data Not Available Using the before Attribute

```
<script type="text/os-template" before="Viewer">
  Loading up your information...
</script>
<script type="text/os-template" before="Friends" require="Viewer">
  ${Viewer.Name}, accessing your friends' info
</script>
```

Continued

```
<script type="text/os-template" require="Viewer, Friends">
  ${Viewer.Name} your friends are <br/>
  <div repeat="Friends">${Cur.Name}</div>
</script>
```

Listener for Data Changes

A developer can "register" a template as needed to be re-rendered when data changes using the `listen` attribute of the `<script>` tag, as shown in Listing 9-17.

Listing 9-17: Re-Rendering of Template Based on the listen Attribute

```
<script type="text/os-template" require="Viewer, Friends">
  ${Viewer.displayName} select one of your friends:
  <div repeat="Friends">
    <button onclick="selectFriend(${id})" value="${displayName}"/>
  </div>
</script>

//only rendered when Viewer and Friend both available
//and re-rendered when Friend changes value
<script type="text/os-template" require="Viewer, Friend"
    listen="Friend">
  <b>${Friend.displayName}</b> has been selected.
</script>


<script type="text/javascript">
  //called when button clicked to get Friend data
  function selectFriend(id) {
    var req = opensocial.newDataRequest();
    req.add(req.newFetchPersonRequest(id, 'Friend');
    req.send(function(data) {
      os.data.DataContext.putDataSet('Friend',
          data.get('Friend'));
    });
  }

  //code to request Viewer and Friends
  function init() {
    //socialDataFromOpenSocialApiCall =
    //OpenSocial API call to get viewer&friends;

    opensocial.template.renderAll
        (socialDataFromOpenSocialApiCall);
  }

  init();
</script>
```

The first template in the listing is rendered when both the `Viewer` and `Friends` data is available and produces a set of buttons associated with the viewer's friends. The last `<script>` block (a JavaScript block) makes the calls to get the `Viewer` and `Friends` OpenSocial data. This JavaScript block also contains a `selectFriend` function that is called when one of the "Friends" buttons is clicked. This will perform an OpenSocial JavaScript call to get the selected `Friends` data. This change to the `Friends` data will trigger the second template in the listing to execute (with the `listen` attribute), which will display information about the selected friend.

Dynamic Request for Data

Developers can choose to resend a previously made data request by using the `os.data.resendRequest` `('key')` method call. All requests made in a `<Content>` block are stored in the `os.data.requests` object and are keyed by the data set key. Listing 9-18 shows an example that resends a request and gets back new results.

Listing 9-18: Resend Request for Set of Friends Using os.data.resendRequest

```
<Content type="profile">
  <!-- Data -->
  <script type="text/os-data">
    <os:FetchPeopleRequest key="Friends"/>
    <os:OwnerRequest key="Viewer" id="VIEWER"/>
     //initial request a dummy request, to be resent
     //with a real id in the
     //JavaScript function selectFriend
    <os:OwnerRequest key="Friend" id="OWNER" profileDetails="ABOUT, BOOKS"/>
  </script>


<script type="text/os-template" require="Viewer, Friends">
  ${Viewer.displayName} select one of your friends:
  <div repeat="Friends">
    <button onclick="selectFriend(${id})" value="${displayName}"/>
  </div>
</script>


//only rendered when Viewer and Friend both available
//and re-rendered when Friend changes value
<script type="text/os-template" require="Viewer, Friend" listen="Friend">
  <b>${Friend.displayName}</b> has been selected.
  <b>About them: ${Friend.About}
</script>


<script type="text/javascript">
  //called when button clicked to get Friend data
  function selectFriend(id) {
      var request = os.data.requests['Friend'];

      request.setAttribute('id', id);
      os.data.resendRequest('Friend');
```

Continued

Listing 9-18: Resend Request for Set of Friends Using os.data.resendRequest
(continued)

```
    }

    //code to render templates
    function init() {
            os.Container.processDocument();
    }

    init();
</script>
```

In this code, the first template contains a data request tag `<os:FetchPeopleRequest>` that has a key value of `Friends`, as well as data requests for the `Viewer`, a request for `Friends`, and a `Friend`. The JavaScript block invokes a `selectFriend` function when a friend is selected via a series of buttons. The `selectFriend` button function uses the user ID of the friend to update the data request associated with the key `Friend`. It resends this request with the `os.data.resendRequest` call.

OpenSocial Template Examples

Figures 9-1 and 9-2 show some samples of OpenSocial templates. Figure 9-1 shows a sample of an OpenSocial template created by the program found at `http://www.google.com/ig/sharetab?hl=en& source=stb&stid=10898705734230152136S4aa9d69edeba3fffa78919d579938c38`. This program installs OpenSocial Template samples on your iGoogle home page.

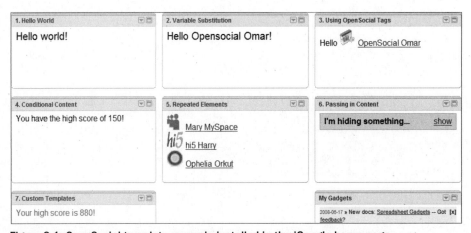

Figure 9-1: OpenSocial template example installed in the iGoogle home page

Figure 9-2 shows an example found at `http://hosting.gmodules.com/ig/gadgets/file/ 10898705734230152136S/examples.html`. A good emulator program can be found at `http://ostemplates-devapp.appspot.com/`.

Figure 9-2: OpenSocial Template example from
`http://hosting.gmodules.com`

OpenSocial Templates Resources

The following are resources related to the OpenSocial Templates Standard:

- ❑ *Web site* — `http://opensocial-templates.org` or `http://ostemplates-demo.appspot.com`

- ❑ *Templates wiki* — `http://wiki.opensocial-templates.org/index.php?title=Main_Page`

- ❑ *Templates discussion group hosted on Yahoo!* — `http://tech.groups.yahoo.com/group/os-templates`

- ❑ *Templates specification* — `http://sites.google.com/a/opensocial.org/opensocial/Technical-Resources/opensocial-templates-spec`

- ❑ *Templates "cookbook"* — `http://ostemplates-demo.appspot.com/cookbook.html`

> ❑ *Information hosted on main OpenSocial wiki* — `http://wiki.opensocial.org/index.php?title=OpenSocial_Templates`
>
> ❑ *Demos/emulator* — `http://ostemplates-devapp.appspot.com` and `http://hosting.gmodules.com/ig/gadgets/file/108987057342301521365/examples.html`

OpenSocial Proxied Content

In Chapter 2, you learned about the different OpenSocial transactional models, including the client-based application, hybrid, and completely server-based application. OpenSocial Proxied Content refers to the creation of an OpenSocial Social network application that is completely server-side. This is the transactional model that is used for development of Facebook applications. In this case, the server-side program generates the HTML (or content) that is returned to the container and integrated (proxied) for delivery to the user. Data is passed to the program from the container via POST variables.

To create an OpenSocial Proxied Content application, the content tag of the OpenSocial XML file that is deployed should resemble the following:

```
<Content href="http://U.com" >
```

In this case, the URL `http://U.com` points to a server-side developer program that receives the POST request and generates the application output. The output can include OSML tags and templates. The application can use OSML to efficiently indicate what data is to be sent to the server program, as shown in the following example where the friends of the owner are sent:

```
<Content href="http://U.com" >
    <os:PeopleRequest  key="ownerFriends" userId="@owner" groupId=
        "@friends" fields="name, aboutme">
</Content>
```

The following represents the shell of a PHP server-side program that is given in the Content href URL, which receives the owner's Friends data and returns some HTML:

```php
<?php

    //return any static html at the start
    echo "<h1>Friend Finder App</h1><br>";


    //grab array of friends and pass into
    //the variable $ownerFriends
    $ownerFriends = $_POST['ownerFriends'];

    //cycle through friends for display in a list
    echo "<ul>";
    foreach($ownerFriends as $person) {
        echo "<li>" . $person["name"] . " says " . $person["aboutme"] . "</li>";
    }
?>
```

Check out `http://wiki.opensocial.org/index.php?title=Proxied_Content` *for more details on this subject.*

Currently, orkut and hi5 (unofficially) are among the containers that support OpenSocial Proxied Content. Yahoo! Open Strategy (Y!OS) and Yahoo! Applications (YAP) also support OpenSocial Proxied Content, as discussed later in this chapter.

OpenSocial Client Libraries

A new project sponsored by Google provides client libraries for the OpenSocial REST API. These can be used in a developer's server-side program, rather than having to create and parse OpenSocial REST requests and responses. Basically, these provide a "wrapper" library for REST calls, and can make it easier to create OpenSocial REST programs.

If you are familiar with Facebook, this is similar to the Facebook API libraries provided for PHP and, in the past, for Java.

Following is an example of the OpenSocial PHP client library in use:

```
$client = $opensocial->os_client;  //create instance of OpenSocialClient
$person = $client->people_getUserInfo($id);  //where id is the user id

$the_profile_imgUrl = $person['entry']['thumbnailUrl'];
$name = $person['entry']['name']['givenName']'
echo 'Welcome'. $name . '<img src='. $the_profile_imgUrl . '>';
```

In this code sample, `os_client` returns an instance of the `OpenSocialClient` class.

For more information about the PHP client library, `OpenSocialClient.php`, *see* `http://code.google.com/p/opensocial-php-client`. *For more information about the Java client library, see* `http://code.google.com/p/opensocial-java-client`.

Table 9-4 shows the current list of methods of the PHP `OpenSocialClient` class. These methods are translated inside the library code to the appropriate OpenSocial REST call. These methods also asynchronously receive the results in JSON format, and return them to the PHP program invoking them.

Yahoo! Open Strategy

Y!OS, Yahoo! Open Strategy (Y!OS) entails the opening of Yahoo!'s social infrastructure to developers, and allowing them to deploy applications hosted on their external Web sites, as well as applications on Yahoo! This includes the development of OpenSocial applications, for which Yahoo! is a big supporter and is member of the OpenSocial Foundation. Through Y!OS, Yahoo! is now an OpenSocial container.

What is unique and appealing about this new strategy is that it is the first real example of a portal becoming explicitly social and allowing social application development. While Google and Yahoo! both have had separate social networks (for example, Google's orkut), neither has explicitly wrapped social networking concepts into its main portals. Yahoo! is inherently a social environment with a rich set of services, so the explicitly social strategy of Y!OS is both intriguing and exciting. The massive audience available to applications via Y!OS through its integration of the many Yahoo! platforms will create new application opportunities.

Table 9-4: Methods of the PHP OpenSocialClient Class

Tag	Meaning
people_getUserInfo	Gets information about people. Can specify an array of user IDs and fields (that is, the @self REST specification).
people_getFriendsInfo	Gets friends and their information. Specify user ID whose friends you wish and the fields array (that is, the @friends REST specification).
people_getAllInfo	Gets all information (that is, the @all REST specification).
people_getGroupFriends	Gets a group of people. Has the group ID specification.
people_getMyInfo	Gets user's information (that is, the @me REST specification). Has a fields array.
group_getUserGroups	Gets groups associated with a user.
activity_getUserActivity	Gets activities generated by the user (user ID specified).
activity_getFriendActivity	Gets activities generated by a user's friends.
appdata_getUserAppData	Gets AppData of user for application. Specify user ID and appid.
appdata_getFriendsAppData	Gets AppData of friends for application. Specify user ID and appid.

A big difference in Yahoo! Applications (YAP) from traditional social network applications is that Yahoo! intends to allow developers to deploy applications to different platforms. So, an application can be deployed to Yahoo! mail, the front page, sports, or the many other platforms. This is an exciting capability that isn't seen on traditional social networks.

Y!OS Architecture

Y!OS is presented by Yahoo! as the "rewiring" of Yahoo! to create a single social base of all of its platforms (search, mail, Flickr, video, and so on), thereby creating an open framework for application developers to get data from and put data not only into this social layer but also into Yahoo!'s services/platforms.

Figure 9-3 shows a diagram of the Y!OS architecture. Across the top are the Yahoo! platforms, including mail, front page, search, media, and partner sites. On the left is a single integration point called Yahoo! Developer Network (YDN) for developers to use these platforms. Below the Yahoo! platforms is a single cross-platform social layer, called the Social Platform. Above this is an Application Platform, which now represents a single framework for developing applications. Finally, access to the individual Yahoo! services is done with one Web service and the Yahoo! Query Language (YQL) layer.

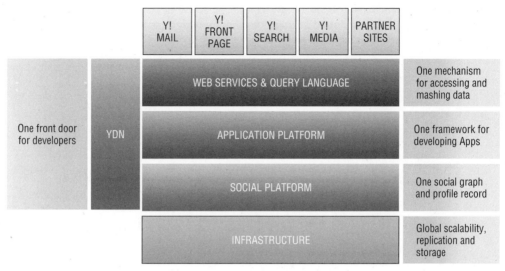

Figure 9-3: Y!OS architecture

Yahoo! Social Platform constructs include the following:

❑   A single social directory

❑   Contacts

❑   User status

❑   Updates

❑   OpenSocial support

To produce a single Yahoo! Social Layer across all of its platforms, Yahoo! stipulates that users be represented with a Global User Identifier (GUID). An application can get information about a user with reference to any Yahoo! platform using this GUID.

Yahoo! User Profiles

Yahoo! users can now create their own Yahoo! Profiles at `http://profiles.yahoo.com`. Figure 9-4 shows a profile on Yahoo! that has many of the features seen on popular social networks. Part of the profile is making connections to other users (friends). Yahoo! makes suggestions automatically based on how a user uses Yahoo! services. For example, in Figure 9-4, suggestions are made based on who the user is frequently emailing. This goes beyond the traditional "suggested friends" that social networks are currently providing. Yahoo! will also look at other properties (such as Yahoo! Messenger) to provide suggestions.

Yahoo! User Updates

Yahoo! user updates can be seen on a user's profile and used in applications. User updates are created as a function of all the Yahoo! platforms that are integrated under Y!OS. Users can choose what updates to allow different connections/friends to see through privacy settings. So, even though the platforms are integrated, a user can choose different settings for different platforms. Figure 9-5 shows a listing of all the Yahoo! platforms for which a user can set permissions.

Check out Yahoo! Messenger and Yahoo! Tech (`http://tech.yahoo.com`*) for links back to user's profiles.*

Figure 9-4: Yahoo! Profile

Yahoo! Applications (YAP)

Development of applications is done using APIs that are part of the Yahoo! Application (YAP) platform. Y!OS is about making Yahoo! social, and opening up data and APIs for application developers to create applications both on and off of Yahoo!.

Applications in YAPs can be based on server-side programs, client-side technologies, or hybrids. The client-side technology features OpenSocial JavaScript support. Other predominately feature technologies include Yahoo! Markup Language (YML), and OAuth. Flash is also a client-side technology suggested for application development.

Similar to other social networks, YAP (regardless of the technology used to implement them) can be discovered via the YAP Gallery (under construction), user updates, and direct invitations.

If the application is hosted externally on a developer's server, and makes calls directly to YAP on behalf of a user, an authentication process using OAuth is necessary, as discussed in the OpenSocial REST API. Yahoo! Senior Director Cody Smith says that support of OpenSocial REST is something that Y!OS is planning in the future. At this point, the YAP proprietary REST services should be used. A PHP SDK is currently provided to ease development.

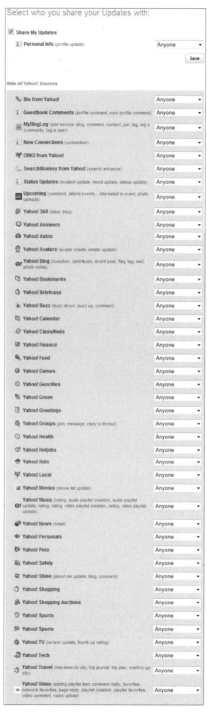

Figure 9-5: Yahoo! platforms for which a
user can set update permissions

Understanding YAP Views

YAP currently supports two views:

- ❑ Small view
- ❑ Full view

The Small view is what can be deployed and embedded into the varied Yahoo! platforms. The Small view is equivalent to the "profile" view in OpenSocial. As of this writing, the Small view must be static and is hosted on Yahoo! Currently, the Small view consists only of HTML, YML, and inline CSS. This allows for quick loading and caching. This is important for integration into Yahoo! platforms such as the Yahoo! front page. The Small view is 300 pixels wide by 250 pixels high.

Yahoo!'s reasoning behind the bar of JavaScript in its Small view is the concern for security. Some discussion of expanding the Small view with dynamic capabilities is ongoing.

A purpose of the Small view is to "launch" into a Full view version of the application. It is important when creating the Small view to have this feature. While this is hosted and cached on Yahoo!, a developer can do periodic customization of the Small view by updating it programmatically with the YAP SetSmallView (with the parameters guid and newYML) method (that is, from a server-side PHP program). The Small view is first created, and then can be updated from the YDN application development interface.

The Full view is meant as the main and currently only functioning view of the application. This is the "canvas" view in OpenSocial. Currently, YAP supports the latest OpenSocial JavaScript API version. Recall that developers can also create non-OpenSocial applications, including Flash-based applications, as well as hybrid or completely server-based applications. In either case, the Full view application is hosted on the developer's server.

The Full view (also called Application view) can be created as an OpenSocial JavaScript application in "canvas" view. Figure 9-6 shows the transactional model.

Server-side programs make calls directly to the YAP, and a YAP SDK must be downloaded. Currently, an SDK for is available for PHP and for AS3 (Action Script, for Flash programming).

The Full view ("canvas") is 760 pixels wide. It is embedded by Yahoo! to run inside of an IFrame. A restriction on all applications (including OpenSocial JavaScript applications) is that they must use Caja (which is a restricted form of JavaScript).

Using Caja

YAP takes all application responses and passes them through a Caja translator. Caja is an Open Source project that translates JavaScript, HTML, and CSS input into a single JavaScript function with no free variables. The goal of this translation (or "cajoling" of the code) is to prevent malicious attacks.

For more information on Caja in YAP, check out `http://developer.yahoo.com/yap/guide/caja-support.html`.

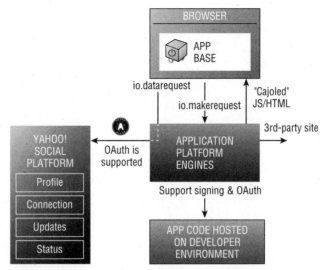

Figure 9-6: Transactional model for client-based Full view application

Restrictions do apply on what JavaScript, HTML, and CSS is allowed. Following are some of the current Caja restrictions enforced by YAP:

❑ Cannot contain arbitrary ActiveX objects

❑ Cannot use `eval` to get around the ActiveX restriction

❑ Cannot use IFrames to get around the `eval` restriction

❑ Cannot use `document.write` (although you can use `innerHTML`)

❑ Must define global variables with `var`

❑ Must include JavaScript and CSS inline in the application (response)

❑ Full support for OpenSocial JavaScript

❑ No support for other libraries (such as YUI, jQuery, and Prototype)

❑ Cannot use `obj.prototype` and constructors except in a way that blocks some common JavaScript idioms (that is, monkey-patching)

After the Caja translation has been performed, the resulting translated JavaScript is run in an IFrame and does not have direct reference to DOM objects outside the frame. Some developers have noted that this translation process leads to larger files, inefficiencies, and, of course, limitations on the function of the JavaScript.

The biggest frustration for OpenSocial JavaScript developers will be learning Caja and understanding its limitations. Debugging is also a challenge in that the output of Caja can yield unexpected results that are difficult to trace. There is some discussion that looks forward to future YAP OpenSocial REST applications as an easier way to develop applications for inexperienced Caja developers.

> **When you are debugging using Firebug, even if you do not see an error icon, look at the Firebug console. Some run-time errors don't raise exceptions but instead show up as plain-text messages in the console, such as the one shown in the following example:**
>
> ```
> Not readable: (Someclass).XXX
> ```
>
> **This means that the application is typically doing something not yet supported.**

YAP Application Development Steps

The developer begins the process of creating an OpenSocial JavaScript YAP application by first creating static HTML (with CSS or YML) for a Small view. The developer then creates a Full view OpenSocial JavaScript XML application with all the code inline.

An important document that discusses application development issues on YAP is located at http://developer.yahoo.com/yap/guide/yap-overview.html.

The following reflects the YAP application lifecycle stages shown in Figure 9-7:

❑ *Development* — The developer specifies the Small and Full view code using the YAP developer toolkit (available at http://developer.yahoo.com). This is accomplished by clicking on My Projects, and creating an "Open Application." You must provide the URL for the Full view and the source for the Small view. Preview mode is available for both. Only the developer can view or run the application.

❑ *Pushed Live* — Using the developer toolkit, you can push "live" the application to allow the application to be shared with others. This is meant for testing between a select set of users. The application does not appear in the Yahoo! Application Gallery.

❑ *Published* — Once published, the application appears in the Yahoo! Application Gallery.

❑ *Installed* — The application is then installed in a "landing page" or platform such as Yahoo! Profiles or Yahoo! Mail. The Small view of the application appears in the landing page. From the Small view, the user can launch the Full view.

❑ *Running* — When the user is using the Small or Full view of the application, YAP renders the application inside of the containing page (platform/landing page, or Full view page).

> **Invest a little time using YML so as to create some feel of customization. Hopefully, in the future, this can be replaced by OSML.**

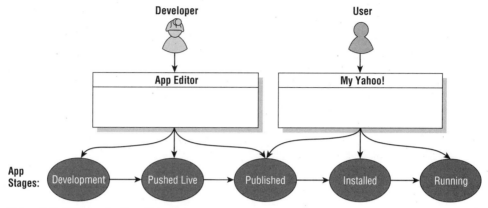

Figure 9-7: YAP application lifecycles

A developer can return to existing applications either through the YDN, or directly at `http://apps.yahoo.com/myapps`. The `myapps` page also has a list of featured applications that can be installed and will eventually link to the Yahoo! Gallery. When an application is selected, it will run in "canvas" view and the URL will have the format `http://apps.yahoo.com/-hIiPNp4o`, where the last part is the application ID.

YAP OpenSocial Application Development

YAP supports only part of the latest OpenSocial version (Gadget API calls). It does not support the OpenSocial RESTful API or the Gadget XML definitions. The Full view Yahoo! application can have only OpenSocial JavaScript API calls.

> Check out `http://developer.yahoo.com/yap/guide/yap-opensocial.html` for updates on YAP's support of OpenSocial.

Currently, YAP supports the following fields:

❑ Activity:

    ❑ Only `opensocial.CreateActivityPriority.LOW` (not `HIGH`)

    ❑ `opensocial.Activity.Field.ID`

    ❑ `opensocial.Activity.Field.TITLE`

    ❑ `opensocial.Activity.Field.BODY`

    ❑ `opensocial.Activity.Field.URL`

    ❑ `opensocial.Activity.Field.USER_ID`

    ❑ `opensocial.Activity.Field.POSTED_TIME`

❑ App Data:

    ❑ Up to 1,024 bytes per key

    ❑ Up to 1MB per application

❏   Messages:

    ❏   No support for either `requestSendMessage` or `requestShareApp`

    ❏   Look at the YML tags `<yml:message>` and `<yml:share>` as alternatives.

❏   Person:

    ❏   `opensocial.Person.Field.ID`

    ❏   `opensocial.Person.Field.NAME`

    ❏   `opensocial.Person.Field.THUMBNAIL_URL`

    ❏   `opensocial.Name.UNSTRUCTURED`

    ❏   `opensocial.Person.Field.PROFILE_URL`

    ❏   `opensocial.Person.Field.ADDRESSES`

    ❏   `opensocial.Address.UNSTRUCTURED_ADDRESS`

    ❏   `opensocial.Person.Field.AGE`

    ❏   `opensocial.Person.Field.GENDER`

    ❏   `opensocial.Person.Field.TIME_ZONE` (not available when fetching friends)

❏   People request fields:

    ❏   `opensocial.DataRequest.PeopleRequestFields.FIRST`

    ❏   `opensocial.DataRequest.PeopleRequestFields.MAX`

    ❏   No support for other `PeopleRequest` fields, including `FILTER`, `PROFILE_DETAILS`, and `SORT_ORDER`. Treats them if set to value of `ALL`.

❏   Gadget API:

    ❏   All of the Core API, but not Preferences, Views, and Feature-Specific APIs.

Listing 9-19 shows a simple OpenSocial application stripped of its Gadget XML that is acceptable for deployment on YAP. This application simply gets the viewer's name and friends list. Figure 9-8 shows the results of running this application in the YAP developer preview mode. This is done in a test Yahoo! account that has one friend/connection.

Listing 9-19: OpenSocial JavaScript Application Acceptable for YAP (with Gadget XML-Stripped)

```
<div id='heading'></div>
<hr />
<div id='main'></div>
<hr >
<div id='friends'></div>
<div id='friend_status'> </div>
```

```
<script>
    var os;
    var dataReqObj;
    var os;
    var html = '';
    var heading = '';
    var friends_html = '';

    function init() {
        dataReqObj = opensocial.newDataRequest();
        var viewerReq = dataReqObj.newFetchPersonRequest('VIEWER');
        dataReqObj.add(viewerReq, 'viewer');

        //get viewer's friends
        var idspec = opensocial.newIdSpec({ "userId" :
            "VIEWER", "groupId" : "FRIENDS" });
        var Req = dataReqObj.newFetchPeopleRequest(idspec);
        dataReqObj.add(Req, 'viewerFriends');

        //send request
        dataReqObj.send(onLoadViewerResponse);
    }

    function onLoadViewerResponse(data) {

        var viewer;

        try{
           viewer = data.get('viewer').getData();
        }catch(err)
        {
           heading = 'Error2 ' + err.description;
           alert (heading);
        }

        heading = viewer.getDisplayName() + ', use Friend Finder
            to find your Friends';
        document.getElementById('heading').innerHTML = heading;

        var viewer_friends = data.get('viewerFriends').getData();
        try{
          friends_html  = 'Your Friends, ' ;
          friends_html = friends_html + '<ul>';

          viewer_friends.each(function(person) {
             friends_html = friends_html +  '<li>' +
             person.getDisplayName()
                  + '</li>';
          });
          friends_html = friends_html + '</ul>';
        } catch(err)
        {  friends_html ='Problem finding friends';
```

Continued

Listing 9-19: OpenSocial JavaScript Application Acceptable for YAP (with Gadget XML-Stripped) *(continued)*

```
            alert(friends_html);
        }


            document.getElementById('friends').innerHTML = friends_html;
    }

        init();
</script>
```

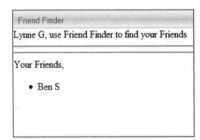

Figure 9-8: OpenSocial application running in YAP

Yahoo! Query Language

The Yahoo! Query Language (YQL) provides an application with access to Yahoo! platforms and their data via an SQL-type language. If you are familiar with Facebook, this is similar to Facebook Query Language (FQL). A big difference is that, with YQL, an application can make queries across Yahoo! platforms. This functionality is something that is currently missing from OpenSocial.

Here are a few simple YQL examples:

```
SELECT * from web.search WHERE query="XXX" LIMIT 4

SELECT * FROM social.profiles WHERE guid = me

SELECT * FROM local.search(100) WHERE query="vegetarian"
AND city="Capitola" LIMIT 100 | sort(field=result.rating)


SELECT * from flickr.search WHERE query="puppy" LIMIT 3
```

YQL can be embedded in both OpenSocial JavaScript YAP applications and YAP server-side applications. Listing 9-20 shows code from `http://developer.yahoo.com/yql/`. This code makes a client-side call to `query.yahooapis.com` using a signed request to service the YQL REST request.

Listing 9-20: Client-Side Call to Perform an YQL Call

```
<script type="text/javascript">

var toQueryString = function(obj) {
    var parts = [];
    for(var each in obj) if (obj.hasOwnProperty(each)) {
        parts.push(encodeURIComponent(each) + '='
            + encodeURIComponent(obj[each]));
    }
    return parts.join('&');
};

var BASE_URI = 'http://query.yahooapis.com/v1/yql';
var runQuery = function(query, handler) {
    gadgets.io.makeRequest(BASE_URI, handler, {
        METHOD: 'POST',
        POST_DATA: toQueryString({q: query, format: 'json'}),
        CONTENT_TYPE: 'JSON',
        AUTHORIZATION: 'OAuth'

    });
};

runQuery("select * from geo.places where text='SFO'", function(resp) {
    document.getElementById('results').innerHTML =
    gadgets.json.stringify(resp.data);
});

</script>
```

You can find a useful test console for YQL at http://developer.yahoo.com/yql/console/.

Understanding the Yahoo! User Interface (YUI)

The Yahoo! User Interface (YUI) is a JavaScript library that uses CSS to provide commonly needed user interface elements. If is free and is provided by Yahoo! Unfortunately, as of this writing, it is not supported by the Caja restrictions and, hence, won't be covered. Discussion of its inclusion in future YAP Caja translation could merit learning it. Some commercial sites using YUI include LinkedIn, JetBlue, Southwest.com, Slashdot.com, Target.com, and more.

Using Yahoo! Markup Language (YML)

The Yahoo! Markup Language (YML) is similar to OSML. Currently, Yahoo! only supports the use of YML and HTML in its Small view applications. Hopefully, Yahoo! will support OSML in the Small view in the future, since the company is involved in the development of OSML through the OpenSocial Foundation.

Details of YML can be found at http://developer.yahoo.com/yap/yml/index.html.

YML offers many nice features like friend selectors, application sharing, messaging, and others. Listing 9-21 shows the modification of some of the HTML from Listing 9-19 to include these basic tags. Figure 9-9 shows the results. As of this writing, sending messages and inviting others to use the application are not supported with OpenSocial API calls. (The main restrictions in OpenSocial support were noted previously.) So, developers will need to use these tags.

Listing 9-21: Modification of HTML to Add YML Tags

```
<div id='friend_status'>
  <yml:friend-selector />
<br>
  Update your friend
  <yml:message name="message-tag">
   <input type="text"  name="status" value="Doing fine :>">
   <input type="submit" value="Update">
  </yml:message>


<br>
  <yml:share > <input type="submit" value="Share Freind Finder now!">
    </yml:share>
</div>
```

Figure 9-9: Results of running
altered code from Listing 9-21

Y!OS Application Examples

Figure 9-10 shows a YAP application called Yahoo! Hot Stocks as it appears in Full view ("canvas"). Figure 9-11 shows a YAP application called America Decides, also shown in Full view ("canvas"). Both applications have common elements seen in social network applications deployed in networks such as MySpace, hi5, and others.

These applications have both client-side and server-side components. Back-end hosting involves edge hosting (CDN). Flash is a key component in both of these applications.

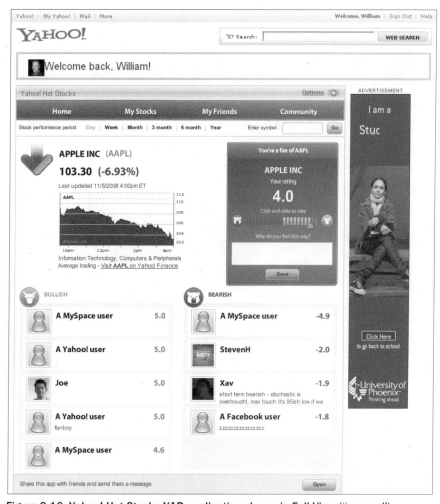

Figure 9-10: Yahoo! Hot Stocks YAP application shown in Full View ("canvas")

iWidgets

iWidgets is a startup company that has created a drag-and-drop integrated development environment (IDE) for social network application development. With iWidgets, a developer can create applications for OpenSocial and Facebook. iWidgets is currently targeting brand companies (such as McDonald's) to make it easier for them to create social network applications.

A developer can also use iWidgets technology to create an application. It is free for use, but iWidgets will put advertising on the "canvas" page (for which they collect revenue). This tool might be useful for doing quick mock-up applications or applications for fee-based clients.

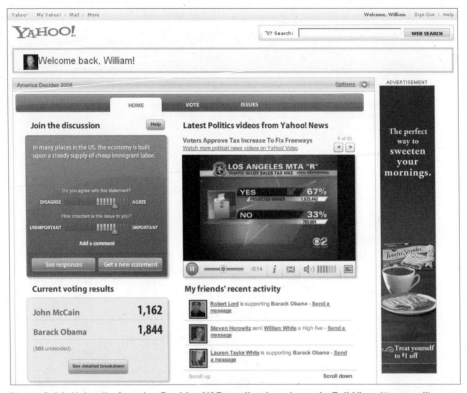

Figure 9-11: Yahoo!'s America Decides YAP application shown in Full View ("canvas")

Zembly

Zembly is a new venture by Sun Microsystems, Inc. that serves as a destination and platform for developers to collaboratively build social applications, services, and widgets that are served from Zembly. With Zembly, the developer can create OpenSocial applications, Facebook applications, and iPhone applications. This takes the "write once, deploy many" philosophy of OpenSocial to a new level.

Another objective of Zembly is to create an environment that is more accessible to new programmers. It achieves this through development of applications via a Web interface, as shown in Figure 9-12. It also hosts applications for developers and publishes them to social networks such as MySpace. Some nice features of the Web interface are items like code completion, syntax checking, and project management (that is, history). A unique and powerful feature of Zembly is the finding and sharing of services and snippets. A self-described catch-phrase to describe Zembly is the "Wikipedia of Social Networks."

The back end of Zembly includes Sun servers, MySQL, a GlassFish application server, Apache, Memcached, and Java. All of this is hosted on www.network.com, Sun's cloud computing infrastructure.

Zembly takes care of scaling and performance issues for your application automatically. Figure 9-12 shows an application running in Zembly. Figure 9-13 shows the underlying architecture Zembly provides for the application.

Figure 9-12: A complex social network application created in Zembly

Currently, Zembly is offering its services for free. In the future, Zembly may possibly add Service Layer Agreements, as well as have monetization and revenue-sharing agreements with developers.

Understanding the Zembly Application Structure

Currently, Zembly applications are created with a mixture of HTML, JavaScript, and CSS. They also include predefined Zembly services, snippets, Web APIs, widgets, and more. JavaScript libraries have been created for developers to use in their code for different social network platforms such as OpenSocial and Facebook.

In the future, Zembly will be adding support for PHP and Python scripting. Developers can create new services, snippets, and widgets for their own applications or to share with other developers.

Understanding a Zembly Service

A *service* is a back-end component that usually wraps some external Web service for applications that developed and then hosted within Zembly. An example of a Zembly service is a "wrapper" service that accesses the Flickr Web service. A Zembly service is created in JavaScript, and the developer defines the parameters that Zembly uses to map to the external service's REST requests. This mapping is done by Zembly through the use of the developer-provided information in a set of Web interface documents and the service's discovery document. (Zembly internally parses all documents to WADL.)

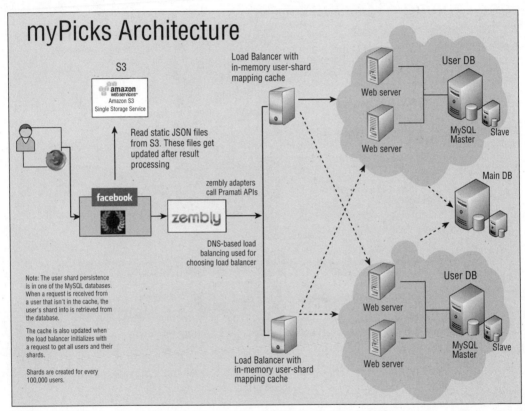

Figure 9-13: Zembly's architecture for the myPicks application in Figure 9-12

Currently, Zembly doesn't support Web services that require a user login to post user-specific data or to get user-specific data to an external Web service. As of this writing, a Zembly service can only post application-specific data, not to a user account on the external service.

For example, the MySpace "mPicks US Election" application (which was developed and is hosted on Zembly, and was shown in Figure 9-12) uses a Twitter service. In this case, the application uses this Zembly-provided service by making Twitter posts to an application Twitter account (meaning a Twitter account owned by the developer). The Zembly Twitter service has only two parameters — `status` (which is the Twitter line the user enters that can be captured by an HTML form) and `key`.

Check out http://wiki.zembly.com/wiki/Getting_Started: *"Creating a Widget Service" for more details on how to create a service. Later in this chapter in the section, "Creating a Simple OpenSocial Application in Zembly," you will see how a Zembly service is incorporated into an application.*

Understanding a Zembly Widget

A *widget* is a front-end component that typically has a GUI component and often will make calls to back-end services. A widget is specific to a platform (for example, OpenSocial or Facebook). Widgets allow for a kind of plug-and-play or drag-and-drop modularity. A widget will encompass both GUI elements and their event handling.

Understanding a Zembly Snippet

Snippets are basically code snippets that can be inserted into the developer's code. For an OpenSocial application, these will be inserted in the JavaScript code. Snippets are typically used to encapsulate commonly used business logic/processes.

Understanding a Zembly Key Chain

A developer's *key chain* is a concept in Zembly that stores keys owned by the developer to external sites. For example, to use a Web service represented by a Zembly service, the developer must obtain a key from the external Web service (for example, Google Maps) and then register this in the Zembly key chain.

When a developer creates a new service, it will commonly have as a parameter a key (because most external services need authentication). Zembly handles the process of authentication using the developer's key when the service is created.

Creating an OpenSocial Application in Zembly

To create an OpenSocial application in Zembly, a developer must first secure an account. After getting an account on Zembly, the developer will go to the "Create Something" pull-down list and choose an OpenSocial application. The developer has the option to use preexisting templates, as shown in Figure 9-14, or to create a blank OpenSocial application. A template has a preexisting layout and application features. This can be a powerful tool to get up and running quickly. Limited selections are available, but more will be available in the future.

At this point, the developer can choose to view or edit the following application elements:

- ❏   CanvasWidget — This is the "canvas" view.
- ❏   HomeWidget — This is the "home" view.
- ❏   PreviewWidget — This is the "preview" view.
- ❏   ProfileWidget — This is the "profile" view.
- ❏   Create — This is used to create either a new widget or a new service.

Figure 9-15 shows the application-creation interface when the CanvasWidget ("canvas" view) is selected. It consists of an editing tab for HTML, CSS, and JavaScript. This has a feel similar to that of the editing tabs available in the MySpace-hosted OpenSocial deployment option discussed earlier in the book.

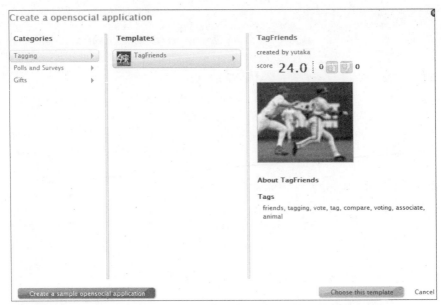

Figure 9-14: Template choices given to developer when creating OpenSocial applications in Zembly

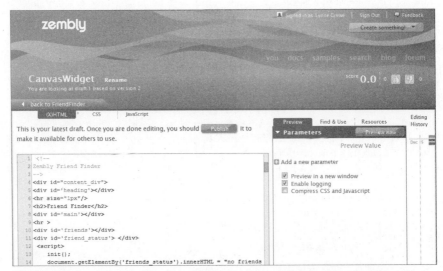

Figure 9-15: Zembly's interface for creating the "canvas" view of the OpenSocial application

A potentially powerful feature offered in Zembly is the service finding and sharing feature. As shown in Figure 9-16, there are currently 161 services that match the search for services under ''Flickr.'' After selecting a service, the result will be the insertion of the JavaScript code necessary to incorporate the service, as shown in the left side JavaScript editing screen of Figure 9-16. The developer must edit this code to pass parameters to the service call, and edit the callback function to handle the response as desired.

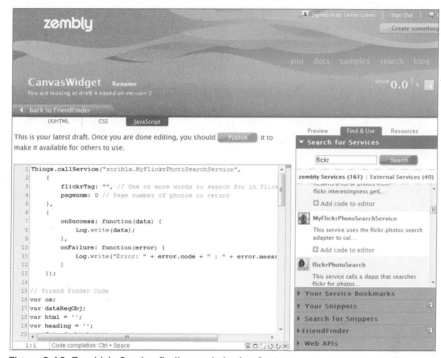

Figure 9-16: Zembly's Service finding and sharing feature

Incorporation of snippets and widgets follows the same transaction as discussed for a service.

Publishing an Application

Publishing an Application on Zembly is simply a matter of clicking a Publish button. This action results in the creation of a URL the developer can use in application deployment on the desired OpenSocial container.

Creating Your Own Service

Developers can create their own services to support modularity, reusability, and the capability to be shared with other developers. From the main application interface, the developer selects the creation of a new service and is taken to the page shown in Figure 9-17. The developer can create as many parameters as desired for the service via the Parameters tab on the right side of the interface. Then, the developer must edit the JavaScript to build out the service. In this case, a service is being created to get the longitude and latitude corresponding to a street address using Google's GeoLocator Web service. The parameter added is an "address," as seen in the JavaScript code.

Figure 9-17: Zembly's Web interface to create a new Service

The Zembly service-creation interface also allows a developer to "test drive" the service before it is published.

Summary

OpenSocial is a powerful platform on which to develop social network applications. It allows the developer to create once and deploy to many OpenSocial containers, including MySpace, hi5, orkut, Netlog, and many others. The list is growing.

OpenSocial is a very important standard, and many corporations have heavily invested in its progress. This chapter highlighted some of the more recent important additions to OpenSocial, as well as some intriguing new technologies like Y!OS and Zembly that feature OpenSocial.

Index

A

Accelerators, Joyent, 298
access, defined (server-side programming), 173
Access Key Identifiers, 295
action requests, 232–233
activities, 130–139
  activity data, 207–208
  activity posting, 134–137
  creating, 135–136
  invitations to install, 137–139
  media items in, 254–258
  messages, 131–134
  REST requests and, 202
adjustHeight method, 104, 106
Adobe Express Install application, 273
advertising, 318–320
Akamai, 290
Amazon Machine Image (AMI), 293
Amazon Simple Storage Server (S3), 296
Amazon Web Services (AWS)
  Amazon Simple Storage Server (S3), 296
  basics, 295
  CloudFront, 296–297
  defined, 292–293
  EBS, 296
  Elastic Compute Cloud (EC2), 293–295
  grid/cluster computing, 296
  Joyent, 298
  pricing, 297–298
analytics, 222, 312–316
AppData
  clearing, 258–259
  data support, 208–210
  requests, 202
appearance, of applications, 17–20
application data, defined, 46
application infrastructures, 304
application servers, 283–284
Application/Client layer, 281
applications. *See also specific* **applications**
  appearance of, 17–20
  brand-based, 39
  communication and, 31. *See also* communications
    applications
  control of. *See* control of applications
  creating, 83–86
  finding, 15–16

friend selector, 241–243
goals of. *See* goals of applications
identity of social networks, 48–50
improvement of, 53
installing, 16–17
JavaScript tools for, 274–275
making social and viral, 29
marketing, 50–53
person/people. *See* person/people applications
publishing (Zembly), 373
retaining users, 53
size for different views, 19–20
social network applications, defined, 14
testing, 78, 79, 221–222
tips for development of, 53–54
trends in. *See* trends in applications
viral channels and features, 46–48
Application Builder interface (MySpace), 69–71
Architectural Styles and the Design of Network-Based Software Architectures, 169, 172
architecture
  OpenSocial RESTful API, 175–176
  REST, 170
  RESTful/RESTful-RPC hybrid, 171
  Web system, 280–282
  Y!OS, 354–355
architecture of OpenSocial, 57–64
  basics, 57–58, 63–64
  client-based API, 58–59
  server-based API, 58, 59–62
asynchronicity (OpenSocial JavaScript API), 114, 116
Atom, 66
attentiveness of application users, 31
attributes. *See also specific* **attributes**
  Content element, 93–94
  ModulePrefs element, 88–91
  UserPrefs element, 91–93
authentication. *See also* **OAuth (OpenSocial REST authorization and authentication)**
  defined, 176
  RESTful architecture and, 175
authorization. *See also* **OAuth (OpenSocial REST authorization and authentication)**
  defined, 176
  RESTful architecture and, 175
authz, 232
AWS. *See* **Amazon Web Services (AWS)**

B

Base URL, calls and, 200
batching requests
  basics, 63–64
  in code for Friend Finder, 114
  multiple requests, 306–307
before attribute, 347–348
blog services, 52
blurbs, creating, 140–144
brand-based applications, 39
browsing indexes (hi5), 15–16
bug-tracking software, 317
build communities, defined, 1
bundles, message, 250–254
buttons for email creation,
    131–132

C

Cache-Control HTTP header, 286
caching
  basics, 284–289
  issues, 228–229
  vs. requests for external files, 309
CAJA, 222, 358–359
calls
  Base URL and, 200
  calling templates, 331–332
  to external resources, 227–228
  Gadget API, 63
  opensocial.getEnvironment() method call,
    259
  os.data.resendRequest ('key') method call,
    349–350
  signed makeRequest calls, 230
  YQL, 365
Canvas view
  application with contents for, 107
  basics, 19, 22
CanvasWidget, 371, 372
case studies
  Jambool, 299–300, 322
  KlickNation, 299, 322
  monetization, 321–322
  RockYou, 299, 322
  ShopIt, 322
  Slide, 300, 322
  social network architecture, 299–300
  Watercooler, 300, 322
CDNs (Content Delivery Networks), 290
certificate caches, 231
check_signature method (OAuth), 188
Chou, Kevin, 173, 300
Cisco Content Delivery Engine/System, 287
client code performance monitoring, 309–311
client libraries, 353
Client URL library (curl), 171, 172
client-based API (OpenSocial), 58–59
cloning, 302
cloud computing, 291

CloudFront, 296–297
code
  hosting on MySpace, 69–71
  performance monitoring, 309–311
  for signed requests, 231
  troubleshooting, 119
  uploading from external servers,
    71–74
Coderunner, 274–275
collections, defined, 65
collocated hosting, 291
communication engagement, 31
communications applications, 246–258
  gadget message bundles, creating,
    250–251
  media items in activities, 254–258
  message and activity templates,
    251–254
  message summaries, 254
  minimessages, creating, 249–250
  signed requests, creating, 247–249
configuring Flash media, 273–274
consumers, defined (OAuth), 176
containers
  application testing and, 221
  compliance, 262–263
  defined, 55
  inquiring about capabilities on, 232
  signed requests and, 231
  support of OpenSocial, 56–57
container-specific extensions, 264–266
Content Delivery Networks (CDNs),
  290
Content element, 93–94
control of applications, 25–29
  developer control, 29
  network control, 25–27
  user control, 28
Core Gadget API, 95–102
cost calculator (Amazon), 298
Cost per Action (CPA), 319
CSS
  image sprites, 312
  style sheets in headers, 308
curl. See Client URL library (curl)
currency, virtual, 320–321
custom tags (OSML), 343

D

data
  accessing with tags (OSML), 343
  including encrypted, 229
  passing to templates, 330–331
  support, 203
data (OpenSocial REST API)
  activity, 207–208
  AppData, 208–210
  group, 207
  messaging, 210

person, 204
retrieving and storing, 202
data formats (OpenSocial), 65–66
data formatting (OpenSocial REST API),
203–210
activity data, 207–208
AppData data, 208–210
group data, 207
messaging data, 210
person data, 204–207
data pipelining, 345–350
data, getting via markup, 345
data access, 346–347
data conditional rendering, 347–348
dynamic request for data, 349–350
listener for data changes, 348–349
databases
database sharding, 301–302
design, 300–302
distributed, 301
DataContext objects, 346–347
DataRequest extension, 266
DataRequest object, 306
debugging
CAJA and, 359–360
errors value and, 228
Firebug and, 303, 360
getErrorMessage() method and,
54, 262
definition files for templates, 333–334
delay, defined, 278
deployment, 67–83
Freebar, 83
Friendster, 80–83
hi5, 74–75
imeem, 78–80
MySpace. *See* MySpace deployment
Netlog, 78
OpenSocial REST API, 212–213
orkut, 75–78
destination applications, 39
developer dashboard (imeem), 78–79
developers
control of applications, 29
signed requests and, 230
tips for developing applications, 53–54
development
YAP, 360–361
YAP OpenSocial applications,
361–364
discovery
OpenSocial RESTful API, 213–216
REST applications and, 175, 176
dismissible minimessage, 249–250
distributed cache, 287–289
distributed database systems, 300
distribution, defined, 31
DNS lookups, reducing number of, 307
Dojo Toolkit, 274
downloads. *See also* **Web sites for downloading**
parallel, 309

dynamic evolution of applications, 32
dynamic requests for data, 349–350

E

EC2 (Elastic Compute Cloud), 293–295
edge servers, 290, 296
efficiency, defined, 278
Elastic Block Store (EBS), 296
Elastic Compute Cloud (EC2), 293–295
elements. *See also specific* **elements; sub-elements**
Atom, 66
Gadget XML, 87–95
XML, 66
XRDS Simple documents, 214
email
example, 131–133
services for marketing, 52
embedFlash method, 272
encrypted data, including, 229
engagement of application users, 30–32
environment (support and domain), 259–261
Environment class, 259
error codes
HTTP, 213
OpenSocial, 263
error handling, 262–263
errors (HTTP), 195, 213
"Evaluating the Scalability of Distributed Systems", 278
examples
activities, creating, 135–136
blurbs, creating, 140–144
buttons, to trigger email creation, 131–132
email messages, 131–133
Info, 122
notification, 133–134
OAuth in PHP, 190–195
people (GetFriends), 119–122
people (Info), 122
people (ViewerData), 117–119
PersonData, 130
templates, 350–352
Y!OS, 366–367
Expires HTTP header, 286
exposure of applications, 31
expressions
defined, 329
templates and, 329–330
Extensible Resource Descriptor Sequence (XRDS)
RESTful architecture and, 176
XRDS Simple, 213–216
extensions, container-specific, 264–266
external resources, 226–232
caching issues, 228–229
calls to, 227–228
POST request, 229
preload, 232
signed request, 230–231

F

Facebook
application trends and, 34–35
gifting feature, 45
programming, 174–175
fans
fan accounts, 317
fan applications, 36–38
Feature-Specific Gadget API,
102–107
Fielding, Roy, 169, 172
fields
individual person fields, 205
to request about people, 123–125
subfields for organizations, 207
subfields for person fields, 206
YAP supported, 361–362
fields extension, 266
files, reducing number of, 307
Firebug, 303, 360
Flash media, 271–275
Flixster hypothetical application,
60–62
flushing server responses, 309
foreign-based social networks, 9–10
forward proxy cache, 286
Freebar
appearance of, 24
basics, 9–11
deployment, 83
Friend Blurb application, 140–143
Friend Finder
batching requests, 114
code for, 112–113
on hi5, 75, 76
makeRequest method, 227–228
on MySpace, 74
navigation tabs, 222–224
on orkut, 77
styled tabs, creating, 226
friends
defined, 116
friend selector application,
241–243
of friends, finding, 246
GetFriends example, 119–122
list of, paginating, 238–239
requesting, 236–238
testing if users are, 243–244
top friends, finding, 244–246
Friendster
appearance of, 23–24
basics, 8–9
deployment, 80–83
styled tabs, creating, 226
traffic on, 48–50
Full view (YAP), 358, 359, 366, 367, 368
future tags (OSML), 339–340

G

Gadget API
calls, 63
core gadget API, 95–102
Feature-Specific Gadget API, 102–107
using, 271–272
gadget message bundles, creating, 250–251
Gadget XML, 87–95
application stripped of, 362–363
defined, 87
elements and sub-elements, 87–95
file for Friend Finder, 112
OpenSocial JavaScript applications and, 87
preload element, 232
specifications, 71–72
gadgets
basics, 87
defined, 59
lifecycle support, 109–110
multiple views, 107–109
Gadgets i18n tool, 270
gadgets.flash object, 102, 106, 272
gadgets.io, 95–97
gadgets.io.getproxyUrl method, 312
gadgets.json, 95, 97
gadgets.MiniMessage Gadget API class, 249
gadgets.MiniMessage.dismissMessage application,
250
gadgets.Prefs, 95, 100
gadgets.skins object, 102, 105–106
gadgets.util, 95, 97–100
gadgets.util.hasFeature method, 232
gadgets.views object, 102–104
gadgets.window object, 102, 104–105
gender-specific pronouns, creating, 240–241
general appeal applications, 35–36
GET method, 229
getDomain method, 259
getErrorMessage method, 263
GetFriends, people example, 119–122
globalization, 267–271
goals of applications, 29–33
dynamic evolution, 32
engagement, 30–32
growth, 30
look and feel, 32
problem solving, 33
relationship building, 33
self expression, 32
social exposure, 33
goods, virtual, 320–321
Google
gadget documentation, 87
Google Analytics, 313–315
Google App Engine, 299
Google Gadget XML. *See* Gadget XML
greetings message, 251
grid computing, 291
grid/cluster computing, 296
grouping requests, 63–64

groups
data groups, support of, 207
requests and, 201
growth of application use, 30
GUI design, 222–226
look and feel, 224–225
navigation tabs, 222–224
social-network specific looks, 225–226
{**guid**}, 200
Guptas, Vikas, 299
GZIP, compressing content with, 308

H

hadError() method, 263
Hadoop, 296
Hansson, David Heinemeier, 171
HAS_APP, 245–246
headers
CSS style sheets in, 308
HTTP, cache and, 285–286
height of applications, adjusting, 106–107
Hello World
with Core Gadget API, 101
height, adjusting, 106–107
including lifecycle support, 110
with ModulePrefs, 94–95
OpenSocial, 64–65
template, constructing, 326–329
template that uses passed parameters, 331
hi5
appearance of, 22
basics, 5–7
browsing index, 15–16
deployment, 74–75
lifecycle extension, 265–266
OAuth and, 196–197
support for OpenSocial REST, 196–198
template library, 225, 266
traffic on, 48–50
history of OpenSocial, 55–56
Home view, 19, 20–21
horizontal partitioning (distributed databases), 301
horizontal scaling, 280
hosting, on MySpace, 69–71
hosting solutions
AWS. *See* Amazon Web Services (AWS)
developer comments/trends, 292
Google App Engine, 299
types of, 290–292
Hot Stocks YAP application, 366, 367
HTML. *See* HyperText Markup Language (HTML)
HTTP. *See* HyperText Transfer Protocol (HTTP)
hybrid applications
client/server OpenSocial, 61–62
OpenSocial JavaScript and RESTful API, 175
Hyper Text Caching Protocol (HTCP), 287
HyperText Markup Language (HTML)
as alternative to media items, 256–258
HTML validators, 222

HyperText Transfer Protocol (HTTP)
errors (OAuth), 195
headers, cache and, 285–286
method type, 210–211
OAuth request parameters and, 180
OAuth tokens and, 181
requests, minimizing number of, 306
REST and, 169, 171, 175
status codes (OpenSocial REST API), 213

I

i18n and L10n, 267
ICP (Internet Cache Protocol), 287
IdSpec, 122–130
IdSpec class, 246
PersonData example, 130
social data, application requesting, 126–129
social data, fields to request, 123–125
if attribute, 332
IFrames, hybrid applications and, 62
I-Jet Media Inc., 322
iLike
length of engagement and, 39–40
on MySpace, 18
image spriting, 312
imeem
appearance of, 24
basics, 9
deployment, 78–80
Info example, 122
information
retrieving, 140–144
storing, 140
Infrastructure layer, 281
init() function, user languages and, 100–101
init() method, 113–114
installing
applications, 16–17
invitations to install, 137–139
instance types (EC2), 293
internationalization
basics, 267–271
marketing applications and, 41–42
OSML and, 344
Internet Cache Protocol (ICP), 287
Internet Security and Acceleration (ISA) server, 287
invitations to install, 137–139
issue-tracking software, 317
iWidgets, 367–368

J

Jambool case study, 299–300, 322
JavaScript. *See also* OpenSocial JavaScript API
CAJA and, 222
code, for Friend Finder, 112–113
code, locating at bottom, 309
minifying, 308
SWFObject JavaScript library, 272–273

JavaScript *(continued)*
  tools for applications, 274–275
  JavaScript Object Notation (JSON)
  basics of, 65–66
  REST responses and, 211–212
Jogalekar, Prasad, 278
Joyent, 298
JSMin filtering program, 308
JSON. *See* **JavaScript Object Notation (JSON)**

K

"Keep Alive On" HTTP feature, 307
key cache (OAuth), 195
key chains (Zembly), 371
Kiss
  internationalization and, 42
  search on, 17
KlickNation case study, 299, 322
Kostarev, Alexey, 45

L

languages (computer). *See also* **JavaScript; OpenSocial**
      Markup Language (OSML)
  language support (OAuth), 196
  work in language of choice, defined, 173
  YML, 365–366
languages (spoken)
  tag for Spanish messages, 344
  user languages, 100–102
Levchin, Max, 322
Leymann, F., 172
libraries
  client, 353
  curl, 171, 172
  hi5 template, 225, 266
  OAuth, 196
  SWFObject JavaScript, 272–273
lifecycles, support for, 109–110
lifecyle events, 109
lighttpd, 289
listen attribute, 348
listener, for data changes, 348–349
load balancing, 284
loading times, 312
localization
  basics, 267–271
  defined, 332
  with templates, 332
longer engagement applications, 39
look and feel
  of applications, 32
  GUI design and, 224–225
  social-network specific looks, 225–226
looping
  repeat attribute for, 332
  through lists, 345

M

Maffia new
  use of media in, 41, 42
  virtual currency and, 50–51
makeRequest method
  caching and, 228
  gadgets.io, 96, 100
  refresh intervals, setting and, 229
  simple invocation of, 227–228
managed dedicated hosting, 291
marketing applications, 50–53
McNulty, Rhet, 322
media
  in applications, 39–41
  HTML as alternative to, 256–258
  using in activities, 254–258
meetups, 304
Memcached system, 287–289
messages
  email message example, 131–133
  gadget message bundles, 250–251
  message and activity templates, 251–254
  message bundles, 252–254
  minimessages, 249–250
  notification example, 133–134
  as option, 202–203
  summaries, 254
  types of, 131
messaging data, 210
methods
  Core Gadget API, 96–100
  Feature-Specific API, 102–106
  HTTP (OpenSocial REST requests), 210
  OAuthRequest class, 182
  OAuthSignatureMethod_RSA_SHA1 class, 190
  OpenSocial, 144–167
  optional parameters, 116
  Y!OS, 354
metrics
  performance, 278
  scalability, 279
micropayments/micro-transactions, 321
Microsoft Internet Security and Acceleration (ISA) server,
      287
micro-transactions, defined, 45
Middleware layer, 281
minified JavaScript, 308
minimessages, creating, 249–250
mobile applications, 45
ModulePrefs
  attributes and sub-elements for, 88–91
  defined, 87
  Hello World with, 94–95
monetization, 318–322
monitoring client code performance, 309–311
monitoring software, 302–303
multiple cache servers, 287
multiple content tags, 108–109
multiple views (applications), 107–109
<myapp:HelloWorld> tag, 342

MySpace
appearance of, 20–22
application trends and, 34
Application Builder interface, 69–71
basics, 2–4
rules for developers, 27
traffic on, 48–50
MySpace deployment, 67–74
code, uploading from external servers,
71–74
getting started, 67–69
hosting on MySpace, 69–71

N

<namespace:templateName/> tag, 342
naming
OpenSocial API and, 116
templates, 328–329
navigation tabs, 222–224
Netlog
appearance of, 24–25
basics, 11
deployment, 78
network control, 25–27
new App Install program, 51
newFetchPersonAppDataRequest method, 140
newUpdatePersonAppDataRequest method,
140, 143
Nginx, 289
non-RESTful, defined, 169
non-social networking applications, 59–62
NOT_IMPLEMENTED error code, 262–263
nothing shared cloning, 302
notification example, 133–134

O

**OAuth (OpenSocial REST authorization and
authentication),** 176–198
basics, 176–177
hi5 authentication scheme, 196–198
HTTP errors, 195
incorporating into OpenSocial REST API, 196
libraries, 196
OAuthSignatureMethod_RSA_SHA1, 189
OpenID, 195
parameters, 179
in PHP. *See* OAuth in PHP
requests, 179–180
signing requests, 180
simple PHP test program, 191–194
steps, 177–178
tokens, 181, 195
OAuth in PHP, 181–195
example, 190–195
OAuthConsumer, 181
OAuthRequest, 182–188
OAuthSignatureMethod, 188–190
OAuthToken, 181–182

objects
Core Gadget API, 95
Feature-Specific API objects, 102–106
OpenSocial, 144–167
received by callback function, 228
Offerpal, 320
onLoadViewerResponse method, 114
Open Group Architectural Framework (TOGAF) Method,
282
open sandbox access, defined, 53
OpenID (OAuth), 195
OpenSocial
AppData as container cache, 307
application sample, 64–65
applications, creating, 83–86
architecture. *See* architecture of OpenSocial
data formats, 65–66
deployment. *See* deployment; MySpace deployment
error codes, 263
get from cache, 312
history, 55–56
introduction to, 1, 55
object, 144–146
performance. *See* performance
programming. *See* OpenSocial programming
supporting networks, 14
tools, 54
OpenSocial JavaScript API, 111–168
activities. *See* activities
architecture, 63–64
basics, 58, 61
client-based API and, 58–59
details, 144–167
features, 115–116
Gadget XML and, 87
people. *See* people
persistence. *See* persistence
simple OpenSocial application, 111–115
OpenSocial Markup Language (OSML), 334–345
basics, 334–335
custom tags, 343
data access with tags, 343
future tags, 339–340
internationalization and, 344
looping through lists, 345
partial content, rendering, 344
proposed tags, 341–342
specifying as required feature, 342
standard tags, 335–338
OpenSocial programming, 221–233
action requests, 232–233
application testing, 221–222
external resources. *See* external resources
GUI design. *See* GUI design
inquiring about capabilities, 232
OpenSocial REST API
data formatting. *See* data formatting (OpenSocial REST
API)
deployment, 212–213
discovery, 213–216
future versions of, 216

OpenSocial REST API *(continued)*
HTTP status codes, 213
incorporating OAuth into, 196
vs. RPC protocol, 216–217
security, 216
specification, 200–203
using, 198, 212
OpenSocial RESTful API, 169–219
architecture, 175–176
authorization and authentication. *See* OAuth (OpenSocial REST authorization and authentication)
basics, 60–62
data formatting. *See* data formatting (OpenSocial REST API)
HTTP method type, 210–211
OpenSocial REST API specification, 200–203
responses, 211–212
REST basics, 169–172
REST request construction, 198–199
RPC protocol and, 216–219
server-side programming, 173–175
OpenSocial Tool/Harness, 222
opensocial.Activity class, 134
opensocial.Activity object, 146–147
opensocial.Activity.Field object, 147–148
opensocial.Address object, 148
opensocial.Address.Field object, 148–149
opensocial.BodyType object, 149
opensocial.BodyType.Field object, 149
opensocial.Collection object, 149–150
opensocial.CreateActivityPriority object, 150
opensocial.DataRequest object, 150–152
opensocial.DataRequest.DataRequestFields object, 152
opensocial.DataRequest.FilterType object, 152–153
opensocial.DataRequest.newUpdatePersonAppData Request method, 258
opensocial.DataRequest.PeopleRequestFields object, 153
opensocial.DataRequest.PeopleRequestFields.FILTER key, 244
opensocial.DataRequest.PeopleRequestFields.FIRST parameter, 236
opensocial.DataRequest.SortOrder object, 153
opensocial.DataResponse object, 153–154
opensocial.Email object, 154
opensocial.Email.Field object, 154
opensocial.Enum object, 154
opensocial.Enum.Drinker object, 154–155
opensocial.Enum.Gender object, 155
Opensocial.Enum.LookingFor object, 155
opensocial.Enum.Presence object, 155–156
opensocial.Environment object, 156
opensocial.Environment.ObjectType object, 157
opensocial.EscapeType object, 157
opensocial.getEnvironment() method call, 259
opensocial.IdSpec object, 157–158
opensocial.IdSpec.Field object, 158
Opensocial.IdSpec.Field.NETWORK_ DISTANCE field, 246
opensocial.IdSpec.PersonId object, 158
opensocial.MediaItem object, 158
opensocial.MediaItem.Field object, 159

opensocial.MediaItem.Type object, 159
opensocial.Message object, 159
opensocial.Message.Field object, 159–160
opensocial.Message.Type object, 160
opensocial.Name.Field object, 160
opensocial.NavigationParameters object, 160–161
opensocial.NavigationParameters.DestinationType object, 161
opensocial.Organization object, 161
opensocial.Organization.Field object, 162
opensocial.Permission object, 162
opensocial.Person object, 162–163
opensocial.Person.Field object, 163–166
opensocial.Phone object, 166
opensocial.Phone.Field object, 166
opensocial.ResponseItem object, 166–167
opensocial.ResponseItem.Error object, 167
opensocial.template.renderAll Templates, 328
opensocial.Url object, 167
opensocial.Url.Field object, 167
optional parameters (OpenSocial methods), 116
ordered lists, defined, 65
orkut
appearance of, 23
basics, 7
deployment, 75–78
os.data.resendRequest ('key') method call, 349–350
os.getTemplate function, 328–329
<os:Locale> tag, 344
OSML. *See* **OpenSocial Markup Language (OSML)**
<os:OwnerRequest> tag, 345
<os:Render> tag, 344
<os:Repeat> tag, 345
owned/proprietary system solution, 291
owners
defined, 116
email message from viewers, 132–133

P

parallel downloads, 309
parameters
calling templates with, 331–332
OAuth, 179, 199
OAuthSignatureMethod, 188
opensocial.Message.Field.*, 131
opensocial.newActivity, 134
optional (OpenSocial methods), 116
request parameters for user validation, 231
partitioning, defined, 284
partnering, 43, 320
Pautasso, C, 172
people, 116–130
basics, 116–117
data, OpenSocial REST support of, 204–207
GetFriends example, 119–122
getting information about, 117
IdSpec. *See* IdSpec
Info example, 122
OpenSocial REST requests and, 200–201

types of, 116
ViewerData example, 117–119
percent encoding (OAuth), 179
performance
defined (server-side programming), 173
improving with preload, 232
metrics, 278
monitoring client code, 309–311
problem areas, 280
performance tuning
AppData as container cache, 307
batching multiple requests, 306–307
caching, 309
client code performance, monitoring, 309–311
CSS style sheets in headers, 308
DNS lookups, reducing number of, 307
files, reducing number of, 307
flushing server responses, 309
GZIP and, 308
HTTP requests and, 306
image sprites, 312
JavaScript, minifying, 308
JavaScript code, locating at bottom, 309
loading times, 312
OpenSocial get from cache, 312
overview, 306
persistence feature in Web servers, 307
preloading content, 311
requests for external files, 309
permissions
asking for, 263–264
checking, 263–264
platforms for, 356, 357
programming and, 232–233
persistence, 139–144
defined, 139
information, retrieving, 140–144
information, storing, 140
in Web servers, 307
personas, creating, 304
PersonData example, 130
person/people applications, 235–246
friend selector application, 241–243
friends list, paginating, 238–239
friends of friends, finding, 246
multiple requests for friends, 236–237
pronouns, creating gender-specific, 240–241
requesting friends, 236, 237–238
testing users as friends, 243–244
top friends, finding, 244–246
PHP. See also **OAuth in PHP**
accepting/verifying signed requests, 247–248
REST program, 172
platforms, 2–14
Freebar, 9–11
Friendster, 8–9
hi5, 5–7
imeem, 9
MySpace, 2–4
Netlog, 11
orkut, 7

other networks, 14
for setting update permissions, 356, 357
Yahoo!, 12–14
Y!OS architecture and, 354–355
YQL and, 364
POST requests, 229
posting of activities, 134–137
pre-fetching, defined, 285
preloading
content, 311
improving performance with, 232
Presentation layers, 281
pricing, Amazon, 297–298
"Principled Design of the Modern Web Architecture",
172
problem of rebalancing, 302
productivity, 279
Profile view
application with contents for, 107
basics, 19, 22
programming. See **OpenSocial programming; social
network programming**
pronouns, creating gender-specific,
240–241
properties
OAuth, 176
REST architecture, 170
proposed tags (OSML), 341–342
proxied content, 352–353
proxy servers, 286
publishing applications
defined, 81
Freebar, 83
Zembly, 373

Q

quality of service, defined, 278
query parameters (OAuth), 199

R

Rabois, Keith, 36
random selection algorithm, 284
reach applications, 35–36
real goods, 321
redundancy, 302
refresh intervals, setting, 229
registerOnLoadHandler method (gadgets.io), 99, 100
relationship building, 33
repeat attribute for looping, 332
replication, 301
Representational State Transfer (REST). See **REST**
requestPermission method, 264
requests
dynamic, for data, 349–350
for HTML resources (PHP REST), 172
OAuth, 179–180
OAuthRequest, 182–188
OAuthToken, 181–182

requests *(continued)*
  rendering templates, 328
  REST request construction, 198–199
require attribute, 347
Require feature, 342
resources. *See also* **Web sites for further information**
  REST, 170, 172
  templates, 351–352
  XRDS Simple, 216
response time, defined, 278
responses
  OAuth, 181
  OpenSocial REST requests and, 211–212
REST. *See also* **OpenSocial REST API; OpenSocial RESTful API**
  basics, 169–172
  non-RESTful, defined, 169
"REST API Specific URL Pattern", 200
RESTful API. *See* **OpenSocial RESTful API**
RESTful Web Services (O'Reilly Media, 2007), 171
"RESTful Web Services vs. Big Web Services: Making the Right Architectural Decision", 172
RESTful-RPC hybrid architecture, 171
retrieving data, 140–144, 202
reverse proxy servers, 286–287
Richardson, Leonard, 171
RockYou
  case study, 299, 322
  self expression and, 43
  slideshow application, 174
role playing, 304
round robin rotation, 284
RPC protocol
  vs. OpenSocial REST API, 216–219
  RESTful/RESTful-RPC hybrid, 171
Ruby, Sam, 171

S

S3
  Amazon Simple Storage Server, 296
  S3Firefox Organizer, 296
sandboxes
  open sandbox access, 53
  running applications in, defined, 9
scalability
defining, 278–279
metrics, 279
scalable user interface design, 316–317
scaling up/out, 280
<script> tag, 347, 348
security (OpenSocial REST API), 216
selector, defined (OpenSocial REST API), 200
self expression
  applications and, 43
  in social networking, 32
Send Good Karma
  jPoints, 44
  partnering and, 43, 44, 320
  virtual goods and, 320

serial order for request processing, 64
server-based API
  OpenSocial, 58, 59–62
  OpenSocial RESTful API, 173–175
servers
  flushing server responses, 309
  multiple cache, 287
  persistence feature in Web servers, 307
  proxy, 286
  reverse proxy, 286–287
  S3, 296
server-side code for signed requests, 231
server-side programming (OpenSocial RESTful API), 173–175
services
  for blogs, 52
  defined, 370
  for email marketing, 52
  finding and sharing, 373
  Zembly, 370–374
sharding, database, 301–302
Share Good Karma, 52
shared disk cloning, 302
shared hosting, 290–291
Shen, Jia, 299
Shindig, 57
ShopIt case study, 322
Shukla, Anu, 320
signatures, checking, 188–190
signed requests, 230–231
signed requests, creating, 247–249
signing requests (OAuth), 180
"Silly is Serious Business", 36
Simple Storage Server, Amazon (S3), 296
Slide case study, 300, 322
Small view (YAP), 358
Smith, Andy, 181
snippets (Zembly), 371
social data
  application requesting, 126–129
  fields requesting, 123–125
  use of in applications, 45–46
social exposure, application growth and, 33
social gadgets, 64
social hooks, 46–48
social network programming
  applications. *See* applications
  identity of social networks, 48–50
  platforms. *See* platforms
  retaining users, 53
social networking
  basics, 1–2
  foreign-based networks, 9–10
social network-provided analytic tools, 316
software
  analytic, 313
  bug-tracking, 317
  issue-tracking, 317
  for monitoring, 302–303
  version control, 305

software design
language choices, 305
overview, 303–304
versioning and, 305
Sometrics, 316
specifications
Google Gadget XML, 71–72
OpenSocial REST API, 200–203
Squid server, 287
standard tags (OSML), 335–338
storing data, 140–143, 202
styles for social networks, 225
subclasses of OAuthSignatureMethod Class, 189
sub-elements, 271–272
Content, 93–94
ModulePrefs, 88–91
OpenSocial REST response, 211
UserPrefs, 91–93
subfields
for organizations, 207
for person fields, 206
subsystems
application servers, 283–284
caching, 284–289
CDNs, 290
load balancing, 284
Web servers, 283
supportsField method, 259, 261
SWFObject JavaScript library, 272–273
swfUrl variable, 272
system support, 317–318

T

tables, social data displayed as, 126–130
tabs
navigation, 222–224
styled, 226
tag="namespace:templateNameX" parameter, 343
tags
accessing data with (OSML), 343
adding (YML), 366
custom (OSML), 343
to define Templates XML file, 333
future (OSML), 339–340
multiple content, 108–109
proposed (OSML), 341–342
standard (OSML), 335–338
targeted applications, 36
targeted social networks, defined, 9
Taylor, Richard, 172
template-based application development, 36–38
template.RenderInto function, 328–329
templates
hi5 template library, 225, 266
message and activity, 251–254
Templates Standard, 325–352
basics, 325–326
calling with parameters, 331–332
conditional tests, 332

construction and use, 327–328
data pipelining. *See* data pipelining
definition files, 333–334
examples, 350–352
expressions and, 329–330
localization with, 332
naming templates, 328–329
OSML. *See* OpenSocial Markup Language (OSML)
repeat attribute for looping, 332
requiring features, 326
variables and passing data, 330–331
testing
applications, 221–222
GetFriends example, 121
tags in templates, 332
Theurer, Tenni, 307
three-layer architecture, 281
throughput, defined, 278
tokens (OAuth)
management of, 195
OAuthToken, 181–182
the response, 181
tools
analytic, 316
Dojo Toolkit, 274
Gadgets i18n, 270
JavaScript, 274–275
OpenSocial, 54
OpenSocial Tool/Harness, 222
for testing code, 222
UML, 304
trends in applications, 33–46
application data and, 46
basics, 33–35
brand-based applications, 39
destination applications, 39
internationalization, 41–42
longer engagement applications, 39
mobile applications, 45
partnering, 43
reach applications, 35–36
self expression, 43
social data and, 45–46
template-based development, 36–38
use of media, 39–41
vertical applications, 36
virtual currencies, goods and points, 43–45

U

Unified Modeling Language (UML) tools, 304
unmanaged leased dedicated hosting, 291
updates
Gadget API updates, 95
OpenSocial, 134–137
update permissions, 356, 357
Yahoo! users, 355
Y!OS users, 355–356
uploading code from external servers,
71–74

URL patterns (OpenSocial REST API)
for activities, 202
for AppData, 203
for groups, 201, 203
for messaging, 202, 203
for people, 201
URLs
avoiding caching and, 229
OpenSocial REST, 198, 200
RESTful-RPC hybrid architecture and, 171
user agent cache, 285
UserPrefs
attributes and sub-elements for, 91–93
defined, 87
users
experience/satisfaction, defined, 278
request parameters for validating, 231
retaining, 53
user control of applications, 28
user ID (OpenSocial REST API), 200
user languages, 100–102
user profiles (Y!os), 355
user support, 317–318
user updates (Y!OS), 355–356

V

value delivered, defined, 279
variables
Core Gadget API, 96–100
Feature-Specific API, 102–106
OpenSocial (listed), 144–167
templates and, 330–331
Varnish Web accelerator, 287
version control software, 305
vertical applications, 36
vertical partitioning (distributed databases), 301
vertical scaling, 280
ViewerData people example, 117–119
viewers
defined, 116
email messages from, 132–133
views
changing dynamically, 109
defined, 107
directing content to different, 108–109
multiple, 107–109
of OpenSocial applications, 19–20
YAP, 358
viral applications, 29, 47–48
viral calculator, 51
viral channels, 46–48
virtual currency
Maffia new and, 50–51
virtual currencies, goods and points, 43–45, 320–321
virtual goods, 45, 320–321
virtual money, 50–51

W

Walton, Ken, 42, 299
Watercooler
applications, 36–38
case study, 300, 322
server-side programming and, 173
Web accelerator, 287
Web proxy caching servers, 286
Web servers, 283
Web sites, for downloading
Adobe Express Install application, 273
Coderunner JavaScript testing application, 274
Dojo Toolkit, 274
lighttpd, 289
Nginx, 289
Varnish Web accelerator, 287
Web sites for further information, 34
Amazon Web Services, 295
analytic software, 313
blogs, 84
bug-tracking software, 317
CAJA, 222, 358
client libraries, 353
CloudFront, 297
curl library, 172
database sharding, 302
developer page (MySpace), 68
extensions for OpenSocial containers, 326
forum on application policies, 27
Freebar deployment, 83
Friendster, 80, 225
Gadget API updates, 95
gadget documentation, 87
Google Analytics, 313
Google App Engine, 299
Hadoop, 296
hi5 Analytics, 316
hi5 developer application, 74–75
hi5 shortcuts to social data, 225
hi5 translation service, 270
HTCP, 287
ICP, 287
imeem deployment, 78
internationalization, 41
Internet trends, 33, 34
issue-tracking software, 317
JSON, 66
key cache, 196
localization resources, 272
meetups, 304
Memcached system, 288
MySpace, 27, 51
Netlog developer contract, 78
OAuth libraries, 196
OpenID, 195
OpenSocial, 14, 83–85
OpenSocial Templates library, 328

orkut, 75, 76, 77
proxied content, 353
RockYou slideshow, 174
rules for developers, 27
S3Firefox Organizer, 296
services, creating, 371
"Silly is Serious Business", 36
software monitoring, 302–303
Sometrics, 316
sprites, 312
SWFObject JavaScript library, 272
templates, 350, 351–352
TOGAF Method, 282
user profiles, 355, 356
XRDS Simple, 216
Yahoo! Web Analytics, 315
YAP, 360, 361
YML, 365
Web system architecture, 280–283
widgets (Zembly), 371
Woodside, Murray, 278

X

X.509 certificates, 295
XML
elements in XRDS-Simple documents, 214
Friend Finder navigation tabs and, 223–224
gadget file for Friend Finder, 112
OpenSocial and, 66
XRDS. *See* **Extensible Resource Descriptor Sequence (XRDS)**

Y

Y!OS. *See* **Yahoo! Open Strategy (Y!OS)**
Yahoo!
basics, 12–14
user profiles, 355
user updates, 355
Yahoo! Social Platform, 355
Yahoo! Applications (YAP)
application development, 361–364
basics, 356–357

CAJA, using, 358–359
development steps, 360–361
views, 358
Yahoo! Markup Language (YML),
365–366
Yahoo! Open Strategy (Y!OS), 353–367
architecture, 354–355
examples, 366–367
methods, 354
OpenSocial and, 353
user profiles, 355
user updates, 355–356
YAP basics, 356–360
YAP development steps, 360–361
YAP OpenSocial application development,
361–364
YML, 365–366
YQL, 364–365
YUI, 365
Yahoo! Query Language (YQL), 364–365
Yahoo! User Interface (YUI), 365
Yahoo! Web Analytics, 315
Yahoo!'s America Decides YAP application,
366, 368
YAP. *See* **Yahoo! Applications (YAP)**
yelp, 59
YML (Yahoo! Markup Language),
365–366
Y!OS. *See* **Yahoo! Open Strategy (Y!OS)**
YQL (Yahoo! Query Language), 364–365
YSlow extension, 309–311
YUI (Yahoo! User Interface), 365

Z

Zembly
application structure, 369–370
applications, publishing, 373
applications in, creating, 371–373
basics, 368–369
key chains, 371
services, 370–371, 373–374
snippets, 371
widgets, 371
Zimmermann, O., 172